The Squid Cinema from Hell

For Tarran and Cordelia

The Squid Cinema from Hell

Kinoteuthis Infernalis and the Emergence of Chthulumedia

William Brown and
David H. Fleming

EDINBURGH
University Press

Edinburgh University Press is one of the leading university presses in the UK. We publish academic books and journals in our selected subject areas across the humanities and social sciences, combining cutting-edge scholarship with high editorial and production values to produce academic works of lasting importance. For more information visit our website: edinburghuniversitypress.com

Edinburgh University Press Ltd
The Tun – Holyrood Road, 12(2f) Jackson's Entry, Edinburgh EH8 8PJ

Typeset in 11/13 Monotype Ehrhardt by
IDSUK (DataConnection) Ltd

A CIP record for this book is available from the British Library

ISBN 978 1 4744 6372 0 (hardback)
ISBN 978 1 4744 6374 4 (webready PDF)
ISBN 978 1 4744 6373 7 (paperback)
ISBN 978 1 4744 6375 1 (epub)

Contents

Figures

Acknowledgments

The Squid Cinema from Hell was written between 2016 and 2019, together and apart, at different speeds and rests, as we wended our way around and between many different places and spaces, including Canada, the People's Republic of China, Italy, Spain, Sweden, the UAE, the UK, and the USA. Along the way, too many people to mention have directly and indirectly impacted us with their generous comments, stimulating ideas, suggestions, and feedback.

Nonetheless, we would like to begin with very special thanks to Gillian Leslie at Edinburgh University Press for her interest and support in publishing what is essentially a very weird book. You are a star.

The journey to EUP involved help from many readers and recommenders, and these include (in alphabetical order) Erick Felinto, Donna J. Haraway, Dominic C. James, Akira Mizuta Lippit, Laura U. Marks, Bill Marshall, David Martin-Jones, Dan Mellamphy, Patricia Pisters, Claudio Rossi, Eugene Thacker, C. Derick Varn, Cary Wolfe, and our anonymous peer reviewers at EUP. Many thanks to all of these for their courtesy, time, and informative feedback, as well as to Eliza Wright at EUP.

Simultaneous to the book's plasmatic peregrinations, we have also been performing *Kinoteuthis* in the flesh as we have prepared for publication. To this end, we would like to extend a huge thanks to Christine Daigle and Terrance McDonald, whose invitation to attend the inaugural Posthumanisms Research Network workshop, "Expressions and Images of the Posthuman," allowed us to road-test work in progress with a range of interdisciplinary thinkers at Brock University, including Nandita Biswas Mellamphy, Lukas Brasiskis, Russell Kilbourn, and Anna Mirzayan.

Various of our eight limbs would also like to thank (again, in alphabetical order) Andrés Bartolomé Leal, Wendy Bednarz, Celestino Deleyto, Andrew deWaard, Kelli Fuery, Graeme Harper, Seung-hoon Jeong, Angelos Koutsourakis, Lars Kristensen, Maja Manojlovic, and Michael Witt, for inviting us to present aspects of this work at research seminars at (from C to Z) Chapman University (funded by Erasmus Mundi), New York University Abu Dhabi, Oakland University, the University College of Skövde, the University of California Los Angeles, the University of Leeds, the University of Roehampton, and the University of Zaragoza (funded by Erasmus+). Thanks must also be extended to Stacey Abbott, Radhika Aggarwal, María del Mar Azcona, Caroline Bainbridge, Alice Bardan, Anita Biressi, Robert Burgoyne, Dennis Chua, Enrica Colusso, Julia Echeverría, Luis Miguel García Mainar, Pablo Gómez, Chris Homewood, Deborah Jermyn, Amos Katz, Aleksandr Krawec, Gillian McIver, Murray Pomerance, Judith Rifeser, Jamie Rogers, Tova Shaban, Gauti Sigthorsson, Eddie Troy, Jamie Uy, and Hunter Vaughan for their interactions and hospitality in and around these sessions.

Thanks equally to the organizers of and delegates at various of the recent Film-Philosophy conferences, especially in Edinburgh (2016), Lancaster (2017), Gothenburg (2018), and Brighton (2019), as well as at La filosofia, il castello e la torre in Ischia in 2018. Across these events, we received valuable feedback on work that now appears in the pages that follow. Special mention here to Anna Backman Rogers, Lucy Bolton, Mashya Boon, Mark Cauchi, John Caruana, George Crosthwait, David Deamer, Elena del Río, Pansy Duncan, Steven Eastwood, Matthew Holtmeier, Joseph Jenner, Laurence Kent, Dario Llinares, Raffaele Mirelli, John Ó Maoilearca, Agnieszka Piotrowska, Chiara Quaranta, Timna Rauch, Richard Rushton, David Sorfa, Francesco Sticchi, Catherine Wheatley, and Dan Yacavone, among many others.

We would also like to thank Adam Knee for forming panels on Scarlett Johansson, respectively with four and then all eight of our limbs, at the Shanghai Theatre Academy (2014) and the University of Nottingham Ningbo China (2015). Likewise to Clifton Evers, who formed a panel with us for the Screen Conference on Animals and Animality at the University of Glasgow back in 2015, and whose ideas have invariably polluted ours. Meanwhile, we are also indebted to Paul Martin, who worked with four of our limbs on an ill-fated interdisciplinary article that remains to emerge in print. Some of the material and research used for this unpublished piece have, with Paul's permission, gained a repurposed afterlife in Chapter 2—and these parts wouldn't have been half as good were it not for their ludic past. Those same four limbs would also like to thank Melissa Brown for bouncing around ideas in a shared office, and for gifting us with beautiful octopus artwork. We would also like to thank Rory Perrott for his concept art, which was inspired by the book's gestation, and which we have used during various presentations and performances around the world since.

DHF would expressly like to thank Mira for her unbending love and support . . . and for enduring so many weird tentacle films during the production of this book. Thanks also to David and Moira, Michael and

Ellen, Ruth and Kenny, Maurice and Anouk, and the wider Fleming clan. Special shout to the Porty Sharks too. Finally, to Phaedra and Tarran, my thunder and lightning.

WJRCB would also like expressly to thank Mila Zuo for reading draft work, engaging in discussions, and bearing moans, with credit also due to the Brown, Bullen, and Cambola clans, together with various other friends.

Once you become "the guys doing the squid book," others send to you pretty much everything they encounter on cephalopods, including films, books, articles, and clickbait. Some clickbait aside, this is a wonderful experience, and so thanks to all of those who have helped to add to our film- and bibliographies (most are named above, but this is also a "sorry if we've forgotten you" moment). Once we get going on the media and mud project that will follow *Kinoteuthis Infernalis* (tentatively titled *Here's Mud in Your Eye!*), surely infinite recommendations are to follow.

FYI, parts of Chapter 7 originally appeared as David H. Fleming and William Brown, "Through a (First) Contact Lens Darkly: *Arrival*, Unreal Time and the Chthulucene," in *Film-Philosophy*, 22:3 (2018), pp. 340–363.

Finally, we know that this book is a bit crazy. And we'll not say outright to what extent its contents constitute a metaphor or a weird reality that we believe in (the more accurate answer is both). Nonetheless, for all our humour (which we use here as a *mètic* method), we also take our work seriously. Thus we must admit, as per academic tradition, that while we hope not to have made any, all errors are nonetheless our own—and are there to remind us and you of our humble humanity. Now, depending on the medium in which you are encountering *Kinoteuthis Infernalis*, flip the pulp or press the plasma, and prepare to be taken into uncharted waters.

We live on a placid island of ignorance in the midst of black seas of infinity, and it was not meant that we should voyage far. The sciences, each straining in its own direction, have hitherto harmed us little; but some day the piecing together of dissociated knowledge will open up such terrifying vistas of reality, and our frightful position therein, that we shall either go mad from the revelation or flee from the deadly light into the peace and safety of a new dark age.

– H. P. Lovecraft

Cephalopods are an island of mental complexity in the sea of invertebrate animals. Because our most recent common ancestor was so simple and lies so far back, cephalopods are an independent experiment in the evolution of large brains and complex behavior. If we can make contact with cephalopods as sentient beings, it is not because of a shared history, not because of kinship, but because evolution built minds twice over. This is probably the closest we will come to meeting an intelligent alien.

– Peter Godfrey-Smith

Just as octopus is delicious to eat but gives one nightmares full of disturbing, weird imaginings (so they say), likewise with poetry too.

– Plutarch

Beaky Prepostface (to sucker you in)

Blood and Thunder! *Kinoteuthis Infernalis* is a portentous and diabolical beast, and the speculative study contained herein blends crazy mixed methods in order to identify an outlandish cine-critter, a mysterious cine-squid from hell ("kino-teuthis infernalis"), that takes us to the end of the world and into a nonhuman multiverse. Our eight-limbed search for this monster enticed us to journey to, and to scour around, a recently formed archipelago, a rare piece of dry terrain from which we write this report, even if the squalling seas still wrack our shores and call us back to the howling infinite. *The Squid Cinema from Hell*: Kinoteuthis Infernalis *and the Emergence of Chthulumedia* thus constitutes a history of our voyage down into the depths of cephalopod cinema and cinema-as-cephalopod, in the process dragging us with its seductive suckers across the dank fields of cryptozoology, evolutionary biology, geology, media theory, astrophysics, (un)natural history, fable, quantum physics, and philosophy—all the while being a work of film and media studies, in that its focus is primarily tentacles in films, films with tentacles, and soft and voluminous media. In the end we hope that the fellow traveler who reads this log will feel, as Charles Darwin once put it, that they, like us, have borne witness to "the first appearance of new beings on this earth" (Darwin 1845: 378). Or perhaps, in the spirit of H. P. Lovecraft, old, nay primeval ones that, like his Cthulhu, are on the rise as humanity faces its final spell on dry land and as the anthropocene is replaced by the chthulucene. Old or new—new and old—our eyes have seen weird, betentacled criptids/cryptids lurking beneath the surface of things, and here, where criticism becomes prophecy as our era of war at a distance ("tele-machus") necessitates the study of distance ("tele-ology"), it is our shamanic duty to report to you our dark illuminations and presentiments—for all of our lives may depend upon "cross[ing] the Rubicon to nonhuman minds" (Sagan 2010: 20). As Luce Irigaray says, "endless rapture awaits whoever trusts the sea" (Irigaray 1991: 13). The emergence of chthulumedia may even be the long-awaited rapture.

CHAPTER 1

Introducing the End

Blast your toplights! Plutarch reports that Diogenes of Sinope—the notorious cynic who not only wanted to learn from animals, but also to base human existence on animality—died on account of eating a "raw octopus," a wild gesture in keeping with his lifelong remonstration against the effects of perverting civilizing forces, especially the "inconvenience of preparing cooked food" (see Onfray 2015: 21). With respect to cookery, Diogenes professedly railed against the treatment of raw flesh or vegetables by fire—that perverse Promethean *technē* purloined from the gods and thereafter setting men apart from, and against, "nature." We shall see humans consume raw octopus later (as well as rare octopus-like creatures eating the odd human), before also considering the Promethean control by humans of fire and, by extension, light. However, at present we wish simply to highlight how Diogenes felt that humans had strayed on to a path of civilized perversion, since we shall look here at the most recent technological "perversions" affecting human civilization—networked computers, software programs, and digital screens—arguing that they mark a strange spiraling return, or reversion, to the world of animals and animality, and in particular the world of cephalopods, which, as Jacob von Uexküll might put it, have their own *umwelt*, or nonhuman world with nonhuman perceptions (see von Uexküll 2010).

Our intention is not just to look at the role that cephalopods—primarily octopuses and squids—play in contemporary media (with an especial emphasis on film). It is also our intention to look at the contemporary media-drenched world from the perspective of/as if it were a cephalopodic universe, since this may help us to understand media not just from a human perspective, but from the perspective of (primarily but not exclusively digital) media themselves. Our aim being to offer up ideas regarding how media themselves think (and act, and invite us to interact, and therefore think). As we shall see, this is necessarily a weird and speculative endeavor, not least because it involves the suggestion that media are alive, an alien presence heralding a new world in which the fate of humans is not necessarily certain as we grow increasingly to recognize the intelligence—and thus the life—of media. Forasmuch weird, though, we believe that the idea of chthulumedia/*Kinoteuthis Infernalis* is one that has legs—perhaps eight of them, to be paradoxically imprecise (eight is a precise figure while "perhaps" signifies ambiguity; we shall also revert shortly to this tension between precision and ambiguity, and paradox, as part of our methodology). For the time being, though, we should say that we do not just want our readers to leave this book with a better understanding of films featuring cephalopods and other tentacled creatures. Such a book would be for the cephalopod/tentacle fetishist at best (although when we consider the popularity of tentacle porn, or that which in Japan is characterized by *shokushu* ["tentacles"] as a form of *hentai* [erotic animation, or literally "perversion"], then that would not be too small a readership). No—our intended readership is much wider than that, and like an octopus clinging to a human with its suckers, we want slowly and softly to lure you into cephalopod thought, putting into place a perverse and weird seduction that hopefully is not without erotic components, as we get you to think like a cephalopod and to find cephalopod thought not just in a ring-fenced selection of movies and other media products that we have carefully selected for cookèd consumption, but raw and everywhere.

In this way, *The Squid Cinema from Hell*: Kinoteuthis Infernalis *and the Emergence of Chthulumedia* is a bit like the change that a human undergoes during puberty, when as a result of hormonal shifts, the adolescent has a novel tendency to find sexual innuendo everywhere (as the adolescent begins to appreciate the erotics of everyday life). Like the adolescent gurgling away in their barely controlled state of sexual overwhelm, we want you to find cephalopods (and their own erotics) everywhere. We want to seduce you as you see/think/feel from the perspective of other minds and bodies. We want to change you as you have flashes of other worlds. And like Diogenes dying from his raw octopus, we cannot say that we do not want to kill you as you taste cephalopod thinking raw rather than cooked. One bite and you may be hooked. But where some fear mind-alteration as dangerous and perhaps even evil, we want to show you that there is nothing to fear. Like puberty, we want you simply to emerge on the other side of our hormonal and cerebral shift as a different being. The old you will be dead (and in this way *Kinoteuthis Infernalis* will have killed you). And yet, we confidently can say that you will still be here, and that one of the things that you will have learned is that death is simply another part of becoming. For, we present here a shimmering ecstasy of a thousand small deaths (or orgasmic *petites morts*) that correspond to each of our thousand tiny glittering sexes (see Deleuze and Guattari 2004: 235). And in the light of which you will be coming and becoming *with* the world.

Armed with these new nonontological cephalopodic perspectives, we believe we can be with the world again—a paradoxical new world within the old world, seeing the world not as fixed but as changing and thus fresh with possibility. By giving you death, then, we give you hope—and hope is a corrective of tingling fear. To get to hope, though, perhaps we must face our fears, we must face what lies beneath, and allow ourselves to become suckered in, and look into the eye (and the partially sighted skin-screen) of squids and octopuses. We must confront Cthulhu. We must stare Roko's basilisk in the eye. (Worry not—the meaning of these strange demonic names and the bestiary that they convey will be revealed in good time—for time as change and becoming is indeed good.)

Why Cephalopods? An Anecdote

There are three preliminary answers to the question as to why we are considering cephalopods, with the first being anecdotal, the second observational-empirical, and the third historical-theoretical.

First, the anecdote. Four of our limbs were on an airplane, traveling long haul, on the type of vessel where, embedded in the back of the headrest of the passenger in front, each traveler is granted their own personal screen (as these days we mostly have outside of airplanes, too). The sort of voyage where a constrained film scholar can catch up on all the latest spineless Hollywood pulp—which is made available through the commercial hauler's onboard intranet (and which no doubt trawls our viewing data as it solicits our "likes"). On this occasion we chanced a seat on an aisle, mid-galley, which granted us a broad vista over a bank of others' headrest-screens—and a porthole aspect onto splinters of the screens in the rows in front, as well as an askew vantage of our starboard neighbor's screen *and* his iPad tablet. Fast-forward a few hours into the flight—after cruising altitude has been maintained and the victuals have been razed and tidied. We remember half-minding a wishy-washy franchise film featuring a British beast-hunting wizard in the USA (*Fantastic Beasts and Where to Find Them*, David Yates, USA/UK, 2016). In a distracted state we were also scouring the cabin to see what we might watch next, using the multiple screens within our field of vision as a material YouTube-style applet bar—albeit one streaming full films and television shows rather than just offering thumbnails.

Then, our ears must have been cued by affective headphone sounds, for our attention was racked back to our assigned headrest-screen. Therein, and not for the first time in this film, a dark billowing smoke monster called an Obscurous—somewhat like the smoke monster seen in the television series *Lost* (J. J. Abrams, Jeffrey Lieber, and Damon Lindelof, USA, 2004–10)—was spiraling around the plasma screen. However, this time something more interesting was happening. For in our peripheral vision we noticed that this black sentient cloudiness was spreading across on to our neighbor's iPad too. On closer scrutiny, though, it transpired that he was not watching *Fantastic Beasts* . . ., but the beginning of the latest modular *Star Trek* series (*Star Trek Beyond*, Justin Lin, USA/Hong Kong/China, 2016), the high-concept opening of which finds a black tendril of inky CGI-smoke sculpting itself into various familiar objects, before deforming, and then re-forming, into a starship, a phaser, a Shatner-era communicator, and so on. As we watched, a sort of flick(er)ing triffid-like tentacle briefly appeared on his touch-screen too. Remarkably, we then noticed *another* screen in front of us showing the Huallywood blockbuster *Xi you ji: Da nao tian gong/The Monkey King* (Pou-Soi Cheang, China/Hong Kong, 2014), and which also featured a curling demonic Obscurous-effect. So, there we were, contingently witnessing three unrelated monitors, each simultaneously billowing the same sort of inky CGI effects. It was as if some invisible squid had suddenly deposited a spiraling ink trail along the whole cabin's screen-tanks as it withdrew down the tube of the deck—and for the rest of our voyage we kept on noticing evermore of the same sort of zeitgeist effects, often coupled with glimpses of weird monsters, demigods, aliens, antennae, and tentacles. This brings us to our observational reasons for why we are writing a book about cephalopods, and which themselves begin to move toward theoretical considerations.

Tentacular Art and Media

We live in tentacular times. Indeed, it seems that tentacles are everywhere. In the realm of literature, this is not simply a case of well-known historical references to cephalopods in the work of Pliny the Elder, Plutarch, Lord Alfred Tennyson, Charles Darwin, Jules Verne, Victor Hugo, Étienne Geoffroy Saint-Hilaire, and the Comte de Lautréamont (see Montgomery 2015: 4–6; Nakajima *et al.* 2018). For, a trip along the vast banks of the Amazon (website) might well also lead you, if you coast into the right forbidden waters, to titles such as *Tentacle: Chameleon 2012* (Albert 2012), *Good Sense of Humour, Must Have Tentacles* (Cramer 2012), *Wrapped up in Tentacles* (Lake 2014), *Squirm: Virgin Captive of the Billionaire Biker Tentacle Monster* (Silverwood 2014), *Tentacle Erotica Mega Bundle* (Trace 2014), *Tentacle Lord: Book 1* (La Mer 2015), *Alien Tentacle Chronicles: Bound* (Styles 2016) and *Seeded by the Alien Tentacle King* (Bright 2017)—to take but eight engrossing titles from the world of pulpy tentacle porn. We should note that many of these are not just soft porn, however, but also soft books, in the sense that they are ebooks, or books without spines. That is, these books are, like their subject matter, invertebrate.

This is not to mention the work of more paper-backed authors such as Matt Ruff, whose *Lovecraft Country* (2016), like China Miéville's *Kraken* (2010), amounts to an apocalyptic conspiracy novel in the tradition of H. P. Lovecraft (about whom more later), and much like Robert Shea and Robert Anton Wilson's earlier Lovecraft-inspired *Illuminatus! Trilogy* (1984), which itself features many subaquatic adventures that are linked to LSD culture and the end of the world. Ruff, Miéville, and Shea/Wilson no doubt also link to the work of Thomas Pynchon, whose *Gravity's Rainbow* (1973) has an octopus, Grigori, at its core in its story of war, piracy, and the development of the early drone technology that was the V-2 rocket. Notably, Alex Ross Perry's film *Impolex* (USA, 2009) is a partial adaptation of *Gravity's Rainbow*, which retains Pynchon's octopus (voiced by Eugene Mirman) as a weird interlocutor for a soldier (Riley O'Bryan), who wanders lost through a forest holding on to the rocket from which the film takes its title.

Beyond these literary manifestations, squid- and octopus-like creatures appear in art galleries, theme parks, architecture, video games, augmented or virtual reality experiences, music videos, television shows, apps, novels, magazines, adverts, online memes, and graphic novels (of which, dear reader, there are enough to overrun this entire book).[1]

Sticking solely to cinema, then, since this is the primary focus of this book, cephalopods have featured in different ways and in numerous films, even though filming underwater is not easy and even though the cephalopod is famous for remaining invisible to the camera/eye as a result of its ability to camouflage itself. Early examples of octopuses and squids onscreen include *The Trail of the Octopus* (Duke Worne, USA, 1919) and *La pieuvre/The Octopus* (Jean Painlevé, France, 1928), with the octopus being revisited by Painlevé nearly forty years later in *Les amours de la pieuvre/Love Life of an Octopus* (Geneviève Hamon and Jean Painlevé, France, 1967). All manner of monster and mutant movies feature cephalopods, from *It Came from Beneath the Sea* (Robert Gordon, USA, 1955) to *Octopussy* (John Glen, UK/USA, 1983) and *Mega Shark vs Giant Octopus* (Ace Hannah, USA, 2009).

Furthermore, if we expand our bestiary to include not just recognized, earthly cephalopods (if cephalopods are indeed earthly), but also betentacled creatures (especially aliens), then we must also consider *It Came from Outer Space* (Jack Arnold, USA, 1953), *The Tingler* (William Castle, USA, 1959), *Possession* (Andrzej Zuławski, France/West Germany, 1981), *Gwoemul/The Host* (Bong Joon-ho, South Korea, 2006), *Monsters* (Gareth

Edwards, UK, 2010), *Spring* (Justin Benson and Aaron Moorhead, USA, 2014), *Arrival* (Denis Villeneuve, USA, 2016), *La región salvaje/ The Untamed* (Amat Escalante, Mexico/Denmark/France/Germany/ Norway/Switzerland, 2016), *Miss Peregrine's Home for Peculiar Children* (Tim Burton, UK/Belgium/USA, 2016), *Life* (Daniel Espinosa, USA, 2017) and *Solo: A Star Wars Story* (Ron Howard, USA, 2018), all of which will merit consideration in what follows, together with films like *Ghost in the Shell* (Rupert Sanders, USA/India/China/Japan/Hong Kong/UK/ New Zealand/Canada/Australia, 2017), which feature other tentacled marine creatures like jellyfish.

Cephalopods and other tentacled creatures are not limited to global horror and/or sci-fi movies, but also play key roles in arthouse movies from around the world, and from among which we shall consider *Hokusai Manga/ Edo Porn* (Kineto Shindô, Japan, 1981), *Maelström* (Denis Villeneuve, Canada, 2000), *L'uomo in più/One Man Up* (Paolo Sorrentino, Italy, 2001), *Oldeuboi/Oldboy* (Park Chan-wook, South Korea, 2003), *Cefalópodo/ Cephalopod* (Rubén Imaz, Mexico, 2010), *Évolution/Evolution* (Lucile Hadžihalilović, France/Belgium/Spain, 2015), *Ah-ga-ssi/The Handmaiden* (Park Chan-wook, South Korea, 2016) and *Kékzsakállú* (Gastón Solnicki, Argentina, 2016). On a related note, the title of *Naissance des pieuvres* (Céline Sciamma, France, 2007), which typically is translated as *Water Lilies*, literally means "birth of the octopuses"—a title that perhaps gives us a far greater clue to the film's meaning than the English translation does. Meanwhile Noah Baumbach's *The Squid and the Whale* (USA, 2005) and the aforementioned *Impolex* both suggest a cephalopodic presence in American indy cinema.

Finally, we shall explore how a relationship between cephalopods and technology is established in *Demonlover* (Olivier Assayas, France, 2002) and *Elle* (Paul Verhoeven, France/Germany/Belgium, 2016), which both feature violent tentacular sex in the cyber realm. Meanwhile, the tentacular Sentinels in *The Matrix* (Andy and Larry Wachowski, USA, 1999) and Dr. Otto Octavius, also known as Dr. Octopus, in *Spider-Man 2* (Sam Raimi, USA, 2004) also convey a sense of how cephalopods are linked to digital technology.[2]

What we hope to have made clear by unfurling this long tentacular list is that there is a bounty of films that feature invertebrates and cephalopods, cephalopod-like creatures, cephalopod-like or cephalopod-inspired technologies, tentacles and/or which draw upon Lovecraftian Cthulhu mythology in order to tell tales wild and weird. These films stretch across cinema's history, extending into different genres and different national/ regional cinemas. While not obvious (perhaps because camouflaged—like an octopus), we wish to suggest, then, that the cephalopod is omnipresent

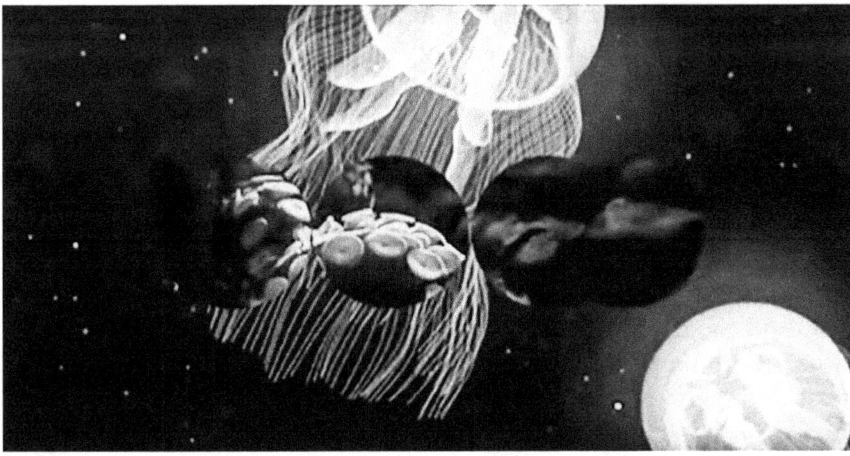

Figure 1.1 Still from Digital Cinema Media ident

in cinema, but more intensely so in the contemporary era, when digital media practices make clear the cephalopodic logic of these forms.

To similar ends, we would like to note that a tendrilled jellyfish and writhing octopus arms feature prominently in the omnipresent big-screen ident for DCM (Digital Cinema Media)—the company that in the UK sells advertising space/time before film screenings (see Figure 1.1). Two things might be worth noting here: firstly, that the octopus welcomed until 2019 virtually all viewers to cinema screenings in the UK (especially at megaplexes run by Virgin, Cineworld, Odeon, and Vue); and secondly, that the logic of advertising is perhaps not so different from the logic of cephalopods, cinema, and of media more generally—in that it wants to lure us in through its chromatophoric displays and through its seductive tentacles, affirming its otherness at the same time as it mesmerizes us.

Loose Metaphorics

Our third answer to *why cephalopods?* is more theoretical. Our previous work on digital effects, digital media and digital environments saw us (individually and collectively) begin theorizing the latest historical ("post-human" and "post-cinematic") modes of moving and imaging afforded by computer-era filmmaking techniques. With regard to cinema, we have written on various occasions about the new forms of fluid movement that are increasingly enabled by the creation of volumetric digital worlds, and which can be navigated in a decidedly nonhuman and non-analog way, not least by permitting a modular point of view to soar through voluminous space as if all within it had melted into water or gas, and/or shift scale at will to pass through tiny holes and/or explore otherwise inaccessible regions (see Brown and Fleming 2011, 2015; Brown 2009a, 2013; Fleming and Brown 2015). However, as we began to rethink these animated gasiform features in light of the seeming omnipresence of cephalopods and tentacles, we suddenly felt that there was a bigger picture, or rather a cephalopodic abstract diagram, lurking within or behind our previous *informe* thoughts. And so, our attention was pricked, and we were on the hunt for new ways and means of proceeding.

Now, animals have of course always been a key part of cinema since its very beginnings, with Rosalind Galt (2015) pointing to the presence of cats in even the earliest films by the Lumière brothers, whose *Sortie de l'usine Lumière à Lyon/Workers Leaving the Factory* (France, 1895) equally features at least two dogs. Nicole Shukin (2009) has explained how early film stock was created through the use of "animal glue," or pulped animals, while various other scholars have recently turned their attention to the animal components of films—in a bid to consider those aspects of cinema that lie beyond simply the human (see, for example, Lippit 2000; Pick 2011; McMahon 2015a; Creed and Reesink 2015). In other words, cinema does not exist without the animal.

What is more, animals and animality have for better and/or for worse played an unquestionably foundational role in the history and structuring of human thought, concept creation, and self-determination more generally. In particular since the nineteenth century, animals have become auspicious figures for thinking through technology and its concomitant transformations of nature. Conversely, and as Akira Mizuta Lippit shows, European modernity can "be defined by the disappearance of wildlife from humanity's habitat and by the reappearance of the same in humanity's reflections of itself: in philosophy, psychoanalysis, and technological media" (Lippit 2000: 2–3). In this way, animals are not only representationally significant to technology but are conceptually and materially implicated in it as well. This is before we even consider tracing a reverse line wherein biological life itself may be understood as always already *technological*, or *technē* proficient, after having initiated processes of becoming-technological qua biotechnological in its primordial appropriation and adaptation of "external" environmental materials and minerals, to form enabling motile structures and prostheses (see, for example, DeLanda 2000: 26; Wills 2008). Accordingly, *Kinoteuthis Infernalis* takes part in the recent "bestial" turn in film and media studies, which harnesses animals and animality in order to "widen the possibilities to think media and technological culture" (Parikka 2010: xiv).

Bearing these material dimensions in mind militates against engaging solely in what Jussi Parikka might term "loose metaphorics," wherein analogy is used "as a method of explanation, [as] we often try to see one phenomenon in the use of some other, usually a familiar one" (Parikka 2010: xxi). Indeed, Parikka's *Insect Media: An Archaeology of Animals and Technology*, from which we have just quoted, demonstrates how insects can come to enrich our understanding of media, as media can perhaps also come to enrich our understanding of insects—such that at times it would appear as though the two are not easily distinguishable one from the other. That is, media might *best* be understood as insects (and insects as media), begging the question anew as to *why cephalopods?* (if insects do the job better, or indeed if one could find commonalities between any two things, much as the adolescent human brain can find sexual innuendo anywhere that it wishes). Or again, cinema and its new media offspring might well have commonalities with cephalopods, but they also have commonalities with insects, cetaceans, arthropods, and pachyderms, to take examples from the animal kingdom alone. Why not equally plastics, plants, mud, the elements more broadly, architecture, music, engineering, ghosts, and religion, which surely also have connections with cinema and media? Why, then, cephalopods and not anything else?

To this we have ready a material and metaphoric answer. For setting out the former we can briefly return to Henri Bergson's writing in *Creative Evolution*, where he contends that for organic life forms, the imagistic perception of any given present moment is always already heavily pregnant with the past (see Bergson 1998). Gilbert Simondon and Michel Serres indicate that such also holds true for technological objects and machinic artifacts, which likewise smuggle their own hidden pasts with them into the present (Serres in/and Simondon 1958: 25–26). The latter elsewhere links this deep and forgotten past to a radical "newness," or the open and transforming future, by framing technologies as "exo-Darwinian" drivers that radically impact human cultures and persons. By becoming free of the need for genes in order to propagate—and free from slowing the time of evolution—human technologies are able rapidly to sculpt the collectives and individuals that previously sculpted them. In other words, our forgetful *despecialized* species attains new behaviors, abilities, and (cultural) intentions with each new tecnologial turn (Serres 2018: 45ff.). As Serres puts it, "[i]ndividual and collective, hardware and software" are all technologies that reveal "cognitive virtues," or at least "mnemonic ones," which act like material memories and change engines (Serres 2018: 47). Among other things, Serres notes how in today's superfast "bioculture," modern technologies drastically "change the scale of time," speeding us up while concomitantly reconnecting us to the deep and forgotten primordial strata of the past. That is, they reconnect us to what Serres terms the Grand Narrative, which includes the history of our species, the evolution of life on Earth more generally, the birth of the planet, and the formation of atoms during the early universe (some 15 billion years ago).

Keeping both this deep, dark history and light-speed acceleration in mind, we might provisionally begin to chart the oft-overlooked role of the cephalopod in the early history of computing development and intelligence. As a first port of call we might remember, as Katherine H. Courage reports, that "back in the 1940s the Marshall Plan lobbed a hunk of money over to Naples, Italy, to see if a lab there could crack the code of the cephalopod brain to make more efficient computers" (Courage 2013: 4). Working in Naples at this time was the outstanding British zoologist and neurophysiologist John Zachary (J.Z.) Young, famed for his groundbreaking comparative studies between the brains, neural intelligence, and memories of common octopuses (*octopus vulgaris*) and humans. Accordingly, Nakajima *et al.* note how during the 1950s

> Young was falling more and more under the influences of cybernetics. The comparative project became the octopus project, and the octopus progressively became a mechanical model—a living computer containing, rather than being characterized by, a memory.
>
> The natural end-point of such a development was the attempt at building a learning machine based on what the researchers had learned about the performances and structure of the animal . . . This machine later came to be subsumed under the wider category of "perceptron," or neural networks and is rather part of the pre-history of artificial intelligence (A.I.) than of its history proper . . . Despite the promises to his patrons (developing a learning computer), what Young had in mind was a comparative study of animal and machine learning, in which not only the animal could provide a blueprint for the machine, but the machine could also help in the interpretation of the structure-function nexus in the octopus. (Nakajima *et al.* 2018: 3)

Cephalopodic forms of thought and intelligence may here be fathomed as entering molecularly into composition with the ancestors of today's digital media assemblages and techno-culture forms, with the cephalopod here becoming the proverbial ghost haunting the computer shell. We shall in the next chapter look at a cephalopodic media archaeology that extends well beyond cinema, before suggesting in our final chapter that an eruption of cephalopodic logic (and alien life) lies at the heart of many (all?) media, from writing to computers. With regard to the former claims we are certainly not the first. In fact, Vilém Flusser had in the 1980s already noted connections between the latest software beings and the "soft intelligence" of cephalopods (to purloin a phrase offered by Jacques-Yves Cousteau; see Cousteau and Diolé 1973). Regarding the term *software*, Flusser maintains that "there can be no doubt that 'soft' alludes to mollusks ('soft animals')," of which cephalopods are of course examples (Flusser and Bec 2012: 67). That is, the cephalopod is inscribed into technology, such that technology—including artificial intelligence—is like a cephalopod. Indeed, tech guru Jaron Lanier suggests that "Cephalopods + Childhood = Humans + Virtual Reality," by which he means that if cephalopods had a human system of parenting, childhood, and the ability for adults to pass knowledge on to children, then they would rule the world, while virtual reality will give to humans the ability to morph, hide, and hunt as a cephalopod (see Lanier 2010: 189).

Beyond the esoteric philosophy of Serres, Flusser, and Lanier, mainstream cultural critics such as Nicholas Carr also proselytize and popularize the idea of digital technologies harboring near-magical abilities to reconfigure and rewire the hyperplastic human brain and nervous systems, moving into daily composition with them, and in the process profoundly transforming what we are both as individuals and as societies (see Carr 2011). But Carr, like Diogenes before him, primarily foregrounds the negative aspects of these transformations, which he sees as making humans shallow and superficial, hence the title of his book, *The Shallows*.

Unlike Carr, however, we do not pine for any "return" to a pristine or prehistoric species origin. Instead, drawing on philosophers like Serres, Flusser, Gilles Deleuze and Félix Guattari, Donna J. Haraway, and Rosi Braidotti, we do not recognize any essential, transcendental, or "pure" human nature to be perverted or polluted by technologies. Rather, as the world itself changes, so "minds change with it," precisely because minds are always already "ecological phenomena" (see Reynolds 2019: 50).

To help symbolize what we see as a false Diogenesian problematic, then, we might in passing draw upon a fitting illustration offered by Guattari in *The Three Ecologies*, where the Frenchman aptly relates a televised experiment with an octopus conducted by Alain Bombard. As Guattari recalls it, Bombard

> produced two glass tanks, one filled with polluted water—of the sort that one might draw from the port of Marseille—containing a healthy, thriving, almost dancing octopus. The other tank contained, pure, unpolluted seawater. Bombard caught the octopus and immersed it in the "normal" water; after a few seconds the animal curled up, sank to the bottom and died. (Guattari 2010: 29)

Similarly, Danna Staaf reports how climate change might be causing various cephalopod populations not to be diminishing in size (in spite of perceived over-fishing), but in fact to be increasing (Staaf 2017: 192). And so, Guattari/Bombard's unfortunate octopus was undone by what many would erroneously consider to be its pure or natural (unpolluted) environment, therefore we do not believe that there is any pure or true pre-technological mindstate for our species to be returned to. There is no "Ctrl-Alt-Del" reset to take us back to some form of Edenic mind.

Thinking of minds, though, we might add that cephalopods have also played a significant mediating role in shaping (contaminating? polluting?) the neuroscientific understanding of our own human brain's function. Indeed, Nakajima *et al.* note how

> in the late 1930s, the Age of the Squid began. Their so-called giant axon—a syncytium, and as such an exception to the strict Cajalian rule of anatomical independence of nerve cells . . . was famously re-discovered by the zoologist John Zachary Young in 1936. The Marine Stations of Plymouth and the Woods Hole (Massachusetts, US) became hothouses for the introduction and development of this model, which was soon adopted by axonologists worldwide. In particular, the giant axon became the experimental model of the Cambridge biophysical school thanks to the work of Alan Hodgkin, Andrew Huxley . . . and Bernhard Katz, all of whom it helped to win the Nobel Prize. As Hodgkin later mused: "It is arguable that the introduction of the squid giant nerve fiber . . . did more for axonology than any other single advance in technique during the last 40 years. Indeed a distinguished neurophysiologist remarked recently at a congress dinner (not, I thought, with the utmost tact) 'It's the squid they really ought to give the Nobel Prize to.'" (Nakajima *et al.* 2018: 2–3; see also Staaf 2017: 4–5)

As we accrue more reasons for why cephalopods merit sustained critical attention in our contemporary media-saturated world, we might nonetheless return to the issue of metaphorics. For, if thought is infinite, then why not think infinitely? That is, if numerous or infinite metaphors enrich our understanding of film and media (media as insects, media as cetaceans, and so on), then why not add another metaphor (media as cephalopods) in order to draw out, thicken or deepen that understanding as the next step in a probably infinite process of greater comprehension? More than this, though, we might suggest that if any two things can be equated if we try soft enough (media as mud, for example), then this is perhaps because we live in a world in which the divisions and separations that are handed down to us do not really exist. Pre-existing language would seem to suggest that cinema is not a cephalopod, since we have different words for these two distinct things (if cinema and cephalopods were the same, then they'd be called the same thing). And yet we can find commonalities, resonances, relationships, and links that upset this separation—just as when it tries hard enough the adolescent mind can find relationships of desire between any two different things. This is not simply a matter of humans and cephalopods enjoying relations of desire—even if, despite the fact that the two species cannot procreate, such perversions do exist (most explicitly in the form of *hentai* involving *shokushu*, as we shall explore in Chapter 5). Rather, the very process of finding commonalities, relationships, and links demonstrates both that we live with a processual world defined by change and in which anything might well become anything else over a long enough timescale (at the very least in the sense of the molecules from a mollusk ending up being part of a computer or a human and *vice versa*), and that the barriers, divisions, borders, and separations between things are an anthropocentric conceit—albeit one that is perhaps necessary for the lifestyle to which many humans have become accustomed (however long that may last). Even though humans like to split creatures into different phyla and species, the tentacles that we see on the so-called "tree of life" demonstrate that all phyla and species are in fact linked (for a good example of this, see the visualization of the tree of life on OneZoom, a software/website designed by James Rosindell and Yan Wong, the latter of whom co-authored *The Ancestor's Tale: A Pilgrimage to the Dawn of Life* with Richard Dawkins; see Rosindell and Wong n.d.; Dawkins and Wong 2017). In other words, "metaphorics," perhaps especially when soft and loose, are perhaps indicative of our tentacular times—and so tentacles become timely metaphors or conceptual beings through which to think . . . tentacles!

Without the conceit of humans being separate from rather than connected with other species and the world as a whole, we contend that humans would not be able to live in the way that many of them do (which, broadly speaking, is to live under capitalism). Perhaps this is made clear by the transition from the anthropocene to the chthulucene, in which capital is demonstrated to be unsustainable. But what presently we wish to suggest is that if humans are interconnected or entangled with the world, then cinema can also be a machine that connects objects, not least through montage, which can be a machine for making otherwise different objects connect, or poetically to rhyme. With its connecting and connected tentacles, and its shape-shifting simulating form, the cephalopod may just be a capital metaphor for cinema, then, as well as for a universe defined not by a Euclidean space split into three dimensions, but a dimensionless and cinematic space-time in which everywhere and everywhen is connected via wormholes to everywhere and everywhen else, being thus a kind of gigantic megabrain that is weird, soft, loose, and other, and where all things do connect (here we might distinguish the cephalopodic brain, from the Greek κεφαλη, meaning "head," from the "head" of capital, from the Latin *caput*, also meaning "head," since the cephalon-brain is, as we shall see, entangled, while the capital-brain is predicated upon a Cartesian split between mind and body and between human and world). Why not use the connected and connecting cephalopod to sum up media that are connected and connecting within a multiverse that is connected and connecting, and where anything can become sexual/erotic, as connections and desire are made across species and perhaps even across life and death?

To further our case for the relevance of the cephalopod, China Miéville has in a critical essay (as opposed to in a fictional story) acknowledged the "spread of the tentacle" in specifically contemporary culture; it is "a limb-type with no Gothic or traditional precedents (in 'Western' aesthetics)." This means that the tentacle has literally gone "from a situation of near total absence in Euro-American teratoculture up to the nineteenth century, to one of being the default monstrous appendage of today"—something that he sees as signaling an epochal "shift to a Weird culture" (Miéville 2008: 105). Furthermore, Nakajima and colleagues describe our intensifying fascination with tentacular octopuses and squids as signaling the creatures' ascendance to "model animals," and our recognition of them as a valuable "boundary object/subject" that helps to draw together thinkers and practitioners from various different fields, including ethology, ecology, neuroscience, genomics, material industry, camouflage technologies, soft robotics, art, gastronomy, and subpopular culture (Nakajima *et al.* 2018). Finally, Slavoj Žižek also seems to cash in on this cephalopodic moment when he asserts that the Kraken is "a perfect image of the global Capital, all-powerful and stupid, cunning and blind, whose tentacles regulate our lives"—even though after introducing this image somewhat glibly at the outset of *Disparities*, he then does not return to it at all over the ensuing 380 pages of fizz and fury, and certainly does not address, as we shall see later, how the image of the octopus as a metaphor of globalized capital has been with us for over a century (see Žižek 2016: 3).

It should be emerging, then, that the cephalopod is perhaps the very meta-metaphor that connotes the truth of metaphoricity, not just in the sense that we live by metaphors, but also in the sense that metaphors themselves connote a world of connection and non-differentiation. In its extra-corporeal organicity and in its extra-organic corporeality (being a body without organs and an organ without bodies), we shall see that the cephalopod—as a protean *mètic* mechanism oozing organic metaphoricity—offers up another mode of thought that helps us to comprehend a world without boundaries, even at a time when humans are rushing to build walls, tighten borders, exclude immigrants and refugees and thus to create boundaries. For those prepared to change, we wish to work here toward a collective process of becoming-animal, or becoming-cephalopod, that is linked to wider changes inculcated by networked software techno-culture, mutations in mediated capitalism more generally, and a developing comprehension of the multiverse and our place within it. If humans are currently rushing to create boundaries, perhaps it is because they are faced with the realization that the world is a world without boundaries, a realization that is strongly linked to the digital techno-culture in which many humans now live. In this sense, the dissolution of boundaries and the subsequent coming into contact with the outside constitutes not just the rise of Cthulhu (a threatening monster who would kill us all), but the arrival of the chthulucene (an opportunity for us not to continue in hatred of the outside, but to make kin with it).

A Soft Touch

The cephalopod is a mollusk and the mollusk is soft (from the Latin *mollis*, meaning soft). Rather than play hard and fast, then, we here play soft and loose. For, as discussed, the boneless octopus is precisely a creature that has no fixed form and which engages in endless becomings that do indeed challenge the distinction between self and other, mind and body, and terrestrial and cosmic, suggesting that everything is linked and that the octopus exists, in the language of Gilles Deleuze and Félix Guattari, in the realm of the Body without Organs (BwO). In specifically the language of sexual innuendo, Deleuze and Guattari suggest that "on it [the BwO] we penetrate and are penetrated; on it we love . . . The BwO: it is already under way the moment the body has had enough of organs and wants to slough them off, or loses them" (Deleuze and Guattari 2004: 166). The Body without Organs, or what Serres refers to as the white or incandescent "stem body" (Serres 2018: 63), is the space (and time) of connection, creation, despecialization and non-differentiation. In some senses, this is the world of the octopus, the world of cinema/media and, as we shall see, the world of the human—even if to assert as much runs against our common-sense understanding of what it means to be human (i.e., a body separate from the rest of the world, or a world separate from the rest of the cosmos). It is perhaps more accurate, after Žižek, to assert therefore that the cephalopod, cinema/media and humans all are not so much Bodies without Organs as Organs without Bodies, in the sense that the octopus is, for example, all eye, all brain, all skin, all tongue and all sex organ—which might equally be a fecund way of thinking about cinema, media, and the human (see Žižek 2003). Or perhaps, best yet, the octopus, cinema, media, and the human are in some senses bodies without organs without bodies (without organs)—or even organs with bodies with organs (with bodies)—an ongoing becoming that takes place in a space of myriad connections and non-differentiation (where the distinction between with and without blurs), a realm that can be defined anthropocentrically and positively as weird and of madness. And here, we already appear to be speedily coasting through the twisted Deleuzo-Guattarian undercurrents of delirium and drift that will in time reveal connections with superpositions and weird quantum vibrations.

Our "soft" form of cephalopodic theory is designed to offset otherwise "hard" science-based methods and all-too-familiar sclerotic, or ossified, humanist thought systems—the priggish sort that usually promote detached and rationally enlightened or logocentric relationships to the objective world, with their discrete and compartmentalized subjects and objects (and their framing devices qua disciplinary lenses). A straw man, perhaps, but one that nonetheless is conceptually contoured as a patriarchal and heterosexual white male, capitalist in fashion, and whose line of sight is standardly Eurocentric in nature (or rather culture). But, even beneath such armoring, we also disband the very frame of an upright (standard) mammalian ape, who, after being weaned on the breast milk of a nurturing mother, is inclined to perceive the frontiers of his galactic home in a predictably milky way. No—with licks of Friedrich Nietzsche (or having Friedrich Nietzsche licked à la Luce Irigaray), we prankishly reject such drawbacks here, in a way commensurate to how, as Miéville puts it, (hard) "scientism rejects the tentacle" (Miéville 2008: 108). A rejection that remains the case a full decade on from when Miéville inked these comments, as can be recognized by the public rejection by Karin Moelling, a professor at the Max Planck Institute of Molecular Genetics, of a multidisciplinary (and thus impressionistic?) review by thirty-three interdisciplinary scientists who suggest that the DNA of the contemporary octopus has extraterrestrial roots thanks to the arrival on Earth of life-bearing (or retrovirus-laden) comets hundreds of millions of years ago (see, inter alia, Gabbatiss 2018; Steele *et al.* 2018). Moelling's rejection of this weird science goes to show how the buttoned-down Royal Science community still cocks a snook at paradigm-shifting (creative) interdisciplinary thought models (which are essentially the mode of all advancement)—in this case dismissing out of hand the Hoyle–Wickramasinghe (H–W) thesis of Cometary Biology, which posits the existence of an expanded interstellar biosphere teeming with *Cosmic Gene Pools*, which literally impact life on Earth and become entangled with the evolution of terrestrial species.

If the more hardened members of the scientific and academic community openly laugh at such "crack-pot" stuff, we here—along with the weird butts of their jokes—return their laugher eightfold in the face of their own rigidity of habit, thought, perception, and action. For, *pace* Henri Bergson, we perceive their stiffness and inflexibility to be utterly comedic, and believe that laughter is both the correct punishment and the key to unleashing our own inner elasticity and flexibility (Bergson 2013: 10). With this in mind, we also suck up all anticipated platitudes and acculturated heckles of our being a "soft touch" or a bit "soft in the head"—not least because the soft outlandish invertebrates from which we draw inspiration (mollusks) are without contradiction formidable muscular hunters and sharp thinkers. Ergo (if not to err as we go, as is all too human) we recognize that without vertebra, things cannot stand. And so, for invertebrate thought there can be no understanding. But just because we cannot understand, this does not mean that we cannot know. (For example, no one can understand death, just as no one can stand death, which leaves us jaw-dropped/open-mouthed and horizontal, before breaking our bones and reducing us to mud. But even if we cannot stand/understand death, we will all come to know it.)

As we shall see, it might be easy also to find and/or to pick holes in what follows, because ours is an argument of the hole, in particular of wormholes and cephalo-holes that connect across space and time, and which the human body perhaps becomes after death, when it is holed out by worms. Furthermore, we also have a grip already on the notion that our approach is spineless, nebulous, protean, and unrigorous—the sort of criticism that has been leveled at many thinkers before us, including Aristotle, whose thought-systems his confused contemporaries and posterior critics accused of being too cephalopodic in nature, in that he worked "like the cuttlefish who obscures himself in his own ink when he feels himself about to be grasped" (see Schmitt 1965: 60, quoted in Derby 2014: 2701). So, against hard-scientific and phallic ("boner") thought we propose to advance with impressionistic intuition and feeling, using a soft, sticky, billowous, and pulpy mode of progressing. One that is perhaps holy.

We shall revert to the figure of the compressed, desiccated, and bony man in due course. But presently, dear reader, it is perhaps a good time to consider that we as authors have been compelled to desire a new *mollusca* methodology. That is, we are ourselves media enrobed in a larger event, and simply excreting or effusing a new form of thinking and moving suitable for adequately diagramming the crepuscular contemporary assemblage of which, no doubt, we are all in some way, shape or form a part. With these ideas in mind, consider here a line of argument offered by Jakub Zdebik regarding the nature of diagrams and assemblages:

> An assemblage, like archipelagos and spinal columns of quadrupeds and cephalopods, relies on the diagrammatic process of abstraction, here described as folding and unfolding, for the connection, based on function, of heterogeneous parts. Most strikingly, the image of a mammal contorting into the shape of a cephalopod drives the point home. We can imagine the bones cracking, the limbs twisting and the body contracting. The squid is the animal that emblematizes the diagrammatic process. (Zdebik 2012: 176)

In other words, through our encounter with the cephalopod, we hope to achieve a mode of thought that is not ossified and bony, but which instead allows us to think in an invertebrate fashion. It is only in so doing that we can fathom invertebrate media and our invertebrate multiverse.

Vampyroteuthis Infernalis

In seeking further to unfold these compressed ideas, we could do worse than to make as our next port of call *Vampyroteuthis Infernalis: A Treatise, with a Report by the Institut Scientifique de Recherche Paranaturaliste*, the biophilosophical masterwork by Vilém Flusser and Louis Bec. There, Flusser notes how humans must share with the squid an ancient ancestor—since all creatures on the tree of life are not separate but connected. For Flusser, this ancestor is a sort of worm, the body of which somehow contained within itself—among a shimmering potential universe of other virtual and compossible larval body maps—the futural topological arrangements for calcified land-dwelling bipedal mammalian vertebrates like us *and* for gelatinous and boneless cephalopods that inhabit the darkest recesses of the ocean. In spite of this common ancestor, however, vampire squids surface as our (and we as their) "physiological antipodes" (Flusser and Bec 2012: 39). That is, these uncustomary sea creatures divulge inverse body–brain–milieu configurations to us, which gesture toward valuably divergent modes of being in and with the world.

Peter Godfrey-Smith makes similar claims in *Other Minds: The Octopus and the Evolution of Intelligent Life* (2016), pointing to how most animals' action-guiding bodies generate specific constraints and opportunities (as with humans' arrangement of their thumbs and fingers, say, or their forward-facing eyes, the angle of their knees, elbows and shoulders, and so forth), which in turn impact and instruct their gestalt modes of cognizing/acting. For some readers, this idea may contain distant echoes of Baruch/Benedict de Spinoza's concept of body and mind "parallelism" (see Spinoza 2001). That is, a non-Cartesian position that refutes a body/mind dualism, and which, with respect to the human species at least, has gained increasing support from ever-new fields of pursuit in the centuries since Spinoza spilt his (cuttlefish) ink.[3] To help illustrate our point, we might gloss/lick George Lakoff and Mark Johnson's *Metaphors We Live By* (2003), to which we alluded earlier and which asks us to prehend how the structures of human language and thought remain deeply grounded in our physical forms, and the manner in which our (acculturated) bodies move, act, become affected and desire. Consider *in this light*, and, if you will, *on the one hand*, notions of *grasping* new concepts, *seeing things from a new perspective*, or simply *advancing through* an argument *toward* a conclusion. Or *on the other hand*, of feeling *in over your head*, *out in the cold*, *left in the dark*, and feeling completely *disoriented* by a vertiginous whirl of alien concepts. Such workaday English phrases and metaphors each betray their epistemic foundations in an embodied and acculturated mode of living and being with the world.

Comparable ideas abound in work by the neuroscientist Antonio Damasio, who across *Descartes' Error* (1994), *The Feeling of What Happens* (1999) and *Looking for Spinoza* (2004) exposes how human organs and their arrangements profoundly inform and shape "higher" levels of thought and cognition. Damasio suggests we must accordingly disavow notions of mind and body dualism, or of a homunculus steering the body, and recognize instead that our "brain's body-furnished, body-minded mind" is the servant of the entire human organism (Damasio 2004: 206). By similar coin, Godfrey-Smith stresses that understanding another animal's action-guided intelligence often presupposes that there *be* a shape to its body in the first place (Godfrey-Smith 2016: 75). But, as is hopefully slowly becoming clear, because cephalopods boast no joints, and various species have no natural angles, nor even fixed distances between what are effectively non-discrete parts, we might begin intuiting that they also come into a soft and malleable ("molleable"?) form of (conceptual?) intelligence (Godfrey-Smith 2016: 75).

In contrasting our diverged phenomenal and ontological experiences, Flusser is moved to observe that whereas we humans are upright and extended, and thus perceive ourselves moving and manipulating objects in an enlightened space, vampire squids by contrast live immersed in a dark watery world, wherein free-floating substances most often stream or tumble into them. He accordingly suggests that where we humans perceive "problems," or "things in our way," the squid derives "impressions" of its world. That is, the squid's method of comprehension is "impressionistic" in nature, with its subvenient mode of existence being a "critique of impressions" (Flusser and

Bec 2012: 39). Taking stock of such ideas—alongside considerations of their *art* of expelling nebulous ink billows into the brine—Flusser deduces (in the tradition of von Uexküll and in a foreshadowing of Lakoff and Johnson and Damasio) that it is simply "unimaginable" for these amorphous beings to conceive of "immutable and eternal" Platonic (or what we might recast here as Eurocentric) forms, such as triangles or circles (Flusser and Bec 2012: 42). Unquestionably, the outlandish geometry and philosophy of *Vampyroteuthis* will likewise appear quite alien to us, too, and therefore difficult to comprehend. Indeed, cephalopods, the octopus in particular, vaunt such a radically "different embodiment" to most other animals that they fundamentally unground and up-end our most basic understandings of brain-based and body-based knowledge distinctions. Godfrey-Smith again:

> [t]he octopus lives outside both the usual pictures. Its embodiment *prevents* it . . . The octopus, in a sense, is *disembodied*. That word makes it sound immaterial, which is not, of course, what I have in mind. It has a body, and is a material object. But the body itself is protean, all possibility; it has none of the costs and gains of a constraining and action-guiding body. The octopus lives outside the usual body/brain divide. (Godfrey-Smith 2016: 75–76)

We have already suggested how "understanding" is perhaps too anthropocentric, mammalian or vertebrate a concept—since the cephalopod has no bones and therefore does not stand. Our failure to understand (but our ability to plumb the depths and to fathom?) shadows (and foreshadows) our impending engagement with H. P. Lovecraft, whose fictional encounters with the outside saw characters come up against the "hard" limits of thought. But this is where our soft theory perhaps empowers us to grasp as many different aspects of the as-yet unknown and unthought as we can (like the limbs of the cephalopod). In this way, cephalopods need not embody (or, as Lakoff and Johnson would put it, live by) a concept of consciously standing (under, among or otherwise) in relation to what a human, in their Euclidean-conceptual *umwelt*, might consider an object or "problem" (see Flusser and Bec 2012: 39). That is, what humans find problematic may not be so for the cephalopod—and *vice versa*. Perhaps, therefore, cephalopodic thought can help us to overcome humanity's problems.[4]

Screwy Logic

While Godfrey-Smith is correct to see protean possibility as the octopus's existential default, Flusser is not wrong to note that these animals share a common action-guiding substratum. For, like all cephalopods and coleoid creatures, Flusser's *Vampyroteuthis* (be it squid or octopus or neither or both; see endnote 4) possesses a coiled or "screw-like" form, and thus harbors a vortexual cavity or "spiral axis" within itself, which allows for a corkscrewing mode of advancing, or retreating (as well as for uncorking its intoxicating wine-ink). This is an idea made vividly apparent by the animated film *Deep*, which shows the giant kraken squid using a twisting-screwing mode of propulsing-advancing—while Hamon and Painlevé's *Love Life of an Octopus* also shows in magisterial and extreme close-up how the infant octopus literally spirals into existence (all set to Pierre Henry's weird electronic score—another early hint of the link between the octopus and the computer).

As Flusser puts it, and as we see in the Hamon/Painlevé film, these animals are inclined to coil, and thus they retain a propensity for "deflectionary dynamism" (Flusser and Bec 2012: 21). By extension, while the quickest route between two points is imagined to be a straight line for us vertebrates (especially those of the logocentric and teleologically acculturated stripe), for cephalopods it is more precisely where the two ends of a coil or spring come together and meet (something that also has consequences for our thinking of time and temporality, as we shall discover in Chapter 7). Appropriately, Flusser contends that if our species bears a tendency to "think linearly ('rightly')," the squid "thinks circularly ('eccentrically')" (Flusser and Bec 2012: 41–42). He continues:

> our respective worlds reflect the difference between our dialectical thinking. Ours is flat and, for us, bodies are simply bulging surfaces (mountains). It lives in a water container, of which the seabed constitutes only one of the walls. For it, then, two-dimensionality is an abstraction of the three-dimensionality of everything that is objective, everything that it licks with its toothy tongue. When it soars, it does not do so from a surface into space, as we do, but rather it shoots into volume. Its soaring is not a breakthrough from a plane into the third dimension, as ours is. It bores through watery volumes like a screw. (Flusser and Bec 2012: 42)

If cephalopods are fundamentally springs/screws that occasionally explode into straight lines, then in trying to meet them halfway on our unmoored voyage here, we might jettison our (preference for) "straight" thinking, and instead embrace a decidedly more *screwy* manner of advancing (and which may well involve some screwing, as per Chapter 5). Or, as David Wills might put it in his study of dorsality, we shall go against vertebrate thought (we shall controvert) and we shall aim instead for something more queer, even if that would be back-breaking (see Wills 2008).

To examine these differences a bit more, we may also note how a cephalopod's bi-directional nervous system, with its "ladder-like" form, works to connect parts that can be paradoxically understood as self and non-self at the same time. Something that results in these intelligent and curious creatures inhabiting a hybrid situation, wherein although we must say that they are sentient, we cannot say that they experience their world because of a "higher" (vertically aligned) level of consciousness, as we typically understand it in ourselves. Octopuses do, for example, have a centralized brain, but this is effectively articulated to eight semi-autonomous peripheral neural-net organs, or "decentralized decision-making areas" that (most often) appear to act and "think" independently of it (see Nakajima *et al.* 2018). For Flusser, the animal's "consciousness" is thus best conceived of as operating underneath a primordial tentacular unconsciousness. A form of (sub)conscious autonomous mind, if you will, located within the usual workaday heteronomous unconscious. The former is only occasionally hailed into sovereign pilot mode (when, say, in pain or peril) in order to take control of the partially non-self limbs and organs that otherwise impressionistically feel their way through the currents and crannies of their supersaturated world. To a similar end, Godfrey-Smith believes that the octopus's central intelligence most often experiences "primordial emotions" such as pain, starvation or suffocation, which impress themselves with "an imperious role when present," in a way that cannot be (sub)consciously ignored (Godfrey-Smith 2016: 98–103). Spiraling back to our model of body–mind parallelism with this sketch in mind, and seeing that *Vampyroteuthis* is both passive to its world but also at times an active reactor or predator, means that such animals acquire

> ontological categories that differ from our own. Its are those of nocturnal passion, ours of diurnal clarity. Not one of wakeful reason, the vampyroteuthic world is rather one of dreams. In this regard our respective *Daseins* are not radically different. As complex beings with complex brains, we are both partially rational and partially oneiric, and yet these two levels of consciousness are inversely proportioned between us. What to us is wakeful consciousness is, to it, the subconscious, a fact that manifests itself phenomenally in its stance toward life: head down, belly up. Its critique of pure reason is our psychoanalysis. (Flusser and Bec 2012: 41)

And here, in the inverse picture of the human sleeper who awakens from a nightmare into a calm, waking reality, the cephalopod experiences an inverted eruption of its tranquil (sub)conscious into an impassioned, nightmarish real(m).

But what could this have to do with chthulumedia and us? Well, even citizens of the first world—as most readers of this speculative philosophical book are wont to be?—are at least dimly aware of a real *alarming* nightmare impressing upon them today. That is, a cacophony of inconvenient truths and telegraphed eco-catastrophes is beginning imperiously to press in on our collective conscious/conscience. News of ongoing and impending disaster often comes courtesy of our tactile digital screens, which at times also function literally as our waking alarms. And this news affectively/effectively threatens our radically comfortable and somnambulistic torpor, even though those self-same digital screens induce that very torpor, caught as we are in the screen's basilisk stare, screen-walking (if not sleep-walking) through our urban landscapes, paying no heed to anyone or anything except our screen. Today humanity is living the dream of screen-saturation—until an angry encounter takes place after a blind collision, with any and all contact with the outside of the screen becoming so traumatic that a new cephalopodic discourse must be invented to "critique its pure reason."

Today, then, our tentacular devices hold our gaze and increasingly relay fragmentary impressions of real primordial states of pain, starvation, suffocation, desperation, and thirst that are most commonly experienced by the not-quite-us, or the less-than-human beings and wretches that are only peripherally articulated to our "post-human" image-worlds (melting ice caps, burning forests, dying animals of all species and stripes, and subaltern humans—boat people, sweat-shop laborers, sex slaves, imprisoned miners, shanghaied pirates, refugees, traffickers, and migrants, the global poor). These are nightmarish but realities all the same, and our software-driven tentacular devices might just yet bring first-world cultures to grips with its denied but conjoined outside—thereby *raising consciousness* from within our mass waking-dream wherein, as Gilles Deleuze has it, life increasingly appears like a bad movie (Deleuze 2005b: 166).[5]

By such means, *The Squid Cinema from Hell* at times connects us to aggressive impressing forces that threaten us all with death, but by doing so it perhaps also innervates new forms of (sub)consciousness-raising life (Cthulhu rises). Thus, and with Diogenes still in mind, we hereafter throw up these alien animals to show how recent technology might have brought humanity to new forms of animality—and how humanity might have brought technology to life (or perhaps technology has brought humanity to life). In this way, we dive (non-cynically) into the withdrawn depths of cephalopods as a means better to fathom our current embrace of transformative digital technologies, which not only seem through their molluskian affects to reconnect twenty-first-century human techno-cultures to the dark ethological universes of cephalopods, but which also bring us to the cusp of a new era of being and thinking. On this note, let us revert as promised to the figure of the compressed, desiccated, and bony man.

Things to Come

Of(f) course, as Spinoza, Bergson, and Flusser's precocious and eccentric attempts have already demonstrated, we *must* do essential violence to ourselves and to our cramped or sedimented modes of habitual thinking and acting if we are to be flexible enough to grow, evolve, increase our affections, and perhaps even acquire more adequate ideas (rational or otherwise) about how best to proceed. As indicated, it is for such reasons that *Kinoteuthis Infernalis* channels the body and—as per the title of Sy Montgomery's study—the soul of an octopus (see Montgomery 2015). Consequently, the soft, many-legged experiment that follows constitutes an immersive sucking up of a large volume of our supersaturated media environment, which we cyclonically churn, and occasionally expel in compressed bursts (to squirt-attack, withdraw or proceed in our screwy manner). From behind our billowing inky screens, our eight decentralized and semi-autonomous tentacles (by which we mean our eight chapters) report back on their independent and impressionistic tickles and tackles with this and that, from here, there, and everywhere.

After this introductory chapter, we shall in the next venture, as mentioned, into a cephalopodic media archaeology ("Pulp Fiction and the Media Archaeology of Space"), establishing the links between cephalopods and screen media in particular as a result of their chromatophoric skins, which can function for purposes of display or camouflage and/or for deimatic purposes, before establishing how the cephalopod's tentacular existence suggests something like a synesthetic/cinesthetic existence, which is linked to the perceived interconnectedness of different spaces. Considering Denis Villeneuve's *Maelström* and Sorrentino's *One Man Up*, we shall then explore how the trope of the octopus gets used in those films precisely to demonstrate the cephalo-logic of the contemporary network narrative (or what we shall generalize as "pulp fiction")—before going on to consider a history/archaeology of other forms of volumetric space, including that of the human body in medical imaging and artistic practice, that of the internet, and that of space in digital cinema. Each of these different types of volumetric space involves an intensified sense of what in some circles might be called immersion, and which we link to the sensual life of the cephalopod.

In the third chapter, "Encounters with a 4DX Kino-Kraken," we build upon the second chapter's investigation into volumetric space in order to look at how the very space of the cinema is itself deployed molecularly to immerse the viewer in a submarine realm during the 4DX experience. After a consideration of William Castle's earlier attempts at multisensory film experiences, especially as they relate to *The Tingler*, we shall look at how contemporary 4DX cinema, which shifts seats around on several axes while simultaneously deploying jets of air and vapor, is indeed a kind of kino-kraken that drags viewers into its realm. However, 4DX cinema is also the "vaporization" of cinema as the use of perfumes and other techniques asks viewers to smell cinema, which is sprayed on to our faces in a strange expression of cinema-as-capital as viewers collectively experience a sort of weird "money shot."

Analyzing the work of Scarlett Johansson, we draw on set theory in Chapter 4, "Actorly Squid/Sets and Cephalopod Realism," to discuss the distinction/overlap between actors and characters, before then considering how, across a series of roles, ScarJo repeatedly plays technologized, shape-shifting (and thus cephalopodic) aliens who seduce and sucker others, typically men, into their dangerous, liquescent world. In particular we suggest that Johansson's work constitutes an example of squid-like somatechnics, wherein body and brain are not separate, but interconnected and integrated with each other, as well as with other technologies that are on or part of the body.

In Chapter 5, we consider "The Erotic Ecstasy of Cthulhu," looking at how the cephalopod enjoys a mucosal, slimy, and yet sensual life, while also in particular analyzing *Hokusai Manga*, *The Handmaiden*, *Oldboy*, and *The Untamed* as examples of a cephalopodic cinema in which the cephalopodic itself (typically the octopus) is related to and redolent of often perverse erotic relationships.

This is followed in Chapter 6, "Cosmic Light, Cosmic Darkness," by a consideration of how the cephalopod is often depicted in conjunction with notions of (human) evolution across a range of films including *Spring*, *Evolution*, and *Life*. The chapter then takes a more theoretical/biophilosophical bent, considering the porosity of the cell, the body, the planet and perhaps even the multiverse to suggest that life is characterized not by separation, but by admixture, or symbiogenesis. We then suggest that our relationship with technology might also be symbiogenetic, looking at how, in tentacled tech films like *Demonlover* and *Elle*, the sexualized digital tentacles that we see suggest the life of digital technology as a possible symbiont, with digital technology itself being a body for capital. We then discuss light and darkness in similar fashion, suggesting that darkness is perhaps the stuff of life in a multiverse that typically we consider only in terms of light.

Our discussion of darkness leads directly into Chapter 7, "The Backwash of Becoming Cthulhu, Or, L∞py, Tentacular Time," since if light is the measure of speed, then darkness must in some senses elude time. Looking primarily at *Arrival*, this chapter argues that it is a dark contact with tentacled aliens that gives to Louise Banks, the film's main protagonist played by Amy Adams, an ability to see time both forwards and backwards. Synthesizing the temporal philosophies of Gilles Deleuze and J. M. E. McTaggart, we suggest that *Arrival* is an example of "3C" cinema, as in that film the future is remembered as if it were the past, suggesting a different approach to time from that found in anthropocentric cinema that features linear causality. We then consider the connection between comets, terrestrial life and time, suggesting the interconnection between deep, galactic time and our human present.

And then finally, in Chapter 8 we consider how the digital era has involved a shift "From the Modern Prometheus to the Modern Medusa," in that digital technology constitutes a tentacular Medusa that petrifies us—as we stare only and always at the ubiquitous screens of digital culture, petrified of any contact with the outside (so-called "real") world. We then relate this to Roko's basilisk, a "dangerous" thought experiment concerning artificial intelligence, and which not only argues that once you start looking at the singularity you cannot stop, but also helps to reinforce our suggestion that cinema and its offspring digital media technologies are already expressions of the singularity. That is, cinema is alive—and perhaps has been for much longer than humans, who are a product of media and not, as we typically think, the other way round.

Or at least, the above is a relatively straight version of what is to follow. As the tentacles actually unfurl, you will see that there are in fact various simultaneous and weird things going on in each chapter, drawing you ever-closer to look into the eye and to feel the suckers of the tentacles of the octopus.

Vert-I-Go

Much as the above-described *divertissements* await, though, we presently have more to discuss regarding our book's unusual mode of moving, as well as its ludic aims to subvert or controvert ossified/ossifying systems of thought. Please note, dear reader, that heretofore our purple patches and green (*vert*) lyrical (*verse*) style hopes to divert, perhaps even to pervert, the more sedimented linear habits of vertebrate thinking (by, among other things, undermining preferences for verticalities or hierarchies, while also discharging the stiff spinal columns of academic argumentation). Henceforward we overtly, rather than covertly, aim to (inter)convert you to our soft, sticky, screwy, and pulpy modes of moving—hoping that you too might in turn advertise our perverse invertebrate methods (that is, if you like it, you might tell people about what you read here). However, we more seriously hope that the section header and the three sentences inked above help to draw out an old but new, visible but invisible (and otherwise hidden in plain sight) dynamic English verb form that we wish to grant new cephalopodic life and meaning. Namely, to *vert*—a dynamic term we take to connote moving off the straight (and narrow) path, in specific relation to something else.

A quick example, to screw home a point: since octopuses use copper instead of iron to carry oxygen around their body, the blood of octopuses is blue-green (Godfrey-Smith 2016: 74). Green and blue (*vert et bleu*) are also colors that lie at the heart of cinema in the digital age, as increasing numbers of images have at their core the green/*vert* screen on to which is digitally painted elements of a dataset *mise-en-scène* after the capturing of human subjects and/or carbon objects. Likely a bit too fanciful for some readers, we might nonetheless posit that like the cephalopod, digital cinema also has "*vert*" blood, the greenness of which equally recalls the economic bottom line of much contemporary cinema (the green of dollar bills), while also implicitly giving reference to the green movement, in the sense of would-be ecological rehabilitation—against which the dictates and demands of contemporary neoliberal capital seem at times to stand. A poetic interpretation of the creature's green/*vert* blood may nonetheless allow us later to explore how the cephalopod and cinema may both indeed combine the twin forces of ecological cataclysm and capitalism. In this, we are not far from David Wills' understanding of *versions*, in that like Wills we shall also use verting, or twisting and turning (from the Proto-Indo-European root *wer-*, meaning to turn or to bend), in order to show how the universe might not be quite as we typically think it (see Wills 2008: 19). Indeed, we shall even show that the universe is a false concept, or at the very least a misnomer, since the verse is multiple and verily we live in a (poetic) multiverse, which has no single version, but only multiple, infinite versions as it twists and bends (the multiverse as bender, with its principal filmmaker being the screwy David Abelevich Kaufman, most commonly known as Dziga Vertov, and whose *Chelovek s kino-apparatom/Man with a Movie Camera* Lev Manovich fittingly considers to be a digital database film *avant la lettre*; see Manovich 2001: xiv–xxxvi).

As Charles Baudelaire demonstrated in "Le Soleil," a poem from his celebrated 1857 collection, *Les Fleurs du Mal*, the *ver*, or worm, is also akin to the *vers*, or line of poetry (see Baudelaire 2018), in that both are, like the octopus's tentacles, "long thin thing[s] possessing a kind of life" (McGrath and Comenetz 2011: 144). In this way, to *vert* is to go into wormholes and to spiral into vertigo, but also to be poetic, to find the poetry that spins throughout our multiverse of ongoing becoming/creation/*poiesis*, even if poetry must involve becoming worm-fodder and death. As we understand it, then, *Kinoteuthis Infernalis* vers, verses, and verts. Or, in its weird and twisted manner it advances in an invertebrate way. It is vertiginous, but ne-ver-theless purposely patterned to invert and willfully pervert our hardwired embodied preferences for vertebrate thinking. In this way, we have written a book that is not very anything, but which is just *very*, and which thus leads us toward veracity, or truth. But this is not a single or singular truth. It is multiple, tentacular, and weird. Indeed, we aver that we have an aversion for any single truth, for there can never be simply a version (singular), but only aversion, or many versions.[6]

Twisting Tentacle Book

It should by now be clear that *The Squid Cinema from Hell* is a neomaterialist study of (bio)media. It situates itself in a tradition inspired by Deleuze and Guattari, who approach media as a realm of potentials, affects, and energies, which materially interconnect human and nonhuman bodies (and brains)—while also allowing intensive and transformative flows to pass between them. Such approaches also inform and inspire an *informe* body of more recent titles such as Rosi Braidotti's *Metamorphoses: Towards a Materialist Theory of Becoming* (2002), Siegfried Zielinski's *Deep Time of the Media: Toward an Archaeology of Seeing and Hearing by Technical Means* (2008), Patricia MacCormack's *Cinesexuality* (2008), Jussi Parikka's *Insect Media* (2010), Patricia Pisters' *The Neuro-Image: A Deleuzian Film-Philosophy of Digital Screen Culture* (2012), William Brown's *Supercinema: Film-Philosophy for the Digital Age* (2013), Sean Cubitt's *The Practice of Light: A Genealogy of Visual Technologies from Prints to Pixels* (2014), and Steven Shaviro's *The Universe of Things: On Speculative Realism* (2014). Like these eight tentacles of thought, we are here primarily concerned with our, and the media's, becoming different/different becomings, and the new possibilities opened up for thought and action through these. Of particular pedagogical interest to us here are Zielinski, Parikka, and Cubitt's media archaeologies. For, by taking ancient coleoid animals as our object of study, *The Squid Cinema from Hell* respects and honors Zielinski's plea "to keep the concept of media as wide open as possible" (Zielinski 2006: 33), and his elliptical call to discover the new in the old (as opposed to the more common scholarly drive of today to catalog the return of the old in the new). This was certainly a prominent theme in our earlier archeological outing exploring the notion of the "skeuomorph" to help us understand digital cinema (Fleming and Brown 2015). However, in ways already outlined above, *The Squid Cinema from Hell* also draws inspiration from Parikka's cry to undertake a "twisted media archaeology," while practicing a bolder "media theory of a nonhuman kind" (Parikka 2010: xxv). In such manner, we treat real octopods (octopuses and deep sea vampyromorpha) and decapods (squid and cuttlefish) not merely as representational metaphors or "icky animals, but as carriers of intensities (potentials) and modes of aesthetic, political, economic, and technological thought" (Parikka 2010: xiii).

In addition to being a neomaterialist study of (bio)media, *The Squid Cinema from Hell* also surfaces as a work of political "biophilosophy." This being a broad and far-reaching label that hauls together the bodies of otherwise unrelated philosophers and thinkers including Flusser, Godfrey-Smith and Eugene Thacker, to name but three beating hearts whose work courses through this book's ink (when in print) and plasma (when on screen). By way of introduction, we might here embrace Thacker, who argues that biophilosophers of all stripes understand life in terms of multiplicity, and therefore are driven to pose ontological, as opposed to epistemological, questions. As he has it, if the philosophy of biology asks "what is Life?," then biophilosophers more often than not also investigate "what is not-life?" (Thacker 2005). Along such spiraling lines the biophilosophy of *The Squid Cinema from Hell* verts into considerations of the non-organic life of film, via what has variously been called object-oriented ontology (OOO), or strange forms of speculative realism (on which, more shortly). Thacker appropriately concedes that the weird (political) ontologies that these undertakings ceaselessly spin out—with regard to the ever-changing nature of the real—mean that (like the shapes and forms of the protean octopus, we might add) none of them are final, "none of them lasting" (Thacker 2005). But this does not mean that they are worthless. For, as Thacker elaborates,

> [b]iophilosophy implies a critique of the dialectics of "life itself." It abandons the concept of "life itself" that is forever caught between the poles of nature and culture, biology and technology, human and machine. Instead it develops concepts that always cut across and that form networks: the molecular, multiplicity, becoming-animal, life-resistance . . . But the point is not to simply repeat Deleuzianisms, but rather to invent or diverge: the autonomy of affect, germinal life, wetwares, prevital transductions, organismic soft control, abstract sex, molecular invasions, geophilosophy, and what Deleuze calls "the mathematico-biological systems of differenc/tiation." (Thacker 2005)

In the spirit of Thacker, then, *The Squid Cinema from Hell* takes from Deleuze (and Guattari) without repeating him (or them), not least because Flusser's influence renders it a biophilosophical quest in the cryptozoology film-philosophy vein (cryptids being unknown, hidden or fabled animals). Indeed, *Kinoteuthis Infernalis* is perhaps a virtual beast, rather than an actual one, believed by some to be hiding from mankind in the manner of Nessie or Big Foot (the definition of cryptozoology is "[t]he search for and study of animals whose existence or survival is disputed or unsubstantiated, such as the Loch Ness monster or yeti"; see English Oxford Living Dictionaries n.d.). From the other direction, however, *The Squid Cinema from Hell* also emerges as an exercise in modern film-philosophy, in the respect that while biophilosophers are driven to ask "what is not-life?," modern film scholars and film-philosophers have increasingly been prompted to ask "what is not cinema?" (Beller 2006; Fan 2015: 222; Brown 2016, 2018a; Nagib 2016; Fleming 2017: 6, 2018). In this vein, we frame squids, octopuses, and cuttlefish as organic forms of "non-cinema," recognizing them as vital and extroverted pop-up brain-screens that index the alien biological processes of becoming-cinema. At the same time, we also form links to digital media and digital culture's own apparent processes of becoming-cephalopod, in its own re-innervated intensive block of becoming-animal.

As if in response to such innervations between the virtual and the actual, there has been a liberal surge in academic and popular literature upon cephalopods of late, as was surveyed in Nakajima *et al.*'s 2018 article mentioned above. With regard to octopuses, we might also enumerate recent monographs on the creatures by Katherine Harmon Courage (2013), Richard Schweid (2013) and Sy Montgomery (2015), as well as Godfrey-Smith (2016), each of which offers an insightful analysis of the lives and in particular the *intelligence* of octopuses (and perhaps cephalopods more generally, although the shell-bearing nautilus is not typically considered to be as smart as the octopus, the cuttlefish or the squid). What is more, the squid forms the focus of Flusser and Bec's aforementioned *Vampyroteuthis Infernalis*, from which we take our title with a large doff of the cap. To Miéville's ongoing fascination for cephalopods (2008, 2010) we might also add the weird speculations of Dan Mellamphy and Nandita Biswas Mellamphy (Mellamphy and Biswas Mellamphy 2014; Mellamphy 2014), which will also twist their tentacular way into what follows. Jane Gilgun's self-published ebook, *The Tentacles of Shame: How Shame Works* (2015), equally conjures cephalopods into the self-help "sheeple" (sheep-people) psychology genre, while Maryanne Wolf's *Proust and the Squid: The Story of Science and the Reading Brain* (2007) harnesses neuroscientific research into the biology of the human brain to reveal how modern interactive computing technologies actively modify and restructure the "open" or "hyperplastic" architecture of the human brain/mind.

More pressingly, however, we should also highlight how squids, suckers, and tentacles form a core component of Thacker's "Horror of Philosophy" series, including *In the Dust of This Planet* (2011), *Starry Speculative Corpse* (2015a) and *Tentacles Longer than Night* (2015b). In particular, the latter argues not for a philosophy of horror, but that horror *is* philosophy. Linking his work to Flusser's, Thacker argues that the way in which horror can offer "the sudden realization of a stark, 'tentacular' alienation from the world in which one is enmeshed" is fundamentally a philosophical experience (Thacker 2015b: 153). John Ó Maoilearca picks up on a similar thread when he argues for a "nonhuman philosophy" in his treatment of "non-philosopher" François Laruelle. Without explaining in full Laruelle's ideas, we wish to acknowledge how Ó Maoilearca ends his book by explaining finally the jellyfish that adorns its cover. "The brightest thing in the world," he writes, "is a jellyfish, a *méduse*, a mutating animal (rather than a 'single arbitrary form'—or [Immanuel] Kant's unchanging animal shape) . . . it is a deep-sea creature that invents its own light within the darkest place in the world" (Ó Maoilearca 2015: 292). Living in a "black universe," the jellyfish/ctenophore is, like the cephalopod, a Medusa-like alien monster, tentacular, shape-shifting/formless and entirely other. In thinking through and perhaps even with the jellyfish, we likewise enter into a philosophical realm of nonhuman thought, where the human is simply one among many, perhaps even an infinity of, weird versions of thinking—with the human as a result losing its privileged position in the universe as it realizes that it is within a multiverse, and no longer understanding itself as separate from the world, but instead knowing that it is simultaneously alienated from and, in Thacker's terms, "enmeshed" with it.

Cthulhu and the Chthulucene

If such thinking sounds weird, then we draw now upon the work of Thacker, Graham Harman, and H. P. Lovecraft in order to demonstrate how it is deliberately and positively so. In his tentacular horror-philosophy, for instance, Thacker perhaps inevitably has recourse to the work of Lovecraft (for example, Thacker 2011: 74–80, 2015b: 110–168), the creator of Cthulhu, a creature from a time before humans and who is described as something like "an octopus, a dragon, and a human caricature" (Lovecraft 2002: 141)—but not so much a combination of these things as somehow all of them at once (see Harman 2012: 57–59). Elsewhere, Cthulhu is "[a] monster of vaguely anthropoid outline, but with an octopus-like head whose face was a mass of feelers, a scaly, rubbery-looking body, prodigious claws on hind and fore feet, and long, narrow wings behind" (Lovecraft 2002: 148). Lovecraft also becomes the focus of Harman's *Weird Realism: Lovecraft and Philosophy*, in which the philosopher argues that the American horror writer is also a philosopher of otherness, who suggests weird realities that lie beyond the realm of human perception. In Lovecraft's own words, which also serve as a frontispiece above:

> [t]he most merciful thing in the world, I think, is the inability of the human mind to correlate all its contents. We live on a placid island of ignorance in the midst of black seas of infinity, and it was not meant that we should voyage far. (Lovecraft 2002: 139; also quoted in Harman 2012: 169)

Humans cannot understand the immensity of the universe—and yet Lovecraft points to it, notably using an octopus-like creature that one day will rise and bring destruction to the human race. The weird, then, is our working method, and the spreading, speculative tentacles of the weird are part of the rise of Cthulhu, or the end of human times.

While she disavows any connection to Lovecraft, Donna J. Haraway nonetheless evokes Cthulhu when she refers to the current era of existence as the "chthulucene"—a period that is supposed to have replaced the anthropocene and in which the human race will diminish in importance, while at the same time learning some humility toward the planet (Haraway 2016: 174). What is more, in *Donna Haraway: Story Telling for Earthly Survival* (Fabrizio Terranova, Belgium/France/Spain, 2016), the American thinker is clearly and repeatedly associated with invertebrates as a soft octopus—a molly mollusk!—sits atop a photo on her desk of a human figure that has lost its legs (and which thus cannot stand in the traditional sense), and as a jellyfish occasionally is seen pulsing past Haraway thanks to the use of green-screen imaging. Haraway deliberately spells her version of Cthulhu differently to Lovecraft, placing an h after the opening c and removing the h after the l in order more concretely to demonstrate that her chthulucene involves a return/reversion of the chthonic—albeit that Lovecraft's orthography also seems to recall this term for the subterranean, the earthly, or that which pertains to the underworld. Haraway's chthulucene will be important for the weird arguments that are to follow. Indeed, we doff our cap to her as to Flusser in subtitling our book *The Emergence of Chthulumedia*. But in refusing her link with Lovecraft, whose Cthulhu she considers to be a "misogynist racial-nightmare monster" (Haraway 2016: 101; see also Houellebecq 2005: 105–109), a problem with Lovecraft to which we shall return, Haraway overlooks the way in which the tentacular, cephalopod qualities of the creature can perhaps help us to think about the chthulucene more clearly, and how the hieroglyphs presented to us in the tentacular "chthulumedia" outlined and analyzed below deliver to us a vision of a radically other, nonhuman universe—even if human figures (whether racist and misogynist or not) remain central to these movies and media.[7]

For, the chthulumedia that we wish to present here, or which after Flusser we also refer to as a *Kinoteuthis Infernalis*, or a "squid cinema from hell," is (collectively if not individually) a horrifically philosophical cinema of tentacles that touches us, and which pulls thought into dark, nonhuman realms, where many of the traditional boundaries, borders, and divisions no longer pertain. It is a weird world of connectivity, and which has strong links to the digital era in which we are living—while also pointing toward a posthuman era of a planet perhaps devoid of humans. It is a world of totally different temporalities to those of the anthropocene, a world of modular ecstasy and yet also a world of death, a desert world in which the oceans rise up to drown us as the sun desiccates the land and renders it barren, and where meteors rain down life and death in equal part. It is a world of immanent darkness, but also a world of immanent light, a world in which we may realize that we have never been human, but at the same time are free to desire all manner of unlawful and public becomings.

The anthropocene is the era in which humanity has not so much lived in "equilibrium" with the planet, but intensified the ways in which it actively changes and shapes the planet—in a fashion that increasingly today is considered to be for the worse as we face global warming, mass extinctions and ecological cataclysm. Perhaps it is ironic, maybe even fitting, that humans are only able to identify the anthropocene at the moment when it is coming to an end, as films like *Trolljegerene/Trollhunter* (André Øvredal, Norway, 2010), *The Hunter* (Daniel Nettheim, Australia, 2011) and *Beasts of the Southern Wild* (Benh Zeitlin, USA, 2012) all suggest—according to David Martin-Jones (2016) and Selmin Kara (2016), respectively (see also Koutsourakis 2017). As Roy Scranton (2015) would posit, it is important that collectively as humans we learn to die in the anthropocene (or perhaps just accept the tossing of the cosmic die in the Nietzschean sense). It may be by embracing the call of Cthulhu, and by thinking tentacularly and/or like a cephalopod (by realizing that we may already be cephalopods), that we can achieve this. Chthulumedia, to which we shall turn shortly, are not just a matter of life and death, then, but perhaps also the very matter of both life and death. Such ideas are most evidently witnessed in the "panspermia"-themed chthulucinema narratives of *The Untamed* and *Annihilation* (Alex Garland, UK/USA, 2018), wherein vital interstellar comets deliver world-changing life forms/forces to Earth.

The former we shall look at in Chapter 5, but with regard to the latter film, the comet tellingly crashes through a phallic lighthouse, and thereafter emits a shimmering and spectrumizing energy field from its womb-like cavern beneath the earth, and which serves to mash-up and to remix the various organic and non-organic forms (DNA and crystalline structures) around the impact zone. As the film's title suggests, this ever-expanding shimmering zone at once annihilates life as we know it, while also giving rise to new alien forms and weird interkingdom admixtures: alligators with shark's teeth, bears that are also sort of human, humans that have snake-like guts, and hybrid plants that roughly inhabit a general kind of human form. Interspecies becomings that find comparable forms of expression in other chthulumedia narratives including *Life*, *Prometheus* and the *Sharktopus* series.

Killing Thee Softly

Before proceeding to identify what Haraway might call the kinship between the cephalopod and cinema/media, a cephalo-kino (head-cinema?) that is all cine-brain/kin(o)brain, we would like to outline another of our key modes of proceeding. For, to suggest that chthulumedia are the matter of life and death is paradoxical, in that we typically think of life and death as separate or compartmentalized states. And yet, perhaps all matter is both life and death at once, with chthulumedia (which may in the fullness of time be understood as all of media) being able verily to show us this, and to make us think and feel as much, too. To create a paradox, or even a plain contradiction in terms (death and life at the same time), runs the risk of being at least weird, and at worst alienating and nonsensical, perhaps even controversial. However, the alienation and the nonsense are partially deliberate and also necessary if we are to grasp the weird world that chthulumedia bring to us. And so, in order to demonstrate the legitimacy of paradox, we turn our attention to Harman's consideration of Lovecraft, since the former analyzes quite clearly how the latter's style depends upon consistent, contradictory-seeming ambiguity.

Harman identifies how Lovecraft "invests a great deal of energy in undercutting his own statements. In this way, Lovecraft's prose generates a gap between reality and its accessibility to us" (Harman 2012: 28). The aforementioned description of Cthulhu can function as a decent example of this. In full, Lovecraft writes the following:

> It seemed to be a sort of monster, or symbol representing a monster, of a form which only a diseased fancy could conceive. If I say that my somewhat extravagant imagination yielded simultaneous pictures of an octopus, a dragon, and a human caricature, I shall not be unfaithful to the spirit of the thing. A pulpy,

> tentacled head surmounted a grotesque and scaly body with rudimentary wings; but it was the *general outline* of the whole which made it most shockingly frightful. (Lovecraft 2002: 141)

Note how Lovecraft's screwy language is rife with ambiguity: it *seemed to be* a *sort of* monster, perhaps even only a symbol. Only a diseased mind could come up with this—and being the product of a diseased mind, the beast may therefore not be real at all! But while the narrator of Lovecraft's story mentions three species of animal (octopus, dragon, human—notably a mix of the real and the fantastical—with the octopus itself perhaps being a combination of the two), this only gives us *the spirit* of the thing.[8] Finally, it is only its *general outline* (the italics here are Lovecraft's) that is frightful. As Harman explains, the horror comes through the ambiguity of the description, as opposed to its details (see again Harman 2012: 57–59). And we should like to add that it is the contradictory nature of the description that exemplifies the method of superposition (or multiple versions) that we shall be using in our discussion of chthulumedia and the *Kinoteuthis Infernalis*. Something that again might resonate with the unconscious impressionistic mode of dream-life that the cephalopod experiences before its nightmarish (sub)conscious awakening.

Ruminate: Lovecraft does not specify that Cthulhu is octopus here and dragon there—even if the beast has a tentacled head and wings. Rather, octopus, dragon, and human seem all to be superposed, or composited (to use the language of digital imaging culture), one atop the other, Cthulhu thus emerging as all of them at once, as opposed to this bit dragon, and that bit human. It may be a monster, it may be a symbol; or perhaps more accurately, Cthulhu is both of these things at once. Of course, we cannot say better even than *perhaps*; but even with this word, we get a sense of chaos, since *perhaps* derives from the Middle English word *per* or *par* meaning "by" or "through," and the plural of *hap*, meaning "chance." That is, *perhaps* means "by chance"—not only in the sense of a cosmic coincidence ("by chance I happened to be walking through Providence, Rhode Island, at the same time as Cthulhu appeared there"), but also in the sense of evoking a random, chaotic universe in which events do not take place by divine decree, but precisely according to chance. Where in the past we have had many peer reviewers telling us to remove ambiguity from our language as we write academic essays that are supposed to be infused with objectivity and thus with certainty, here we willfully adopt the language of ambiguity and chaos, for this form seems better to suit our subject matter. *Perhaps, perhaps, perhaps . . .* we move from hard theory to soft mutiny. Killing thee softly is par for our (off-)course.

Superposition

Superposition—whereby a phenomenon can be in two different, supposedly contradictory states at once—is by now a widely understood notion that we can borrow from physics to illustrate our style. For, much as a photon can be both a wave and a particle, so might Cthulhu be both an octopus and a human. Of course, as per(haps?) the famous "uncertainty principle" of Werner Heisenberg, the observer helps to determine whether the photon be wave or particle, thereby in some senses eliminating that ambiguity (it may have been a wave and a particle, but now that we have had a look and affected it, we can say that the photon is now a particle; see Heisenberg 2000). However, given that the observer determines the result of the experiment, and that the knowledge of the photon's status as a particle is dependent on the experiment and the experimenter themselves, our uncertainty is a more accurate description than the ensuing seeming-certainty, since the latter is temporary at best, and illusory at worst. Reality in the "objective" sense is thus perhaps reductive, and certainly impoverished, a version of the truth, but in denial of the very versions of truth. In the footsteps of Niels Bohr, it is not, thus, that there exists some realm of reality in which the photon finally does exist as either a wave or as a particle; on the contrary, we and it exist in the same realm, a realm determined by change as we affect photons and as photons affect us—a realm defined by both complementarity and entanglement (see Bohr 1937; Barad 2007). This is a realm in which a cat can famously be both dead and alive at the same time (see Trimmer 1980)—even if such a smudged "state" boggles conventional logic.

One of the debates surrounding Erwin Schrödinger's cat is that its being simultaneously alive and dead is a metaphor. For Schrödinger, the cat was actually one of dead or alive—it's just that the person conducting the experiment would not be able to tell until opening the box in which the cat had been placed. However, feminist physicist Karen Barad suggests that the experiment is not just a question of epistemology (we cannot know whether the cat is dead or alive) but that it is also a question of ontology (the cat actually *is* both dead and alive; see Barad 2007: 275–284). Famously, for Schrödinger, the cat's death or life is determined by whether an atom of a radioactive substance decays over the course of an hour; if it decays, a charge is released that causes a hammer to fall on a flask of cyanide; as the hammer smashes the flask, so the released cyanide kills the cat. As Heisenberg appeals to a reality of which we cannot be certain, so, too, does Schrödinger imagine that there is a realm of truth—the cat is one of dead or alive—but that we cannot access it. However, as Heisenberg is incorrect to suppose that there is an objective world somewhere beyond our reach, so, too, is Schrödinger incorrect to imagine that the cat is only metaphorically both dead and alive. In a universe of quantum entanglement, the cat is both dead and alive as the photon is both particle and wave—and while this superposition of states (dead and alive as opposed to dead or alive) runs against common-sense logic, perhaps it is a more accurate interpretation of our universe, since our entanglement with the radioactive atom and with the cat, as per our entanglement with the photon, would suggest that where the cat begins and ends is not clear, and that we are better off comprehending our universe as one not made up of boundaries between separate entities and/or states (dead or alive, duck or rabbit), but as a multiverse of interconnected and inseparable phenomena (dead and alive, duck and rabbit, octopus and dragon and human).[9]

If we were momentarily to err on the side of a technological determinist—such as Friedrich Kittler, say, who convincingly argues that our "media determine our situation" (Kittler 1999: xxxix), or even Zielinski, who harbors an interest in "imaginary media" more generally (Zielinski 2006)—we might sense that, in taking stock of today's cultural assemblages (including science-fictional imaginings of fantasy technologies), the above ideas unconceal their own "real-world" technological models and modi operandi. For, if the computers that defined the sociocultural assemblages at the end of the twentieth century (at the end of the anthropocene) operated upon binary systems composed of ones and zeroes (openings and closings, ons and offs), today's cutting-edge quantum computers now push us into the substratal realms of quantum probabilities and operational superpositions. In actual fact, if rendered crudely, today's (chthulucene) quantum computing exploits "weird" or "quantum" vibrations to analyze and read what are called "quibits" (quantum-bits), "that can be set to zero, one, or, bizarrely zero and one at the same time" (Cho 2018). And this fact virtually ensures that there are consequences for more than simply the programmers of super-expensive Hadron colliders and Wall Street algorithms.

Indeed, as has already been well illustrated by Lewis Mumford in *Technics and Civilization* (2010 [1934]) and in both volumes of *The Myth of the Machine*, namely *Technics and Human Development* (1967) and *The Pentagon of Power* (1970), the addition of new technologies, modes, machines, and practices into a dynamic cultural assemblage necessarily leads to the emergence and crystallization of new and different patterns of collective organization, action, axiomatics, metaphor, and conceptualizing (or, ways of living, speaking/enunciating and thinking)—which in turn modify what it means to be "human" at any given time. Eurocentric studies surrounding the emergence and embrace of the Greek alphabet, or later the printing presses under evolving systems of European capitalism (and its subsidiary technologies)—as per work by Marshall McLuhan (1962), Benedict Anderson (1983), Flusser (2011 [1987]) and Serres (2018)—make such ideas all too clear. Taking heed of such thoughts, our ecological and impressionistic argument would do well to acknowledge that today's quantum computers and networked technologies demand ever-new practical skills (*technē*) and knowledge (*epistēmē*) to build, program, and operate them. And that this, too, will entail their own manifold knock-on butterfly affects/effects (and forms of cross-pollination and innervating encounters) in-between the always already overlapping and interconnected domains of economics, war, medicine, organizational development, environmental engineering, the arts and gaming.

In the above messy and fractalized pictures there is no satisfactory distinction or hierarchy between different "levels" of the theoretical and technical, between *epistēmē* and *technē*, and between the metaphorical and the ontological. As mentioned in reference to Lakoff and Johnson, we "live by" metaphors (while metaphors live by us). Of course, recognition of these determinable horizons has in the past accounted for "heroic" efforts to break out of the all-too-human (magic) circle. From Zhuannzhi's unshackled dreams of being a butterfly to Spinoza's crystalline geometric method of philosophy, right through to the speculative currents of today—which provoke us to consider what it might be like to be a bat (Nagel 1974), a wolf (Deleuze and Guattari 2004), a squid (Flusser and Bec 2012), an inanimate thing (Bogost 2012), an electrical grid (Bennett 2010), global warming (Morton 2013) or a computer, an alien, slime mold and a human being (Shaviro 2016)—countless other ways of experiencing the world are entering into circulation. What does an electron think? Individually and collectively, or in superposition, these other *umwelten* attempt to get us to think differently and to realize that our embodied perspective on the universe is an affordance of our physical existence with it, and the things in it, and not because of some objective insight into it made from a separate and disconnected standpoint. In this way, perhaps the boundaries between the metaphoric and the literal and between the epistemological and the ontological also begin to break down—and fictions as per(haps) Flusser and Bec's can tell us as much about reality as "hard scientific" and "documentary evidence" can. As per the title of the collected works of Jean Painlevé, himself a noted student of the octopus, science is fiction (and *vice versa*).

Perhaps, then, perverse or perverted philosophical science fiction is just our shtick. If so, we're in good company. Flusser himself writes of *Vampyroteuthis Infernalis* that "a 'philosophy of fantasy' . . . might become a discipline 'as rigorous as phenomenology'" (quoted in Jue 2014: 94). In some senses, then, our consideration of chthulumedia and the *Kinoteuthis Infernalis* might equally offer a film-philosophical-fantastical-phenomenological account of contemporary and other cinema(s) and media, putting into practice the superpositional and superpositive style (yes!) that is found in Lovecraft, who like Flusser creates a philosophy of cephalopods and by extension of the chthulucene—which is itself a period to be understood via superposition, paradox, and seeming contradiction. As Haraway blends fiction and theory in *Staying with the Trouble* (a trope also pursued by Serres; see Serres 1995), so, too, might we invert fiction and philosophy/theory—not by interpolating specifically and deliberately fictional elements into this work (not least because the creative work of most theorists who dabble in fiction, poetry and/or filmmaking—including perhaps the authors of this book—is perhaps perceived not to be as "good" as their "purely" theoretical work), but by demonstrating that the ill-defined "borders" between theory and fiction—and between fiction and truth—are highly porous, impressionistic and molleable/malleable.

So . . . having set the scene, let us advance with our weird speculations and investigate the ways in which we might grasp the contemporary media scene as a *Kinoteuthis Infernalis*, rising like Cthulhu from the deep in order to raise our cephalopodic consciousness, and weirdly to signal the arrival of the chthulucene.

Notes

1. As we shall discuss in Chapter 5, Katsushika Hokusai is a key artist to have explored the octopus in his work, which strongly influenced the likes of Félicien Rops, Pablo Picasso, and Gustav Klimt. Cephalopods also have a clear presence in today's art world, featuring in the work of Miquel Barceló and Zak Smith (see Schweid 2013: 143–144), as well as in the work of Yutaka Mukoyama, who produces "incredibly detailed photorealistic oil paintings of squids," which Ryuat Nakajima and colleagues describe as "stunning and mesmerizing" (Nakajima *et al.* 2018: 9). Among various other exhibitions and installations, cephalopods recently surfaced as a popular motif in the *What about the Art?* exhibition curated by Chinese artist Cai Guo-Qiang at the Qatar Museum in 2016, which featured a giant sea monster created by Huang Yong Ping, while Takashi Murakami's *The Octopus Eats Its Own Leg* exhibition enjoyed record-breaking audiences at Chicago's Museum of Contemporary Art in 2017. Finally, we might also mention the chromatophore-inspired installations/simulations of Todd Anderson (for more on these exhibitions, see Nakajima *et al.* 2018: 9).

In the world of graphic novels and manga, meanwhile, the recent *The Fall of Cthulhu: Godwar* (Michael Alan Nelson *et al.*, 2008–), *Fatale* (Ed Brubaker *et al.*, 2012), *Neonomicon* (Jacen Burrows and Alan Moore, 2013–), *The Squidder* (Ben Templesmith, 2014), *The Wake* (Scott Snyder and Sean Murphy, 2014), *Monstress* (Marjorie Liu and Sana Takeda, 2016–), *L'appel de Cthulhu* (François Baranger, 2017–), and *Providence* (Jacen Burrows and Alan Moore, 2017) stand out as eight further examples of erotic and/or eradicating interdimensional tentacle beings. Why eight? As David Foster Wallace puts it in his short story, "Octet," "best of British luck explaining to anyone why" (Foster Wallace 2001: 124).

Finally, to give but one example from the realm of virtual reality (VR), we note that the Eurostar between London and various cities in France and Belgium has since 2017 offered an in-train VR experience called *Eurostar Odyssey*, which involves looking at (digitally rendered) aquatic life, including octopuses, while traveling under the English Channel. Designed with digital agency AKQA, the entire experience involves putting one's smartphone inside a set of special glasses that one can buy from vending machines at the various Eurostar terminals, and which also prominently feature models of octopuses (see Tan 2017).

2. Further audiovisual media products that feature cephalopods, cephalopod-like creatures, and/or prominent tentacles—but which we do not have space to consider more fully—include: *The Navigator* (Donald Crisp and Buster Keaton, USA, 1924), *Mare Nostrum* (Rex Ingram, USA, 1926), *20,000 Leagues under the Sea* (Richard Fleisher, USA, 1954), *Bride of the Monster* (Edward D. Wood Jr., USA, 1955), *Tentacoli/Tentacles* (Oliver Hellman, Italy/USA, 1977), *Deep Rising* (Stephen Sommers, USA/Canada, 1998), *Octopus* (John Eyres, USA, 2000), *Octopus 2: River of Fear* (Yossi Wein, USA, 2001), *Hellboy* (Guillermo del Toro, USA, 2004), *Kraken: Tentacles of the Deep* (Tibor Takacs, USA/Canada, 2006), *Pirates of the Caribbean: Dead Man's Chest* (Gore Verbinski, USA, 2006), *Slither* (James Gunn, Canada/USA, 2006), *The Mist* (Frank Darabont, USA, 2007), *Pirates of the Caribbean: At World's End* (Gore Verbinski, USA, 2007), *ReGOREgitated Sacrifice* (Lucifer Valentine, Canada, 2008), *Sharktopus* (Declan O'Brien, USA, 2010), *Grabbers* (Jon Wright, Ireland/UK, 2012), *Prometheus* (Ridley Scott, USA/UK, 2012), *Pacific Rim* (Guillermo del Toro, USA, 2013), *Kiseijuu/Parasyte* (Takashi Yamazaki, Japan, 2014), *Monsters: Dark Continent* (Tom Green, UK, 2014), *Bermuda Tentacles* (Nick Lyon, USA, 2014), *Sharktopus vs. Pteracuda* (Kevin O'Neill, USA, 2014), *Transcendence* (Wally Pfister, UK/China/USA, 2014), *Sharktopus vs. Whalewolf* (Kevin O'Neill, USA, 2015), *The Void* (Jeremy Gillespie and Steven Kostanski, USA/UK/Canada, 2016), *Guardians of the Galaxy Vol. 2* (James Gunn, USA/New Zealand/Canada, 2017), *Hagane no renkinjutsushi/Fullmetal Alchemist* (Fumihiko Sori, Japan, 2017), *Pirates of the Caribbean: Dead Men Tell No Tales* (Joachim Rønning and Espen Sandberg, USA, 2017), *The Cloverfield Paradox* (Julius Onah, USA, 2018), *Pacific Rim:*

Uprising (Steven S. DeKnight, USA/China/UK/Japan, 2018), *A Wrinkle in Time* (Ava DuVernay, USA, 2018), and *Captain Marvel* (Anna Boden and Ryan Fleck, USA, 2019).

We might also tally here the tentacles of planetary beings that rise from the earth in films like *Thor: Ragnarok* (Taika Waititi, USA, 2017), *Transformers: The Last Knight* (Michael Bay, USA/China/Canada, 2017), and *Valerian and the City of a Thousand Planets* (Luc Besson, France/China/Belgium/Germany/UAE/USA, 2017). Furthermore, we could also throw into the mix tentacular monopods that rise from the earth—as per the worms in *Dune* (David Lynch, USA, 1984) or *Tremors* (Ron Underwood, USA, 1990).

In kids' cinema, noteworthy examples include the Kraken, dumbo octopus, and all-singing, all-dancing vampire squid who have inherited an otherwise abandoned and polluted Earth in *Deep* (Julio Soto Gurpide, Spain/Belgium/Switzerland/USA/China/UK, 2017), the terrifying neon squid and astonishing *mètic* octopus named Hank (Ed O'Neill) in *Finding Dory* (Andrew Stanton and Angus MacLane, USA, 2016), and the haughty Squidward Q. Tentacles (Rodger Bumpass) from *The Spongebob Square Pants Movie* (Stephen Hillenburg and Mark Osborne, USA, 2004). This is not to mention the tentacle-beings threading throughout an array of shorts, including Alejandro Suarez Lozano's *The Fisherman* (Spain, 2015) and animated shorts including *Oktapodi* (Julien Bocabeille, François-Xavier Chanioux, Olivier Delabarre, Thierry Marchand, Quentin Marmier, and Emud Mokhberi, France, 2007), *Catharsis* (Marine Brun, Jean-Guillaume Culot, Sébastien Dusart, Antoine Foulot, Pauline Giraudel, and Floriane Hetru, France, 2015), and *Goutte d'or* (Christophe Peladan, Denmark/France, 2016).

What is more, cephalopods have also recently appeared in documentaries like *The Life and Times of Paul the Psychic Octopus* (Alexandre O. Philippe, USA, 2012), a film about the octopus that famously predicted various results for the 2010 football World Cup, as well as *All You Can Eat Bouddha* (Ian Lagarde, Canada/Cuba, 2017), a surrealist tale of a French tourist in Cuba who achieves something like enlightenment after an encounter with an octopus that he frees from a fishing net. *La villa/House by the Sea* (Robert Guédiguian, France, 2017) also features octopuses at key points during its story of intergenerational desire and the onset of global capital on the outskirts of Marseille.

Finally, beyond such big-screen appearances there are of course the squid-faced Ood from *Dr Who* (Sydney Newman, UK, 1963–), the megalomaniacal tentacle aliens Kang and Kodos Johnson from *The Simpsons* (James L. Brooks, Matt Groening, and Sam Simon, USA, 1989–), the 16-foot telepathic interdimensional Pacific octopus "Old Night" from *The O.A.* (Zal Batmanglij and Brit Marling, USA, 2016–), and (with a stretch) the octo-pod groups of posthumans in *Sense8* (J. Michael Straczynski, Lana and Lilly Wachowski, USA, 2015), which are all shows that have aired on what is still referred to as television, while also being widely available online. Similarly, the concept band Gorillaz use cephalopod and jellyfish imagery in a number of the songs from their 2010 album *Plastic Beach*, which includes a single called "Superfast Jellyfish," creatures that subsequently reappear in the video for "On Melancholy Hill," where one of the band's main characters, guitarist Noodle, is on a ship that is sunk by two attacking Vought F4U Corsair fighter planes. Noodle climbs on to a life raft with her guitar, before the video goes under water and inside a shark-shaped submarine piloted by the band's bassist, Murdoc Niccals. Here, Virtual Noodle (a digitally animated version of the regular, 2D Noodle) wakes up from a slumber and vomits an octopus with a huge eye. As the shark machine is joined by a fleet of further submarines, among whose pilots are well-known musicians like Lou Reed, Snoop Dogg, and Gruff Rhys, one piloted by De La Soul smacks into a (Vilém?) fluther of Superfast Jellyfish, churning some of them up in its propellers, thereby leaving a cloud of black ink in its wake. The submarines surface to find a dead manatee on a small, tower-like rock island, with a character known as the boogieman trying to steal its corpse. Virtual Noodle fires a shotgun, but the boogieman escapes. A thick fog descends, through which emerges Plastic Beach, the fictional island after which the album is named. With its cephalopodic digital imagery and its oblique narratives, the videos from *Plastic Beach*, as well as the album as a whole, speak of a world choking on the plastics made from fossil fuels by humans. We shall leave for another occasion a more complete analysis of the videos/album, but as will become clear from the rest of this book, Gorillaz are surely dealing with various key themes that are linked to the chthulucene (cephalopods, pollution, digital culture, extinction, the rising oceans, and more).

Beyond such examples, we feel that each reader will naturally be thinking of many more, some known to us and many more almost certainly not. We leave it to those readers to become writers and to offer other analyses of chthulumedia in its numerous iterations.

3. In our attempts to discover what form of ink Spinoza used, we ran up against a lack of any real scientific or historical evidence. Our initial searches online and through literature on Spinoza turned up naught. However, our personal correspondences with the Spinozahuis Society and Professor Piet Steenbakkers of Utrecht University offered a tantalizingly inky trail. Steenbakkers notes that "nothing has been published about the ink [Spinoza] used, nor about the paper, for that matter. In the inventory of his belongings, drawn up by a public notary after his death, there is no mention of ink; the only item that may be relevant in this context is a 'Cantoortrechtertje' (an office funnel): one imagines him using that to pour ink from a bottle in the inkwell" (Steenbakkers 2018). Steenbakkers also believes that Spinoza purchased his bottled ink from local apothecaries. To this end, we have ascertained that Mediterranean cuttlefish ink, or *sepia* (the scientific name for the common cuttlefish is *Sepia officinalis*), began popularly to be used for drawing as well as for writing in Holland during the 1700s, as was iron gall ink (made from vegetal matter). Our examination of Spinoza's handwriting in scans of

existing manuscripts reveal the ink to be brownish in color. While brown coloration is a distinctive feature of sepia, this could also perhaps be a property of aged iron gall ink, which is black when applied. Until more advanced tests can be done, we speculate that Spinoza probably did use cuttlefish ink at some point during his lifetime, which coincided with the popularization of sepia (see, for example, Ward 2008: 282).

4. The lack of fixity regarding *Vampyroteuthis Infernalis* even extends to its categorization as a species, regarding which there seems to be much confusion. Regularly considered to be a squid (*teuthis*), Danna Staaf explains that it is in fact an octopus (Staaf 2017: 118), while Cousteau and Diolé claim that it is "neither a squid nor an octopus. It has the consistency of a jellyfish and is dark violet in colour" (Cousteau and Diolé 1973: 275). Björn Kröger and colleagues are no less clear when they argue that "[c]oleoids [i.e., soft-bodied cephalopods, which includes squid, octopuses and cuttlefish, but not nautiluses, which retain their shells] are the most diverse cephalopod group today and are divided into two groups—the ten-armed Decabrachia and the eight-armed Vampyropoda. The latter group comprises the familiar octopods as well as the Vampire squids, which actually have ten arms, but two arms are reduced to sensory filaments" (Kröger *et al.* 2011: 603). Octopus, not squid; neither octopus nor squid; both octopus and squid—the *Vampyroteuthis Infernalis* suitably breaks down the boundaries of hard scientific categorization in a way that is in keeping with the soft logic that we seek to develop here.
5. Today in the global north, spineless Hollywood-style movies and social network screens most often flood us with a self-deceptive point of view that appears to be our own. And here, we might draw yet more links with Flusser's fabled *Vampyroteuthis*. For, *Vampyroteuthis* lives in darkness, but is able, like other cephalopods, to activate bioluminescent chromatophoric pixels on its screen-like skin to illuminate objects and others in the pitch black. Philosophically speaking, Flusser notes that while we humans "have to penetrate behind appearances in order to free things from the veil of light (*aletheia* = unveiling = truth)," *Vampyroteuthis* instead "irradiates the world with its own point of view." But, because the animal's bioluminescence serves to "engender appearances, that is, phenomena," it lives in a world of "self-generated deception" (Flusser and Bec 2012: 39). It was for similar reasons that Flusser claimed that during the video and computing explosion of the 1980s, we were already on the cusp of "vampyroteuthizing" our own art and culture.
6. As one of our EUP peer reviewers pointed out, Michel Serres makes similar puns when he points us to how the meaning of the word *universe* and the more troubled term *universality* mean "turned (versus) in such a way as to form a single (unus) whole" (Serres 2018: 173). He continues: "The Latin verb *vertere* signifies 'turning' or 'veering,' 'changing,' but also 'translating' sometimes. The French and English words deriving from it designate a single direction (*averter* [to warn], *vers* and adversary, noted by the Anglo-Latin *versus*), then its change (inversion, subversion, *versatile* [changeable], conversion), lastly every possible

direction, from the diverse to the universal. Direction—spatial, temporal or semantic—is produced and organized, dispersed and concentrated, totalized or lost in conversation as well as in flocks of starlings" (Serres 2018: 175).

Perhaps our shared desire for *verting* and *versing* reveals our various ethical projects taking parallel paths of screwy evolution. Or do our labyrinthine impressionistic books rather form fragments of a mosaic mirror reflecting the same "soft," morphological, and malleable species reshaping and recoding itself in the event of its latest fractal tools? In other words, might our bifurcating books sway and dance to the same background noises and music, verifying the same seachange from within a changing system?

7. Notably, in a letter written in response to Jenny Turner's review of *Staying with the Trouble* in the *London Review of Books*, Haraway laments: "I wish I had used the term Chthonocene" (Haraway 2017)—precisely because Turner brings her work back to Lovecraft, a connection that Haraway denies, but which we hope can be developed in a productive fashion (see also Turner 2017).
8. Nakajima *et al.* point out how the myth of the kraken is a retelling of the myth of St George and the dragon (Nakajima *et al.* 2018: 11). In other words, the dragon is potentially a relative of the cephalopod, with dragon–human combinations à la Cthulhu conspicuously present in various ongoing "television" series on Netflix, HBO, and SKY. The snake-cum-dragon symbol coiled into an infinity ∞/8 is central to Netflix Originals films and series such as *Annihilation* and *Altered Carbon* (Laeta Kalogridis, USA, 2018–), while also playing a significant role in HBO's *Game of Thrones* (David Benioff and D. B. Weiss, USA/UK, 2011–).
9. Another quantum physicist, Paul Dirac, perhaps emerges here as another important forebear. For in his development of matrices, Dirac in effect wrote superposition and the simultaneous coexistence of different versions into our knowledge of the world. That is, matrices mark the shift from a definite universe to a probabilistic multiverse. What is more, Kurt Gödel's famous "incompleteness theorem" makes clear Bertrand Russell's suggestion that "pure mathematics is the subject in which we do not know what we are talking about, or whether what we are saying is true," since things can be both true and false at the same time (see Nagel and Newman 2005: 9).

CHAPTER 2

Pulp Fiction and the Media Archaeology of Space

WE ARE DEADLY serious when we suggest that cephalopods are media—and so let us open this chapter by looking at how this is so, before going on to consider cephalopodic conceptions of (volumetric or voluminous) space in cinema and other media. Nandita Biswas Mellamphy describes cephalopods as having "[c]unning intelligence" before outlining what she calls their "mètic mentality," which denotes the way in which they function through ruses and crafty manipulation (see Biswas Mellamphy 2015). The crafty manipulation that she describes can be seen in how giant cuttlefish boast "about ten million chromatophores" on their signaletic bodies (Godfrey-Smith 2016: 111). As a result, cephalopods "in general (not all, but a great many) are skilled color changers" (Godfrey-Smith 2016: 108). That is,

> [t]he skin of a cephalopod is a layered screen controlled directly by the brain. Neurons reach from the brain through the body into the skin, where they control muscles. The muscles, in turn, control millions of pixel-like sacs of color. A cuttlefish senses or decides something, and its color changes in an instant . . . very roughly, we can think of that layer of the animal's skin as a ten mega-pixel screen. (Godfrey-Smith 2016: 109–111)

The "dynamic" patterns and images projected on to their biomedia bodies are tellingly described often as screen-savers or "movies played on the screen of the [animal's] skin" (Godfrey-Smith 2016: 112), except that here the "video screen is tied directly to the brain" (Godfrey-Smith 2016: 132) and can be sculpted into different shapes and textures.[1] Perhaps it goes without saying, then, that the pixelated, sculptable skin of the cephalopod recalls the camera, computer screen and/or the projector, as well as today's "4D" architecture-anatomy, which combined constitute the major pieces of equipment and apparatuses that help cinema to function (see the next chapter on 4DX cinema for more). Furthermore, the digital era has seen the cinematic image shift from being understood as made up of frames (with each frame being a unit of time) to being understood as made up of pixels (with each pixel being a unit of space), with the screen itself also shifting increasingly from being a static and rigid rectangle to being foldable and flexible, as per the latest smartphone screens. We shall revert later to this transformed relationship between space and time, where world is no longer picture, but for the time being we wish simply to assert that the cephalopod is a kind of living movie machine, which like a movie in the digital era can be understood as "colors changing in time"—in the sense that the computer simply changes the color of the image's pixels rather than thinking about what is in the image (see Manovich 2001: 302).

Perhaps after Manovich, who defines digital cinema not so much as a kino-eye but as a kino-brush, we might more precisely frame this ability as cephalopodic "painting in time," or as biomedia digital animation (Manovich 2001: 308). Flusser certainly makes a comparable point when he describes his *Vampyroteuthis Infernalis* as partaking in expressive acts of "epidermal painting" (Flusser and Bec 2012: 3)—ideas also germane to Godfrey-Smith, who names two dynamic cuttlefish Kandinsky and Matisse on account of their breathtakingly expressive pixelated skin-art. Elsewhere, a composited comparison between a close-up of Georges Seurat's *Le Crotoy, amont/View of Le Crotoy from Upstream* (1889) with a microscopic photograph of dense and colorful octopus chromatophores and iridophores also screws home this notion (see Nakajima *et al.* 2018: 10). On account of such properties, Godfrey-Smith suggests that cephalopods are "immensely expressive animals, animals with a lot to say" (Godfrey-Smith 2016: 108). Flusser even suggests that cephalopods might be communicating through their animated skin using a visual language comparable to cinema or television (Flusser and Bec 2012: 21ff.; see also Godfrey-Smith 2016: 130), an idea that is hijacked and literalized in the biomedia art project, *Insane in the Chromatophores*. For this, the Backyard Brains group hooked an iPod headphone wire to the fin nerve of a Longfin Inshore Squid (*Loligo pealeii*), hacking its nervous system and ostensibly turning the animal's skin-screen into a living, biocybernetic music-video machine, with the results posted on YouTube (see Backyard Brains 2012).

Furthermore, the cephalopod's skin is often observed changing color not only for the purposes of display—for example, for attracting a mate via a virtuoso spectacle of color, as might do a peacock—but also for the purposes of camouflage (or "cryptic" display). That is, the cephalopod changes color not so as to be seen or to communicate, but precisely in order to remain unseen. And while we tend to think of screen media uniquely as a system of display, might we not also begin—as a result of our conceptual encounter with cephalopods—to think about chthulumedia also as a system of camouflage or conning? Consider the latest "ambient mode televisions," which today boast a display feature that allows them, like a camouflaged octopus, to merge into the wall or wallpaper upon which they have been mounted, so that instead of seeing an empty black rectangle, they become indistinguishable from the background *mise-en-scène* (even if this means that the device is never turned off, and thus always burning electricity, perhaps even more than the unblinking red dot-eye of older resting/observing televisions). As the recent Samsung advertisement says: "[y]ou won't notice the TV on the wall as it blends perfectly with your décor."

Similar cephalopodic features are also worth billions to military camouflage engineers, who have been busy researching and developing 3D "biomimetic artificial skin able not only to match its background but also to fast adapt to a changing environment, all this, without losing flexibility" (Nakajima *et al.* 2018: 7). Such ideas find science-fictional extrapolation and expression in chthulumedia stories such as the American remake of *Ghost in the Shell*, where the Major (Scarlett Johansson) dons a cloak that renders her invisible as she blends into the background, using this technology as a means of hunting and averting her opponents.

We shall revert to *Ghost in the Shell* and to the wider work of Johansson (and her "deepfake" clones) in Chapter 4, but presently we should like to add a third category of cephalopodic display, one that seemingly combines elements of the other two (signaling/communication and camouflage). These are called *deimatic* displays, which are variously designed to trick, confuse, startle, threaten or make hesitate (Mather *et al.* 2010: 105; Godfrey-Smith 2016: 125). In squid species, common deimatic displays include the sudden use of intense neon coloring or wave-form disorienting color patterns, which can be combined with a rearrangement of body shape and size. The first encounter with a deep-sea squid in *Finding Dory* perfectly actualizes these features of display, as it first looms up in the dark frame as an unblinking neon blue eye, which then becomes surrounded by throbbing patches of hypnotic blue light, before it suddenly bursts into existence as an expansive overhead umbrella of tentacles, somewhat like an alien spacecraft.

Beyond such CGI animations, real octopuses have been known to bulk up into the shape of a barrel as images of large eyes become projected on to their chromatophoric skin-screen, suggesting the presence of a large staring monster head (perhaps even that of Cthulhu!). As mentioned, such deimatic displays are recognized as "an attempt to startle or confuse the foe," or

> to suddenly look different, and weird, in a way that might lead the predator to pause or lose its bearings. Here, the display is supposed to be noticed, but it does not send information to a receiver. It is merely supposed to be confusing or disruptive. (Godfrey-Smith 2016: 125)

Perhaps, then, our own perception of *Kinoteuthis Infernalis* might be accounted for as the perception of a (virtual) deimatic display, which is not dissimilar to what Timothy Morton terms a hyperobject, as we shall discuss presently.

Bracing for *Kinoteuthis*' Embrace

Embracing the tentacular, or having the tentacular embrace you, inevitably leads to the creation of stringy and knotted concept-creatures—the sort of thing Morton describes as a nonlocal entity, which might appear radically distributed across vast tracts of (phase) space and (deep) time. He calls these amorphous things *hyperobjects*, which constitute complex meshes of *interobjectivity*, wherein "nothing is ever experienced directly, but only as mediated through other entities in some shared sensual space" (Morton 2013: 86). The *Kinoteuthis Infernalis* we seek here is unquestionably a viscous interobjective organism, which emerges (emitting its own time and space) through a form of feeling-encounter between many parts within a conglomerated cultural system or assemblage. As if anticipating and echoing this idea, Morton notes how for human observers, the "octopus of the hyperobject emits a cloud of ink as it withdraws from access" (Morton 2013: 39). The inky cloud we are left to experience in the wake of the octopus is one of "effects and affects" that stick to us, as we become entangled with(in) it (Morton 2013: 39). That is, "[its] causal traces float in front of it, in the real of appearance, the aesthetic dimension" (Morton 2013: 90). Theorizing the octopus of the hyperobject leads Morton to see himself as a tentacular thinking-being, too: "as an object-oriented ontologist I hold that all entities (including 'myself') are shy, retiring octopuses that squirt out ink as they withdraw into the ontological shadows" (Morton 2013: 3–4). Such thoughts resonate with our reference to the obscured and ungraspable, or withdrawing like that cuttlefish Aristotle (see Schmitt 1965: 60, quoted in Derby 2014: 2701), while also indicating stringy connections between Morton's project and that of Flusser, who similarly discovers himself (and humanity) reflected within the vampire squid, qua becoming vampyroteuthian. As pursuers of a hyperobject cryptid (namely, the *Kinoteuthis Infernalis*), we, too, increasingly find ourselves to have become soft, betentacled beings. Thus, as with Herman Melville's *Moby Dick* (1851), *The Squid Cinema from Hell* might be read as a journal tracing our own processes of becoming-animal.

However, *Kinoteuthis Infernalis* is not just a hyperobject in the sense that Morton discusses. No—it is perhaps more precisely what we might call a cloud-expelling *hypercryptid*, or a *hypoobject* (the prefix "hypo-" meaning beneath, down or under, and more on which below). To such ends, we might note that the inky clouds dispelled by real octopuses during their drawbacks have often been described—by biologists, artists, and philosophers alike—as a form of 3D sculpture or self-portrait. Jennifer A. Mather, Roland C. Anderson and James B. Wood, for example, note how the expelled bio-ink, when blended with another thickening bio-mucus, serves to leave a lingering form of octopodal "pseudomorph" suspended in the brine (Mather *et al.* 2010: 107; see also Derby 2014: 12). Flusser adds that there is clearly more to the artful story of the "floating cloud of ink, which they shape into their own image" than simply misleading their enemies (Flusser and Bec 2012: 51–52). Indeed, while most octopuses typically beat a rapid withdrawal behind these obscuring inky screens (à la Morton, and Aristotle), a few creative creatures have also been known simultaneously to flush their own chromatophoric skin-screens into an inky black display while distending their bodies and hanging still in the water so that they themselves become mistaken for the "phantom squid blob," or self-portrait-sculpture, that they expel into the water. In terms of deimatic displays, this becomes a ludic quadruple bluff as they change their color to look like they are emitting ink and withdrawing, while in fact remaining on the spot, in the process somehow becoming their own (non-) decoy (Mather *et al.* 2010: 107).[2] In such artful dodging behavior, or deep fakery, these animals expressively combine three different forms of screen art: that of the blocking ink-screen, the (camouflaging) projecting skin-screen, and deimatic display (perhaps also with intoxicating or toxicating chemical attributes, on which more later).

In this way, cephalopods are in various ways what Biswas Mellamphy terms *mètic*, not least because the Greek term implies resident aliens, from *meta*, meaning change, and *oikos*, meaning dwelling (they are from another home). Furthermore, drawing like Biswas Mellamphy on Marcel Detienne and Jean-Pierre Vernant, Amber Jacobs argues that the *mètic* is octopus-like, suggesting also that Metis herself, who in Greek mythology was a threat to Zeus such that he raped and ate her, is "a [maternal] figure signifying laws and practices not reducible to phallic logic" (Jacobs

2010: 2; see also Detienne and Vernant 1991). We shall in time revert to maternity and the non-phallic, in particular in our eighth and final chapter. But for the time being, we wish simply to use the *mètic* to suggest that cephalopods have moved home to be here—a notion taken literally by the scientists who inked the aforementioned panspermia essay on the alien origins of octopuses (a suggestion that we shall take further in later chapters by arguing that all life on Earth is extraterrestrial; see Steele *et al.* 2018). Indeed, writer after writer considers the cephalopod to be "the closest we [humans] will come to meeting an intelligent alien" (Godfrey-Smith 2016: 9), and that they (quite literally) are "aliens living on Earth" (Vlasits 2017; see also Montgomery 2015: 2). What is more, these aliens also gaze knowingly and existentially back at us, with curious "sentient eyes" (Courage 2013: 1; see also Cousteau and Diolé 1973: 13; Nakajima *et al.* 2018). Erika Balsom argues with reference to oceanic life that "we need not leave our earthly planet to encounter alien wonder" (Balsom 2018: 28). Perhaps this is because alien wonder has come to our planet, or, better, that our planet and its inhabitants (including humans) are always already alien.

If cephalopods are like cinema displays of color, then might cinema also, like a cephalopod, be "alien"? Or, if cinema is, like the cephalopod, camouflage and deimatics as much as if not more than it is communication/display, then might we ask what it is that cinema is hiding/hiding from and/or what it is trying to put off? That is, cinema may well present to us so many monsters on the screen-skin surface of a dispersed body of chthulucene films, and these onscreen monsters do constitute a display. But they also camouflage the presence of a different creature—and this is our *Kinoteuthis Infernalis*. What, therefore, is *Kinoteuthis Infernalis*? This hypo-object (or this hyperobject from below) is not simply the sum of "hidden" ideological messages within films, for example, that capitalism and individualism are good—even if we recognize the need for ideological critique in the contemporary era. Rather, we wish to suggest that cinema may also be hiding beneath its typically representational skin a fundamental otherness that the cephalopod also shares. That is, we wish to suggest that cinema is an intelligent alien disguising itself as a mere representation of our world. It is in some senses Cthulhu. Or, as we shall come to see in our final chapter, cinema and media are already a manifestation of what artificial intelligence experts might call the singularity.

We have a long way to go in order to convince you of this outrageous-seeming suggestion, and we need to proceed slowly if we are to get anywhere beyond loose if thought-provoking metaphorics. But this is where we are heading, and so let us continue with our preliminary comparisons between cephalopods and cinema.

Cinesthetic Squids

In addition to its "cinematic skin" that changes color, evidence from cuttlefish also suggests that the skin of cephalopods contains "gene sequences usually expressed only in the retina of the eye," meaning that they might be able to "see" with their skin (Montgomery 2015: 50). As we have seen, what is not subsequently clear is whether the "skin's sensing is communicated to the brain, or whether the information remains local" (Godfrey-Smith 2016: 121). To this end, Godfrey-Smith explains,

> [i]f the skin's sensing is carried to the brain, then the animal's visual sensitivity would extend in all directions, beyond where the eyes can reach. If the skin's sensing does not reach the brain, then each arm might see for itself, and keep what it sees to itself. (Godfrey-Smith 2016: 121)

Interestingly, in their comprehensive survey of the scientific literature on cephalopodic "skin perception," Nakajima *et al.* note that the octopus's ability to detect environmental illumination through its skin helps to clarify how these otherwise colorblind animals expertly blend into their surroundings, even if their chromatophore organs are "light-activated in a manner completely independent of the central nervous system" (Nakajima *et al.* 2018: 8).

The reason for discussing the embodied vision of the cephalopod here is because studies of film and new media have increasingly acknowledged how film itself has a "skin" that is photosensitive, as is made clear by the French term *pellicule*, which refers to a film strip while also meaning "little skin" (see Nancy 2008). Furthermore, the "skin of the film" has come to stand for how our relationship with cinema as viewers is not dependent solely on the senses of sight and hearing, but that it also involves a multimodal engagement that at the very least includes touch (or a haptic engagement with film; see Sobchack 1992, 2004; Marks 2000, 2002; Barker 2009a; Elsaesser and Hagener 2010), if not more of our senses. Indeed, various scholars have since Gene Youngblood (1970) tried to fathom cinema as a fundamentally synesthetic experience, with Vivian Sobchack also coining the term "cinesthetic subject" as someone who might "see" a film with their fingers (Sobchack 2004: 53–84). This cinesthetic subjectivity is nicely captured in the febrile music video for Valentino Khan's "Deep Down Low" (Ian Pons Jewell, USA, 2015), where within a piscine-saturated Japanese *mise-en-scène* we discover a digital image-world full of dynamic octopus-like shape-shifters. In one potent sequence, a female dancer has two dancing tentacles burst forth from her eye sockets, and which sway in rhythmic harmony with the immersive electronic dance track

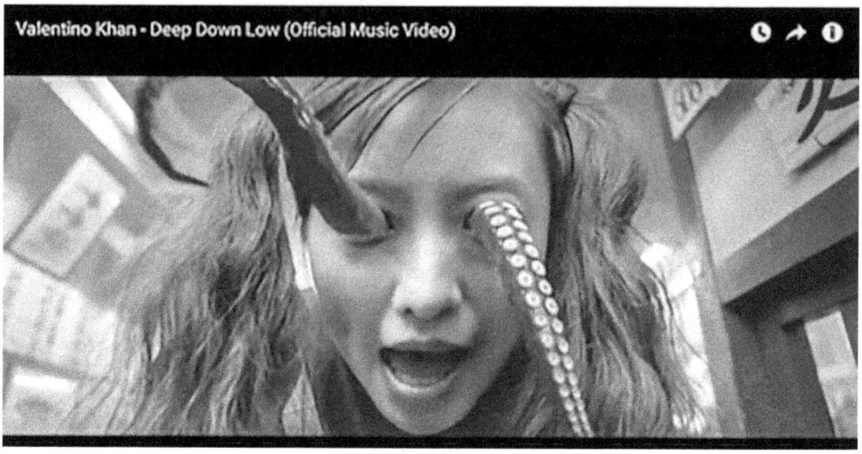

Figure 2.1 Tentacular dancing in the video for Valentino Khan's "Deep Down Low"

(Figure 2.1). In this example, we find a clear expression of how the eye feels and how the tentacle perhaps also sees (the octopus's arm is both eye and feeler—and more).

In other words, the cephalopod is always already a "cinesthetic subject," and as such functions as an as-yet unused metaphor for the film viewer, who briefly becomes a cephalopod of sorts when she finds herself immersed in a film as the octopus is immersed in the sea.

Beyond the octopus's protean and *mètic* seeing skin, the cephalopod is also famous for its numerous arms and/or tentacles (cuttlefish and squid both have eight arms and two extra tentacles, while octopuses have eight arms—the distinction typically being that a cephalopod arm has suckers all along it, while a tentacle only has suckers at the end, if at all). As Haraway notes, "tentacle" derives from the Latin "*tentaculum*, meaning 'feeler,' and *tentare*, meaning 'to feel' and 'to try'" (Haraway 2016: 31). The cephalopod does not just use these multiple limbs to feel—as the notion of "trying" suggests, since it has connotations of other sensory modes, such as tasting or smelling (to try a new food or perfume). Perhaps unsurprisingly, then, we should add that octopuses are essentially able also to taste with their skin, even if "this sense is most exquisitely developed in their suckers" (Montgomery 2015: 5). By such means, these animals' tentacles are not just eyes and arms, but they are also long, probing, and gripping tongues, which taste/smell/lick the objects and molecules with which they come into contact. The way in which humans move their soft boneless tongues—to tie a knot in a cherry stem, say, or to probe into a lover's slimy orifice—thus finds parallels in the muscular cephalopodic

Figure 2.2 The tentacle-tongue hydrostats of the Hollowgasts

limb, with both being examples of *hydrostats*, or "limbs . . . almost entirely composed of muscle and connective tissue used both for force production and as structural support. They can bend in any direction and change the stiffness at any point of the entire arm length" (Nakajima *et al.* 2018: 6). This idea is made somewhat explicit by the betentacled Hollowgasts in *Miss Peregrine's Home for Peculiar Children*, where the mouths of these creatures appear alive with curious tongue-like tentacles (see Figure 2.2). Of course, the seeing-touching-tasting-smelling tentacle is still only a limited picture when we recall that in the real world, cephalopods' non-discreet multi-organ limbs are not just eyes, tongues, and arms, but also legs, brains, and sexual organs (about which more later).

The tentacle thus becomes a pertinent image for the modern thinker-philosopher, who must at least try to think new thoughts with this form of multi-organ without body, or multi-body without organ, or more precisely multi-organ-body within multi-body-organ. Eugene Thacker makes a comparable point, noting how outstanding weird practitioners such as Lovecraft and Edgar Allen Poe attempt to grope and to feel around strange unknowable realms that stimulate novel forms of feeling-thought, which in turn help to give shape to the unrepresentable and unknowable (Thacker 2015b). The broader noological sense of groping around, or feeling out, and getting a taste for (different styles and possibilities) ties perfectly into the recent tide of speculative realisms, posthuman philosophies and object-oriented ontologies chumming today's academic currents courtesy of writers like Jane Bennett, Ian Bogost, Iain Hamilton Grant, Graham Harman, Quentin Meillassoux, Timothy Morton, Steven Shaviro and Patricia Ticineto Clough (to name but eight). Appropriately, and as if summarizing the connections between such vast and varied projects, Haraway reminds us that the "tentacular are also nets and networks," and that "[t]entacularity is about life lived along lines—and such a wealth of lines—not at points, not in spheres" (Haraway 2016: 32). It is along such coiling lines, such verted lines of flight, and through such wormholes, that we track *Kinoteuthis Infernalis*, whose obscuring cloud—expelled as images into our collective cross-cultural assemblages—constitutes a dark indexical sign that signals this hypercryptid or hypoobject's with-drawing retreat. As we follow the trail of the octopus, we take many chthulumedia expressions as a singular-plural sign or hieroglyph. And in so doing, we remain open to the possibility that within this befuddling and intoxicating cloudy cocktail, we might just brush up against, feel, or become touched by, the sticky and pulpy beast that ejected them, namely *Kinoteuthis Infernalis* itself.

The Trail of the Octopus

Cinesthetic film viewing, in which the film touches us as we touch, taste, and see the film suggests not distance but interconnectedness (a film is not something over there that we observe detachedly, but something here with which we are connected). If our relationship with cinema involves touch across space (cinema as glossy tongue-tentacle), then space itself is not simply a backdrop or a neutral medium through which this relationship takes place. Rather, space, too, is interconnected, something that we grow increasingly to realize in the era of globalization, digital technology and chaos theory. Not only does cinema reflect this, but it may also play a key role in globalization, as well as in our burgeoning comprehension of our interconnectedness. That is, cinema might be an alien that gives to us a new language that allows us to understand the world in new ways, as per the story of *Arrival* and its tentacled aliens that also provide humanity with a new language. We shall consider *Arrival* in more detail in Chapter 6, but here we wish to look at a succession of films that use the trope of the octopus precisely to demonstrate the interconnected nature of space (and time). This will include another film by Denis Villeneuve, namely *Maelström*, but let us start with the 1919 silent serial, *The Trail of the Octopus*, which in its date clearly demonstrates that the idea of the octopus/Kraken as a symbol of modernity long predates the fashionably glib use to which Žižek puts it in *Disparities*.[3]

Duke Worne's serial is an *Indiana Jones*-style adventure that involves a cult called the Sacred Twelve in search of the Sacred Talisman of Set (the Egyptian god of the desert), which was plundered from the ancient Temple of Death in Egypt by Dr Reid Stanhope (Howard Crampton). Stanhope's daughter Ruth (Neva Gerber) becomes caught up in a plot to find nine daggers (including the talisman), which when combined will bring great power to their owner (or something like that—the plot is in fact nonsensical and confusing at times, and not simply because some scenes are missing from various episodes). Ruth and her father encounter criminologist Carter Holmes (Ben F. Wilson), who is also working on the case and whose name evokes not only Arthur Conan Doyle's Sherlock Holmes and Edgar Rice Burroughs' John Carter, but also H. P. Lovecraft's Randolph Carter, whom Lovecraft created in 1919—the year that *The Trail of the Octopus* was released.

As the fifteen-part serial continues, Ruth and Holmes cross the globe, taking in numerous supposed locations, from Egypt to Paris to China to San Francisco, and getting into all manner of scrapes, including multiple abductions and rescues. Various parties from various places are in search of the daggers, including Jan Al-Kasim (Al Ernest Garcia, credited as Allen Garcia) from Tunis, the psychic Zora Rularde (Marie Pavis), who seems to be French, and Stanhope's rival American academic Raoul Bornay (Harry Archer). However, it is Chinese Buddhist Wang Foo (also Al Ernest Garcia, but here credited as Ernest Garcia) who emerges as the sinister master criminal seeking global domination through the extermination of the white race (those evil Buddhists!). Defined in the penultimate episode as a "quantum villain," who with a mere stare can control minds (but not that of Holmes, thank god!), Wang Foo at one point masterminds an attempt to crash Mars into Earth, while also having cloned himself. As we shall see, such themes of cloning, planetary collisions and the quantum world will reappear throughout this book—with the serial even linking these indirectly to the cephalopod by calling the final episode "The Yellow Octopus." This is an unflattering reference to Wang Foo, with this title conveying clearly how the racism of the serial reflects a Lovecraftian hatred for the other (Chinamen and to a lesser extent Arabs threaten the whites, who nonetheless feel empowered enough to go and plunder sacred treasures from wherever they wish).

This rejection of the other is a far cry from Haraway's desire to see the other as kin. But what is important here is not just that this otherness is conveyed through the image of the octopus (Wang Foo as "yellow octopus"), but also how this cephalopodic and threatening otherness is an expression of an increasing awareness of different cultures, for example globalization and the attendant power struggles that this involves (whose globalization is this?).[4] Furthermore, in trotting the globe, as well as in having episodes that prominently feature trains, boats, and telephones, the serial communicates a world of shrinking spaces and greater interconnectivity. And even if Wang Foo is an evil "octopus," the serial nonetheless engages consciously with the idea of tentacular entanglement as the prologue sequence of each episode sees the tentacles of an octopus wrap themselves around and then reel in both Ruth and Holmes. That is, they are connected with Egypt, China, France, and the USA, which are themselves connected—whether they like it or not.

A similar logic of globalized power struggles is at work across all of the James Bond films, but *Octopussy* is in some senses a crystallization of the franchise's cephalopodic logic of globalization, cinema, and capital. Bond (here Roger Moore) must get to the bottom of a plot by Soviet general Orlov (Steven Berkoff) to raise money to buy a nuclear weapon that in turn can be used as an excuse to trigger not so much World War Three as a Soviet invasion of Europe. For, by making it seem like an accident that the nuclear device detonated at a circus on an American airbase in Germany, the Western powers would surely sue for nuclear disarmament, which would then allow the Soviets to invade Europe, since without nuclear weapons Europe would not have the military strength to protect itself from the vastly greater numbers of Soviet soldiers and tank divisions.

Octopussy demonstrates clearly the tentacular logic of interconnected and globalized space, as the film takes in Havana, London, Udaipur, and Berlin, among other locations. But where the octopus is an evil other in Duke Worne's serial, the octopus here is morally more ambiguous. Octopussy (Maud Adams) is a British jewel smuggler and businesswoman based in India, where she leads an all-female octopus cult gang (we shall explore further the link between octopuses and jewels in relation to the myth of the *Taishokan* in Chapter 5). Octopussy smuggles treasure for the exiled Afghan prince Kamal Khan (Louis Jourdan), who, unbeknownst to her, is in league with Orlov. When Bond infiltrates her island base, he recognizes her as the daughter of Major Dexter-Smythe, a British traitor whom Bond was supposed to arrest, but whom Bond allowed to commit suicide rather than face the indignity of a public trial. For this, Octopussy thanks Bond and invites him to be her guest. There commences an uneasy relationship, which only fully resolves when Bond convinces Octopussy that Khan is aiding Orlov, at which point she helps him in deactivating the nuclear warhead that is about to explode at the circus. Khan takes Octopussy hostage in a bid to save his own skin, but Bond ultimately rescues her and the two close the film in a clinch on board her yacht. By being a woman who is associated with treachery, criminality, and foreignness (Octopussy lives in India, while Maud Adams is Swedish), the figure of the octopus here continues to connote an otherness to the nation, the law and to patriarchal masculinity. It is perhaps unsurprising that the film's narrative involves the seduction of Octopussy back into Bond's patriarchal and nationalistic order (Bond as phallic boner), with Bond at one point claiming chauvinistically that her all-female octopus cult is guilty of sexual discrimination. But even if Octopussy ultimately falls for her father's captor (Bond as replacement daddy), the figure of the octopus is still expressing difference under globalization. And we can push this logic yet further by turning our attention to *Maelström*.

Pulp Fiction

In *Maelström*, model and fashion designer Bibiane Champagne (Marie-Josée Croze) goes for lunch with her friend Claire (Stephanie Morgenstern). They order octopus, which is their usual, but on this occasion a shocked Claire sends the octopus back because it is too tough ("*la poulpe est coriace*," i.e., like leather). The couple continue to lunch, Bibiane distracted as a result of her life, which is falling apart after being fired from her own family's business and after a one-night stand with a random man less than a week after getting an abortion. We have also seen Bibi run over a man while drunk-driving—but we are not sure how much of this she remembers. Indeed, it is only having read in the newspaper that the man subsequently died that she drives her car to a port and tries to push it into the water after removing the license plate—in a bid to cover up her crime. When she fails to achieve this, the film's narrator, a fish, voiced by Pierre Lebeau and which on occasion we see being chopped up on a fishmonger's table, announces that "[l]ife gives her a second chance. If she survives, she will give herself the right to live." We then see Bibi climb inside the car and drive it into the sea. We hold on its dark waters before cutting to the fish-narrator, which resumes the story. It is at this point that we revert to the same restaurant where Bibi and Claire ordered the octopus. We see the octopus scene play out a second time, except that now we also see the consequences of Claire's refusal of the food: the restaurant manager (Khanh Hua) tells the waiter (Paul Brian Impéchette) to reprimand the chef (Jean Chen), before calling up his supplier (John Dunn-Hill) to give him an angry earful, too.

The supplier does not understand the restaurant manager's Vietnamese, and so gets his employee Bélinda (Belinda Hum) to translate: "your octopus is like cement," she says, before the fishmonger grabs the phone and claims that his octopus is the best there is. The fishmonger then goes into his warehouse and addresses his employees: who has been bringing in this substandard octopus? We cut to the fishmonger with an employee, Miguel (Alejandro Morán), who explains that he has been buying the octopus these past few days because the usual buyer, Head-Annstein Karlsen (Klimbo), has not come to work. This is because Head has died after spending several days at home trying to recover from injuries sustained from . . . getting run over by Bibi. We then see Bibi emerge from the water and climb a ladder back up to the port's quayside.

It is not just that *Maelström* demonstrates a circular logic when Bibi is served bad octopus as a result of her inadvertent murder of the best supplier in Montreal. As far as "just deserts" go, to be served tough octopus is hardly the comeuppance that murder typically receives. Rather, it is that the octopus serves here both as a plot device and as a metaphor for the entangled lives of the characters of *Maelström*. For, it will be at Head's cremation that Bibi will meet the former's son, Evian (Jean-Nicolas Verreault), with whom she will fall in love. We could read the film as telling us that Montreal is a small city where such coincidences happen (as also suggested in a film like *Starbuck*, Ken Scott, Canada, 2011, in which it transpires that 142 people from Montreal are all children of the same man). But rather than suggesting an insular, nay incestuous Québecois world, we would suggest that *Maelström* suggests a world of interconnection—and that this interconnection is materialized through the octopus.

With its eight multisensory limbs, an octopus does indeed suggest connection and entanglement as it connects with far more things than any human can (Montgomery describes a moment in which an octopus, aptly called Octavia, interacts simultaneously with six different human beings and distracts them sufficiently to be able to use her remaining arms to steal a bucket of fish from right under the noses of the six—and without any of them noticing; see Montgomery 2015: 48). That is, cephalopod perception would suggest an understanding of the interconnected as opposed to separated nature of events in the world. What seem to humans as distant and separate events are in fact connected to each other, as per(haps) chaos theory's famous butterfly beating its wings in Argentina and thus changing weather patterns in the USA (see Gleick 1998), and as per(haps) the "spooky action at a distance" that sees two particles, especially those with matching polarization, react to each other simultaneously and across distances that it would take light longer to travel—as a result of quantum entanglement (see Zeilinger 2003).

Thinking like a cephalopod, then, helps us to account for this connective, chaotic world in which a car accident leads to the retrieval of bad-quality octopuses for lunchtime consumption. With its fish-narrator and its insistent images of the sea, *Maelström* would seem deliberately to convey a different, less dry, and more "liquid" kind of thought, or intelligence—as per that which Melody Jue (2014) attributes to Flusser, and which we also see in the marine intelligence of octopuses themselves, as per the analysis of Godfrey-Smith (2016). The word *maelström* is itself the name of a whirlpool in Norwegian, suggesting that the "grinding-stream" of the water (from the Dutch *malen*, meaning to grind, and *stroom*, meaning stream, itself from the Proto-Indo-European root *sreu-*, meaning to flow) is a chaos of connectivity. Meanwhile, Harman explains how Lovecraft "can be dismissed as a pulp writer only under the presupposition that *all* writing about otherworldly monsters is doomed to be nothing but pulp" (Harman 2012: vii). But Harman here misses a trick. For as one of the French words for octopus is *poulpe* (as in Spanish it is *pulpo*), Lovecraft is in some senses precisely a pulp writer, and what he produces is precisely *pulp fiction*: a fiction that in tentacular fashion links the outer and dark reaches of the universe to the mundane world of New England academia. But more than this: as many authors have come to discuss how contemporary cinema (and television) involves "forking plots" (Bordwell 2002; Branigan 2002), fractal films (Everett 2005), complexity (Mittell 2006; Staiger 2006; Harper 2005), puzzles (Panek 2006; Buckland 2009, 2014), and modular narratives (Cameron 2008)—all of which might also be seen to fit under the umbrella of "post-classical narration" (Thanouli 2006)—so might we understand all of these to be indicative of a "chthulucinema": a tentacular cinema that demonstrates a cephalopod-like perception of a connective, entangled multi-strand world. If such narrative tropes demonstrate a "Tarantino effect" (Ramírez Berg 2006), it is not because in *Pulp Fiction* (USA, 1994) Quentin Tarantino created the *ur*-movie of our times, but because in naming his film about the intersecting and interconnected lives of various Angelinos *Pulp Fiction*, Tarantino was inadvertently expressing the cephalopod logic of the chthulucene.[5]

Wormhole Cinema

Let us revert to the scene of Bibi's attempted suicide in *Maelström*. It is not just that after her suicide we go back to the restaurant and see it play out in a different way. More pertinently, the fish-narrator announces as Bibi tries to push her car into the sea that "life gives her a second chance." And yet, at this precise moment, Bibi is not attempting suicide; she is simply trying to dispose of her car so that evidence of running Head down is disappeared. It is only after the fish-narrator has said this that we see Bibi climb into the car and drive it off the quay and into the water herself. In other words, tentacular cephalopod logic does not just suggest an interconnectivity of space, but also an interconnectivity of time, which emerges thus as nonlinear: Bibi has not yet attempted suicide, but it is recounted to us as if it were so, as if it were a fait accompli, and as if fate itself were telling us that what will come to pass has in fact already (per)happened (it is *fait*/fate). This is not necessarily a teleological form of narration (for if Bibi survives the crash into the water, she will then have a second chance—but her survival is not yet clear). But it does suggest that all moments in time—past, present, and future(s)—coexist simultaneously when witnessed from the "liquid" perspective of the fish-narrator, and that moments in time affect each other not just forwards (as per classical linear causality), but in all directions (the future affects the past)—an idea that will find more distilled expression in Villeneuve's *Arrival*, as we shall demonstrate later. Perhaps it comes as no surprise, then, that quantum entanglement happens not just across space—as polarized atoms move in union in a "spooky" fashion that defies the supposedly absolute measure of the speed of light—but also across time. That is, photons have been demonstrated to affect each other's behavior both backwards and forwards across time, or what physicists refer to as "quantum steering into the past" (Ma *et al.* 2012; Megidish *et al.* 2013; Price and Wharton 2016). Verily we do seem to live in a weird universe that the "alien" cephalopod might fathom better than the standard human.

Indeed, the octopus has been adopted as the image of the structure of wormholes, which can be considered portals across space and time, and which perhaps are the stuff of the multiverse. For, physicists Juan Maldacena and Leonard Susskind recently contended that wormholes, which connect distant points in space-time and which often are referred to as Einstein–Rosen bridges, are equivalent to quantum entangled particles such as those described previously, and which also are referred to as Einstein–Podolsky–Rosen pairs—these phenomena being named after Albert Einstein, Boris Podolsky, and Nathan Rosen respectively. The resulting equation, ER = EPR, would suggest that black holes are not necessarily phenomena from which no information can escape (their blackness derives from the fact that even light cannot escape from them), but rather that information can travel through black holes via the wormholes that connect them (see Maldacena and Susskind 2013; Wolchover 2017). If you will, black holes are the entrances to wormholes, suggesting the interconnected nature of the universe as entangled particles interact at speeds faster than light (or in a realm without light and thus without speed and without time—and thus in darkness, or amidst a black optics). But more than this, according to Maldacena's model, wormholes are also the heat that black holes slowly give off and which typically is called Hawking radiation, after Stephen Hawking. In effect, each wormhole is a tentacle of Hawking radiation seeping out of the black hole and re-entering space-time as we know it at a point completely different from where it entered the black hole (see Figure 2.3).

By this token, the monopod wormhole should now also be replaced by the multipod cephalo-hole, as is the case with the aptly named "Maelstrom" of *Solo: A Star Wars Story*. Not dissimilar to the cyclonic maelstrom of Villeneuve's film, in *Solo* the maelstrom is a time-space anomaly where, of course, a tentacular time-monster feeds off black-hole energy.

What is more, Christopher Nolan's *Interstellar* (USA/UK/Canada/Iceland, 2014) similarly gives cinematic expression to the "timelessness" of

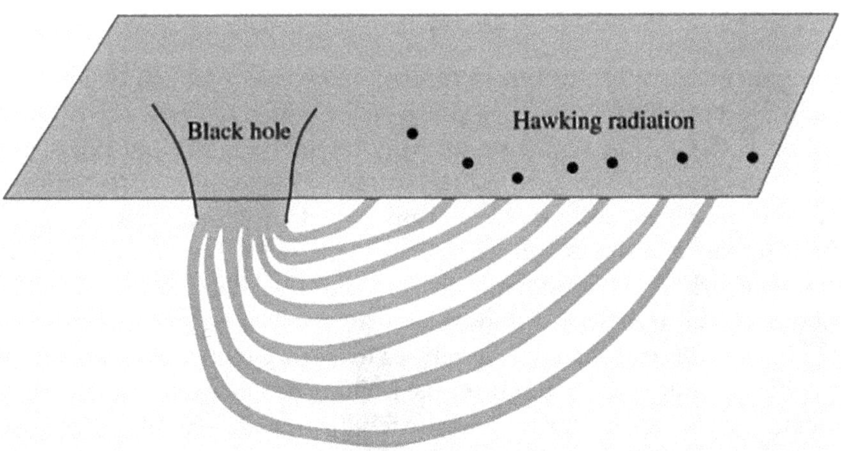

A sketch known as the "octopus" that expresses the ER = EPR idea.

—

arXiv:1306.0533v2 **[hep-th]**

Figure 2.3 Note that Maldacena and Susskind's sketch involves not eight legs but seven, making of it a heptapod à la *Arrival*

existence in the black hole, as Cooper (Matthew McConaughey) emerges after a period of time inside a black hole to find his daughter Murph (Ellen Burstyn) significantly more aged than him. That is, Cooper has traveled through time by traveling through the black hole, suggesting that the past is not separate from the future, but that the two coexist simultaneously and interconnect with each other. Perhaps it is only fitting, then, that the late Mark Fisher connects Nolan's films to the work of H. P. Lovecraft by considering them both in his book on *The Weird and the Eerie* (Fisher 2016). Even though Lovecraft is given as an example of the former (weird) and Nolan an example of the latter (eerie), we might nonetheless further this link between Nolan and tentacular thinking not just because of his time-sprawling and complex ("pulp") narratives, but also through his Batman films, *Batman Begins* (USA/UK, 2005), *The Dark Knight* (USA/UK, 2008), and *The Dark Knight Rises* (UK/USA, 2012). For, as H. P. Lovecraft sets a number of his stories in the fictional Massachusetts town of Arkham, so is Arkham Asylum—named after Lovecraft—a key location in the Batman mythos, being the insane asylum to which most of Batman's nemeses are sent and from which they escape at one point or another. Chthulucinema is a cinema of insanity!

One Man Up

A second example of this time-warping, multiverse logic can be found in Paolo Sorrentino's *L'uomo in più* (Italy, 2001), which typically is translated as *One Man Up*. The film is set partially in Naples in the late 1980s, and it tells the story of two men called Antonio Pisapia. The first, typically referred to as Toni and played by Toni Servillo, is a crooner with a penchant for sex and drugs and who gets caught *in flagrante delicto* with an underage girl. The second, typically referred to as Antonio and played by Andrea Renzi, is a Serie A footballer who scores a bicycle-kick wonder goal in an important match, who refuses to throw a game, and who may or may not be injured deliberately on the training ground—but which injury nonetheless brings his career prematurely to an end. The film then basically charts the demise of both men, as Toni the crooner struggles to make a comeback post-prison, and as Antonio goes through a divorce, fails to hold down any new relationships, and is nary given a chance to show his skills as a manager, even though he believes that he has devised a revolutionary and attacking form of play that he refers to as *l'uomo in più*.

Despite sharing the same name, the two halves of Sorrentino's film do not particularly connect, and so the oblique structure of Sorrentino's narrative becomes hard to explain—unless we understand the film through its references to octopuses. For, Toni regularly expresses his dislike of octopuses, even though he loves seafood and to cook fish. The reason for this, we discover, is that Toni's brother supposedly died in an accident featuring an octopus, a moment that we see at the beginning of the film, even though its meaning and relevance are not at that time clear. However, as Toni gets further down on his luck, he decides to face his fears. Entering a covered market, Toni buys an octopus, and it is on his way out of the market that Toni—for the only time in the film—crosses paths with Antonio. However, it is not as if their meeting is particularly momentous. Indeed, the two just look at each other somewhat curiously . . . and then continue on their separate ways.

What are we to make of this? Well, since the two men share the same name, it would seem that the two halves of the film's narrative are two different versions of the same story, or two different ways in which Toni's life might have played out. More than this, we might suggest that the two halves of the narrative are parallel universes—one in which Toni survives the diving accident with the octopus, and one in which Antonio survives the diving accident with the octopus, as if the two were different versions of the same person, or dead brothers living in weirdly different but connected worlds. And it is the octopus that brings these two otherwise separate universes together, suggesting that from the cephalopod's perspective, or when we go through the cephalo-hole, we exist in a multiverse, in which multiple universes are entangled across multiple times, some of which from the human perspective are actual, and some of which are virtual—but which for the *Kinoteuthis Infernalis*, or the squid cinema from hell, share an equal ontological value.

Notably, the universes are linked not just by the octopus, but also by media: Toni also sees Antonio on the television show *Confessioni pubbliche*, with the latter staring out from the television as if he sees Toni, or as if the television itself were an octopus connecting otherwise disparate worlds, flattening out their ontology. Toni calls the television show demanding Antonio's number, but the show refuses to give it out, perhaps because he is really just asking for his own number or because Antonio is a figment of his imagination, or a ghost looking on from a different dimension. Either way, Toni then dreams of seeing Antonio in a diving costume similar to the one that we saw at the film's opening, as Antonio sits on the beach with Toni's mother (Angela Goodwin). The presence of Toni's mother at the scene of the brother's death would suggest that it is not Antonio who is dead, but Toni, who here realizes that he is already dead, and that it was his brother Antonio who survived the octopus attack (as per Zhuannzhi's query that the butterfly may be dreaming of him rather than him dreaming of the butterfly, perhaps Antonio dreams Toni as Toni dreams Antonio).

Toni then wakes up from this dream and takes a bath, hearing news of Antonio's death via the radio (or perhaps in his head). Toni then attends a funeral, presumably that of Antonio since the latter's ex-wife is present, before Toni then arranges himself to be on *Confessioni pubbliche*. However, this is not before he stabs to death Antonio's former club chairman, who had refused to give the former footballer a break as a coach (although how Toni knows this is not especially clear). And so, while Toni professes on the television show to be free, he ends the film in prison, where he prepares fish for other inmates.

If in *One Man Up* the octopus is connected to media, dreams, and parallel universes, what is perhaps also of interest is how this invertebrate universe of the octopus is one in which phallic masculinity crumbles, as both Toni and Antonio are brought low, even if the latter tries to use his spine to stand upright and even if the former claims to be a free man. While *l'uomo in più* is translated as one man up, what the title connotes above and beyond a football formation is the excess of masculinity—there is more man than we need in the world, and perhaps even in the multiverse, as is reflected in the film's double narrative, as well as in its double critique of slightly different types of men (Toni as cynical womanizer; Antonio as somewhat ineffectual naïf). In Sorrentino's pulp fiction, then, we not only see the back of masculinity broken, but also that of a singular timeline, as the invertebrate world instead connects many universes (to suggest a multiverse) via its connecting tentacles.

In his study of cephalopods, Godfrey-Smith asserts that "[d]oing philosophy is largely a matter of trying to *put things together*, trying to get the pieces of very large puzzles to make some sense. Good philosophy is opportunistic; it uses whatever information and whatever tools look useful" (Godfrey-Smith 2016: 12). For Daniel Reynolds, meanwhile, philosophy is also a matter of groping around, "feeling through the world," like a tentacle being or blind person with a "tap-tapping" cane. Furthermore, philosophy is best used to help discover our changing position within a world in flux—today accelerated by the transactional blurring of digital technology, the environment, and organisms (Reynolds 2019: 41–47). That is, philosophy becomes "a kind of probing action" designed to help us "feel our way through a concept with spoken language or with words on a page" (Reynolds 2019: 47). Such tentacular groping and grasping will help to create a portrait of the *Kinoteuthis Infernalis*, which can only be rendered impressionistically because the cephalopod is, with the philosophy of Georges Bataille in mind, *informe*, or without shape (see also Balsom 2018: 31). Indeed, superpositionally this portrait is, like Cthulhu, all at once map, abstract diagram, index, and camouflage cape (of good hope?).

With this in mind, we might add that if Michel Foucault saw the carceral panopticon as the abstract diagram of earlier disciplinary societies (Foucault 1991), Gilles Deleuze noted that the enclosed, burrowing mole was its metaphoric token animal. In his writing on modern control societies, however, Deleuze argued that with the third generation of digital (but not necessarily binary) machines, the old mole was becoming usurped by a coiling snake: "[a] snake's coils are even more intricate than a mole's burrows" (Deleuze 1995: 182). However, as is by now clear, we would in our digital era of liquescent topologies, oceanic computing (see Greenspan 2015), and volumetric informatics, suggest that the snake's single tentacle remains evocative, but that it is not as fitting a creature as the betentacled octopus. Indeed, while we certainly have sea snakes, these tend not to be coiling restrictors, even if that is how Deleuze wanted to imagine the critter. The cephalopod, then, is the animal for us, not just because it provides us with a method for investigating our present technological forms, but also because it functions as a conceptual tool that can help us to understand the nature of websites, social media, medical imaging, 3D printing, and digital imaging as deployed in art and cinema—all of which we shall consider below.

Tentacles R Us—in Volumetric Space

A fresh vector: while discussions of soft(ware) bodies and coiling wet(ware) tentacles may be metaphorical, it is interesting to note how ubiquitous such metaphors have become in the digital realm. To take just one of innumerable examples, the downloadable creative "mind map" launched online by sportswear company Adidas in 2016 features a schematic that functions here as another verting point of departure and another sign of our cryptid's retreat/presence (see Figures 2.4 and 2.5).

Surrounded by an inky pool of blackness, the central clickbait section in Figure 2.5 suckers users into navigating through hyperlinks, which (as with many or even most websites) form potential lines through a volume rather than constituting objects to be moved over or around.[6]

Worth recalling here is that for Martin Heidegger, earlier modes of "thinking about" simply reflected modernity's "conquest of the world as picture" (Heidegger 1977: 134), through a practice that ultimately left the subject distanced and alienated from the world. Conversely, we would argue that computational image forms, with which we increasingly interact

Figure 2.4 Adidas's creative octopus

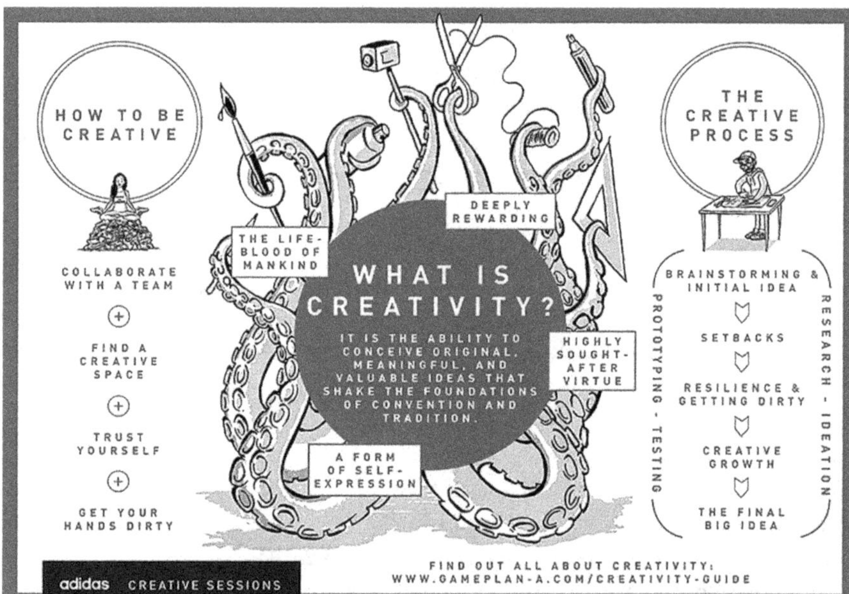

Figure 2.5 Creativity as cephalopodic

(as per the Adidas website), help to erode and to deterritorialize the bedrock substrates of older modernist views of the "world as picture" (for the privileged eyes)—replacing this with more fluid and immersive volumetric image-forms that we navigate through with our fingers and bodies as much as with our eyes. Like a squid or an octopus, we might move not (only) from

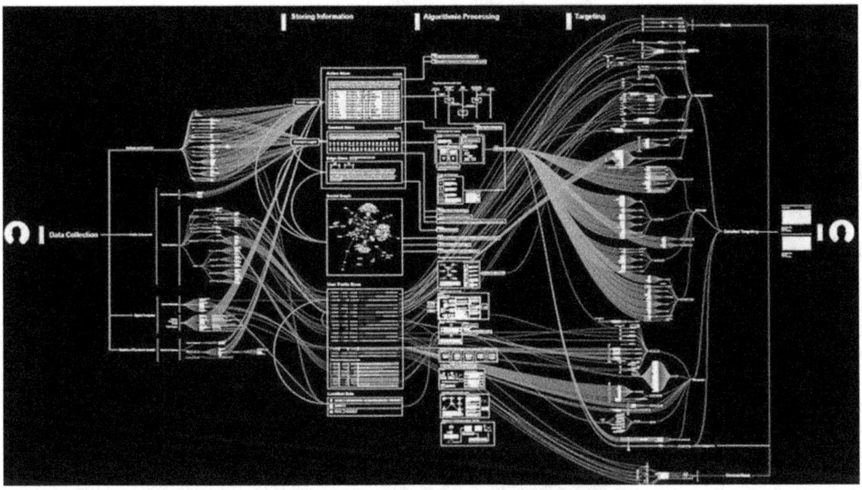

Figure 2.6 Facebook's tentacles

the surface and down ("hypoverting"), but from within. That is, just as the octopus propels itself backwards through its own jet propulsion system, so might we navigate the site in multiple directions (backwards and forwards), touching our way through one or many enfolded screen interfaces.

Moving on to social media, consider how a 2017 article for the BBC exclaims "[h]ow Facebook's tentacles reach further than you think" (Miller 2017). Of pertinence here, the image—or more precisely the digital informatic schematic—accompanying this article betrays its own anatomical resemblance to our cephalopod totems (see Figure 2.6). And as if confirming such intuitions, the Share Lab (who generated the informatic image) emblazon images of octopuses and the fabled Kraken on their website, through which users pass in order to access information about the control and manipulation practices enabled by today's networked machines and autonomous software programs (Figure 2.7).

In even more recent stories about Facebook's compliance with the notorious Cambridge Analytica during the American presidential election campaign for Donald J. Trump, reportage highlighted how in the epoch of computerized control, these organizations colluded to use volumetric data capture, combined with methods of "deception" and "electronic brainwashing"—which Flusser recognized as the modus operandi of vampyroteuthian art (Figure 2.8). Even before this story broke, the tentacular Cthulhu was already linked conceptually to the Twitter-enabled presidency of Trump as a result of numerous memes that promote Cthulhu for America and Cthulhu for President 2016 (and already for 2020), thereby

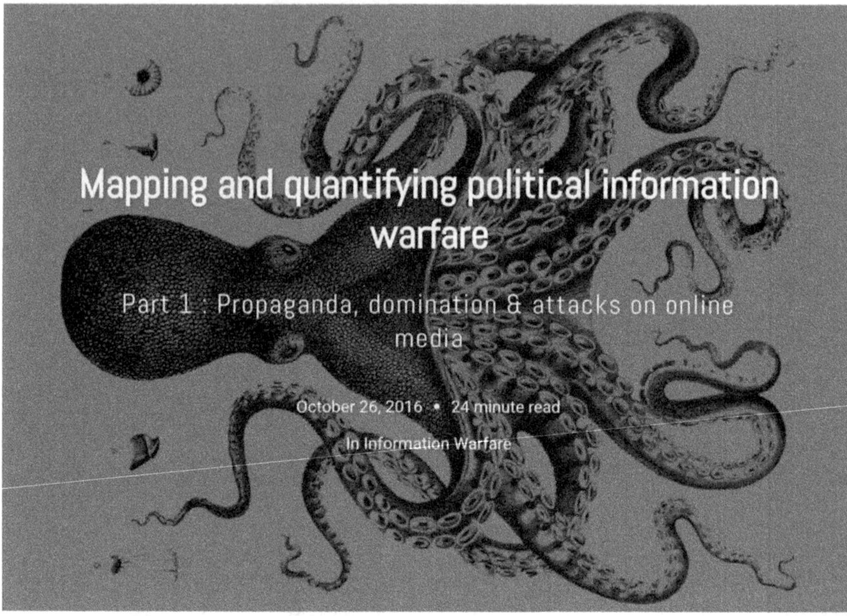

Figure 2.7 Share Lab website

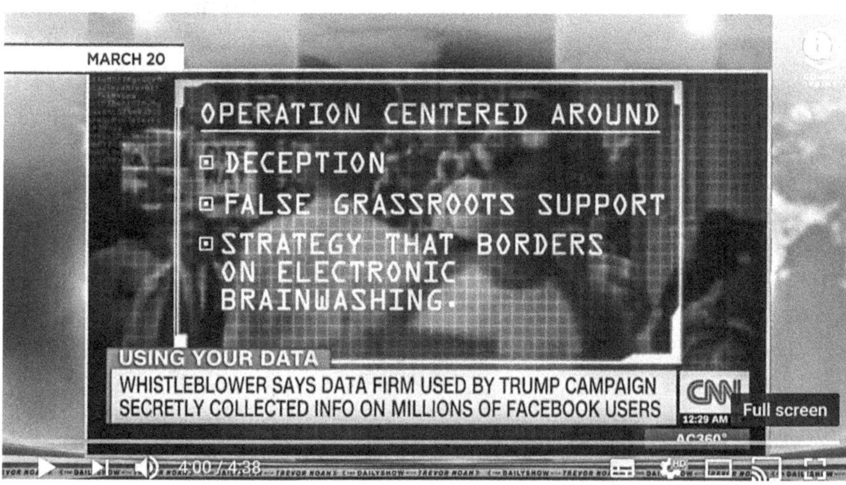

Figure 2.8 Facebook and Cambridge Analytica modus operandi

linking Trump and his exclusive, combative, and anti-ecological policies to impending apocalypse. As the posters playfully ask: why vote for the lesser evil? (See Figures 2.9, 2.10, and 2.11.)

Similar things can be said of a less reliable informatic schematic found in the vampyroteuthian conspiracy zones of YouTube. For example, Richard

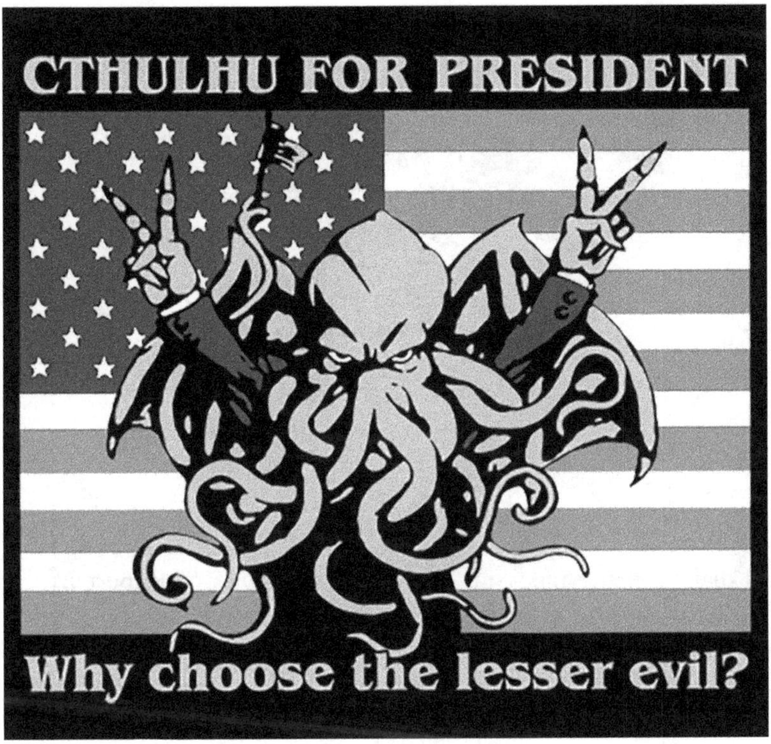

Figure 2.9 Cthulhu for President

Figure 2.10 Trump octopus

Figure 2.11 Trump peril

Hall's diagrammatic mock-up of the media empire of Rupert Murdoch (a God-hero for Trump) offers one such cephalopodic case in point, channeling both the deceptive nature of the animal and its tentacular spread to make a point about the nature of Murdoch's grasp on the contemporary mediascape—in this instance to argue that the public have been greatly deceived about the case of Madeleine McCann, a three-year-old girl who went missing in Portugal in 2007 (see Figure 2.12). If media power and data knowledge are synonymous with the cephalopod, then small wonder that Ned Fleming (Bryan Cranston) describes Laird Mayhew (James Franco) as an octopus in *Why Him?* (John Hamburg, USA/Cambodia, 2016), since the latter plays a Silicon Valley millionaire who has made his money through new technologies that bear a loose similarity to data tycoons like Facebook's Mark Zuckerberg.

With this in mind, the Facebook schematic and organizational structure created by Share Lab provides another interesting vector with our model animals. For, the "tentacles" of Facebook loosely mirror the bilateral neural arrangement of octopus intelligence, which is often described in terms of an interaction between bi-directional information waves linked by a "ladder-like" arrangement in their nervous system—with the majority of octopus neurons being found in their arms (see Godfrey-Smith 2016: 51, 65). As previously discussed, we can think of each octopus tentacle as a kind of independent thinking brain (as well as eye, tongue, arm, leg, and clitoris/penis), seeing, groping, tasting, feeling, and responding independently of any centralized intelligence. However, the various tentacles' impressionistic perceptions and actions

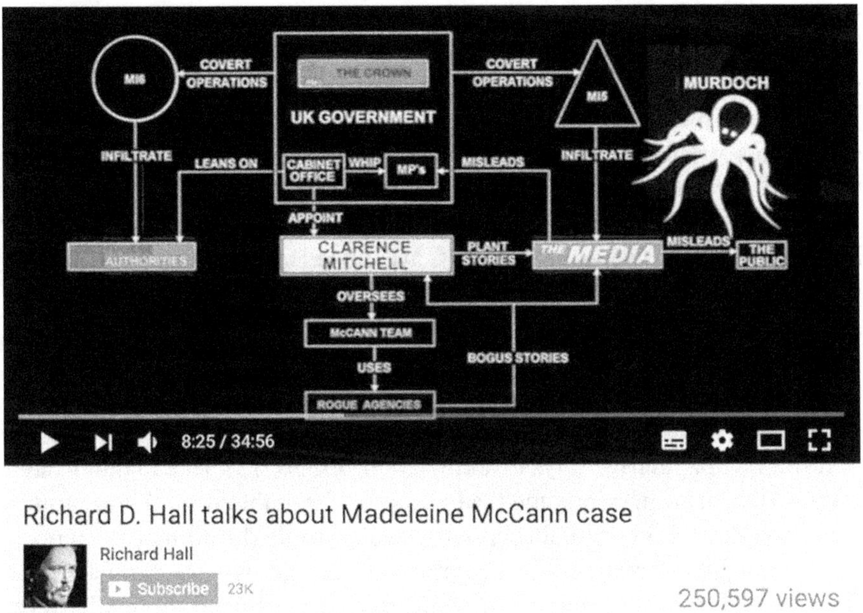

Figure 2.12 Murdoch's media octopus

can feed back up the ladder into the central intelligence, which can, in turn, and if need be, fine-tune, (re)direct, or even execute control of it/them. Thus, it appears that "two forms of control are working in tandem," to the extent that the octopus finds itself in a hybrid situation (Godfrey-Smith 2016: 69). Is this not a comparable model to the organization of Facebook, in that a given Facebooker may well feel like an independent intelligence or autonomous being, while also being party to the organization's centralized policies and laws, which can override and direct, by blocking movements, sending targeted material, or encouraging certain forms of expression/action? Thus, as with an octopus, Facebook's "arms are partially *self*—they can be directed and used to manipulate things. But from the central brain's perspective, they are partially *non-self* too, partially agents of their own" (Godfrey-Smith 2016: 103).

Fleshed-out Volumetric Man

In 1993, Texan prisoner Joseph Paul Jernigan became the digital era's informatics Adam—albeit after his execution by lethal injection. Jernigan's corpse—which he donated to medical science—was frozen solid, and then planed/ground down into a series of 1mm axial layers, each of which was digitally photographed and scanned into a series of tomographic planar sections. The images were subsequently uploaded and recombined by computer software into a gridded 3D (replete with x, y, and z axes) anatomical image of a volumetric human cadaver "amenable to computer vision" and animated interaction (Waldby 2000: 9). Cathy Waldby notes how this "material assemblage of corpse and computer," known as the Visible Human Project, overcame the problem of the human body's self-enclosedness by first "transluminating" the body's interior and transforming the dataset into a new morphable form of digital terrain, which could easily be navigated *through* as a geometric volume—either manually or via pre-programmed "flythroughs" (or soar-throughs). This dataset also allowed for the digital body to be taken apart and recombined in novel or imaginative ways (Waldby 2000: 15, 58, 72). In a manner radically different to previous medical stiffs, this mutable digital body interface also allowed the virtual corpse to have multiple durational existences, as it could be "animated and programmed for interactive simulation of trauma, or human movement, of fluid dynamics and of surgery." Here, the biomedia dataset could be set up as a range of transactive "operable images" programmable for simulated surgeries replete with haptic interfaces and affective qualities of resistance and/or drag for interactive users (Waldby 2000: 15–21, 73).

What is more, the imaging software could now also allow for medium-specific forms of scale-shifting interface, permitting an endoscope-style point-of-view to shrink down so that users could navigate through microscopic ventricles that actual physical instruments simply could not—in a manner that recalls how boneless cephalopods can pass easily through tiny gaps and spaces. Cybernetic features also allowed the software lumen to display different deportments in a way that recalls how octopuses malleably change the shape and size of their own soft bodies. Within this 3D volumetric lumen, the fourth animated dimension of time is also infinitely pliable and morphable, so that diseases or traumas can be generated, developed, rewound, replayed, reoperated upon, or reprogrammed ad infinitum (see Waldby 2000: 73).

Apart from the direct benefits to scientific knowledge, the reconstitution of a human body on a web applet also allows for the commodification of this body, in which users can navigate the image across one axis for free or across multiple axes for a price (see Micheau and Hoa 2017). This demonstrates the tentacular flexibility of this sort of computational image in its ability effortlessly to articulate itself to other domains (education, entertainment, play, and, as we shall shortly see, cinema). There is also perhaps a strictly poetic resonance here, with the entirely non-reversible radical fragmentation of Jernigan's human body guaranteeing an altogether more stable and integrated posthuman data-body or informatic "afterlife."

From 3D Printing to Digital Art

3D printing arguably gives us an inverted or reversed image of the planar destruction of Jernigan's body and the creation of a digital volumetric dataset. For, 3D printing originally emerged as a concept modeling system (Dimitrov *et al.* 2006) that has increasingly grown to become a catch-all term encapsulating a wide range of processes that transmit and transform virtual digital information into "real world atoms" in an additive layer-by-layer real-time printing process known as "growing." To grow the desired object/organ or "product," 3D printers utilize a heterogeneous combination of industrial plastics, ceramics, metal alloys, polymer filaments, nylon, glass, carbon, gas, gels, "exotic fluids," and organic materials that are stored in printer feedstock cells (Birtchnell *et al.* 2013: 2–11; Faulkner-Jones *et al.* 2013). The process of printing or growing for industrial or commercial products can involve a variety of techniques and practices including "heated extrusion, laser sintering, electron beam melting, [and] chemical binding" (Birtchnell *et al.* 2013: 11). The manufacture of metal tools, for instance, "can be made by printing in stainless steel powder, sintering and infiltrating with bronze" as the object is printed in real time (Dimitrov *et al.* 2006: 141). What is more, squid chitin has in recent years become a key ingredient for the biothermoplastic used in 3D printing (as well as in the creation of prosthetics for amputees; see Staaf 2017: 104).

But beyond the material role played by cephalopods in tomographic 3D printing, we might suggest that the medium is a highly significant sociopolitical and cultural game-changer, with its modular as opposed to molded modes of production providing an entirely new "scope to print fully assembled gadgets with multiple materials, different colors, embedded electronics and moving parts" (Birtchnell *et al.* 2013: 14). As indicated, these printouts may also be novel forms of what Eugene Thacker has termed "biomedia" (see Thacker 2004). In the field of medical sciences, for example, an inchoate era of "biofabrication" dawns, employing similar "electrohydrodynamic jet printing" techniques that utilize "nanolitre dispensing systems" and "bio-ink" feeders made up of human (or posthuman, depending on your preference) embryonic stem cells (Faulkner-Jones *et al.* 2013: 2–3). By 2006, Dimitrov and colleagues thus proclaimed that 3D printed implants, which included bone and soft tissue, were already "a reality," and as such presented "obvious major advantages in reconstructive surgery," as when "growing the implants, different polymer binders can be deposited at required locations, thereby encouraging cell migration into specific areas of the implant" (Dimitrov *et al.* 2006: 143). Echoing Thacker's work, Thomas Elsaesser frames the uses of printable enzymes and proteins—the new "building blocks" of bio products, alongside the digital mapping of genomes and the commercial patenting of plant species—as signaling a collapse between long-standing and otherwise inveterate (but always already spurious) nature/culture divisions (Elsaesser 2008: 16–17).

Looking at Angela Palmer's *Brain of the Artist* series (2012) allows us to further these considerations of 3D images and objects. *The Brain of the Artist* consists of five 3D "self-portraiture" sculpture-images, with each being constructed by Palmer joining together various panes of glass, each of which includes an engraving (or drawing) on each of their flat edges. The images are based on volumetric magnetic resonance imaging (MRI) and computed tomography (CT) scans taken at University College, London, and which were thereafter subdivided into an appropriate number of planar sections representing a thin topological slice-through of the artist's brain—not dissimilar to the navigable body of Joseph Paul Jernigan. When properly (re)aligned, these various engravings form a ladder-like block of riven glass, somewhat like a tank, which contains (or generates) a floating 3D image of (parts or the whole of) the artist's brain suspended within. The portrait-sculpture tanks are today presented on a plinth about 150cm tall, so that the volumetric images can be walked around and viewed from any angle, including from above (viewer height permitting).

The information accompanying the sculpture at the National Portrait Gallery in Edinburgh in 2018 notes that this "most unusual form of self-portraiture . . . is an elegant, ethereal work which develops in a challenging way the concept of self-representation," and which is linked to Palmer's broader desire to "map," as can be seen in her work more generally. Such mapping practices accord with Steven Shaviro's perception that technologies such as functional MRI and transcranial magnetic stimulation (TMS) mark a shift away from philosophical and scientific models of understanding the psychological, to engineering-based modeling of the physiological. These machines thus also help to broker a broader movement "from technologies that serve as metaphors for the mind, to technologies that themselves *literally* act upon the mind, by measuring the flow of blood in the brain, and by stimulating or inhibiting particular neurons in determinate ways" (Shaviro 2016: 115–116).

We would add that in the context of the Scottish National Portrait Gallery, which is full of older historical portraits and self-portraits, Palmer's composited MRI sculpture works to unconceal a wider shift in thinking about the self/subject. For, in having a transparent image of the artist's brain before us, viewers can literally see through it to the surrounding historical portraiture, which draws into relief a new shift from a preoccupation with the biographical self (*bios*) of the (historical-present) subjective mind to a concern with objective, "bare life" (*zoë*) aspects of the self (or the not-quite-self). Or: these portraits do not so much capture the self as a version/person, which the mind (of the artist) typically reads and recognizes, but instead they offer up an alien(ating) inhuman tech-image of the biological body/brain, just as the 3D printer offers up an object that combines biology and technology, and which points to the volumetric, interconnected nature of space in the contemporary world. This is not to say that the mind or perspective of the artist is not present as a prosthetic medium, but rather that there is here a certain foregrounding of a nonhuman or posthuman perspective, which averts us away from a singular version and toward multiple versions of the self—or which constitutes a with-drawal of the self (as unified) as much as it does a drawing of the self (it is a self-portrait).

Indeed, the Spanish word for portrait is *retrato* (with *retrait* also being a now-obsolete term for portrait in French), suggesting that the drawing of the self (with ink) constitutes a retreat as much as it does an advance (drawing is thus understood as withdrawing). In this way, portraiture is tied not only to a history of ink, but also to a history of withdrawing/retreating. That is, the portrait, and perhaps pictorial art more generally, is a camouflage as much as a revelation. As if highlighting the work's posthuman perspective, the isolation of the left hemisphere of Palmer's brain in a piece called *Edition 2* results in an image that at once resembles a dissected (map of a) brain in a vat *and* a kind of suspended cephalopod-like alien creature, perhaps making it the National Portrait Gallery's chthulumedia-era portrait par excellence.

A second example of chthulumedia art that expresses itself through both form and content is the performance/installation piece *Octopus Brainstorming: Empathy* (2017–) by artist Victoria Vesna and neuroscientist Mark Cohen. This piece demands that viewer-user-performers wear real-time brain scanners that are tellingly disguised as bioluminescent octopuses. Wearing these cephalopod devices thereafter allows participants to communicate with each other through their brainwaves, which are connected to the cephalopodic skin-lights—not unlike the fictional SQUID devices from *Strange Days* (Kathryn Bigelow, USA, 1995), where

SQUIDs are soft, wiry devices worn on the head and used to record and to play back, as if lived, the experiences of other people (SQUID stands for Superconducting QUantum Interference Device). In *Octopus Brainstorming: Empathy*, brainwaves become translated into light and color on the wearable biomedia skin-screen (see, for example, Sommer 2017; Nakajima *et al.* 2018: 9). By such means, the tech-art installation again illuminates another biological sense of self that is tied more to *zoë* (our corporeal existence, language rendered not as a means of communicating but as a means of licking, or speaking [in] tongues) than it is to *bios* (the visible human body and spoken language as supposed communication).[7]

Digital Cinema

Le cinquième élément/The Fifth Element (Luc Besson, France, 1997) foreshadowed 3D printing by featuring a then-science-fictional organic 3D printer, which used the computer-generated imagery of the Visible Human Project's digital-dataset-body (that is Jernigan's planed body) to realize/ give flesh to the meaty 3D growth/printing of an alien being named Leeloo, played by Milla Jovovich (see Waldby 2000: 2)—a process not too dissimilar from that currently featured in the high concept opening of the latest *Westworld* series (various directors, USA, 2016–). However, if Besson's pioneering film used the informatic dataset as a special effect, or as mere diegetic *content*, subsequent waves of digital cinema have begun to turn this databody logic inside out, exploring/exploiting the potentials of these new immersive media for the film bodies themselves. For example, two years after the release of *The Fifth Element*, the cinematic spaces, objects, bodies, and worlds of *Fight Club* (David Fincher, USA, 1999) were suddenly rendered as navigable mathematical volumes, through which new skeuomorphic "cameras" or points of view were able to soar in a manner reminiscent to the pre-programmed flythroughs of the digital Adam dataset of Joseph Paul Jernigan. As we have argued elsewhere, these consequently shifted the abilities of a previously "humanist" cinema into posthuman realms (see Brown 2009a, 2013; Brown and Fleming 2011, 2015).

In short, *Fight Club*'s famous opening shot moves us effortlessly, and without a cut, from inside the fear center of the narrator's brain/wetware—where we observe his microscopic bioluminescent tentacular neurons firing in electro-chemical storms—through the meat and bone of his brain and skull, into a drop of his sweat, which then passes through a pore in the skin of his scalp, before we track down his face and along the barrel of a gun pushed inside his mouth. Meanwhile, Gaspar Noé's *Enter the Void* (France/ Germany/Italy/ Canada, 2009) consists of a 142-minute seemingly single shot that shifts from a living human to a necrotic posthuman perspective as the lead character Oscar (Nathaniel Brown) dies and then floats around Tokyo (and through time) to see his past and what happens in the future after his death. One virtuoso scene sees the free-floating point of view pass into a character's skull and brain-screen as he has intercourse with his lover, before then seamlessly passing into the woman's uterus to capture the tip of the male's erect penis ejaculating sperm into her body. The modular long take then proceeds to shift scale down into the microscopic realms so as better to trace the path of embodied spermatozoa swimming up the oceanic fallopian tubes and into the ovum where the life process begins. In these instances, the aesthetics of digitally enabled imaging technology allow for a new form of "gaseous continuity" that no longer thinks space "as fragmented into objects *and* that which divides them," but which rather shows space and matter as a single interconnected volumetric continuum (see Brown and Fleming 2011, 2015; Fleming and Brown 2015). Simultaneously, throughout the film the screen surface itself appears to signal viewers' brains in a manner reminiscent of a cephalopodic deimatic display. Consider in this light David Deamer's recent discussion of the film's opening hallucinogenic trip:

> Like a cloud, millions of star systems orbiting around a galactic central axis. A dispersive amorphous map of smoke pulsates: purples morph into orange morph into white morph into red. Like an eye—a big, bloodshot eye—staring down at you, looking into your skull, gazing into your mind. Like jellyfish swarming in the night sea, thousands of teeming tentacles in the invisible movement of the water. (Deamer 2016: 337)

Jennifer M. Barker notes how similar CGI, geometrically strange image regimes—whose "undulating movements" appear to be more about "flow than fixity"—help blur the lines "between visual and non-visual senses" (Barker 2009b: 312–323). For example, Barker maintains that in films like *Perfume: The Story of a Murderer* (Tom Tykwer, Germany/France/Spain/USA, 2006) and *Sweeney Todd: The Demon Barber of Fleet Street* (Tim Burton, USA/UK, 2007), the sensational image forms—which she also ties to what Brian Massumi calls *biograms*—are "as muscular and haptic as [they are] aural," meaning that they help to generate a startling "foreground-surround" effect that surfaces as "a trick centre twisting into an all-encompassing periphery" (Barker 2009b: 323). Such features clearly resonate with our diagram of flexible and malleable cephalopod bodies, as do Barker's claims that these image forms function somewhat like "*synaesthesia in motion*" (Barker 2009b: 323).

In a similar vein, Evan Calder Williams notes that the "stunner of an opening" of *Deadpool* (Tim Miller, USA, 2016) sees viewers

> share the view of a more fantastic and biologically improbable creature, exiting backwards out of the centre hole of a car cigarette lighter, through the lid of a coffee cup, and on from there, worming its way without gravity, size, or mass through the gathered debris of a halted moment of collision, including more than a few glistening glass fragments. (Calder Williams 2017: 180)

The moment clearly recalls cephalopodic modes of soaring though navigable volumetric space, while Calder Williams' later description of flexible CGI surfaces as a form of "skin that has been applied as cladding and wrap to a set of disaggregated forms beneath" evokes a kind of protean octopus body, which "encloses nothing other than a [virtual] skeletal frame over which it is stretched and the empty volume within" (Calder Williams 2017: 181).

Chthulumedia Archaeology

By constellating different images drawn from our contemporary cultural *assemblage* (the internet, social media, medical imaging, artistic practices, cinema), we necessarily conjure and channel the work of Michel Foucault, whose own archaeology of knowledge can be understood in terms of freezing history and addressing itself "to the general space of knowledge, its configurations, and the modes of being of the things that appear in it"—all the while recognizing in them common "systems of simultaneity" linked to their shared characteristics, qualities, and/or properties (see Foucault 2004: xxv). However, as philosophers like Gilles Deleuze and Alain Badiou teach us, science, politics, art, and philosophy all have different relationships to events, thought, and (the creation of new) truth. In *What is Philosophy?*, for example, Deleuze and Guattari argue that science, art, and philosophy formulate the three beating hearts of human culture, with each displaying its own unique relation to thought and to broader events (Deleuze and Guattari 1994). Artists work to create novel bundles of sensations, for instance, so that their artworks promote or provoke thinking (of the event) courtesy of an innervating constellation of affects and percepts. Scientists (and engineers) by contrast generate operations and functions, while philosophers fashion concepts—which are the *images* of thought. The different practitioners live and die (and toss their die) embedded within their own interleaving planes of consistency.

From a media archaeology perspective, then, we can be thought of as here conducting a techno-*image* survey of the present, and, like Foucault,

Deleuze and Guattari, and Godfrey-Smith, as employing philosophical concepts to criss-cross or (zig-zag in-between) the unknown interstices and gaps in our newly formed archipelago. That said, we wish to re-shape and to re-arm some of the terms we are using/putting into play. For example, we are no longer deploying the term "image" in its usual workaday form. Indeed, we hope to re-vert to an older usage by recalling to mind that the original meaning of "image" was drawn from the psychology of perception, wherein "to have an image of something is to have a mental copy of it" (see Badiou 2013: 222). As Badiou reminds us, "image" is best understood in terms of "a relationship between knowledge and reality" (Badiou 2013: 222)—an idea that becomes particularly pertinent to our comprehension of the above assemblage where, and like many before us, we take images to formulate entangled material aspects of subjectivity, and thus approach them as machinic agents that materially stretch the agency of thought beyond (and before) the purely human.

In turn, our conceptualization of "assemblage" draws first and foremost upon Deleuze and Guattari's philosophical use of the concept (translated from the French *agencement*, which some argue is better deciphered as a processual "arrangement" [see, for example, Philips 2006; Buchanan 2015]). However, we also reactivate and pull together a range of different nuanced meanings likewise evoked by the application of the term assemblage within other non-philosophical fields and zones. Beyond the term's mobilization in the spheres of art and architecture, which are clearly relevant, J. Macgregor Wise informs us that Deleuze and Guattari's concept gathers associations from paleontology, ecology, and archaeology—where it relates to a group of organisms or artifacts that only contingently share a common habitat (Wise 2011: 91). Furthermore, in geology the notion of an assemblage is used to refer to groupings of fossils that appear together and which "characterize a particular stratum" (Wise 2011: 91).

One further point worth mentioning with regard to our assemblage of imagistic "technologies of the self" relates to the writing of Gilbert Simondon, who proposes that there is a "transductive unity" whenever a human–technology relationship highlights that the "*living individual is a system of individuation, an individuating system and also a system that individuates itself*" (Simondon 1992: 305–311, italics in original). The human here simultaneously becomes an "agent" and a "theatre of ontogenetic individuation," by instituting a "primordial process of participation" that brings the "individual-milieu dyad" to light (Simondon 1992: 300). Today, thinkers such as Patricia Pisters update such models (via Deleuze), arguing that the vortex of omnipresent modern screens constitute "synthetic thoughts," meaning that nowadays "images *as images* . . . are a 'political player'" (Pisters 2012: 193, 245)—ideas given flesh in the era of Cambridge Analytica, Presidential Tweets, and VAR (video action replay) decision-making during sports events.

Of particular relevance and appeal here is Pisters' interpretation of new "omnidirectional" image forms, which she picks up from Deleuze's observations/anticipations at the end of *Cinema 2: The Time-Image* (Deleuze 2005b), where the Frenchman posits a newly emerging image of space that no longer foregrounds any privileged directions, actively unraveling notions of an "outside" or an "out-of-field." In recalibrating Deleuze for our present digital epoch, Pisters argues that

> the screen itself can no longer be considered a window or a painting, but it rather constitutes a table of information, a surface inscribed with "data," where information replaces nature. In Deleuze's terms: "the image is constantly being cut to another image, being printed through a visible mesh, sliding over other images in an 'incessant stream of messages,' and the shot itself is less like an eye than an overloaded brain endlessly absorbing information: it is the brain-information, brain-city couple that replaces the eye-Nature." (Pisters 2012: 188)

Various thinkers, including Steven Shaviro and Ron Burnett, have likewise tentacularly groped toward similar notions, appending neologisms such as "turborealism" (Shaviro 2013) or "imographic spaces" (Burnett 2008) to help account for computerized image forms that increasingly open up new frontiers or phenomenologies of perception-(inter)action. Slightly modifying these concepts here, we more specifically delineate this turn as a new cephalopodic thinking which lies with(in) immersive but navigable matter-space, and which overtakes earlier ways of thinking *about it*.

To risk stating the obvious, each of our chthulumedia examples touched upon above is computationally defined, thus allowing all or most aspects of the image to be highly manipulable by creators, end-users, or both. And it is our contention that these forms of image are somehow cephalopodic, or at least encourage and inculcate cephalopod-like modes of navigating and inhabiting (info/data) "space." Or again, the technological-wetware individuation-interface can be understood as "bringing forth" a new "posthuman" perception that is simultaneously an unconcealing of an alternative nonhuman perspective upon conceiving of and navigating through an immersive volumetric time-space.

Having made this argument in relation to various contemporary imaging practices, we wish in the next chapter to pursue the *Kinoteuthis Infernalis* by looking further at volumetric spaces of cinema, including most particularly that of 4DX cinema. To crack an infernal pun: it's Kraken stuff . . .

Notes

1. Cephalopod skin might look like screensavers, but those who have seen various screensavers and iTunes visualization animations might note that many take on a kind of tentacular form as chromatophoric shapes float across the otherwise black screen.
2. The squid appears capable of making thick gelatinous or thin cloudy blobs depending on what is needed. Certain glamorous species (for example, *heteroteuthis dispar*) even dispel bioluminescent clouds of bacteria that startle and confuse (see Mather *et al.* 2010: 108).
3. An even earlier example of this cephalopod logic is *The Octopus: A Story of California*, a novel written by Frank Norris in 1901, two years after his *McTeague* (1899), which famously would be adapted into Erich von Stroheim's *Greed* (USA, 1924). The octopus of the novel's title refers explicitly to the railroad, which shrinks time and space and the tentacles of which spread across the USA (together with information wires that provide the novel's Californian farmers with near-real-time information about the global wheat market). As we shall see, by being set in California, *The Octopus* is also announcing a psychogeographic connection between technology (perhaps especially information technology), cephalopods, and capitalism (see Norris 1994).
4. Terrible cephalopods also appear in another cinema serial, namely *Flash Gordon* (Frederick Stephani, USA, 1936). The way in which the serial announces 100 years in advance the contemporary "quality television" series, as "binge consumed" on Netflix, HBO, Amazon Prime, and elsewhere, perhaps goes without saying. Nonetheless, in chapters 3 and 4 of *Flash Gordon*, the titular hero (Buster Crabbe) is forced by King Kala (Duke York Jr.) to fight an octosak, a sort of extraterrestrial octopus that is an enemy of Kala's Shark Men on the planet Mongo. Notably, *Flash Gordon* also tells the story of planets colliding as Flash's whole adventure is set in motion by the impending collision into Earth of another planet . . .
5. More tentacles: employing a slightly different tentacular animal as its model, *Meduzot/Jellyfish* (Shira Geffen and Etgar Keret, Israel/France, 2007) is, as A. O. Scott (2008) notes, another complex movie "in which the accidental connections between lonely city dwellers are given a magical glow of serendipity"—alongside films like *Thirteen Conversations about One Thing* (Jill Sprecher, USA, 2001) and *Me and You and Everyone We Know* (Miranda July, USA/UK, 2005). On a slightly different note, Tarantino himself comes back, at least inadvertently, to octo-thinking in his film, *The Hateful Eight* (USA, 2015).
6. In an essay on Flusser and digital culture, in which he also discusses *Arrival*, Erick Felinto writes of how the digital era is characterized by marine metaphors, like navigation, liquidity, piracy, and the helmsman, or *timoneiro* in Portuguese (see Felinto 2017: 12).

7. Let us not overlook how in the realm of engineering the jet-propulsion system of the cephalopod has also been key to the development of contemporary air and space travel, thereby furthering the shrinking of space and time beyond simply land masses (as was achieved by Norris's railroad octopus), and even beyond the Earth itself. As Sir Frank Whittle, the man widely credited with the invention of the modern jet engine, said in 1981, "the idea [of jet propulsion] is as old as nature: the squid" (see Zito 1981). Indeed, in the aftermath of World War II, the American military created Project SQUID, which was designed to improve jet propulsion and rocket mechanisms after the capture of the Germans' V-1 during the war, and which led the Americans to design the cruise missile. No wonder Pynchon links an octopus to the V-2 rocket in *Gravity's Rainbow* (in which the alien substance "imipolex" also plays a key part, as we shall see in a later note).

CHAPTER 3

Encounters with a 4DX Kino-Kraken

> Technology is not human; in a specific sense, it is deeply inhuman.
>
> – Siegfried Zielinski

> It is as if the relations of the outside folded back to create a doubling, allowing a relation to oneself to emerge, and constitute an inside which is hollowed out and develops its own unique dimension.
>
> – Gilles Deleuze

> There's no escape; you're part of the film.
>
> – Tim Grierson

APOLLO'S BREATH! SOMETHING new is afoot, which enfolds consequences for all that is ahead. For, last night we entered the dazzling and gripping atavistic kingdom not just of the shadows, but of 4DX cinema, a cinema of the coleoids, that subclass of cephalopods that continues to include our beloved octopuses, squid, and cuttlefish. If you only knew how strange it is to be there—like Maxim Gorky's first contact with cinema, but to the im-mersive-max.

Spinal Tap

When we say that 4DX is "new," we naturally do not want to overlook previous attempts to make cinema a more "immersive" and multisensory experience, not least through the addition of performing audience members, as per Lettrist filmmakers like Isidore Isou and Maurice Lemaître (see Cabañas 2017: 115–117), or, more particularly, through the use of moving seats, wind machines, smells, and sprays. Indeed, William Castle stands out as the major figure in the history of "gimmick" filmmaking and exhibition thanks to his various experiments in shocking audiences (see Leeder 2011; for a fictional version of Castle's approach to filmmaking, readers might also take a look at *Matinee*, Joe Dante, USA, 1993). For example, Castle had objects emerge from the screen via a system referred to as the Emergo for *House on Haunted Hill* (USA, 1959), which involved a skeleton flying above the audience. Meanwhile, Castle also asked audience members to decide on the outcome of *Mr. Sardonicus* (USA, 1961) by getting them to take part in a "Punishment Poll" regarding the fate of the film's eponymous villain (Guy Rolfe), who could with clemency be cured of his permanently horrified countenance, or suffer at the hands of vengeful physician, Robert Cargrave, played by Ronald Lewis (apparently audiences rarely if ever saw the "happy" ending, choosing almost universally to see Sardonicus punished). More specifically, though, we wish at present to discuss *The Tingler*, which is a film that features a strange tentacled beast (that also looks something like a cross between a giant centipede and a crayfish), and the Percepto effects for which the film is famous, and which share similarities with 4DX cinema today.

The Tingler tells the story of Warren Chapin (Vincent Price), a doctor obsessed with identifying how fear in humans takes on a flesh-and-blood form, referred to as the tingler, and which in turn kills people if they are not able to alleviate their fear, for example, through screaming (or perhaps from shuddering, much as one seeks to shake the devil off one's back, perhaps even by dancing). Having carried out an autopsy on the brother-in-law of Ollie Higgins (Philip Coolidge), who runs a cinema that still shows silent movies and who has a penchant for beer, Warren meets Ollie's deaf-mute wife, Martha (Judith Evelyn). Discovering that Martha cannot scream even though she is terrified by the sight of blood, Warren decides to drug her with LSD (having tested the drug on himself), only for Martha then to die from a series of seeming hallucinations that are in fact Ollie dressed up as a monster.

Warren removes from Martha's spine the titular tingler, which seems indestructible, even if it is easily contained in its tentacular attacks by the sound of human screams. Deciding that the only way to destroy the tingler is to put it back into Martha's body, Warren returns with Ollie to the latter's house, only for the tingler to escape into the downstairs cinema, where *Tol'able David* (John G. Blystone, USA, 1921) is playing. Humans scream in darkness as the tingler attacks them, only for Warren and Ollie to recapture it in the projection booth. Upon Warren replacing the tingler in Martha's body, Ollie confesses to having scared Martha to death after hearing Warren's (at that point unproven) theory about the tingler, and he threatens to kill Warren as his witness—but ultimately cannot, as Warren simply walks away. Ollie is left with Martha, whose body rises up and attacks him. The screen goes black as Ollie tries but does not manage to scream.

The Tingler is interesting for several reasons. Firstly, the film suggests that fear can take on a material form, in effect giving flesh to a creature from a different dimension (demonstrating the tentacular interconnectivity of dimensions that humans know little about—perhaps not wholly different from a 3D printer). Secondly, the tingler itself is of course tentacular, but also silent, wrapping its fore tentacles around any part of a human that it can find, especially the neck, a form of attack that constrains the voice, thereby increasing the tingler's chances of killing its prey. While inside the human body, however, the tingler kills by paralyzing the spine, a maneuver that seems to have a similar silencing effect—something that Warren discovers after frightening, drugging, and then taking X-rays of the tingler as it manifests itself in his wife, Isabel (Patricia Cutts), with whom he has an antagonistic relationship. It is the spine, then, that allows the human to scream, but when the spine becomes too ossified, the human dies of fear. In other words, the spine may give to the human a voice (while the cephalopod and the tingler alike remain silent). But the spine also gives to humans fear—while the cephalopod perhaps does not know fear in the same way because invertebrates do not have a spine.

Drawing on André Leroi-Gourhan, David Wills explains how it was the human spine that allowed the human brain to develop, since the human's upright posture took downward pressure away from the skull, which in turn had to rebalance, leading to "room for more brain" (Wills 2008: 8). The intelligence of the cephalopod must be alien, then, to that of the human, since the former has developed its intelligence without the aid of bones. However, much as it is the spine that allows for intelligence, fear of the outside creates this tingling other that in turn kills the human, who in some respects dies from rigidity, stiffness, or what we are calling ossification. "He's behind you!" we shout at pantomimes to actors oblivious of their impending fate, suggesting that fear also is a result of our inability to see behind us (perhaps the habit of taking selfies is not so much a desire to look at the self, but to surveil what is behind our backs). Our spine and its concomitant fear thus in some senses blind us, in that they prevent us from being able to adjust our field of vision, allowing only for confrontation (looking at things front-on), rather than for a more dorsal encounter (perhaps the existence of the spine in the bipedal human is also what leads to monogamous love as we find another human to "watch our back," forming a beast with two backs in the process). The cephalopod, meanwhile, senses in all directions at once, with no behind and perhaps no limit to its ability to love. Where we get tingles in our spines, the cephalopod exists in a state of pure sensuality.

When the tingler breaks free and into Ollie's cinema, perhaps inevitably the creature appears on the screen as it crawls across the front of the projector in the booth. Not only is the film announcing, then, that cinema itself is perhaps a tentacled, spineless, and sensual creature (that also is most apparent when, like *Tol'able David*, it is silent; that *The Tingler* features a scene from *Tol'able David* in which a man makes unwelcome advances toward a woman might also suggest that cinema-as-cephalopod poses a sexual threat). But the sequence also reminds us that cinema is in some senses a fear machine, since the image is projected from behind us, even if it appears on the screen in front of us. That is, cinema is always behind our backs, in an invisible zone where grows fear, a tentacled creature from another dimension that climbs up our spines, ossifying us to the point of death.

Meanwhile, the Percepto was a system that Castle developed to give shocks to the audience in their seats during screenings of *The Tingler*. Surprising audiences from underneath, the Percepto clearly brings a corporeal dimension to the film-viewing experience (see Littau 2003: 49), putting us into contact with the space of the film as per our discussion of volumetric space in the last chapter. Creating a tingling in the spine, or a spinal tap, the Percepto relies on the human backbone to function, but it also serves as a reminder of cinema's otherness (it's behind you!). In this way, *The Tingler* and Castle's Percepto system function, along with a history of phantom rides and ride-films (for more on these, see Holmberg 2003 and King 2000 respectively), as important and tentacular precursors to 4DX cinema, to which we shall now turn our attention.

Entering the Kino-Kraken

Dear reader, we must report that going to the 4DX in the In Time mall in Yinzhou, China, the audience is first sucked up into the long thin body of a hall, narrower than most traditional auditoriums, consisting only of three columns of chairs, which are the embedded hearts of this outlandish space. The middle column is the broadest, comprising a solid couch with four elevated seating units. Meanwhile, the two rows flanking it are composed of three seats, each adorned with the same tight-stretched and gleaming synthetic skins. Along each row, red chords striate like arteries the blocky-stepped seating tiers. On the back of each seating unit and upon the headrest are numerous hollows, nubbins, nozzles, jets, and spraying valves. Several more concealed glands and cloaked anatomical rudiments—secreted within each membranous seating unit—are covertly aimed at our backs and legs. Above us, where the wall and ceiling converge, is a rig of strobe lights and surround-sound speakers, in-mixed with a corniced cresting of ceiling fans, ten in total, each trained downwards, but not yet circulating.

Standing inside the cavernous hollow of this anatomical amphitheater, one feels like Jonah after being consumed by some infernal kino-Kraken. When the chamber's lights (and our posthuman 3D spectacles) go down, and the IMAX D3D projector begins volumetrically to swell the succulent "Z-screen" (replete with "xyz axis"), what strange life begins to bubble around us![1] Inside this digestible architecture, as the cavern's magic screen-dermis flushes with layered chromatophore-like displays, we become prey to the arts of squirting, fumbling, jetting, and billowing. Animatedly, a whole raft of motors and organs begins to act and move in concert as seats drift and jolt. Almost immediately our stomachs rise up to our throats, as a fluid aerial drone-shot begins subtly moving through the film's spatial volume in tandem with a yawing seat, ostensibly tipping us forward over a slippery abyss, wherefrom a headlong wind blows into our face. Cool stuff. And it isn't long before the vital life of the anatomical auditorium begins spasmodically hauling and probing, gassing and immersing us all in wave after wave of wild visceral sensations. Fast-flowing molecular currents rush around our heads. Aromas and odors seep from below the nosegay seats. Once, during a violent in-screen struggle, we found ourselves rocked, rolled, shaken, jolted, tilted, tingled, gassed, and propulsed by spraying exocrine glands and myriad other expressive agential contraptions. Our legs are blasted by high-pressure releases of compressed gas, we seem to recall, as a kick landed in-screen. Befuddling hazes spewed forth from the foot of the volumetric display-screen, oozily clouding the "there-then" and the "here-now" of the screen–space continuum (where does the film begin and end?). As our wetware collectively nerves with the intense affects of this living leviathan, we hear the squeals, gasps, and laughs of our fellow consumed consumers.

Only after being excreted back out into the light of the foyer are we virtually (if not actually) convinced that this 4DX ensemble presents the world with a new form of monster/monstrator, a *Kinoteuthis* from the depths.

4DX Marketing and Machines

Since the sea constitutes (1) an environment in which one can become fully immersed (it does, after all, contain *mer*, the French term for the sea), (2) a dynamic restless surface, and (3) a vast volumetric body that formulates an exploratory biosphere, much of the advertising for 4DX cinema employs oceanic metonymies and metaphors. Unquestionably, the elemental depths, surfaces, and adventure-enticing horizons associated with the sea provide an apt range of attributes with which to promote this latest attraction in the supersaturated "economy of affections" (see Jenkins 2016). In one online image for a 4DX cinema from the USA, for example, we discover an ecstatic heterosexual couple in SCUBA-like 3D goggles, being delightedly sprayed by (CGI) water and bubbles (see Figure 3.1). In another from South Korea, four women experience their conjoined seating block viscerally heaving up and away (spraying one moviegoer's popcorn everywhere) as a huge tsunami surges up behind them. In a third, a couple skip from left to right over a series of choppy waves on a jet-ski-like seating unit (Figure 3.2). In yet another, an entirely submerged audience stretches out in wonder to touch a torrent of underwater bubbles left in the wake of a SCUBA diver, as a white pointer shark stalks him back into the screen, just a few feet above the bottom-feeders/viewers in the front row (Figure 3.3).

Incidentally (rather than coincidently), movies with marine themes often (strategically or tactically) become associated with the format's launch, promotion, expansion, and spread to far-flung geopolitical locations. James Cameron's deep-sea, bioluminescent *Avatar* (USA, 2009) aesthetic initially helped to promote the 4DX model in its South Korean home, for example, while his *Titanic 3D* (USA, 2012) served to launch China's first 4DX theater. Mexico City got its first encounter with 4DX affections the previous year courtesy of *Pirates of the Caribbean: On Stranger Tides* (Gore Verbinski, USA/UK, 2011). Through such

Figure 3.1 Submarine vision

Figure 3.2 Dynamic surfaces in 4DX

Figure 3.3 Immersive depths in 4DX

advertising images and movie tie-ins, the technology is clearly marketed as a new, exciting, and adventurous "mode" of film viewing, offering intense and immersive moviegoing experiences that are relatively unique within the crowded digital and affective marketplace/economy. But what exactly is 4DX?

4DX is a corporate brand, or a registered and trademarked acronym that is shorthand for "Four-Dimensional Experience." It specifically relates to an expanded range of "extrasensory enhancers" (Keegan 2012) and technological apparatuses bolted on to the more "conventional" digital 3D (D3D) movie experience. 4DX specifically refers to the interactive environmental movie-going architecture, a "unique selling point" that helps to blur the lines between kinetic theme-park ride and D3D movie. In this manner, the 4DX equipment points toward what we might call, after Nigel Thrift, a form of *digestible environment*, wherein "technologies of public intimacy" allow participants to negotiate various territories of sensation after stacking numerous affective fields, tactile objects, and signaletic aesthetics together (see Thrift 2010: 292–295). In this way, 4DX perhaps becomes a cheaper and more flexible workaday version of the fully immersive "dark rides" like *Pirates of the Caribbean: Battle for the Sunken Treasure* (China, 2016), which theme-park visitors can experience at the Shanghai Disney Resort. Therein, invisible magnetic forces are used to implicate rafts of guests into an inland water park surrounded by all-encompassing environmental screens, animatronic hosts, and powerful eye-popping projectors capable of creating thrilling vection illusions that viscerally destabilize the divisions between reality and simulation.[2]

Unlike other marketplace competitors (such as MX4D or D-Box), 4DX apparatuses are installed and assembled by the South Korean company CJ4DPLEX, a subsidiary of the Cheil Jedang conglomerate. The company's website informs visitors that

> [e]ach 4DX® auditorium incorporates motion-based seating synchronized with over 20 different effects and optimized by a team of skilled editors, maximizing the feeling of immersion within the movie. It presents an all-five-senses absolute cinema experience allowing everyone to connect with the movie and experience special effects through motion, vibration, water, wind, bubbles, fog, rain, lightning, and scents that enhance the visuals onscreen.

Gimmicks from phantom rides to the Percepto system suggest that such experiments are constant throughout cinema's history (see, for example, Gunning 2006: 383; McGee 2001: 20–28). However, unique to today's array of sensational machines is the 4DX software "track," which has to be generated and layered over, or programmed into/on to, the film's existing digital audiovisual tracks so as to become orchestrated and aligned with a given movie. In this sense, an additional "symbiotic" or "parasitic" software-being further converges with and remediates the unadorned D3D audio and video tracks, bringing to bear the additional 4DX apparatuses, which move into a mutually modifying affective concert with the seated participants (see Figure 3.4). Courtesy of its corporate origins, we accordingly frame 4DX as an attempt to *incorporate* viewers into mainstream film experiences.

Figure 3.4 4DX effects

Ethological Incorporation: Actual and Virtual, Body and World

Jennifer M. Barker comments that the addition of digital SurroundSound technology into the moviegoing experience historically constituted a new "kind of embrace or envelopment," which she describes as the "film's way of drawing us close to its body" (Barker 2009b: 110). By similar coin, we see 4DX as revealing (the desire for) an even more intimate embrace, with an even more manifold body increasing its draw by sucking viewers even closer in(side). Indeed, as the masthead review of a 4DX experience puts it, with 4DX "[t]here's no escape; you're part of the film" (Grierson: 2014). Or, as the viewer in a recent megaplex poster campaign exclaims: "I'm in the movie!" Certainly, in other recent reports about 4DX, the mode's intimate affective features appear most often to be singled out for praise or comment. For instance, in a gushing 2014 article from *Rolling Stone*, entitled "8 Things You Need to Know about the 4DX Theatre Experience" (the number fittingly reflects our octopod argument!), Tim Grierson claims that the "best" part of 4DX is "the fans" (that is, the tentacular overhead air blowers, not fanatical audience members): "[d]uring scenes when cars or planes are zipping through space, the overhead fans kick on, and it's like you're zooming down the highway with the wind in your hair. It's an oddly liberating, freeing feeling" (Grierson 2014). Further down his chart of special affects (to pirate Eric S. Jenkins' term; see Jenkins 2016), Grierson remarks upon some of the olfactory aromas released into the 4DX environment, which add "an extra layer of immediacy" (Grierson 2014). A year or so later, Kervyn Cloete generates a malodorous survey of her experiences, noting how a range of new (humorous) additions have been added to the earlier 4DX bouquet of environmental aromas. These, she notes, are pumped out courtesy of "a nozzle mounted underneath the seat which lets out a choice of 11 different smells to simulate the environments seen on screen . . . and farts. Yes, it really does fart smells" (Cloete 2015).

In such manner we can understand the auditorium becoming a quasi-aquarium, or a volumetric environment replete with moving currents and miasmic molecular atmospheres linked to the immersive sensory experience. We might also recognize resonances here between the incorporated 4DX spectator experience and the passive squid's impressionistic relationship with its objective world—wherein matter, tastes, and molecules tumble into it in a passionate manner that is distinct from a detached ocularcentric framing of the world as picture "out there" (see Flusser 2012: 39). Confronting these molecular, sensual, and *bioaesthetic* (Kennedy 2002: 28) dimensions of the 4DX experience signals the extent to which we need to adopt an all-round "ethological" approach to these latest mediated milieux (see, for example, Fleming 2017: 138). That is, we must think about the enmeshed entanglement of bodies within larger messy conglomerate worlds.

4DX Bodies

Following Spinoza, Gilles Deleuze provokes us to expand thought to recognize almost anything as a body: "it can be an animal, a body of sounds, a mind or an idea; it can be a linguistic corpus, a social body, a collectivity" (Deleuze 1988: 127). Here, we might add 4DX environments to this list of body forms. But of course, in recognizing such things as bodies, we must remain aware that these are always already entangled with "a world" (rather than the world), and that they are never neatly bounded or enclosed beings:

> [e]very point has its counterpoints: the plant and the rain, the spider and the fly. So an animal, a thing is never separable from its relations with the world. The interior is only a selected exterior, and the exterior, a projected interior. (Deleuze 1988: 125)

Or again, as Sara Ahmed more concisely renders it: "[b]odies take the shape of the very contact they have with objects and others" (Ahmed 2014: 1).

In adopting an ethological body-based approach to 4DX mediated environments (with their literal projected interiors and viewer exteriors), we here follow in the wake of a broader range of thinkers and (bio)philosophers such as Thrift, Jenkins, Flusser, Massumi, Parikka, and Zielinski, who individually and collectively demand that we acknowledge the complex knottings or connections found binding together media, mediated environments, and manifold bodies (objects and subjects), within distributed eco-webs or environments. For example, regarding the complex enfolding of exterior and interior and of subject and object that environments occasion, Flusser points out that, "[i]n succinct and concrete terms, the environment is that which we experience and we, in turn, are that in which the environment is experienced: Reality is a web of concrete relations" (Flusser and Bec 2012: 31). As such, any given body (an organism or otherwise) can be recognized as being "a stratified memory constructed of superimposed suppressions, somewhat like geological formations" (Flusser and Bec 2012: 27). To zoom out for a moment and to consider the human as a molar species, Flusser argues that the objects in our environments, while instituting concrete relations, literally modify and mediate our ability to act, think, communicate, and remember. From this perspective, we are always already transhuman knottings of subjects-objects and of bodies-environments:

> [b]oth the environment and the organism are abstract extrapolations from the actuality of their entwined relations. An organism mirrors its environment; an environment mirrors its organism; and if the arena of their relations is altered in some way, neither the environment nor the organism will be left unchanged. (Flusser and Bec 2012: 31)

With regard to art and technology, it follows that the material objects in our environments (such as stones, iron, letters, cinema, and databases) "shape all of human experience and thought." So much so, in fact, that it

> is not the case that we first experience or think something and, subsequently, scour the vicinity for an object with which to record it. Rather, it is *already* as sculptors, filmmakers, authors—as artists—that we begin to experience and think. (Flusser and Bec 2012: 62)

Interestingly, Godfrey-Smith argues that squids and octopuses have a comparable manner of understanding their world, in that they, too, "carve [the stuff of their world] up into objects" that have use-value and exploitable properties, and which "can be re-identified despite ongoing changes in how those objects present themselves" (Godfrey-Smith 2016: 74). To update Flusser, we could say that because theatrical players such as 4DX, electronic music, social networking, and (so-called) smartphones exist in today's supersaturated wave-form environments, these mediate/individuate with us, and co-constitute our being, altering what the human-world assemblage actually is. In this sense, we are all chthulumedia.

Consider, then, Zielinski's remark that today the "case of media is similar to [Otto] Roessler the endophysicist's relation to consciousness: we swim in it like the fish in the ocean, it is essential for us, and for this reason it is ultimately inaccessible to us" (Zielinski 2008: 33). Anyone seeing a shoal of smartphone users harvesting data in an invisible wifi eddy will be in no doubt about this idea, especially during the night, when their faces light up like free-floating bioluminescent creatures courtesy of their screens—for example, as they gather together to await the release of new prey while playing *Pokémon GO* (Tatsuo Nomura, Japan/USA, 2016). As mentioned in the first chapter, Parikka similarly notes that we should begin practicing a "media-studies of a nonhuman kind" (Parikka 2010: xxv). Such ideas become especially valuable to think through their relation to an abstract notion of 4DX cinema (as a technological media body and as an incorporating environment) and its entangled viewer relations—as organisms and consumers (and as consuming/consumed animals).

To do this first means actively erasing traditional bounded distinctions between the natural and the artificial, while transactionally reframing the incurving or isomorphic world "as a specific kind of assemblage of technology + biology + nature + politics + economics + *n*" (Parikka 2010: 160). As already intimated, Parikka for this reason literally treats animals as media, and media as quasi-animals:

> Media are a contraction of forces of the world into specific resonating milieus: internal milieus with their resonation, external milieus affording their rhythms as part of that resonation. An animal has to find a common tune with its environment, and a technology has to work through rhythmic relations with other force fields such as politics and economics. In this context, sensations, percepts, and affects become the primary vectors through which entities are co-created at the same time as their environmental relations. (Parikka 2010: xiv)

To begin framing the 4DX apparatus as a "body," we must see it as being entangled with, and inseparable from, its relations with "a world" (see Deleuze 1988: 125), which in this instance becomes the phenomenological universe of the human filmgoer's body-brain (and the wider in-curving milieu of affective economies, commercial attractions, and all the other associated flowing desires). Lest we forget the teachings of Deleuze and Spinoza, we would do well to frame the coming together of our cryptid's affections/affects, sensations, percepts, and actions as (instituting) a new *mode*—much as a comparable *modal* approach to animation permits Jenkins to see historical apparatuses as formulating posthuman or virtual bodies, linked to debates surrounding "affect and the cyborg" (Jenkins 2016: 2). For if Jenkins is interested in the history of Disney entertainment, it is his discussion of their ever-evolving animated forms and their innervating processes that makes new forms of consumer visible. Such a process unquestionably shares parallels with the latest 4DX moviegoing experiences, which can be thought of as more accessible versions of Disney's most up-to-date "dark rides." After apprehending such a strange cyborg body, which, after Flusser, we honor with the name *Vampyroteuthis Virtualis*, we might now undertake an anatomical comparison of this media creature with its biomedia cousins.

Vampyroteuthis Virtualis

As discussed, Flusser holds up the vampire squid as both the inverse and the uncanny specular double of the modern human. In making his case, he exquisitely unfolds and refolds our parallel evolutions along the deep timeline of the phylogenetic rhizome-tree—in a distant echo of the comparative anatomy debate between Georges Cuvier and Étienne Geoffroy Saint-Hilaire (more on which shortly). But while the divergent becomings of humans and squids seemingly branched ever further away from their common primordial worm ancestor, Flusser catalogs the various "analogous," "homologous," and "converging" organs that developed upon and between these different environmentally entangled species. Homology here specifically refers to a range of organs that appear to have the same evolutionary origins, even if they display "different functions," as is the case with wings on a bird and arms on a human. Meanwhile, an analogous (as opposed to a homologous) organ is described in terms of having "the same function as a comparable organ in another species but a phylogenetically different origin" (Flusser and Bec 2012: 23). Flusser offers the "photographic" eyes of the human and the octopus as an illustrative case in point, since although they emerge from two quite distinct courses of development, they effectively arrive at the same function (Flusser and Bec 2012: 24). That is, "nature" or evolution devised the same solution to *seeing* in two radically different worlds or environments.

Godfrey-Smith makes a comparable point when he describes the remarkable anatomical similarities found in humanoid and octopus eyes. Both are "like cameras," he notes, with an adjustable lens, that serves to focus an image onto a retina, even if the brains behind these eyes, which process these images, are radically different "on almost every scale" (Godfrey-Smith 2016: 10). While the brains and structures of the cephalopod and the human brain diverge radically, and illustrate that life developed intelligent minds twice over, Flusser and Godfrey-Smith still see the two species as having many things in common. Best to describe this uncanny similarity, Flusser introduces a third important term, "convergence" (increasingly fashionable in media studies today, as per the foundational work of Henry Jenkins; see Jenkins 2008), which he recognizes as "part of life's agenda" (Flusser and Bec 2012: 24). Flusser thereafter notes how the squid's brain

> is both analogous and homologous to ours. In the lowermost levels of its brain, its mental faculty shares a common origin with our own, and yet its thinking differs from ours: homology. In the uppermost levels of its brain the origin of its mental faculty differs from our own, and yet its thinking resembles ours: analogy. Our existences converge. (Flusser and Bec 2012: 24)

But what does this recognition of convergence mean with respect to our discussion of cyborgian 4DX bodies and worlds? Common to both Godfrey-Smith and Flusser's projects are (Heideggerian) attempts to unfold and then refold together the alien worlds of humans and squids. In thinking about radically different worlds and bodies, though, we argue that while organic cephalopods and inorganic 4DX cinema boast very different types of bodies (biological and media-machine), there nevertheless remain significant parts and abilities that become strangely convergent and loosely homologous.

On account of this, we propose that actual 4DX arenas—the agential assemblages—can be thought of as a becoming-animal of cinema, and as being subtended by a virtual vampyroteuthian hypercryptid or hypo-object (which communicates from beneath the material surface of our world). To illustrate how, and perhaps why, we need now necessarily to conjure up (even though it has all along been hiding in plain sight) a second cephalopodic spirit or species to help guide us—this time from the warm shallows, rather than the dark depths: *Thaumoctopus mimicus*, or the mimic octopus, whose famed abilities for mimicry not only extend to morphing into the shapes and forms of various other animals living in her environment, but also to impersonating their manifold markings and behaviors, including complex motile actions. As the reader will soon discover, we channel the spirit of this animal for quite different reasons to that of *Vampyroteuthis Infernalis.*

4DXtensive Attributes, Affects, and Affections

So far, we have hunted and tracked the virtual vampyroteuthian spirit of 4DX cinema. What remains now is to begin outlaying an exploded anatomical diagram of this extensive hybrid-monster, while surveying its intensive relationships and articulations. To do so, we employ Deleuze and Guattari's notion of *longitudes* and *latitudes* to guide us: "*latitudes* [*are*] *made up of intensive parts falling under a capacity, and longitudes of extensive parts falling under relation*" (Deleuze and Guattari 2004: 283, emphasis in original). This method necessarily puts us back into communication with Deleuze and Guattari's assemblage theory—or *agencement*—wherein bodies are thought in terms of multiplicities, or as a parliament of disparate machines, actors, agents, forces, and enunciations that, although impermanent, appear to come together for varying periods of time, to "do things" (differently). Deleuze and Guattari remind us that

> [w]e know nothing of a body until we can know what it can do, in other words, what its affects are, how they can or cannot enter into composition with other affects, with the affects of another body . . . either to exchange actions and passions with it or to join with it in composing a more powerful body. (Deleuze and Guattari 2004: 284)

Form follows function.

Further to this, and as Deleuze likes to point out in his discussions of animals via Spinoza, "animals are defined less by abstract notions of genus and species than [they are] by a capacity for being affected, by the affections of which they are 'capable'" (Deleuze 1988: 27). For this reason, Deleuze and Guattari famously remark that "[a] racehorse is more different from a workhorse than a workhorse is from an ox" (Deleuze and Guattari 2004: 283). That is, when we consider not what their abstract family trees are, nor their similarities in appearance, but rather what these animals do, we can produce another form of taxonomy or mode of categorizing bodies.

In the above section we offered a preliminary survey of the twenty or so additional moving and expressing machines and features that account for the extensive anatomy of the 4DX monstrator. However, we can fruitfully gloss over these affective elements once again to help us perceive the strange convergences emerging between biological creatures and our mediated monster. To best do this, we can plunge back into Flusser's vivid description of *Vampyroteuthis Infernalis*' fabled (but based on real) anatomy, which includes a

> gland, near the anus, [that] secretes an ink-like liquid ("sepia") and shoots it forcibly into the water to form a cloud. These clouds of ink can, in turn, be shaped into sculptures by the "arms" of the animal (*Tintenfisch*, "ink-fish"). An additional gland, this located in the mouth, excretes a poison that disables whatever it circumscribes. Yet another produces a gelatinous compound, the excretion of which renders the body translucent. Finally, there are glands on the surface of the skin that emit light and others that allow the animal to change color. In short, the digestive system serves purposes far beyond digestion. (Flusser and Bec 2012: 19)

We might further recall that Flusser literally sees these glandular body parts as *media*: "[t]hese media are glands," meaning that "vampyroteuthic history is a glandular history, a history of secretions" (Flusser and Bec 2012: 51). In the spirit of *Thaumoctopus mimicus*, we might now turn to our 4DX media-body. For, rewriting Flusser, it has a

> gland, near the screen, [that] secretes a fog-like liquid (carbon-dioxide or "stage smoke") and shoots it forcibly into the auditorium to form a cloud. These clouds of smoke can, in turn, be shaped into sculptures by the "fans" of the auditorium (ten air tentacles). An additional nozzle, this located in the front, excretes bubbles that float around whoever it circumscribes. Yet another produces a liquescent compound, the excretion of which renders the spectator's face lustrous. Finally, there are stroboscopic lights on the walls and ceilings that emit pulses of light and others that allow the auditorium to change color. In short, the digestive environment serves a purpose far beyond projection.

Too much? Recall here that for Deleuze, affects constitute pre-conscious intensities, which derive and arrive courtesy of a body's ability to affect and be affected (à la Spinoza). We might here recognize such immersive cinematic experiences as resonating with our earlier discussions of media ethologies—entangled assemblages of bodies and worlds—and topological (en)foldings. That is, we might recognize 4DX as a *modality*. Or as Jenkins (Eric S.) might put it, we can understand this *mode* linking together "a manner of relating" with the "flip-side of affects" in a way that joins actual to virtual and subjects to objects (Jenkins 2016: 15). This also gives us a sense of what Timothy Morton means when he describes the sensual spaces of interobjectivity in his descriptions of sticky hyperobjects, which force thought to leap from the actual to the virtual, from the known to the unknown, and from the thought to the unthought.

Longitudinally speaking, then, the 4DX viewer must also be reframed and counted as part of the embodied and extended cyborg-being as their nervous and sensory-motor system becomes disseminated across the extensive arrangements of the automated auditorium, the D3D screen, and a given film's constellated bundles of special sensational effects and affects. In concert, these institute an intimate arrangement of constellated sensations. Or put differently, the 4DX assemblage and the viewer come to constitute a sticky body–media–milieu continuum. Recognition of this brings us closer to the dark heart of our virtual cryptid and its intensive-extensive relations. For, in our example, the given arrangement of actual components (squirting chairs, billowing smoke machines, sculpting fans, nosegay nozzles, and so on) gives rise to a whole galaxy of virtual potentialities that connote "a virtual orientation between bodies, with affections being the actualizations of these virtual fields, the intensities that flow forth from the engagement of the mode" (Jenkins 2016: 15). Put differently, the environmental exterior reflects and inverts the hollowed-out viewer interior. Jenkins similarly posits that, historically speaking, emerging mediated *modes* can fruitfully be thought in terms of

> an orientation for the folding of bodies into a distributed body, a folding that produces a crease—a line along which new neural and affective pathways may run. Because of the crease, cognitive, perceptual and affective surfaces may rub against one another differently, producing friction and at times a spark. (Jenkins 2016: 15)

With regard to 4DX bodies, these affective modalities patently do lead to "sparks" of enjoyment (joyous affection?), which can be imagined occurring within, and because of, the novel meshes of mediated arrangements. We think here of the laughter, screams, and smiles of fellow patrons. In such ways, 4DX exploits the novel and interobjective enfolding of sensory motor mechanisms and complementary sensing surfaces (surround sound and ear, eye and glasses and screen, gas and nose–tongue, water and skin, stage smoke and nose and eye and ear), thus making new consumer beings perceptible (4DX aficionados).

So if 4DX's extensive and affective arrangements give shape to our hybrid cyborg-body's longitudes, what of this body's latitudes? Well, as Deleuze describes them, latitudes pertain to a "set of affects that occupy a body at each moment, that is, the intensive states of an anonymous force (force for existing, capacity for being affected)" (Deleuze 1988: 127). We can perhaps best comprehend a given body's latitudes in terms of its *unformed elements*, or as "the set of relations of speeds and slowness, of motion and rest, between particles that compose [the body]" (Deleuze 1988: 127). To best grasp what this means, we might pick up on our earlier discussion of topologies and foldings, albeit here plicating them with a series of discussions from Deleuze and Guattari's *A Thousand Plateaus* dealing with folding humans into cephalopods. The first of these occurs in the chapter entitled "10,000 B.C.: Geology of Morals (Who Does the Earth Think It Is?)," where Deleuze and Guattari curate a (science-fictional) debate between Professor Challenger and his assembled audience regarding the Earth as a living organism. The debating participants include the naturalists and zoologists Georges Cuvier and Étienne Geoffroy Saint-Hilaire, whose earth-shattering debates in the early nineteenth century spiraled around the comparative anatomies of humans and cephalopods (see Nakajima *et al.* 2018). Of relevance to our argument, the latter exclaims that

> [t]he proof that there is isomorphism is that you can always get from one form on the organic stratum to another, however different they may be, by means of "folding." To go from vertebrate to the cephalopod, bring the two sides of the vertebrate's backbone together, bend its head down to its feet and its pelvis up to the nape of its neck. (Deleuze and Guattari 2004: 51–52)

In another entry in the chapter entitled "1730: Becoming-Intense, Becoming-Animal, Becoming Imperceptible . . ." the debate between Geoffroy and Cuvier again raises its head—with Deleuze and Guattari using them in this wave to debate the "hidden plan(e) of organization, a structure or genesis" (Deleuze and Guattari 2004: 281). Geoffroy here contends that we must move beyond analogies between "organs and functions to abstract elements he terms 'anatomical'" (Deleuze and Guattari 2004: 281). In this passage our attention to structure once again shifts from a consideration of actual longitudes to intensive latitudes, and cedes to a consideration of speed and slowness, movement and rest. A vantage from which we are invited to think that there is but one

> fixed plane of life upon which everything stirs, slows down or accelerates. A single abstract Animal for all the assemblages that effectuate it. A unique plane of consistency or composition for the cephalopod and the vertebrate: for the vertebrate to become an Octopus or Cuttlefish, all it would have to do is fold itself in two fast enough to fuse the elements of the halves of its back together, then bring its pelvis up to the nape of the neck and gather its limbs together into one of its extremities, like "a clown who throws his head and shoulders back and walks on his head and hands." *Plication*. (Deleuze and Guattari 2004: 281)

As is hopefully becoming clear, *Vampyroteuthis* becomes our abstract animal, effectuating the 4DX body (*Kinoteuthis*), and within which an enfolded and plicated human sensorium resides. In this inverted way we posit that the introduction of 4DX-like environments, which most often screen spineless Hollywood blockbusters (or busted blocks of spine?), inculcate or intensify processes of becoming-animal within contemporary culture—a process that we also link to the rise of Cthulhu and the inescapable suckers of capital as we progress through the next few chapters. This interkingdom entangling of the human and digestive environments in turn reveals a shimmering molecular vibration passing across the plane of immanence, in-between the worlds of *vampyroteutha* and humans (via their becoming with digital media).

As if deepening this connection, the blockbuster movies most often granted 4DX life become eerily reminiscent of the vampire squid's sexual "festivals," which "involve, among other things, choreographed dances, light shows, chemical orchestrations, and exhibitions of color" (Flusser and Bec 2012: 22). The 4DX experience extends cinema into bestial architecture, then, suggesting a becoming-smart and a becoming-animal of arenas and anatomical architecture, such that the very buildings in which we watch films take part in this mating ritual (recalling Deleuze and Guattari's argument regarding the block of becoming interlinking the wasp and the orchid, wherein the insect becomes part of the flower's sexual reproduction, and the flower begins to display images and to smell attractive to the wasp). As we shall see, 4DX plays a role, then, in the immanentization of passionate cinema, or the increase of environs designed to sucker our attention and incorporate us, rendering us incapable of anything other than absorbing the porous screens, in the process rendering us immobile, or petrified as happens when sharing a gaze with a basilisk or Medusa. Cinema's tentacles extend not just from specialized screens, then, but from the very architecture that we inhabit, as all space is organized for cinema/capital, for the arrival of Cthulhu, for the arrival of alien life, for the arrival of the singularity. In this way, 4DX plays a part in the rise of Cthulhu.

The Vaporization of Cinema

"Psssst." When four of our limbs watched *Guardians of the Galaxy, Vol. 2* at a 4DX screening in 2017, they and their associated two nostrils eagerly inhaled a broad bouquet of aromas from a forest, which were like an amusing Magic Tree approximation of synthetic "nature." When smells are released during 4DX screenings, one can overhear the hissing sound of gas being released into the auditorium ("psssst"), an aural cue that quickly leads to habitually responding with a deep nasal inhalation. As such, we have already begun to rearrange our sedimented movie-going attitudes, reactions, and postures, and now when watching films in the regular as opposed to 4DX format, we often wonder what missing smells might have been activated by them (even if four of our limbs have also synesthetically experienced smells of places depicted at regular movie screenings, without the need for aromatic prompts; see Brown 2014).

What is more, four of our limbs also encountered in 2017 a flagrant synthetic smell associated with the skin suit of the Major, the name of the main protagonist played by Scarlett Johansson, or ScarJo, at a 4DX screening of the American remake of *Ghost in the Shell*. This synthetic smell tumbled into two of our nostrils as the cyborg wafted by our four limbs at key points in the movie. As a naff sommelier, one has no vivid reference points to describe what this smell was or is like. But when we recall it now, its piercing artificial tones make us think of what the posthuman ScarJo must smell like.

We hope that it is not too great a leap of the imagination to suspect that 4DX cinema will—if it is not doing so already—peddle out smells that have a commercial component. That is, since ScarJo is the female face of Dolce & Gabbana's The One perfume, it would make sense for 4DX at some point to team up with D&G (the evil but inevitable bastard child of Deleuze and Guattari?) to pump that scent into the auditorium/aquarium when her characters appear onscreen, such that there does indeed become an association between star and smell—and all in a bid for audience members to buy the perfume (available by waving a card or smartphone over the invisible magnetic waves of the armrest) so that they, too, can smell (like) ScarJo and thus make their otherwise dull lives that little bit more cinematic.

It is perhaps ironic that 2017 also saw ScarJo perform for Saturday Night Live in a spoof advert, in which she impersonates Ivanka Trump for a perfume called "Complicit." As ScarJo/Ivanka walks dreamily/emptyheadedly around a champagne reception, a voice tells us over canned laughter about how this is, with reference to the controversial presidency of Donald J. Trump, "the fragrance for the woman who could stop all this, but won't." That is, if Trump is Cthulhu, then Ivanka is a high priestess in a Cthulhu cult hoping to accelerate his arrival and thus the end of times. However, forasmuch amusing and parodic, "complicit" conceivably also summarizes ScarJo's own role in the immanentization of cinema and thus of capital, or the rise of Cthulhu (more on which in the next chapter). For, via our imagined (or perhaps real) aroma-sponsored 4DX cinema, via her advertising work and via the roles that she plays in many of her films, ScarJo helps to spray us all with scents that will further in us the sense of cents—by which we mean the immanentization of capital such that it is, as it were, The (only) One. In other words, ScarJo, who is the focus of our next chapter, is covered and covers us with the odor of lucre, rendering us also complicit with capital and Cthulhu. To recite Flusser: "[y]et another [gland] produces a gelatinous compound, the excretion of which renders the body translucent" (Flusser and Bec 2012: 19).

In this sense, as our bodies are sprayed during the 4DX screening, so does cinema carry out a kind of "money shot," literally jizzing mucosal liquid-capital all over us. This is not simply a masculine performance of domination—a demonstration that patriarchy has an endless supply of jizz to spray around (see Figure 3.5). But the reason why it is not a demonstration of patriarchal power is not simply because the use of

Figure 3.5 Spraying capital

spray is dressed up in the supposedly female guise of Johansson (indeed, the rising interest in women who squirt during sex would suggest that the desire to spray is not uniquely masculine at all, even if this is yet another performative externalization and visualization/commodification of an internal process that the porn industry surely already knows how to fake). Rather, the money shot here (as per the pornographic money shot in general) is a sign of patriarchy on the wane. For, as the human male often ejaculates on the point of death in one final bid to get his seed out into the world in the vain hope of reproduction, so might this facial squirt from 4DX cinema be the dying spray of cinema—and perhaps also of capital and patriarchy more generally, the last hurrah of a solid penis that is about to become soft and mollusk-like.[3] The *petite mort* of soft, spineless cinema. If after Karl Marx all that is solid melts into air, then perhaps it necessarily goes through a vapor stage on its way through—a meteorological analogy to which we shall revert shortly.

The upshot is that ScarJo and 4DX remind us of cephalopods, because the latter also use a spraying mechanism both to maneuver when under water and more playfully to soak the humans with which they interact above water (see Montgomery 2015: 9–10). Furthermore, sprays and other waves of vapor can immerse us into an inky fog of confused, complicit immobility as we are folded (as we are rendered *com-pli-cit*) with capital via tentacles from which we cannot easily extricate ourselves (if extrication is tricky, complication is easy, and can only be remedied by explication, which perhaps is what this book is trying to unfold).

Fittingly, then, vaporwave is the name given to a genre of music that involves remixing existing music—but in ways that expose the act of remixing, for example by taking otherwise "pleasant-sounding" and highly produced music and looping it in an insistent, repetitive fashion while at the same time not hiding any blips on the soundtrack as the music reaches the end of one loop and the beginning of another. As a result, vaporwave in principle brings to our attention the workings of capitalism as it makes annoying, mundane, and perhaps even anti-musical the music that otherwise forms part of the soundtrack of our lives under capital.

Grafton Tanner writes of vaporwave that it is a kind of musical "horror" genre, inducing dread in its listeners as they notice in everyday music a kind of emptiness that otherwise is covered over. Indeed, Tanner even aligns vaporwave with the writing of H. P. Lovecraft as this musical micro-genre reminds us of the horrific and alien nature of the would-be familiar world of neoliberal capital (see Tanner 2016: 19). Tentacles, tendrils, the weird, and *hentai* (which we shall consider in Chapter 5) all pervade Tanner's book as he explains how vaporwave presents original songs "in an alien way . . . as cultural trash, as jokes, as actually beautiful pieces of music" (Tanner 2016: 12). However, vaporwave is perhaps something of a misnomer, in that the music created by the movement's most prominent figures, which include artists like James Ferraro, g h o s t i n g, Internet Club, Macintosh Plus, Midnight Television and Chuck Person, is not itself "vapor" so much as a critique of the vapid nature of mainstream culture. In other words, it is the mainstream culture that is like a vapor, sprayed from the glands of capital on to consumers such that they stink of it and can smell it wherever they go.

A brief discussion of vaporwave is useful for our discussion of spray as deployed in 4DX cinema—and cinema more generally in the digital age. For, as vaporwave involves the remixing of mainstream music, so increasingly are movies remixed in the era of the mash-up, with the academic digital video-essay also playing a role in this process. As we move increasingly into a culture in which movies are streamed (if not mainstreamed), it stands to reason that those relentless streams of network flicks (*Sharktopus* and *Annihilation*) and on-demand "quality television" (*Altered Carbon*, *The O.A.*, and *Stranger Things*, Matt Duffer and Ross Duffer, USA, 2016–) on top of YouTube channels (like Smosh and PewDiePie) will throw up vapor in the form of reworked concepts and film footage. In particular, video remixes and video-essays might both constitute a form of cinematic vaporwave.

That said, when Tanner outlines how vaporwave involves "a grassroots approach that shows [that] musical history can still occur without the industrial tentacles of the music-business-at-large constricting every stage of artistic creation in the name of the dollar" (Tanner 2016: 46), he forgets that music has always been able to do this via its most traditional means, namely when played live. Here we reach an important distinction between cinema and music: while music can be played live—and while live music can thus like vaporwave avoid music-as-capital—cinema cannot in the same way be played live without ceasing to be cinema. Acknowledging that film audiences are on the whole living people, meaning that they interact "live" with the otherwise pre-recorded film (and a pre-recorded 4DX track), the pre-recorded nature of cinema, as opposed to live music (and live musical accompaniments to films?), means arguably that cinema lends itself less readily to non-commercialization (in this way, the live interactions carried out by planted audience members during the Lettrist film screenings constitute a genuine attempt to render cinema non-commercial).

As an aside, it is worth noting here how music is often adopted as a metaphor to help describe the cinematic and existential nature of the cephalopodic body-brain. For example, in trying to describe their body-screen performances, Godfrey-Smith says "I realized that these colors were changing in a concerted way, and changing in more ways than I could track. It reminded me of music, or chords changing amid and over each other. [The animal] would shift several colors in sequence or together" (Godfrey-Smith 2016: 133). Backyard Brains' *Insane in the Chromatophores*, which we mentioned in the introduction, also makes this process clear as the technological interface ostensibly turns an expressive animalistic ability into a repeatable and replayable product for the attention economy. Beyond the music video nature of their silent screens, though, the cephalopodic body-brain organization also invites comparisons with different musical styles and arrangements. Indeed, the centralized brain is described by Godfrey-Smith as a musical conductor, albeit one challenged with directing the semi-autonomous betentacled-net organs that are compared in turn to free-form jazz musicians. Godfrey-Smith thus throws up the image of a high culture classical conductor guiding various jazz players, who are forever "inclined to improvisation, [and] will accept only so much direction" (Godfrey-Smith 2016: 105)—an image that reworks a more familiar pastoral-managerial image of herding cats, which is not conducive to rationalized industries under capitalism.

In comparison to this musical picture, cinema is perhaps always capitalist—meaning that the mash-up and the academic video-essay alike are generally complicit with cinema and thus with capital, except when like vaporwave they seek to expose rather than to celebrate the workings of cinema-capital. In this way, the now-established connection between academic video-essays and cinephilia is perhaps misleading (see Keathley

2011; Stork 2012; Grant 2014). For, if video-essays love cinema (if they are cinephiliac), then surely they are complicit with capital—with only those video-essays that are at the very least ambivalent about cinema involving some possible form of resistance to capital. (Or if this resistance is inherent to and thus true of the academic video-essay as a form, then cinephilia is perhaps not the correct framework through which to understand it.) Complicit rather than critical mash-ups and video-essays, then, could form part of what Tanner might term the tradition of "YouTube Poop," the inevitable shit that comes as a result of the endless consumption of moving images and sounds (see Tanner 2016: 24).[4]

Laura Kipnis describes most mainstream blockbusters as "vapid," the vapor-like existence of which is perhaps inevitable in a world where temperatures are rising and thus sucking vapor from the never-ending streams of moving images and sounds (Kipnis 1998: 604). More than this, vaporization is the next stage in the transformation of a film from a thing to a part of a stream to a vapor in the air to being part of a formless cloud, i.e., vapor is the next stage in the transition from movies streaming to movies sitting in the computer cloud that is the increasing digitization of the world (which is not to mention movies being projected on to clouds; even clouds can be put to work for cinema-capital). This computer cloud may hang low in the air, like a miasmic fog that disorients and confuses us, allowing the *Kinoteuthis Infernalis* to maneuver unseen. Or it may simply take on vapor until it is pregnant with rain. If during 4DX screenings we feel some spray, perhaps this is only a foretaste of the deluge that is to come as the clouds break, as the rain falls (as cinema reigns), as the water levels rise, and as humans thus are soaked to the bone before drowning in images as Cthulhu emerges from the depths.

A wary reader will have noted that we seem to employ contradictory metaphors, in that at one moment we suggest that the spray is a squid's ink and capitalism's last hurrah, before then arguing that the spray signals the onset of the flood and the rise of Cthulhu. As we shall discuss in more detail in Chapter 8, chthulucinema is all of these at once—but not quite via the contradictory method of superposition that we discussed in the introduction. For, the rise of Cthulhu is both the end of humanity (and thus of human capitalism) and the realization/continuation of capital without humans, of capital as a living alien. Before we explore these issues in more detail, however, we should like to revert to Scarlett Johansson to discuss how in her alien becomings and in her eight-limbed dualities, she constitutes something of the posthuman poster-squid for *Kinoteuthis Infernalis*.

Notes

1. Z-screens are matte silver screens replete with an "xyz axis" that enables the interleaving of negative parallax images (images that penetrate into the auditorium), with more traditional, converged frame-plane images, and enfolded positive parallax images (located within the depths of the screen; see Zone 2012).
2. Indeed, when four of our limbs visited the Disney Resort in Shanghai to undertake this dark ride, its immersive nature rippled through the form and content of the experience. To draw a science-fiction reference, the experience of *Battle for the Sunken Treasure* is at times like the holodeck from *Star Trek: The Next Generation* (Gene Roddenberry, USA, 1987–94) as it becomes difficult to reality test, or to distinguish between props and projections. At other times, although one cognitively knows what the difference is, it feels as though the opposite is true. For example, at one point the audience/crew appears to be at the bottom of the ocean. We know that we are not, because we are dry and can breathe. However, we can also see the surface of the ocean far above us, where ships sail past. As we move quietly across a lake, a massive Kraken lifts off the ocean floor and swims over us, a homage to Disney's earlier *20,000 Leagues under the Sea*, no doubt. And soon after, an animatronic and then a projected squid-faced Davy Jones conjures an armada of sunken ships, which rise off the ocean floor and float up to the surface to join in an overhead sea battle. Our own projected rise from the ocean floor, up to and then through the surface is a total rush. Everyone in the raft physically feels the upward surge as an embodied vection illusion, as ubiquitous motion fills their perceptual field, with many people screaming on the occasion of our visit.
3. As a hydrostat, the human penis is, along with the tongue, perhaps the appendage most similar to the cephalopod tentacle. Ejaculation might also be understood as an eruption of chaotic life, as per the inability of humans to bottle blood via menstruation (see endnote 10 of Chapter 8). However, in the effort to dominate via the money-shot, and in the search for permanent hardness (the penis as boner), this hydrostatic potential is subjugated to hard capital rather than working positively with softness.
4. Similarly, academic video-essays could be masturbatory videos that ask the viewer to behold the hard penis of cinema as it ejaculates its spray on to yet further audiences. An important aspect of vaporwave's critique of mainstream music is that it is quasi-anonymous, such that "vaporwave erases the notion of authorship altogether" (Tanner 2016: 12). The same holds for many mash-ups, but the insistence of/on authorship in video-essay culture (under the neoliberal pressures within academia of publish-or-perish, i.e., one must not be anonymous, but instead one must make oneself visible) suggest that as a form it is a kind of "vapor" that accompanies rather than critiques a vapid mainstream cinema that is always already complicit with capital.

CHAPTER 4

Actorly Squid/Sets and Cephalopod Realism

> And when you think you see
> Someone who looks like me
> Be aware it's a grand illusion
>
> – J. Ralph ("One Whole Hour," covered by Scarlett Johansson)

> I have come 500 miles
> Just to see a halo
> Come from St. Petersburg
> Scarlett and me
> Well I open my eyes
> I was blind as can be
> When you give a man luck
> He must fall in the sea
>
> – Tom Waits ("Falling Down," covered by Scarlett Johansson)

IN THIS CHAPTER we make our fourth *pars pro toto* case for the existence of *Kinoteuthis Infernalis*, trusting that the whole will become discernible via an examination of a fractalized part, the macro pattern courtesy of a micro detail, the general through a consideration of the specific, and the multiversal discovered shining through a case of the particular. We also here pick up where the previous chapter left off, by turning our attention to one of contemporary global cinema's most commanding lead performers, Scarlett Johansson, an actor (micro), whom we see as constituting a small Benjaminian "crystal of the total event" (macro; see Benjamin 1999). We focus in particular on Johansson's growing corpus of science-fiction work, which we believe renders cephalopodic forms of thought "immanent to the image" (Deleuze 2005b: 168), thereby making them easily graspable. Starting from the notion that digital cinema is *theorematic*, we specifically engage with what we might here call digital cinema's cephalopod *somatechnics*, openly borrowing the notion of theorematic cinema from Deleuze, who was well attuned to the manner in which the technological capabilities and aesthetic properties of the image, in concert with other formal choices, impinge upon thought. Put differently, the viewer's ability to think or feel along with any given film is comprised or compromised, innervated or impeded in the material encounter between brain and screen by the range and quality of affects afforded to filmmakers by their *technē* (art or craft) and its sensational possibilities (shot lengths, focal lengths, camera mobility, sound recording, color quality, light exposures, and more).

As mentioned, we elsewhere discuss some of the novel potentials opened up by the digital event for filmmakers and viewers alike. These include the possibility for digital cameras to record for longer, for small digital cameras to access more intimate places, for expansive networks cheaply and simultaneously to record action, for skeuomorphic "cameras" to pass through solid objects within digital spaces as if they were navigable volumes, and for digital films to have a morphogenic and malleable *mise-en-scène*—meaning that the film's setting can change at any given moment in time. We have also discussed how actual and virtual space-times are seen to be coexisting within digital cinema, and for digital cinema as a result to place the viewer equally in an ambiguous position (i.e., uncertain of the truth-value of anything that she sees). We have also discussed how bodies within digital films are equally malleable, and even how the body of the actor is in digital cinema a hybrid of flesh and machine (see Brown 2013, 2018a; Fleming 2012, 2013, 2017; Brown and Fleming 2011, 2015; Fleming and Brown 2015). Such ideas are even more pronounced at the time of writing, as newer forms of AI image rendering, such as "deepfake" (a portmanteau brand combining "deep learning" and "fake"), allow computer users to superimpose, composite, or synthesize facial images, so that the look and gestures of one person replace those of another. The compositing and mapping technique has most recently become infamous through its deployment in so-called "revenge" and "fake celebrity" porn, of which Johansson has herself become a hapless high-profile victim (Harwell 2018).[1] With this in mind we shall hone in on Johansson's star image in order better to expose the extent to which its specific attributes, qualities, and properties have become composited into and indexically expressive of the soft molluskian intelligence of digital coding.

We thus primarily zoom in on notions of persona, acting, and performance in the digital era in order to expose multiple articulations of cephalopod animality, and further eruptions and expressions of becoming-cephalopod—on different scales and registers—of our present digital culture. In this way we explore how Johansson's star image (both endorsed and counterfeit examples) and various of her science-fiction (chthulu-cinema) characters bring to mind protean and *mètic* squid-like abilities, including the ability to alter at will their shape, texture, appearance, color, movements, and more, while also blending and camouflaging with viewers, in addition to signaling to them, both inside and beyond the screen, via posthuman digital-dermal body-tech.

As we shall see, it appears that the propensity of "soft and fully muscular" cephalopodic animals to deceive, to make hesitate, to seduce, and to kill is channeled by many of the cyborgian characters that Johansson embodies, especially in her science-fiction work (see Nakajima *et al.* 2018: 1). Before beginning our analysis, however, it is worth pausing minimally to establish some of the many meanings and associations freighted forth by the conceptual figure of the "cyborg." Indeed, of particular relevance to our arguments below is LeiLani Nishime's descriptions of these human–tech hybrids as archetypal "boundary crossers" that—because they still "inspire fascination and dread" à la Donna J. Haraway—should properly be understood as a type of *monster* (Nishime 2016: 694; see also Haraway 1991: 2). Fittingly, this notion resonates with the writing of Gilles Deleuze on film actors, whom he likewise describes in terms of hybrid monsters, in that "monsters are born of cinematic actors" (Deleuze 2005b: 70). That is, actors and their characters are chthonic and crepuscular "Siamese twins," each with their own face, even if there is a constant flipping between the two as actual and virtual poles of a crystal. As David Deamer explains, "the virtual image of the character becomes actual, or limpid, as the actual image of the actor becomes opaque, or virtual; and reciprocally, actual-virtual, limpid and opaque are ongoing exchanges throughout the film" (Deamer 2016: 312). In what follows, we ultimately seek to track the two sides of a crystalline circuit erected between Johansson the monstrous actor and the monstrous (cyborgian) characters that she embodies—the latter being, for Deleuze, "the great dark stage of the aquarium of monsters, [which] rises in silence and grows as the first one becomes vague or blurred" (Deleuze 2005b: 71).

Zeitgeist Starlet

Scarlett Johansson garnered much inky attention in the 2010s. Beyond the usual column inches and reportage one would expect of a Hollywood star, together with countless tweets and posts, Johansson was also the focus of edited collections (Monaghan *et al.* 2019), special dossiers (issue 57 of *Jump Cut*), and a cascade of academic essays, talks, and panels (Knee and Fleming 2014; Ng 2014; Brown *et al.* 2015; Fleming 2015, 2018; Herzog 2016;

Brown and Fleming 2019). Broadly speaking, many of these latter works foreground/highlight Johansson's celebrity mutability, her cinematic timelessness, her commercial and professional adaptability, her meme-etic modularity, her cultural capital, her political activism, and myriad other matters and events. However, in this outing we wish to focus on the weird nonhuman and posthuman roles that Johansson fleshes out in various of her fantasy and science-fiction films, including *The Island* (Michael Bay, USA, 2005), *Her* (Spike Jonze, USA, 2013), *Under the Skin* (Jonathan Glazer, UK/USA/Switzerland/Poland, 2013), *Lucy* (Luc Besson, France/Taiwan/Germany, 2014), *The Jungle Book* (Jon Favreau, UK/USA, 2016), and *Ghost in the Shell* (the 4DX version of which we discussed briefly in the last chapter), as well as her various performances as Natasha Romanoff, or the Black Widow, from the Marvel cinematic universe (*The Avengers*, Joss Whedon, USA, 2012; *Captain America: The Winter Soldier*, Anthony and Joe Russo, USA, 2014; *Avengers: Age of Ultron*, Joss Whedon, USA, 2015; *Captain America: Civil War*, Anthony and Joe Russo, USA/Germany, 2016; *Avengers: Infinity War*, Anthony and Joe Russo, USA, 2018; *Avengers: Endgame*, Anthony and Joe Russo, USA, 2019).

With Black Widow in mind, Haraway notably describes octopuses as "spiders of the seas" (Haraway 2016: 55), meaning that spiders are reciprocally the octopuses of the lands (seeing as life in the sea predates life on the land). As the Russian double-agent Black Widow, and thus as an octopus of the land, Johansson emerges as a fittingly tentacular subject for enquiry, as does the fact that her ever-expanding body of science-fiction work is very much about bodies and their parallel brains, human identity/nature, and the complex relationships (and/or becomings) that these have with alien and/or inhuman technologies. For example, *The Island* sees Johansson play Jordan Two Delta, a clone grown for the purposes of providing organs and other body parts for Sarah Jordan, her "real"-world celebrity double, while in *Her*, Johansson provides the voice of Samantha, an AI that befriends lonely would-be writer Theodore Twombly (Joaquin Phoenix) in a vaguely dystopian near-future Los Angeles (sequences of which were filmed in Shanghai). In *Under the Skin*, Johansson plays an alien who travels around Scotland in a van, seducing men and inviting them back to her lair, where they are trapped and killed for their material resources, while in *Lucy*, Johansson's eponymous character ingests some CPH4, a superdrug that she smuggles on to an airplane after having been roped into acting as a mule, and which turns her into a super-intelligent entity that can control and manipulate space-time and matter-energy. In *The Jungle Book* Johansson voices Kaa, a hypnotic, seductress python (or a single tentacle with mesmerizing, cinematic-basilisk eyes) that attempts to eat Mowgli (Neel Sethi), while in *Ghost in the Shell*, she plays the Major, a technologically enhanced law-enforcement agent who discovers her former identity as a technophobic dissident, which otherwise had been kept secret from her.

While the Black Widow might be a sort of octopus, and while Kaa might be a kind of Gorgon-like basilisk-tentacle, we wish more specifically to argue that across these films the performances of the world's most highly remunerated female film actor (see Robehmed 2016; Harwell 2018) involve a return/reversion of squid-like somatechnics, which more generally form a key aspect of individuated identity in our supersaturated digital era. To do so we hone in on three intersectional aspects of contemporary somatechnics, linked respectively to the brain, to the body, and to thought. This tripartite exploration (of which each part already has many parts) of the squid or squid-like aspects of Johansson's work takes up questions raised by the discourse that surrounds her star image, and allows us to explore how the digital nature of today's somatechnics nudge us to think about the digital in relation to cephalopods and our thinking/theorizing of cinematic animality more generally. In this way, we specifically reframe the above set of films as an important body of contemporary *sci phi*—a term coined by Gregory Flaxman to draw out the parallels emerging between works of science fiction and (Nietzschean and Deleuzian) creative philosophy (for a similar argument, see also Shaviro 2016: esp. 54). Certainly, Johansson's shape-shifting body of work presents us with fleeting glimpses "of the alien world beneath the normal order of things," and this also serves to raise important "what if" questions relevant to our present and futures (see O'Sullivan and Zepke 2018: 18–19).

With this in mind, we here harness some of the vacillating and polysemous meanings bound up with the term *soma*, which suggests a nexus of interrelated applications to, and critical insertions into, Johansson's ever-growing *oeuvre*. On account of complex interferences between the different levels of reality and fiction, star and character, we begin by posing timely ontological questions regarding the nature of Johansson as a star body in this supersaturated digital era, which includes so much (deep)fake imagery, and what our cephalopodic lines of flight entail for our thinking of celebrity and identity in the digital present.

To Greek Metamorphoses via Rabbits and Ducks

Our first port of call with regard to Johansson's cephalopodic somatechnics occasions a brief reversion to ancient Greece, where *sōma/σῶμα* delivers us to (because it literally means) "the body." However, when we articulate our thinking of the body/σῶμα with *technics* or *technos*, and in particular digital-cinematic *technē*, we are already compelled critically to acknowledge and grapple with four distinct yet interleaving aspects of somatechnical analysis. These can be broadly adumbrated here as corresponding to the intersectionalities of: (1) the fictional bodies of the (inhuman or posthuman) characters that we see in the sci phi scenarios of Johansson's films (as outlined above); (2) the technologically assisted or mediated star body that appears and performs in these films (and/or paratextual media, including deepfake porn); (3) the flickering "signaletic material," or theorematic "film body" (to intercept a common phrase; see, for example, Deleuze 2000: 368 and Sobchack 1992: 219), with which Johansson's kinetic performances assemble (and co-constitute); and (4) the embodied sensorium of the viewer with whom the affective film bodies (including the star-character performances) move into composition during the screening encounter. In order to explore these intersectionalities, we shall focus presently on the strange liminal world of the star-character body, and the monstrous cyborgian frontiers that trouble our understanding of various interfacing ontological categories.

Having briefly glossed/licked Deleuze's monstrous take on actors and characters as having diverging and converging ontologies, we now opportunely re-vert to the writing of Johannes Riis, who similarly aids us in thinking through Johansson's intriguingly (and increasingly) technologically determined star performances and roles, the most relevant of which constitute what Riis respectively calls the "duck/rabbit" and "realist" models of understanding performance (see Riis 2009). Importantly, Riis acknowledges the fact that in our era of ubiquitous CGI filmmaking, acting and performance have increasingly become associated with the domain of images and imaging (recall Badiou's earlier sense of an image as a "mental copy"). In light of this, Riis returns us to, and road-tests, two historically popular models used for conceptualizing the complex immingling or intermeshing of the actor persona and the character performance.

The duck/rabbit model is so-named because of its associations with a well-known and centuries-old optical illusion, which became a popular illustration among perceptual and cognitive philosophers in the nineteenth and twentieth centuries—perhaps most famously by Ludwig Wittgenstein in his *Philosophical Investigations* (2009 [1953]), where he uses this "ambiguous image" to help draw out a distinction between passive *seeing* and active *interpreting*. Speaking generally, viewers typically see/interpret either a duck or a rabbit at any one time during their encounter with the illusionary image. As a result, the model implicitly evokes a "top-down" understanding of cognitive perception, wherein an image is seen/interpreted as corresponding to an already known concept or category (rather than being a "bottom-up" hybrid image beheld by the perceiver as-it-is). However, while the duck and rabbit aspects might appear as mutually exclusive perceptions/perspectives (with viewers seeing it as either one animal or the other at any given moment), the perceiver is recognized as having the mental capacity willfully to flit between each category/concept (and thus to remain intellectually aware of perceiving an ambiguous "duckrabbit" image that occasions, or is conducive to, shifting perspectival perceptions).

When applied to the realm of film acting and performance, though, the duck/rabbit image is redeployed as a material metaphor corresponding to the apparent ambiguities that emerge between actor identity and their role-playing performance, qua the "photographic and dramatic" levels of representation, which likewise trouble as much as they reaffirm a form of actor and character *dualism* (see Riis 2009: 5). In Deleuzian language, we might here understand one image becoming opaque or shadowy as the other becomes luminous or limpid, with one pole becoming actual as the other recedes toward the virtual courtesy of the crystalline cinema machine (Deleuze 2005b: 70–71). While this model ostensibly helps to account for the mutually exclusive perspectives upon the star or the character that viewers apparently adopt at any given moment of film viewing (now I see Scarlett Johansson, now I see Natasha Romanoff), Riis argues that the dualistic duck/rabbit star/actor paradigm ultimately implies a kind of perceptual mistake. For such reasons, he instead favors an alternative "realist" model of (or perspective upon) the actor/character, which offers a more plausible or *realistic* understanding of this complex intrarelationship—and of how we actually perceive the star/character when we encounter their image in and around a film.

In short, and in contrast with the troublesome duck/rabbit model, a realist model concedes that whenever we see a film performer, we remain aware of and/or affected by past encounters with that given actor's image (including their previous roles and/or promotional materials). What is more, this previously encountered assemblage delimits a horizon of expectations, which comes into play whenever the actor might be cast in a new role, or given a new set of circumstances with which to engage (Riis 2009: 6–7). There are clear echoes here of Leo Braudy's assertion that film stars develop a "residual" self-image over the course of their career, and which snowballs from film to film, "creating an image with which the actor, the scriptwriter, and the director can play as they wish" (Braudy 1977: 197–198). There are likewise reverberations here with Stanley Cavell's discussion of Humphrey Bogart's star "type," whereby "'Bogart' comes to *mean* 'the figure created in a given set of films'" (Cavell 1979: 28–29).

From such realist vantages, we can better conceive of any given Johansson character as being subordinate to, or a subcategory of, the superior star persona. What is more, such approaches to stars also conjure affinities with Alain Badiou's philosophical appropriations of axiomatic, or Zermelo-Fraenkel, mathematical theory (see, for example, Ling 2011: 63–65), which in turn opens up new potentials for understanding actors in our digital era. To explain how and why, we must first recognize Johansson as a form of *set* {}, or a plurality in unit form, and within which unit all of her characters belong (∈) or become members (or even subsets, in the sense that Johansson's science-fiction characters would become a subset of the set of Johansson's appearances as a celebrity image). According to this model, Johansson surfaces as the image that one-ifies/unifies all the residual character-members, which demonstrate a tentacular belonging to this larger category (∈ as a symbol that involves tentacles; see Badiou 2007: esp. 81–120).[2]

If the star carries with her virtual images or memories from her previous roles, then to view a star is in some senses always to view an image of time—in that, like astronomers observing the light from stars, the past is visible alongside the present (and perhaps the future, too). In a certain sense, then, we can also rehabilitate the duck/rabbit image as providing us with an image of time. For, if the human observer can only see either a duck or a rabbit at any given moment in time, the crystalline "duckrabbit" nonetheless itself remains both at once. That is, the duckrabbit presents to us two (or more) moments in time at once, giving to us a sense of how all moments in time exist simultaneously, and of how a virtual time (it could be either a duck or a rabbit) surrounds and accompanies all actual moments in/of time (we see either a duck or a rabbit as a result of our conditioned modes of viewing the world in a chronological order). Consider in this light David H. Fleming's observations elsewhere that Johansson's star image emanates a weird form of cinematic timelessness and hypermutability, which at once encompasses pre-, past-, present-, and even post-cinematic thresholds. How? For one thing, Johansson has embodied or inhabited (camouflaged herself as)

> a pre-cinematic "star" in the period film *Girl with a Pearl Earring* (Peter Webber, UK/Luxembourg, 2003), where she plays the muse of Johannes Vermeer (Colin Firth), the Flemish master who captures her image through his proto-photographic *camera obscura* machine. (Fleming 2015)

However, she has also

> played a quintessential 1940s *femme fatale* in Brian De Palma's nostalgic neo noir *The Black Dahlia* (Brian De Palma, Germany/USA/France, 2006), and an archetypal 1950s blonde bombshell in Joel and Ethan Coen's meta-cinematic ode to the golden

> era studio system, *Hail, Caesar!* (UK/Japan/USA, 2016). Johansson's on- and off-screen celebrity image has likewise witnessed her morphologically actualize two or three of the twentieth century's most famous on-screen "blondes," at once realizing an iconic Marilyn Monroe-cum-Madonna image for her Dolce and Gabbana lipstick commercials, and personifying Janet Leigh in *Hitchcock* (Sacha Gervasi, UK/USA, 2012), another meta-cinematic film about Hollywood filmmaking. Meanwhile, Johansson became a bona fide star and muse in her own right, as can be evidenced by her appearance in a string of millennial Woody Allen films including *Match Point* (UK/Ireland/Luxembourg, 2005), *Scoop* (UK/USA, 2006), and *Vicky Cristina Barcelona* (Spain/USA, 2008). (Fleming forthcoming-a)

Furthermore, Johansson can also be recognized today as a post-cinematic star who still pilots old-school Hollywood blockbusters, wherein she commonly plays posthuman characters (Knee and Fleming 2014). We might thus also revert here to our friend, the mimic octopus (*Thaumoctopus mimicus*), who similarly and for various reasons often takes on the shape and movements of an other (such as a striped sea snake or a toxic flatfish), remaining an octopus even when performing, and thus being perceived as, the other.

To aid our discussion of these issues, let us draw a conceptual distinction between the star, which we might label *ScarJo* (a moniker that the actor purportedly does not like, but which becomes useful for highlighting how a celebrity image is a commodity that is often owned and manipulated by others; see Herzog 2016), and any given character that Johansson, with the help of technology, embodies—and which for bilateral symmetry we might here label *CharJo* (with the alien from *Under the Skin*, the Black Widow, Lucy, Samantha, Kaa and the Major here delimiting a predominantly science-fiction subset of CharJo characters/CharJos). By thus dividing the star and her characters into entangled ScarJo/CharJo poles (which remain derived but distinct from the actual biological human and mortal subject known as Scarlett Johansson), we can become better attuned to certain somatechnical convergences and resonances that play out on and between these different levels or registers.

Similar themes and issues actually appear as loaded subtexts or prominent themes raised by many of ScarJo's science-fiction films, thereby, after Deleuze, stimulating the becomings of thought. Amy Herzog's recent engagement with the Johansson star image hints toward this idea, while painting ScarJo as a peculiarly modern assemblage whose tendrils penetrate into different actual and virtual dimensions of contemporary life. Herzog foregrounds the extent to which Johansson essentially becomes a kind of "living commodity," whose "current zeitgeist as an idealized non-or-superhuman avatar" is expressed throughout many of her science-fiction films (Herzog 2016). Individually and collectively, films such as *Under the Skin*, *Lucy*, and *Her* seem to needle viewers to pose a raft of philosophical questions, including: "what does it mean to perform as an instrument for use by another? Can one consent within a system that remains unknowable? And how might the very machinations of commercial cinema be entwined with these practices?" (upon which, more shortly).

Johansson already raises a comparable set of questions in *The Island*, which playfully explores the intensified convergences between the realms of *bios*, *zoë*, and *technos*. As mentioned, Johansson here plays a divided or doubled role, at once embodying the commodity-clone Jordan Two Delta, an unwitting biocybernetic replica that has been ordered, grown, and imprisoned in a corporate holding facility (a CharJo), and her real-world donor/owner, Sarah Jordan, a media celebrity and an (un)timely fictional Johansson proxy or double, whose initials suggest that this second CharJo can be read as an implied ScarJo surrogate. Within the film, Jordan Two Delta escapes the fleshfarm, but while on the run in the city she encounters a series of video and poster images depicting the commoditized face and body of Jordan, her celebrity owner/double. The CharJo here peers transfixed through a high-end shop window at a screen-within-the-screen, captivated and disarmed by Sarah Jordan, her eerie real-world doppelgänger whose slick mediated image is harnessed and commoditized by some futural fashion brand. We are here cast into a disorienting crystalline hall of mirrors, with rotating dark and light sides. In other words, the moment exposes a circuit of affective deimatic display and hesitating effect—for Jordan Two Delta and for us, because these mediated diegetic images "ostensibly look like real world adverts for Calvin Klein or Dolce & Gabbana (in whose advertising campaigns Johansson has herself featured)," meaning that Johansson's star body can be understood as operating and performing "simultaneously as image, commodity, product, and clone," at once diegetically and extra-diegetically at the same time (see Brown and Fleming 2019). Or again, the real star, like the fictional clone, is always already what W. J. T. Mitchell might refer to as a living image—in the same way that a clone like Dolly the sheep is a replicant or facsimile of an other (see Mitchell 2005: 14, 309ff.), and in a fashion that speaks forward to Johansson's own troubling encounters with deepfake images of herself, as we shall see. Within the biopolitical-biomedia science-fiction story, however, Jordan Two Delta appears as another form of biomedia *image*, even if a living one, in whose cloned-commodity organs and womb the fictional star (another commodity/image) and/or her agent invest in order to prolong the celebrity-commodity's own image-life (through either organ harvest and transfer or through surrogate parenthood).

There are other overt instances when fictional CharJos regard a divided or inhuman self-image, or moments when CharJos look back at ScarJo (if not *vice versa*), suggesting that this becomes a trope interconnecting Johansson's wider science-fiction *oeuvre*. In *Ghost in the Shell*, for example, the Major (CharJo) stares intently at a real-time 3D hologrammatic projection of her own cyborg shell's living image, while after having been attacked and exposed as a black alien in *Under the Skin*, the hybrid creature looks back at the living human image-mask that has been ripped from it—meaning that the alien CharJo is again confronted with the ScarJo image. As if anticipating Johansson's encounters with deepfake porn images, Marc Francis writes of this disturbing moment of split embodiment in *Under the Skin*: "[t]he eyes of the mask that is Johansson's face even blink to remind us that the human component to this alien can be shed but not so easily annihilated—it exists independently of the body that wears it" (Francis 2016). Similarly, Amy Herzog argues that such moments recall and recast Pierre Klossowski's considerations of the "industrial slave," which in turn prompt thought to encounter the conjoined images of "the slave" and "the prostitute," two key vectors that likewise increasingly become thought with or bound up within the ScarJo–CharJo commodity-image across a range of different films and paratextual media—while also conjuring forth Walter Benjamin's idea from "Central Park" that when the commodity sees itself, it sees a whore: "[t]he commodity attempts to look itself in the face. It celebrates its becoming human in the whore" (quoted in Herzog 2016).

In this way, ScarJo ultimately begins to surface as "a living commodity," albeit one who constantly "attempts to look itself in the face," even if it finds there only "a slick surface, no point of origin, a simulacrum, endlessly circulating" (see Herzog 2016).[3] For us, such instances of dividing and doubling appear to acknowledge and knowingly to play with the idea that the ScarJo/CharJo celebrity persona always already operates as a singular-multiple commodity (sex-slave) image. With regard to the (Greek) somatechnics associated with the doubled-down sci phi Johansson image, then, we might note that both the fictional (CharJos/ScarJos) and the extra-diegetic body performances (ScarJos qua celebrity set) reveal a clear convergence and merging with digital technologies. Reverting to Riis's theories about screen acting, we might accordingly argue that a modified or modularized duck/rabbit model *and* a set/realist model become helpful for our understanding of the micro (fictional) and macro (celebrity) levels of Johansson's singular–plural, or particle–wave, star–character continuum.

This notion of the star as a commodified Benjaminian "sex-slave" only becomes more telling when we consider the surfeit of deepfake porn films that feature ScarJo, or at least her likeness, and which circulate online. Lev Manovich noted in the early millennium that algorithms (alongside databases) ultimately constitute the complementary interlocking half "of the ontology of the world according to a computer" (Manovich 2001: 223). But while algorithmic/database films directed by AI were relative novelties during the first decade of the millennium, the end of its second decade has seen deepfake porn videos surge to such an extent that Johansson, whose face has been made to appear in many such videos, believes that the tide is impossible to fight against or to stem (see, for example, Harwell 2018). If Manovich notes that the more complex and larger the dataset, then the simpler the algorithm will be that is needed to work with it (and *vice versa*), then today the face-swapped Johansson deepfake films are made possible by free software and easy-to-use apps that employ

> machine-learning algorithms to analyse photographs of a target subject, "learning" the map of the target subject's face (the more photographs, the more accurate the portrayal), and then superimposing the target subject's "face" onto a video, sometimes producing extremely convincing results). (Black *et al.* 2018)

What is more, this technology has advanced to the degree that even a limited set, and sometimes even a single photograph, can produce relatively (if not "extremely") convincing results (see, for example, Neild 2019). These deepfake videos, then, are the products of users (for example, mrdeepfakes) with access to free image databanks and AI, who then upload the videos to porn databases such as PornHub and/or to social media websites like Reddit, where multiple users can view them. In relation to Johansson, this means that her star persona becomes a sprawling hypertext body or dataset, with her star "sex-symbol" status no doubt helping to account for her enduring popularity as a target of (sex-slave commodity for) these trick films.

Furthermore, since these videos involve ScarJo images in a fake context, but where we do not strictly see a CharJo (since the idea/fantasy that the videos wish to convey is that ScarJo herself is engaged in these pro-camera sex acts, and not a character that she is playing), then these deepfake videos become examples of hybrid ScarJo–CharJos. Or, rather than a duck/rabbit, let us imagine a molecularly entangled squid-human that recalls the fused hybrid being encountered in David Cronenberg's science-fiction horror, *The Fly* (USA/UK/Canada, 1986), which is not to mention Lovecraft's Cthulhu, which is at once a composition/superposition of sea monster, dragon, and human, but nowhere specifically any of them. However, where the Brundle-Fly is entangled at the level of DNA coding, we here posit the hybrid ScarJo–CharJo as entangled at the level of CGI coding. If you will, the latest deepfake images signal that nowadays we are able to perceive a form of technologically enabled "duckrabbit" precisely because these products are perceived and mentally processed in such a way that negates the Johansson image at the moment of its perception. Or put differently, the brain perceives and conceives of an always already ambiguous image wherein we both see and conceptually "unsee" Johansson at the moment of viewing (CharJo~~ScarJo~~, in the sense that we seem to be seeing Scarlett Johansson, but it is not her).

Having arrived at the superpositional (Cthulhu) or converged (Brundle-Fly) portrait of our Scar–Char, wherein is revealed the drive for (patriarchal) cinema-capital to turn all (women's?) bodies into commodities/sex slaves, we can now feed the CharJo~~ScarJo~~ into another sort of software program in order to derive a further molecularized and fractalized (databased and algorithmic) *image*—the type of digital-era photomontage that generates celebrity/character portraits that are themselves composed of thousands of smaller images of the same star/character. This might in turn be rendered as one of those scrambled "magic-eye" (stereogram) patterns that gains depth and solidity when we adjust or "diverge" our eyes to stare beyond its surface manifestations. If we further imagine this "magic-eye" image in animated form at different scales of composition, then we can see an endlessly shifting modular-monadic being composed of smaller and moving pixelated images, cycling through different Scar-Char looks, at once wave and particle across different scales, depths, and registers. The name that we give to this (fractalized, impressionistic, volumetric, modular, databased, algorithmic set) chthulumedia being is {Schar-JØ}—a composition/superposition of both real and "fake" ScarJos and CharJos, and which somehow is and is not at the same time (hence the Ø). The {Schar-JØ} is a cephalopodic being with tentacular links to many different cultural products (including the inky tattoo industry) and networked software entities (deepfake porn), which in turn begin to impinge upon a second dimension of squid somatechnics relevant to our study, and to which we turn presently.[4]

Squid-like Body, Brain, Thought

Across his writings, Deleuze was undoubtedly one of the first to argue that the molecular biology of the brain offers far more to the analysis of cinema than linguistics or psychoanalysis. Rethinking Spinoza's notion of mind and body parallelism in light of the (then-)latest biological understandings of the brain, Deleuze famously asserts that "the brain is unity. The brain is the screen" (Deleuze 2000: 366). Deleuze here recognizes how the molecular movement of images on the screen is capable of directly affecting and innervating the viewer's central and peripheral nervous system(s), while effectively tracing new circuits in their brain, and thus modifying their subjectivities. As Patricia Pisters puts it in reference to cinema's ability to stimulate the human body's so-called mirror-neuron system, cinema can here be understood as "a programme that is run on a processor, which is the mind," with the film displaying an ability to "modify our subjectivities such that the brain and mind are one" (Pisters 2012: 31).

In these film-thought models we encounter a cyborgian convergence, or a *modal* ontological individuation of an inhuman technological body (as discussed in the last chapter), together with the molecular soma of a biological nervous system, which registers affections and actions (hence somatechnics). Importantly, the term *soma* is most often deployed nowadays in discourses surrounding neurology and the biology of the brain (which, as mentioned in the introduction, was first investigated through octopus biology), where it is used to describe the anatomical or molecular "body" structure of neurons (see, for example, Dharani 2015; OpenStax 2015). With this in mind, it is sci phi cinema's dermal ability to put our brains into a relation with the unknown, the unthought, the new, and the unfamiliar that sees it as a privileged site/sight for stimulating novel forms of thought in the mind. Our current point of departure can thus be Deleuze's Spinozist understanding of how cinema communicates techno-somatically with the viewer's nervous system:

> "Give me a body then": this is the formula of philosophical reversal. The body is no longer the obstacle that separates thought from itself, that which it has to overcome to reach thinking. It is on the contrary that which it plunges into or must plunge into, in order to reach the unthought, that is life. Not that the body thinks, but, obstinate and stubborn, it forces us to think, and forces us to think what is concealed from thought, life. (Deleuze 2005b: 182)

As mentioned, the body politics of our {Schar-JØ}'s singular-plural performances have themselves become a popular theme in recent film and celebrity studies, with one tendril of these appearing particularly relevant to our larger discussion here, namely the hybridized "animal-cum-machine" vector invoked by many of her science-fiction performances. For example, using Haraway's feminist writings to describe the contradictory creatures that ScarJo performs, Francis notes how the star's queer "cyborgian" performances belong "to no one" and yet often harbor an "equal potential to be used as a force of oppression or disobedience" (Francis 2016). Meanwhile, Fleming draws upon Rosi Braidotti to suggest that the {Schar-JØ} (the set of

ScarJo and CharJos, and perhaps Scarlett Johansson herself and her deepfake clones) exposes an "unholy marriage of *bios* and *zoë* with *technos*" (which respectively are life as qualified or narrated [bio-graphical life], bare life or the life of the cellular organism, and technological life and/or life skills). Finally, Lucy Bolton draws upon Mary Ann Doane and Luce Irigaray to read both the CharJo Charlotte from *Lost in Translation* (Sofia Coppola, USA/Japan, 2003) and ScarJo herself as embodiments of a feminine masquerade, in which sex/gender take on a performative dimension that, we might add, conveys a sense of further, hidden depths of thoughtfulness and thinking, or intelligence (see Bolton 2015: 119–123). In other words, ScarJo's digitally enabled star performances, and in particular the legitimate science-fiction {Schar-JØ}s , are linked to shimmering "deceptive appearances, which are typically employed to conceal a 'true' identity or nature behind a misleading façade or body-form" (see Fleming forthcoming-a).

Now, we potentially are entering dangerous waters when we suggest a link, via Bolton, between feminine masquerade and issues of deception. The aim is not to make any misogynist (Lovecraftian) claims that women are "essentially" deceitful, monstrous, and so on (although we shall return to such themes in our final chapter, where we take up the mythological Medusa as a tentacular monster that helps us to think about the Chthulucene). Indeed, we should make clear that mrdeepfake's {Schar-JØ} porn reinforces the patriarchal oppression of women's bodies even as it exposes the pornographic underside of the star system by disobeying the tendency for patriarchy to keep hidden its treatment of women as sex slaves. That is, mrdeepfake exposes the star system (and capital more generally) as a system of sexual slavery, the very unspoken nature of which is key to its success, as years of "unknown" (that is, unspoken) abuse by the likes of Harvey Weinstein make clear. In this sense, Cthulhu really is a figuration of man's fear of woman.

As this book twists and verts onwards, we shall demonstrate that there are aspects of chthulumedia, including the {Schar-JØ}, that pose a challenge to masculinist, phallic, vertebrate ("boner") systems of thought and action. But we wish for the time being simply to suggest that the often deceitful shapeshifting of the {Schar-JØ}, in terms of both its authorized and unauthorized performances, is readily linked not only to Deleuze and Guattari's notion of becoming-animal, but it more specifically finds parallels in Flusser's *Vampyroteuthis Infernalis*, which morphologically shifts shape and engages in expressive chromatophoric skin performances. For, as if anticipating the issues surrounding deepfake porn, Flusser ultimately concludes that the squid's skin art "is a mode of rape and hatred—of deception, fiction, and lies: it is a delusive affectation, that is to say, it is 'beauty'" (Flusser and Bec 2012: 65). In other words, beauty for Flusser is an attractive deception put in place/performed for the purposes of sex-murder—and in this way the deepfake images of ScarJo enact a reactionary sexual enslavement of Scarlett Johansson that stands in contrast to her seemingly more empowered "authorized" performances.

The alien in *Under the Skin* looms large here, especially because it is essentially a decoy-being that seduces and lures men to their deaths in a dark oceanic abyss. After becoming suspended in this dark liquescent alien afterlife, the human prey are literally digested from within, leaving only a flaccid invertebrate (and thus squid-like) skin bag floating in the abysmal depths, an image that is rendered as a CGI effect. Meanwhile, the Black Widow offers us similar examples of willful deception, not least by wearing a hologrammatic mask to deceive her targets of assassination in *Captain America: The Winter Soldier*, where this CharJo emerges from behind a face-swapping skin-screen/mask that displays an image of what was thought to be another character/actor, namely Councilwoman Hawley (Jenny Agutter). Lucy is likewise able to morph and change form at will, disguising herself as anything or anyone in her environment, while in *Her*, Samantha is a superhuman software being (a soft algorithmic body/mollusk) that only deceptively appears human thanks to ScarJo's embodied voice performance. Furthermore, the Major in *Ghost in the Shell* is a hybrid military cyborg who not only "deep dives" into the software of other beings (plugging into a drone in order to scan its files), but who also finds solace by literally diving beneath the ocean (where she floats alongside jellyfish and other tentacular beings). Finally, this beautiful assassin and murderer wears a shimmering (and in 4DX, synthetic-smelling!) somatechnic hologrammatic skin-suit (referred to in the film as thermoptic camouflage), which allows the Major to cloak, or blend into her background, to evade detection.

These beautiful, murderous deceptions and cyborg beings can be understood as beautiful vampyroteuthic monsters, then, since their exhibitions and displays of light and color primarily serve "to mask the demonic predator's will to power" (Flusser and Bec 2012: 53). But while this might make of ScarJo (or more accurately of Scarlett Johansson when subjected to the technologies of authorized and unauthorized filmmaking) a "demonic predator," these deceptive appearances also prompt us to reflect upon how today's digital cinema more generally uses digital skin renderings to flesh out characters. That is, viewers of digital cinema commonly see CGI skin renderings when they watch (or think that they are watching) pro-filmic human performances. In a reversal of the real-world online deepfake deceptors, it is Johansson's body, rather than her face, that is performatively "fake" in *Ghost in the Shell.* And what this tells us is that Johansson and film stars in the digital age more generally are always already "deepfake"—and the somatechnical dimension of such Photoshop-era modification is made clear through the term *rendering*. For, as Nicole Shukin has explained, rendering is a term also used in the treatment of animals for human ends (for example, rendering fat and the gelatine that was the base of celluloid film; see Shukin 2009: 104; also quoted in McMahon 2015b: 82). The body is both technologized and animalized through rendering, which is the term that digital artists use to describe the generation of digital/digitally modified images. Involving both the body (soma) and technology, the result is somatechnics.

In sum, we repeatedly see the (enslaved and prostituted?) CharJos possessing a machine-cum-squid-like ability to camouflage, to communicate with, and/or to confuse others within (and beyond) the supersaturated oceanic digi-worlds of film and fiction. In rendering this digital skin on screen, the makers of these films forge yet more links to the cephalopod's biomediated abilities to secrete shifting bioluminescent chromatophore pigments on their signaletic epidermal surface. This in turn reveals similarities with ScarJo's digitally realized star body and technologically augmented performances.

Hollywood Soma: On Drone-Clone Violence and the Obliteration of (Asian) Others

We shall end this chapter by considering a third interfacing notion of cephalopod somatechnics, which arrives courtesy of our encounters with ancient Hindu thought and modern Huxleyan science fiction, wherein *soma* draws associations with intoxicants, opiates, and chemical stimulants that activate reactions and/or feelings of pleasure/confusion at the expense of clear perception (rational/critical thinking/reflection). We have already discussed how cephalopods produce weird *mètic* and *deimatic* displays that fall in-between communication (screen-signaling) and camouflage (screen-invisibility), but these vectors can also be stretched to include the (al)chemical abilities of cephalopods to influence the perceptions and behavior of their kin and prey by injecting into the water affective cocktails of "tyrosine, dopamine and DOPA, and enzymes, such as tyrosinases, peroxidases and dopachrome-rearranging enzymes" (Derby 2014: 2710; see also Flusser 2012: 51).[5]

The narcotic somatechnic dimensions and properties of squid ink are relevant to our reading of {Schar-JØ}'s Hollywood work firstly because Big Pharma and chemical-narcotic vectors appear courtesy of the content of her blockbuster films (Lucy is a drug mule; the Major takes drugs to suppress her memories), and secondly because the form of Hollywood cinema itself still presents the dominant and dominating image of global cinema today, having often been described as an imperially imposed "spiritual opium" in places like China (see, for example, Ying Song, quoted in Su 2011: 191). With this in mind, we frame these big-budget Hollywood spectacles as hegemonic somatechnical examples of chthulucinema, which more often than not serve to block, rather than to stimulate, clear or critical thinking about the historical and ideological practices of the American military-entertainment complex that produced them, and which also trade in (and normalize) unethical images of white violence against Asian and other others—even if in a problematically sexy and mindless manner.

If various CharJos are beautifully and deceptively murderous (the alien in *Under the Skin*, the Major in *Ghost in the Shell*, Black Widow), might not the {Schar-JØ}'s Hollywood movies also be thought of as camouflaging or disguising themselves as one thing, while attempting clandestinely to operate, or to move through the world, as another—often while delivering pleasurable opiate-like sensations to the viewer's nervous system (pumped into the air via 4DX's nozzle sprays). In this way, the {Schar-JØ} itself functions as a quasi-posterchild for all of the Hollywood blockbusters produced by the world's largest "military-entertainment complex" (see Elsaesser 2011): they profess to entertain, but they also do violence, rape minds, and bring war.

By taking such a tack we here resonate with a range of works that undertake critical race readings of science-fiction narratives, and by so doing expose troubling parallels and convergences between the history and practices of colonialism—and its racial and racist politics of white supremacy—operating within or beneath the surface of what Darryl A. Smith refers to as the "broader [science-fiction] megatext" (Smith 2007; see also inter alia Dery 1994; Bould 2007; 2014; Lavender III 2007, 2011; Rieder 2008; Ramírez 2008; Reid 2009; De Witt 2010). In order to demonstrate how this is so, let us look at both *Lucy* and *Ghost in the Shell*, which contain protracted action scenes of the {Schar-JØ} doing violence to Asian characters at the same time as these Western productions do an ethico-aesthetic violence to Asian characters and themes at a different level or register. For example, *Ghost in the Shell* is a live-action remake of an earlier anime, *Kôkaku Kidôtai/Ghost in the Shell* (Mamoru Oshii, Japan, 1995), and which famously became embroiled in debates of Hollywood "white-washing" (see, for example, Child 2016; Ahern 2017). Putting to one side debates surrounding adaptation, appropriation, and transculturation (which potentially are complicated by animator Mamoru Oshii deliberately giving more Caucasian characteristics to his anime characters, which is not to mention the style of the earlier graphic novel series), the remake's main conceit is that the Japanese anti-technology terrorist Motoko Kusanagi is killed, and that her brain (or "ghost") is transplanted into the cyborg body of the Major, this film's CharJo. This cyborg "weapons technology" is thereafter encouraged to take a memory-repressing chemical substance (soma) in order to subdue and plicate her recollections of her past (Japanese) life. This includes no longer thinking or speaking in her native Japanese, as the Major speaks in English throughout the film—even if she can still understand Japanese when it is spoken by Aramaki ("Beat" Takeshi), the only Japanese-speaking character. This suppression of memory in the film is linked to the suppression of Japan by the film, with ScarJo, like the Major, thus taking up a complicit role (as a clone/drone) that encourages viewers uncritically to celebrate and/or to perpetuate the spectacle of (US or white) violence (in this case upon Asian others).

While different forms of cephalopod somatechnics are used by the Major to obliterate (with relish) several undesirable Japanese characters from the fictional story, at a meta-fictional level, the Hollywood film's body concomitantly works almost entirely to obliterate all things Japanese from the scene, with *Ghost in the Shell* having been filmed on location in Hong Kong and New Zealand, even though the film is supposed to be set in Japan and even though it trades in generic images of anime-inspired "Japaneseness." (To be precise, the physical features, the architecture, and the geography of Niihama—meaning The New Port City—were in the "original" 1995 anime supposed to recall Hong Kong, and thus to evoke a future Japan. Nonetheless, the American remake is complicit in and accelerates this erasure of Japan; see Brown and Fleming [2019].) Meanwhile in *Lucy*, we similarly find the {Schar-JØ} taking revenge on a series of Asian bodies, albeit this time Korean gangsters who used her as a fleshy transportation device for a narcotic commodity.

If the {Schar-JØ} becomes uncritically complicit as a deimatic screening device for her violent military-corporate masters in and beyond these films, this is not necessarily the case for *Under the Skin*, which is an independent European film, and where the CharJo's seductively violent nature appears perfectly befitting of an alien killer-consumer (Hollywood star and commodity image) masquerading as a human. Put differently, *Under the Skin* attunes us to seeing/thinking the danger lurking beneath/under the skin of the seductive and desirable image-surface, or the façade of a {Schar-JØ} body-rendering. On this level, *Under the Skin* appears to assert that ScarJo is in and of herself a dangerous and seductive alien, in that there is always already a sinister alien war machine lurking beneath or behind her hegemonic Hollywood "action babe" rendering (see, for example, O'Day 2004). That this sinister alien is figured as black points perhaps to how blackness is rendered other and inhuman (to render is to other; to render is to render inhuman), and this alien otherness can most pointedly be seen in how the {Schar-JØ} often appears stripped of all maternal and human instincts, with the scene on the waterfront in *Under the Skin* arguably offering the most visceral example, as ScarJo's non-maternal and inhuman monster manifestly disregards the desperate cries of a stranded baby on the beach, ultimately leaving the infant for dead as the sun sets. Without maternal instincts or feminine sexuality, her character also appears stripped of both a womb and vagina—much like the Major in *Ghost in the Shell*. Even though clad in a tight leather uniform (i.e., sexy), the technologically enhanced Natasha Romanoff likewise appears more killer than nurturer, as her professional name, the Black Widow, suggests.

In this way, the tentacular {Schar-JØ} helps us to image, if not to imagine, the somatechnical convergence of the human and the squid through digital media. This being is not necessarily a squid–human hybrid in the same sense that the Brundle-Fly is a fly-human. Indeed, as Flusser makes overt, the result of a reciprocal indoctrination between the worlds of the human and the cephalopod does not necessarily always present us with "a spherical being with eight arms and two faces—as Plato proposed—but rather a self-mutilating hybrid, a cybernetic Nazism" (Flusser and Bec 2012: 71). It is in this sense that we must be wary—not of Scarlett Johansson, nor necessarily of the {Schar-JØ} and its likes, which is to say the hybrid entities that emerge from the conjunction of humans and filmmaking technology. For these beautiful and seductive entities are the shape-shifting posterchildren of chthulucinema—and it is chthulucinema, or the *Kinoteuthis Infernalis* itself, of which we should be wary. For this creature, which might also go by the name of white patriarchal capital, will perhaps bring about the end of humanity, not least if it meets white patriarchy's hatred of otherness (the reduction of women, other races, animals, and technology alike to the status of slaves) with its own murderous hatred, even as the end of white patriarchy and a world defined by hard lines and hatred must itself be brought to an end and replaced by a multiverse of kinship and love. For if in these largely white and patriarchal movies the {Schar-JØ} lacks maternal instincts and love (it is a hated and/or hateful other, the product of a racist and misogynist Lovecraftian worldview), this does not mean that there is not a whole erotic dimension to our relationship with the *Kinoteuthis Infernalis* and with chthulumedia more generally. And it is to this erotic appeal that we shall turn in the next chapter.

Notes

1. Deepfake has also increasingly been used to generate alternative versions of existing films and trailers, such as layering Harrison Ford's face and facial performances over Alden Ehrenreich as the lead character in *Solo: A Star Wars Story* (see Gartenberg 2018). In an echo of the famous scene from *Being John Malkovich* (Spike Jonze, USA, 1999), where the eponymous actor passes through a portal into his own brain, the face of Nicolas Cage has also been used to replace the entire cast of *The Lord of the Rings: Fellowship of the Ring* (Peter Jackson, New Zealand/USA, 2001; see Price 2018).
2. As a concept, the set displays certain overlaps with another paradigmatic tool of our digital times: the database, which is a *dispositif* that has increasingly become the "centre of the creative process in the digital age" (Manovich 2001: 277). The Internet Movie Database looms large when we think of actors and their personae today, with Johansson's IMDb profile granting us immediate access to all the different characters and narratives that the actor has played in her career, thereby helping us to delimit a Johansson "hypernarrative" or set.
3. The reflexive moments when science-fiction CharJos look back at ScarJo as a living commodity somewhat confirm a condition of slavery, with the Major seeking out the company of precisely a prostitute (Adwoa Aboah) moments after attempting to look into the face of her own hollow/hologrammatic projection in *Ghost in the Shell*. Both moments would seem to constitute attempts by the Major to know herself, which process means understanding herself as simultaneously military-industrial slave and a sexy "mulatto cyborg" whore—in another foreshadowing of deepfake Johansson performances.

   Using a critical-race reading of the cyborg figure, Nishime understands much cyborg science fiction to be playing with and working through racial themes of "miscegenation" and "passing" in a manner that continues and reworks interracial melodramas and narratives of the twentieth century (see Nishime 2016). In this light, it is interesting to note that the Major in *Ghost in the Shell* is essentially a Japanese character (or brain) that has been placed inside an ethnically white cyborg shell. The Major's encounter with the prostitute, played by Ghanaian-British model Adwoa Aboah, seems further to acknowledge such themes, casting new racial meanings on the question that she asks: "What are you?" Of course, there is a similarly raced and problematic moment when the CharJo from *Under the Skin* is revealed to be a black body inside the ScarJo persona.
4. As a celebrity influencer, Johansson's body ink is often celebrated as part of her edgy and unique star image (see Body Art Guru n.d.).
5. Charles D. Derby suggests that in lab conditions squids have been observed using amino acids mixed with other secretions to provide the animals with toxic chemical defenses, granting their ink "phagomimetic properties" that

account for increases in "misdirected attacks," "startle behaviour," and the "abandonment of attacks" (Derby 2014: 2712–2713). With regard to their seaworld conspecifics, the function of expelled DOPA or dopamine in cephalopod ink is also believed to evoke jetting or flight responses (Derby 2014: 2714–2715). On a related note, squid ink is utilized as a psychedelic vision-inducing drug in China Miéville's *Kraken*.

CHAPTER 5

The Erotic Ecstasy of Cthulhu

LIKE *MAELSTRÖM*, *ARRIVAL* hinges on an encounter between cephalopod-like creatures (referred to in the film as heptapods) and a woman (here, linguist Louise Banks) who is wondering whether or not to have a child—although in *Arrival* Louise ends up having her baby, while Bibi has an abortion at the opening of *Maelström*. In other words, it seems clear that Villeneuve, like Park Chan-wook, is a director attracted to cephalo-stories (and motherhood)—with Guillermo del Toro perhaps emerging as a third cephal-*auteur* (and for more on del Toro's links with Lovecraft, see Janicker 2014 and Wetmore Jr. 2015). We shall revert later to the possibility that the stories of these films might simply take place in the heads of their main protagonists (as mentioned in relation to *Maelström*, the Greek *κεφαλή*, from which the first half of the word cephalopod derives, means head), meaning that the stories are as much the product of those protagonists' minds as they are of their embodied existence in the worlds that the films depict (as our reality is itself the product of our minds as much as it is the product of our embodied existence on Earth—if we can tell our mental and our physical experiences apart). Furthermore, we shall also revert later to *Arrival* to discuss in more detail its chthulucenic take on space and time. But for the time being, though, we should like to concentrate on the link between cephalopods and sex—implied in both *Arrival* and *Maelström* via the thematic link between octopuses and reproduction.

Most cephalopods have relatively short lifespans and only reproduce once (although they may mate several times; exceptionally, the *Vampyroteuthis Infernalis* has multiple reproductive cycles; see Hoving *et al.* 2015). In relation to octopuses, reproduction therefore tends to happen toward the end of the female life cycle, with the final months of the female's life taken up by tending her fertilized eggs (which can be up to 100,000 in number; see Montgomery 2015: 95). These eggs then drift in the sea amid plankton, before hatching. Clearly a minority of the fertilized eggs survive into life—otherwise our oceans would be teeming with octopuses. Indeed, without the protective shell that other species of mollusk enjoy, the life of an octopus seems precarious from start to finish.

Edo Porn?

While in reality semelparous (i.e., they mate only once), octopuses nonetheless are strongly sexualized in human culture. This is most famously rendered in Katsushika Hokusai's *Tako to ama/Octopuses and Shell Diver*, which is often referred to as *The Dream of the Fisherman's Wife*, and which appeared in Hokusai's album *Kinoe no komatsu/Young Pines* in 1814. This *ukiyo-e*, or woodblock print, which also belongs to the *shunga* or erotic artistic tradition, depicts a woman with a giant octopus performing cunnilingus on her, as a smaller octopus (which in the accompanying text on the print refers to the larger octopus as its relative) supports her neck, fondles her breasts, and inserts its beak into her mouth. The text explicitly refers to the sexual ecstasy that the woman experiences as both octopuses vaunt their sexual prowess, with the larger octopus promising to take the woman to the Dragon King once he is done with her.

This reference to the Dragon King places the story clearly within the tradition of the *Taishokan*, a Japanese myth in which Ryūjin, the dragon god, steals a precious jewel as it is in transit between China and Japan, where it will be presented as a gift to Fujiwara no Kamatari, whose daughter, Kōhaku, has married the Chinese emperor Taizong. In order to retrieve the jewel, Kamatari (although different versions claim that it was one of his sons or grandsons) travels to Fusazaki in Shido-no-ura Bay in Sanuki Province and marries an *ama*, a shell-diving woman called Tamatori. As Kamatari distracts the Dragon King with a song and dance show at surface level, Tamatori dives down into his realm and retrieves the jewel. Pursued by various sea monsters, including octopuses, Tamatori cuts open her breast and hides the jewel within her so as to free up her arm to swim better. Tamatori is killed as she reaches the surface, but Kamatari retrieves the jewel from her corpse and returns to his position of power. Hokusai clearly is playing fast and loose with this myth, parodying it perhaps because *tako*, which is the Japanese for octopus, and *awabi*, which are jewels that the diving *ama* would retrieve from the sea, are both synonyms for vagina and thus equally function as sexual symbols (for more on this, see Bru 2009: 55–58).

Kaneto Shindô's *Hokusai Manga/Edo Porn* follows the story of Hokusai's life and the creation of *The Dream of the Fisherman's Wife*, while also displacing and charting Japan's contemporaneous political inwardness and cultural conservatism during a period of stable economic growth and global development (projecting back into the Edo period, which is generally considered to have lasted between 1603 and 1868, with Hokusai dying in 1849, just four years before Commodore Matthew C. Perry arrived like an alien in Japan to demand that it open up to foreign trade). The film opens with widowed artist Tetsuzo (Ken Ogata)—who later takes on the name Katsushika Hokusai—and his daughter Ōei (Yûko Tanaka) eking out a meager living above a friend's *geta* (wooden footwear) workshop, to whom they go into increasing financial debt. The film then follows the long life of the struggling artist as he gradually earns his master status (including through the production of his famous *Kanagawa-oki nami ura/The Great Wave off Kanagawa*, from around 1830, to which we shall revert in the next chapter), using his intense love of the enigmatic prostitute Ōnao (Kanako Higuchi) as a key focal point. Ōnao is a mysterious, cold, and sadistic woman, who in the tradition of Japanese ghost stories and folk tales may be coded as a spirit or otherworldly being. She certainly enchants and tortures men, including Hokusai's father-in-law, Nakajima (Furankî Sakai), the Shogunate mirror-maker who eventually commits suicide on account of his obsession with her.

Hokusai also becomes unhealthily obsessed with Ōnao, who inspires his early success as a *shunga* artist. What is more, she tellingly becomes emblematic of time out of joint. Indeed, with shades of *Vertigo* (Alfred Hitchcock, USA, 1958), a film to which we shall also revert later on, Ōei discovers Ōnao's eerie doppelgänger (also played by Kanako Higuchi), whom she brings to her father, now 89 years of age, to try to reignite his artistic passions. After dressing the girl as Ōnao was in the past, the film's key scene thereafter dramatizes the creation of Hokusai's most (in)famous woodblock print. As Hokusai and Ōei stage the now well-known bestial threesome using real octopuses, the artistic set-up serves to catapult the film into a dark fantasy realm, where moving octopus puppets perform tentacular oral sex and penetration upon the *ama*/Ōnao's body within a black featureless space. In other words, the film anachronistically flips us from the realms of the real to fantasy, from the actual to the virtual, and from creatures to cryptids (see Figure 5.1).

In its blurring of fantasy and earthly erotics, meanwhile, *The Dream of the Fisherman's Wife* has achieved something of a cult following, and has clearly influenced many European artists, including Félicien Rops (see *La pieuvre/The Octopus* from 1882) and Pablo Picasso (*Mujer y pulpo/Woman and Octopus* from 1903)—as we mentioned in the introduction. Ricard Bru also points to how the Hokusai print influenced, for example, Victor Hugo's *Travailleurs de la mer/Toilers of the Sea* (1866), in which

Figure 5.1 A recreation of *The Dream of the Fisherman's Wife* in *Hokusai Manga*

the "Devil-Fish" that is the nemesis of main protagonist Gilliatt is clearly supposed to be an octopus, even if that term is never used (see also Bru 2009: 59–63).[1] The idea of women smuggling jewels recalls the plot of *Octopussy*, while in the Hokusai print, and in *Hokusai Manga*'s reanimation thereof, the shell-diver moans out about the ecstasy that she experiences as a result of the suckers that line the octopuses' arms and which suck on her skin. Indeed, Hugo describes how the victim of the devil-fish is "oppressed by a vacuum drawing at numberless points: it is not a clawing or a biting, but an indescribable scarification" (Hugo 2010: 294). In this way, the octopus's tentacles signal both love and death (Bru 2009: 59).[2]

That love and death are linked is of course made clear by the French term for orgasm, *petite mort*, which literally means little death, with Joris-Karl Huysmans describing the woman in *The Dream of the Fisherman's Wife* as being "as though in death" (quoted in Schweid 2013: 129). But the sexual encounter between human and octopus might also be understood as *weird*, as per Harman's analysis of Lovecraft, with the Japanese *manga* genre of *hentai*, which has also been heavily influenced by Hokusai's woodblock, deriving its name from the kanji 変/*hen*, meaning change or weird, and 態/*tai*, meaning appearance or condition, with *hentai* as a whole commonly being translated as *perversion*. Nakajima *et al.* note that strict censorship banned the representation of genitalia in 1980s Japan, meaning that Toshio Maeda's *Urotsukidoji* (1987) was the first to use "tentacles to replace both male genitalia and bondage expression," with the two-volume *manga* thereafter expanding into "15 video series, two featured movies, video games, and special feature books." Since the release of the original series, *shokushu* (meaning tentacle) has become "one of the dominant genres in Japanese pornographic and non-pornographic anime alike" (see Nakajima *et al.* 2018: 8–9). The hardcore *urotsukidoji* trope is thus paradigmatically described today in terms of "an incomprehensible phantasmagoria punctuated by teen girls suffering rapes in all available orifices from the tentacle-penises of demons" (Powell Dahlquist and Vigilant 2004: 93). If demons with tentacle-penises in some senses recall Lovecraft's Cthulhu, then perhaps their weirdness becomes less "incomprehensible."

More than this, though, we might imagine that the perversion is even less weird when we think about the sensual aspects of the encounter. Let us start with the suckers on the shell-diver's skin. For humans to suck, they must use their mouths, with sucking being a common action in human sexual practices, from the colloquialized practices of sucking cock and sucking face to the more generalized practice of leaving bruises (or "love bites") on one's partner by sucking on various parts of their skin. In this latter practice, we also get a sense of the porous distinction between pleasure and pain. Since a single sucking mouth can yield such pleasure, imagine what sensations one might experience when sucked upon simultaneously by the *c.*1,600 suckers of an octopus. Indeed, as Alfred Tennyson describes these suckers as "[u]nnumbered and enormous polypi" (see Montgomery 2015: 6), so might we make a pun and say that the touch of an octopus is like the kiss of many/poly lips. What is more, the ability of octopuses to taste through their suckers, which are positioned upon their muscular hydrostat arms, also suggests that the tentacle is something of a tongue, which delivers forth yet more probing pleasure. This is not to mention the fact that three of an octopus's tentacles are also penises or clitorises depending on the specific creature's sex. As per Irigaray, whom we quoted in our beaky prepostface, rapture verily does await those who trust the sea.

In her analysis of octopuses, Sy Montgomery at one point explains to a friend, Jody, that octopuses are covered in slime. Jody finds this repulsive, while Montgomery explains the use of slime: it keeps octopuses moist when they leave water, while also ensuring their ability to slip and to squeeze through small spaces. "Slime doesn't wreck anything," Montgomery continues to Jody. "'After all . . . slime is part of the two greatest pleasurable experiences known to humankind.' // She thought for a moment. // 'What's the other one?' she asked. // 'Eating,' I replied" (Montgomery 2015: 76). Montgomery clearly is referring to sex as she reports this exchange. As the octopus encounter might involve a thousand simultaneous kisses and eight licking tongues, so might we understand that the creature's whole body carries the "sliminess" that provokes such pleasure during sex.

We shall revert imminently to the idea that the octopus's entire body might be understood as a sensuous if not an outright sexual organ, in spite of the creature's limited reproductive abilities and the fact that octopuses seemingly do not, unlike humans, have sex for fun. But first, we shall analyze how *The Handmaiden* and to a greater extent *The Untamed* explore the link between octopuses and sex and the possibility that the encounter with numerous slimy tentacles might indeed involve sexual ecstasy that merges pleasure and pain, and sex and death, as the human ecstatically passes from the anthropocene to the chthulucene.

From *The Handmaiden to Oldboy*

Park Chan-wook's *The Handmaiden* and Amat Escalante's *The Untamed* are not the only films that link octopuses with sex, in particular emphasizing the queer dimensions of cephalopod-inspired desire. Jean Painlevé, the surrealist pioneer of underwater documentary filmmaking, returned repeatedly to octopuses, linking them first with death (where we see an octopus crawl past a skull in *The Octopus*) and then with sex in *Love Life of the Octopus*. Notably, Painlevé's film compares octopuses' mating rituals to hunting, a concept to which we shall revert in the final chapter, while also featuring a remarkable sequence (also discussed in the introduction) in which we see an octopus embryo grow at a speed 1,400 times faster than real time, and in which we see the embryo come to be a miniature octopus as a result of rotations in and of the egg. As the smallest quantities of matter, quarks, are defined by their spin (see Greene 2000: 9, 172), so does it seem that the octopus is a creature that comes into existence through spin, as if it arrived in our world by spinning in via a wormhole from a different dimension, much like the tentacular Lovecraftian beasts that emerge from portals to other dimensions in the depths of the ocean in *Pacific Rim*. We might also note Céline Sciamma's *Water Lilies*, which as mentioned is a mistranslation of the film's original title, *Naissance des pieuvres* ("birth of the octopuses"). A tale about teenage girls taking part in a synchronized swimming team, and thus also a film that links water with different temporalities/synchronies, the film is also a coming out film about Marie (Pauline Acquart) and Anne (Louise Blachère), the former of whom has a crush on Floriane (Adèle Haenel), the coolest kid on the team, but whom various people consider to be a slut. In exploring nascent sexuality, the "octopuses" that are born are thus clearly sexual beings, whose sexuality is notably not wholly straight.

But while various films make clear the link between octopuses and sex, and while *Hokusai Manga* is notable not just for the explicit scenes that are staged by Hokusai in order to create his masterpiece, but also for its nonlinear treatment of time (about which, more later), perhaps no films are as explicit in linking octopuses with sex as *The Handmaiden* and *The Untamed*.[3] Indeed, the former makes clear its debt to Hokusai when Park names one of the main characters Count Fujiwara (Ha Jung-woo)—invoking the character of Fujiwara no Kamatari from the *Taishokan*. Indeed, while the film is nominally based upon Sarah Waters' 2002 novel, *Fingersmith*, it is also in some senses a retelling of the *Taishokan*. We can see how this is so in various ways. Firstly, in Park's film Fujiwara, a conman posing as a count, engages the light-fingered Sook-hee (Kim Tae-ri) to infiltrate the household of Lady Hideko (Kim Min-hee) and her controlling uncle Kouzuki (Jo Jin-woong) in order that he might marry Hideko and then make off with her riches. Fujiwara's engagement of Sook-hee, then, echoes Kamatari's engagement of Tamatori in the Japanese myth in order to send her into the "underworld" to retrieve the lost jewels stolen by the Dragon King. This parallel is furthered when Sook-hee changes her name to Tamako when in disguise in Lady Hideko's household: Tamako clearly is homophonous with Tamatori, with both names featuring the word *tama* (珠), meaning a gem or a jewel in Japanese. What is more, Kouzuki controls Hideko by continuously telling her to "remember the basement"—a space that we eventually discover to be Kouzuki's vast library, in which he keeps esoteric and occult texts, including ones that reveal the secrets of carnal bliss. Notably, it is also in his basement library that Kouzuki keeps a giant octopus in a tank, evoking further the maritime elements of the *Taishokan*, while also linking Kouzuki in some senses with the Dragon King, whom we see represented as surrounded by octopuses in Utagawa Kuniyoshi's famous woodblock painting, *Tamatori Chased by a Dragon* (1853, the year of Commodore Perry's arrival).

Now, nothing is as it appears in Park's film (or in Waters' novel), as Fujiwara has in fact set Sook-hee up by getting her to become Hideko's handmaiden. Having fallen in love with Hideko, Fujiwara and she plan to get married and then for Hideko to feign insanity, which will lead to her being committed to a mental asylum. Instead of Hideko being sectioned, though, she and Fujiwara have Sook-hee placed in the asylum, leaving them free to escape the controlling arms of Kouzuki, who for years has been forcing Hideko (and her mother before her) to read the erotic texts in his library to aristocratic guests at their vast mansion. Kouzuki, as the octopus-linked Dragon King, is also a tyrant who has had sexually abusive relationships with both Hideko and her mother, thereby suggesting an erotic link between the octopus and sex, as per Hokusai's *Dream of the Fisherman's Wife*.

However, the story does not end there. For, unforeseen to all is the fact that Hideko and Sook-hee fall in love with each other, especially as the latter prepares the former for marriage with Fujiwara via an erotic relationship of their own. Having been committed in Hideko's place, Sook-hee uses her light fingers in order to escape from the asylum, and she joins Hideko at her honeymoon hotel, where the newly wed poisons Fujiwara, allowing them to escape together to China. In searching for his niece, Kouzuki finds Fujiwara and takes him to his basement, where under pain of torture he makes him recount his sexual relationship with Hideko. Fujiwara lies—for he has not in fact slept with Hideko (a lie that finds a parallel in *Naissance des pieuvres*, where Floriane also lies about having sex with a young boy, François, played by Warren Jacquin). What is more, Fujiwara also gets his captor to light the mercury-laced cigarettes that he keeps on his person. Both Kouzuki and Fujiwara die, then, with Sook-hee and Hideko making love on their ferry to Shanghai.

If Sook-hee as Tamako reminds us of Tamatori, the shell-diver who retrieves the jewels for Fujiwara, then it would seem that the jewel that she finally rescues from the Dragon King/Kouzuki is Hideko herself. This potentially gives to the myth various novel edges, in that Sook-hee is a poor Korean woman who rescues a Japanese aristocrat from her sexually corrupt world. Given that *The Handmaiden* is set during the Japanese occupation of Korea during the 1930s, the film itself might involve a Korean filmmaker purloining/"rescuing" a Japanese myth—under the cover of being an adaptation/wearing the camouflage of a British novel—which in turn allows the film to thumb its nose at the historical domination of Korea by Japan. It is not that these readings are definitive, and we have no wish to overstate them. But they seem to be suggested by the various elements that we have outlined above (the names Fujiwara and Tamako, the presence of the octopus, the fact that Japan looms so large in this Korean film).

Furthermore, it seems clear that director Park has an interest in octopuses, since *Oldboy* also features lead character Oh Dae-su (Choi Min-sik) eating a live octopus in a sushi restaurant after escaping from being held in captivity for fifteen years. "I want to eat something alive," he declares to sushi chef Mi-do (Kang Hye-jeong), before being served the creature, from which his teeth tear the head as the octopus's tentacles continue to writhe and cling to his hands and face. While *san-nakji* is a traditional Korean dish in which octopus is eaten raw after being chopped up (although the arms can still move around), typically the creature is not eaten whole. Oh

Dae-su's devouring of the octopus, then, would seem to suggest more than simply culinary habits that are strange to Western eyes. Not only does it suggest Oh Dae-su's animality, but the octopus also would suggest in some ways the interconnection of all things ("pulp fiction") as *Oldboy*'s plot weaves together the fates of Oh Dae-su, Lee Woo-jin (Yoo Ji-tae), an old classmate bent on revenge for the bullying that he and his sister endured while at school, and Mi-do, with whom Oh Dae-su begins a relationship and yet who turns out to be his own daughter. Indeed, Lee so precisely manipulates Oh into his relationship with Mi-do that it would appear as if all moments in time, too, were interconnected such that we cannot escape our fate—much like the myth of Oedipus with which *Oldboy* bears some resemblance and with whose name the film's title loosely rhymes when spoken by a Korean (Oh notably removes not his eyes at the film's end, however, but his tongue-tentacle). Rather than avoid our fate, we can instead learn from it.

Not only does the octopus become associated with incest and sexual depravity in both *Oldboy* and *The Handmaiden*, as Oh Dae-su sleeps with Mi-do and as Kouzuki abuses and is obsessed to learn about sex with Hideko from Fujiwara, but the films also are both ambivalent about the meaning of this. Of course, Kouzuki gets his comeuppance and dies and Oh Dae-su is so horrified at his actions after Mi-do is revealed as his daughter that he does indeed cut out his tongue. Nonetheless, the notorious octopus-eating scene from the latter film is not as gruesome to Mi-do as it is to many viewers, with the sushi chef looking on with a curious smile on her face, announcing that she must be "a different breed of woman" since her hands are cold—at which point she places her hand on Oh Dae-su's, as the latter still has an octopus arm protruding from his mouth ("why is she doing this?" we hear him whisper in voice-over). That is, she would seem somehow even to be turned on by Oh Dae-su's actions. Meanwhile, if Kouzuki is evil, *The Handmaiden* does also endorse (and perhaps too voyeuristically makes a spectacle of) the cross-national and cross-class lesbian relationship between Sook-hee and Hideko. In other words, while the octopus is linked to animality and to a sense of "complex" and nonlinear storytelling in both films, where the fates of various characters are proven to be not separate but closely interlinked, there is also a link between the octopus and sexual desire in Park's films, a desire that does not respect the typical barriers of family, gender, or sex, but which instead demonstrates how desire is, like the cephalopod as we are theorizing it here, ignorant of boundaries, existing on a plane beyond the typical sexual mores/moralities, and freely flowing and connecting with whatever it comes into contact with—a sense affirmed by *Naissance des pieuvres*, *Hokusai Manga*, and *The Untamed*, to which we shall turn our attention presently.

In the Wild Region

If the perceived "weirdness" of Park's films is in part symbolized by the octopuses that feature in their *mises-en-scène*, a weirdness that includes perceived sexual "perversion," then Amat Escalante's film takes matters further by not just using tentacles symbolically, but rather literally as practically every character within the film embarks on a specifically sexual relationship with a tentacled beast from outer space, which bears some close resemblance to a cephalopod. If Park only alludes to (dreams of?) Hokusai's *Dream of the Fisherman's Wife*, Escalante goes further and reproduces it—while at the same time offering up his version of Lovecraft's "Color Out of Space" (1927), in which monstrous life forms are also linked to meteoroid impacts.

Escalante's fourth feature film tells the story of Verónica (Simone Bucio), who one day emerges from the countryside with what appears to be a dog bite on her side and who is treated in hospital by Fabián (Eden Villavicencio), a nurse with whom she strikes up a friendship. Fabián's sister, Alejandra, or Ale for short (Ruth Ramos), is in a problematic relationship with her husband, Ángel (Jesús Maza), who is something of a machista archetype—even though he is also having an affair with Fabián, who is openly gay. Verónica takes Fabián to the countryside and instructs him to follow a path until he reaches a cabin, where resides a couple, Iván and Marta Vega (Oscar Escalante and Bernarda Trueba), who are looking after and observing the behavior of . . . a tentacled alien that has arrived on Earth via a meteor impact. First Verónica, then Fabián, and then Ale and then Ángel—all embark upon sexual encounters with the monster, with each experiencing such ecstasy with the alien that they cannot but return for more encounters, while also adjusting their sexual behavior outwith their liaisons in the Vegas' cabin.

However, as per Verónica's injury at the opening, the alien can and does hurt those with whom it interacts, even if that is not understood to be its intention (Ale explains at one point, owing to the intensity of her relationship with the creature, that it "only gives pleasure" and that it can "never hurt anyone"). Indeed, Ángel's relationship with the alien seems eventually to cost him his life—although exactly how is unclear as Escalante's narration is often opaque, with the creature itself often relegated to the shadows or heard off screen, and Ángel simply being discovered naked in a ditch not far from the Vegas' cabin. There is, however, one graphic encounter between the alien and Ale, which seemingly caresses her body and penetrates her various orifices with its manifold, slimy-seeming (but not suckered) tentacles. Thus, where Park only does so thematically, Escalante visually recalls Hokusai's woodblock of the *ama* and the octopuses.

To view characters in pursuit of sexual ecstasy can make for uncomfortable viewing in prurient societies. Sexual desire is regularly something that is occulted—perhaps because it demonstrates too great a physical and "base" existence, rather than helping to sustain the belief that humans have "risen above"—or at least can rise above—corporeal drives. In this way, the repression of sexual desire is the creation of a boundary that is supposed to demonstrate the separation of humans from "mere" animals, since through consciousness they can control and tame such basic instincts. Those who liberate their sexual desire are conversely untamed, with *The Untamed* being precisely the English translation of Escalante's film title.

Typically, humans close off their bodies from the world, as they also try to close off their bodies from their minds. That is, humans typically are invited to keep their mouths shut and to suppress from sight all leaks that might take place. The person who spits as they speak is considered unpleasant, while sweat is rendered invisible and incontinence is the target for many a joke across the globe. Humans are highly porous (we are wholly holy), with between five and seven holes (two ears, two nostrils, a mouth and perhaps two eyes) on their heads, an anus, a meatus for males, a vagina and a urethra for females, and countless pores through which grow hairs and/or sweat is secreted. And yet, this porosity is hidden in favor of a consistent and perceived "solid" existence that neither leaks nor is penetrated.

When it comes to sex, however, things change. The body opens up as we secrete fluids of all kinds—from sweat to semen to saliva, and from vagina lubrication to pre-ejaculate. Sex thus involves numerous fluids that render the experience pleasantly slimy—as Montgomery suggests above. As an expression of desire, sex is also open in the sense of involving penetration: lips and tongues penetrate various orifices, while of course the male penis also often penetrates the orifices of a sexual partner. What was inside the body now comes out, as bodies intermingle and interpenetrate, such that sex involves a blurring of the distinction between self and other, an impression that can also take place as a result of eye contact. Sex, therefore, can involve a transition from a static and closed-off self to an ecstatic and open blurring of the boundary between self and other. In some senses, the sexual encounter involves violence—although we must make clear that this is of a different order to the willed violence that takes place during sexual abuse and/or instances of rape (even if simulations of such situations can also be pleasurable for some people). For, as the static self becomes an ecstatic blurring of self and other—as the self in effect dissolves—so can we understand this process as being a violent one: I as such "die" temporarily (or experience a "little death"), or at least am penetrated and penetrate as I combine with another. Furthermore, it is through physical contact that we come to experience pleasure. Rubbing, licking, biting, slapping, gripping, twisting: there is a violence involved in much sex that clearly is closely linked to pleasure. And yet, if sex involves an opening up of the self, such that the very perceived existence of the self is challenged, then this runs counter to the notion of the self as closed and autonomous. It is small wonder, then, that in capitalist societies where the idea of the self is upheld as almost sacrosanct, sex is so markedly repressed. Openness is countered by all manner of closures—and the sliminess of mutual pleasure is replaced by the dryness of rape, which becomes the logical sexual expression of the patriarchal drive for personal sovereignty and separation, with slime thus functioning as a marker of connection between two bodies, as a marker of life, and as a marker of love. As Ben Woodard puts it in his study of slime (which curiously he insists on finding disgusting), sexual procreation is "an obvious example of the disgusting yet generative articulation of slime-as-life and life-as-slime" (Woodard 2012: 1).

We wish to develop two separate but linked strands of thought here. The first relates to sex and the human body, while the second relates to the drive toward ecstasy—and ultimately toward death—in the chthulucene. With regard to the former, let us revert to the cephalopod. Sex is a theme that runs throughout Flusser and Bec's *Vampyroteuthis Infernalis*, with orgasm in particular being related to release from fixed identity. For Flusser, drawing upon Wilhelm Reich, "[o]rganisms are accumulations of suppressed drives, and psychology is the analysis of organisms" (Flusser and Bec 2012: 27). Like the layers of bark that wrap themselves around a tree's trunk, so, too, does an organism accumulate layers that in turn suppress/ossify it—even as they nominally protect it. Beyond Flusser, we might think simply of cell walls and other layers of "protection" that in fact contain (i.e., delimit) life in even the most "simple" of forms. And as the multiplication of the cell must involve a breach in its wall, so might all sexual reproduction (and sensuous contact) involve the breaching of an otherwise closed system. In Flusser's language, what in humans is "known as 'personality' is . . . a matter of muscle cramping and individual posture" (Flusser and Bec 2012: 28): we surround ourselves by "character armor" in order to protect ourselves, and in the process we suppress our potential for all manner of different becomings. As Flusser puts it:

> [a]n organism, then, is . . . a bomb, laden with potential energy, in which the sum of pressures, accumulated over the course of one life and over the course of the entire development of life, has been stored. An organism is a ball of bioenergetic force that explodes when the cramp—which is life itself—is released. Reich refers to this explosion as "orgasm" and the energy in question as "orgone." (Flusser and Bec 2012: 28)

The repression and closure of the body leads to rigidification, militancy, and eventually to death ("rigor mortis"), while the loosening and opening of the body "leads to love and selflessness—to orgasm" (Flusser and Bec 2012: 28).

Let us think now of the octopus and the squid, two creatures that are mollusks, and yet which, unlike many mollusks—from the snail to the oyster that Tamatori dived for—do not have shells. That is, the octopus and the squid have both managed to avoid much of the "armor" and the "cramp" that characterizes most other life forms, and which can be seen in their fellow mollusks in the form of the shell that each creature must carry around with it. (In "overcoming" its genetic history in this way, perhaps it comes as no surprise that the octopus and the squid can—much to the surprise of many a biologist—"edit" their RNA to reprogram their DNA, about which, more later; see Liscovitch-Brauer *et al.* 2017). Boneless (invertebrate), the squid and the octopus can be understood, then, as experiencing near-constant orgasm according to the terms laid out by Flusser after Reich. As Flusser himself suggests: "[t]he world arouses the *Vampyroteuthis* sexually: It conceives the world with its penis or clitoris, and its conceptions—unlike our sexually neutral and existentially bland conceptions—induce it toward orgasm" (Flusser and Bec 2012: 41). Where the human (per)happens upon the world, the world (per)happens upon the *Vampyroteuthis*, which, like the octopuses analyzed earlier, can smell, see, and even digest with its arms/tentacles, while Flusser also suggests that "the sexual organs are [also] partially located on its tentacles and, like its eyes, they are directly connected to its brain" (see Flusser and Bec 2012: 39–40). Where we consider ourselves separate from the world, then, the *Vampyroteuthis* only senses entanglement as it "receives optic, tactile, and sexual impressions as already coordinated (processed) and unified bits of information" (Flusser and Bec 2012: 40). Where the human self/other binarism reflects numerous other contradictions that we encounter—such as those between true and false, good and evil, and body and wave—the *Vampyroteuthis* can negotiate these contradictions "only by means of coitus" (from the Latin, *co-itus*, meaning to go with; where we fight against it, the cephalopod "goes with" the flow). "The resolution of contradictions is its orgasm . . . In short, vampyroteuthic theory is not contemplative [i.e., observation from a perceived distance] but orgasmic—not philosophical tranquility but philosophical frenzy" (Flusser and Bec 2012: 42).

Since the *Vampyroteuthis* in effect thinks through orgasm, sex and sensuality are at the center of its existence—even if other cephalopods mate but once. Perhaps contrary to Flusser, it would seem that the orgasmic existence of the *Vampyroteuthis*—and by extension also the octopus—does not come at the expense of personality, since Montgomery attests to the individuality of the octopuses that she encounters. Nonetheless, it is small wonder that such a body-driven creature would come to be associated with the demonic: the *Vampyroteuthis* is a "passionate 'devil'" in the sense that it experiences the world rather than considering it a container for activity as the human does (Flusser and Bec 2012: 41). That is, the *Vampyroteuthis* cannot conceive of a divine beyond the surface that the humans inhabit—with humans conceiving of the divine precisely because they only inhabit the surface. Rather, the *Vampyroteuthis* only understands a corporeal here and now of the depths. The personalities of the creatures only make them more uncanny: the *Vampyroteuthis* is both analogous/similar to the human (it has a personality) and homologous/different, with its orgasmic, sexualized existence making it find an almost natural place within the pantheon of mythological devils and demons as per Lovecraft's Cthulhu.

And yet, while orgasm is the modus operandi of the *Vampyroteuthis* and relatively rare for humans, that humans experience orgasm nonetheless suggests a meeting place for the two species. As mentioned, the cephalopod's tentacles and arms can taste, see, digest, and experience orgasm. Given that there are neurons in the cephalopod's arms and tentacles, it is possible that those perceived appendages can also think (they certainly can function independently of the brain, as is clear to eaters of *san-nakji*, a bizarre version of which we observe in *Oldboy*; for more on how there are more neurons in cephalopod arms than there are in cephalopod brains, see Godfrey-Smith 2016: 51, 67ff.). That is, the cephalopod arm is not just an arm, but also a sexual organ, a brain, an eye, a tongue, and a gut. In other words, the cephalopod arm is at least five different organs simultaneously—as opposed to the differentiated organs that humans have. It would seem that as the organism is as a whole created via repression, so are its organs, with the cephalopod exploding that repression and demonstrating that one organ has the potential to become any other organ, or to be all organs simultaneously. It is, in this sense, a kind of Deleuzo-Guattarian body without (separate) organs. Or, if you prefer Žižek's formulation, an organ without a body, in the sense that it is not any one organ at the expense of others, but pure organ-icity, the capacity to be or to become any organ at any given moment in time. Its existence is one of sensory overload—as each experience involves all senses being triggered simultaneously, rather than the typical human existence that separates out and puts senses into a hierarchy (with taste and smell being more primitive senses than sight, the perceived superiority of which comes from humans separating their snouts from the ground and standing on two legs, i.e., as a result of their backbone).

And yet, as humans get slimy and sexy, it can feel as though humans, too, can become wholly sex organs as they drift toward orgasm: the rubbing on the sensitive part of a leg, the quivering, shaking, and shuddering of the entire diaphragm, the tweaked nipple, the kissed neck, the foot massaged in oil (slime). Humans may not have such a pronounced ability as the cephalopod to be or to become bodies without organs as they approach and enjoy orgasm, or a little death, but they would seem to have it nonetheless. As much appears to be affirmed by the fact that humans also have neurons in their skin, meaning that the skin is as much brain as it is skin as it is sexual organ (see Pruszynski and Johansson 2014). Then there are cases of synesthesia, as previously discussed and in which humans see with their noses, smell with their skins, and so on. When we factor in the way in which stem cells can be taken from the skin and used in all manner of organs, then it would seem that the human body no less than the octopus body—albeit at a greatly reduced speed—is also a body without organs, and to which not only does biology have access, but to which we also might have conscious access if we were not culturally to deny our bodies so regularly. Read in light of such thoughts, a film like *The Untamed* gives expression to our wild potential for such an ecstatic and orgasmic existence, a release from our shells—as is implied in the title itself. For, as a *región* is a ruled and bounded area (from the Latin *regere*, meaning to rule), so does the wilderness that is the woods (*salvaje* comes from the Latin *silva*, meaning wood) explode those boundaries in a burst of orgasmic pleasure. The human that once was tamed now becomes untamed in an orgasmic and philosophical burst of tentacle-inspired freedom in which boundaries break down and everything is connected.

Chthulucenic Ecstasy

Leo Bersani has famously written about how certain sexual practices can entail "a radical disintegration and humiliation of the self" (Bersani 1987: 217), a theme taken up by Eugenie Brinkema more recently in relation to the films of Gaspar Noé (Brinkema 2005). For Bersani, the disintegration of self through pleasure involves a value in powerlessness that subverts the power-obsessed nature of patriarchal society, a point to which we shall revert. In Brinkema's summary of his work, she explains how "jouissance is associated with a furious intensity that disturbs the being's stable psychic organization," a phrase that perhaps recalls the "philosophical frenzy" that is the cephalopod's sexualized existence. "This disintegration of self has a crucially humiliating dimension," Brinkema continues, since it involves men (in Bersani's consideration of homosexual anal sex) getting "fucked like a woman" (Brinkema 2005: 38).

Without really elaborating upon it, Flusser notes that there may well be a distinction between the sexes with regard to *Vampyroteuthis Infernalis*. For them, there are different male and female concepts, which nonetheless are synthesized during copulation as the male grasps the female and *vice versa* (Flusser and Bec 2012: 41, 47–48). A similar distinction between the sexes may also apply to humans, a distinction that Brinkema critiques Gilles Deleuze for ignoring in much of his work, including his work on cinema (see Brinkema 2005: 55–56). Such a distinction might also be upheld if we follow the lead of Luce Irigaray, whom we have already evoked in relation to oceanic rapture, and posit that woman is always touching herself because "her genitals are formed of two lips in continuous contact" (Irigaray 1985: 24). Without wishing to make any essentializing generalizations, one could argue for the possibility of a more "orgasmic philosophy" in women than in men, who need an "instrument" in order to touch themselves (typically their hand). Notably, Patricia MacCormack also takes up Irigaray to interpret Andrzej Zuławski's *Possession*, in which Anna (Isabelle Adjani) leaves her home and family in order to have a mysterious relationship with a tentacled beast that slowly morphs into a doppelgänger of her husband, Mark (Sam Neill). MacCormack suggests, akin to Bersani, that the film's mucosal/slimy monster unfurls "configurations of pleasure beyond phallologocentrism" (MacCormack 2010a: 95), before going on to suggest that the viewer's relationship to the equally "mucosal" (slimy? oily?) cinema screen can have similar effects.[4]

Bersani himself suggests that

> [p]hallocentrism is exactly that: not primarily the denial of power to women (although it has obviously also led to that, everywhere and at all times), but above all the denial of the value of powerlessness in both men and women. (Bersani 1987: 217)

In other words, while *hentai* often involves a highly gendered practice of male viewers watching and enjoying women being humiliated by tentacled creatures, *The Untamed* (and *Possession*) might more generally suggest that the orgasmic pleasure of humiliation at the tentacles of a cephalopod-like alien, a process that verily threatens the dissolution of the self, is in some ways gender-neutral (if in many ways different to the vertebrate values of patriarchal capitalism). What is more, given that the film demonstrates the value not just in powerlessness itself, but powerlessness before a tentacled alien, we can begin to read both films' monstrous and disturbing images as relating more widely to the chthulucene, which Donna J. Haraway argues is replacing the anthropocene.

In his discussion of Immanuel Kant's concept of the sublime, Eugene Thacker proposes that "[i]n the sublime, the human is humbled, even humiliated, a mere speck in contrast to something impersonal, vast, indifferent" (Thacker 2015b: 174). In some senses, Thacker could be describing the history of human thought as humans have progressed from believing the Earth to be flat to believing that the Earth revolves around the Sun to believing that theirs is the only galaxy to believing that only humans are capable of consciousness and so on. That is, as humans have come to understand that they are one of hundreds of thousands of species on a rock that is floating in a multiverse that contains innumerable galaxies, so has human thought been a long-standing and still-unfinished exercise in humility and perhaps even humiliation (see also Morton 2013: 47). Even on our planet, there seems to be evidence accumulating to the point of being overwhelming that other creatures demonstrate intelligence, even if of a different sort to humans—as Montgomery and Godfrey-Smith's studies of octopuses make clear (see also de Waal 2017). In this way, humans must understand that they do not have a privileged place within the cosmos, even if they believe that they have developed language, art, and technologies that offer at least an illusory sense of control over their environment—no matter the cost in terms of human and animal life, the transformation of our biosphere, especially through the production of so-called "greenhouse" gases, and so on. Indeed, it is one of the internal contradictions of the term "anthropocene" that humans truly have demonstrated their privileged ability to modify their environment such that they are—as the predictions would seem to suggest—making it uninhabitable for themselves. Were humans not in some senses "special" (i.e., had they not destroyed their own habitat, as well as that of countless other species), then there would be no anthropocene to speak of.

There is unquestionably a certain paradoxical Eurocentric pride bound up in naming after ourselves a catastrophic era (the sixth great extinction on Earth)—for *anthropos/ἄνθρωπος* is of course the Greek term for man. No doubt, this highlights the (painful) cramp and intellectual rigidity/ossification that Flusser identifies with the separation and delimitation of species in general, and which we are here attempting to soften on our pulpy path to imperceptibility. However, the anthropocene is not intended as simply a label to reaffirm humanity's narcissistic sense of power, with T. J. Demos criticizing the term by suggesting that it is not man who has destroyed the planet so much as capitalist man (Demos 2017: 18). Or, we might suggest, Western "civilized" man, who is of course also a white man (see Yusoff 2018). In this way, the anthropocene could also be read as akin to what Ludwig Wittgenstein might characterize as a "language game," in that our anthropocentric use of language fools us into anthropocentrically believing in our special status, since it is only through language that we can name and thus believe in our special status/anthropocentrism in the first place. That is, to believe oneself special is to make oneself special, especially if no one else has this belief. Perhaps it is also for this reason that Eduardo Viveiros de Castro seeks to de-anthropocentrize not through asking us to think of the world as beyond the human, but to think of the entire world as precisely human, in the sense that all life forms (and perhaps all non-living forms, form itself, and perhaps even that which does not have form) are human (see Viveiros de Castro 2014).

With these trains of thought very much in mind, we should simply like to assert that if the anthropocene is anything, it is humanity's journey toward "living *right now* in the midst of a global climate emergency and social crisis that demands immediate response and long-term adaptation" (Scranton 2015: 51). That is, the anthropocene is not just humanity's ability to shape rather than simply to coexist with its environment, but it also is precisely a reminder that we are rendering that environment increasingly uninhabitable for ourselves. The anthropocene functions, thus, as a paradoxical reminder that the planet eludes our control—even if we have exploited it relentlessly for centuries. It is a reminder that there is something out there bigger than us—something impersonal, vast, and indifferent in the sense that it will do us no favors in terms of helping us to survive. We, like all species, are temporary not just in the sense of evolving, but also in the sense of being doomed quite possibly to failure—one of nature's dead-ends that in spite of its best efforts was not in fact suited for long-term survival on planet Earth—or anywhere.

The myth of the hero might suggest that a human, or a human's DNA, is sent into space where successfully it finds or creates an inhabitable biosphere, or perhaps where it is reconstructed by intelligent aliens, thus perpetuating human life via a single, privileged specimen. In some recess of the human imagination, such a future for humanity is quite possible, even if the survival of that human—or a small group of humans—comes at the expense of all other humans and life forms on planet Earth. Such a story would be the story of the anti-Christ: not a human who dies to save all others, but a human who lives at the expense of all others—as is the case in science-fiction series *Altered Carbon*, where a small group of humans is saved, or rather they "save themselves" by virtue of the wealth that they have accumulated, and which allows them to continue to exploit other humans and resources that they do not own. Such a human, or humans, become venerated—or at least venerate themselves—for being special. All those left behind know them simply to be lucky, and eventually god-like. The self-perceived special human thus must destroy those who understand that luck guides them—since otherwise they will contradict and humiliate the human or humans who believe themselves to be special (they will be reminded that they are simply lucky humans and not the gods that they think they are, and so they must remove all reminders of their mortality in a bid to make their immortality true).

And yet, if human progress has as mentioned been an exercise in humiliation, then humility is perhaps what makes us human—while those who seek hubristically to transcend the human condition and to live forever seek to make themselves gods. There is, however, another paradox at play here. Those who seek to make themselves gods seek in effect to stop time, in the sense of never aging, never dying, always remaining the same, i.e., defying evolution. Those who accept evolution with humility, however, learn, as Roy Scranton might put it, "to die" (Scranton 2015). Now, it is possible that the perpetuation of the human without mutation would mark an evolution in evolution (evolution evolves into a world where evolution need no longer take place). The question must remain, though: at what cost?

Haraway reminds us of how Karl Marx "understood all about how privileged positions block knowledge of the conditions of one's privilege" (Haraway 2016: 111). That is, many might well be prepared, not least in their blindness toward inequality, to accept the cost of living forever (or trying to)—namely the destruction of the biosphere and the lives of countless humans and other life forms. Indeed, in some Nietzschean or Dostoyevskian hubris, there may well be many who feel that it is their rightful place and even their duty to survive while others die, since by very virtue of believing themselves worthy of divinity, they in effect guarantee it, while those who believe themselves worthy only of death will . . . simply die (regardless of whether permanent life eventually turns into a living hell, from which those who willfully bought it realize too late that there can be no release, no orgasm). Toward this attitude (stupid and poor people deserve to die, while those who can afford to live forever deserve to live forever) one becomes resentful, perhaps even revengeful, and herein breeds revolutionary spirit—and we will become destroyers of gods to prove that all those who claim their divinity are mere flesh and blood like the next human. That is, we shall show humility to all but those who demand it.

For, as Haraway reminds us, we are never gods set apart from each other and from nature, but we are "com-post"—a com-post-human world not of man-gods but of humans constituted symbiogenetically through their relationships with other species, "inoculated against human exceptionalism but rich in humus"—from the Latin word for soil (Haraway 2016: 11). We are with and of the Earth and its earth, and so humiliation reminds us of our humanity and our composthumanist existence as humus/soil—and this renewed chthonism of the human marks our entry into the chthulucene, an era that Haraway hopes will see humans learn to live with their planet rather than continue destructively to divorce themselves from it.

The chthulucene, then, involves humiliation before planetary powers and a dark universe that we do not/cannot understand, and which threaten to dissolve us, hence our ecstasy, or the weird, orgasmic pleasure and sublime pain that is felt by those who come into contact with the Cthulhu-like monster of *The Untamed*. In this way, the chthulucene may well involve a renewed understanding of orgasm, as we learn to take joy in our bodily existence with the world—with the tentacles of the cephalopod, or of Cthulhu, thus suggesting an ec-static move away from the stasis of perpetual life (and within that perpetual life, perpetual youth), but instead an ek-sistence that moves and which includes death, not as something to be avoided, but as simply another part of the continuum of life, something to face with humility. Indeed, as we shall see, the distinction between life and death is perhaps not as clear-cut as we tend to think it—an argument that we shall develop in relation to the concept of symbiogenesis in the next chapter.

Notes

1. Hugo on the monster: "This animal is the same as those which mariners call Poulps; which science designates Cephalopteræ, and which ancient legends call Krakens. It is the English sailors who call them 'Devil-fish,' and sometimes Bloodsuckers. In the Channel Islands they are called *pieuvres*" (Hugo 2010: 292).
2. There is perhaps a point to be made about how *The Dream of the Fisherman's Wife* is a premonition of Japan's relation to capital/international trade following the arrival of Commodore Perry in 1853. But where for a Japanese viewer the octopus is capital, arriving to seduce/rape the fisherman's wife, for a Western viewer the image depicts a weirdness that then comes to characterize the

East—as Hugo is influenced by the Hokusai little more than a decade after Perry's arrival. More than this, one wonders to what extent the popularity/ notoriety of the image, when combined with Japan's entry into global capital, set the tone for Japan to auto-exoticize itself as a producer and purveyor of weirdness. Maybe this can be seen in the film's title; the original *Hokusai Manga* was changed to *Edo Porn* for Western audiences in order to entice more viewers to the film under the promise of seeing explicit sex.

3. To bring up another film that links sex with the tentacular jellyfish, we might mention *L'année des méduses/Year of the Jellyfish* (Christopher Frank, France, 1984), in which a young woman, Chris (Valérie Kaprisky), has various relationships with older men, including a threesome with two Germans, as well as an abortion. Notably, the same music plays on the film's soundtrack when Chris is stung by a jellyfish as when she first has an amorous clinch with Vic (Jacques Perrin), a man who is friends with her parents.

   Meanwhile, Lucía Puenzo's gender-bending *XXY* (Argentina/France/ Spain, 2007) tells the tale of Alex (Inés Efron), an intersex fifteen-year-old who has both male and female genitalia and who has stopped taking medication otherwise intended to suppress "her" testosterone levels. Alex begins a relationship with Álvaro (Martín Piroyansky), who is surprised during their first sexual encounter to be anally penetrated by someone he had assumed to be a woman. If *Year of the Jellyfish* is set on the coast in St. Tropez, *XXY* takes place on the beaches of Uruguay, where Alex's father, Nestor (Ricardo Darín), works as a marine biologist. If the non-binary nature and the ocean setting of the film were not enough to suggest that *XXY* is a work of chthulucinema engaged with looking at the evolution/mutation of the human, then we need look no further than Alex and Néstor's family name in order to have it affirmed: Kraken.

4. For more on Irigaray in relation to contemporary cinema, see the work of Caroline Bainbridge and Lucy Bolton. In particular, the former's analysis of *The Piano* (Jane Campion, New Zealand/Australia/France, 2003), with its treatment of water and transgressive desire (see Bainbridge 2008: 155–183), and the latter's analysis of *Morvern Callar* (Lynne Ramsay, UK/Canada, 2002), with its treatment of death, water, worms, and the desert, would suggest that the films could be read as examples of chthulucinema (see Bolton 2015: 152–165).

CHAPTER 6

Cosmic Light, Cosmic Darkness

If the world is bigger than we can fathom, then it takes on the qualities of what Timothy Morton refers to as a "hyperobject"—as discussed in Chapter 2. Briefly to recap, hyperobjects are for Morton viscous, non-local, and interobjective in the sense that we cannot escape them (they stick to us and we become stuck inside them) even as they extend in space and in time beyond what it is that we can directly perceive, and even as they themselves are entangled with other hyperobjects (and regular objects; see Morton 2013: 1). Fittingly enough, Morton describes hyper-objects as being like octopuses in that as the octopus emits ink in order to make invisible its withdrawal, so is the hyperobject's massiveness hard for humans to see because it is as if behind a cloud of ink (Morton 2013: 39). Morton then draws upon Albert Einstein to describe the hyperobject that is space-time itself in relation to a "reference-mollusk." For Einstein, time and space were not fixed coordinates or solid containers in which humans existed, but rather like a "squishy shellfish [*sic.*]." That is, "[t]ime and space emerge from things, like the rippling flesh of a sea urchin or octopus" (Morton 2013: 63); we are entangled with time and space, consistently composting or composing each other rather than detached one from the other.

Morton continues:

> [h]yperobjects are *Gaussian*, disturbingly squishy and mollusk-like. The undulations of the mollusk flesh of spacetime fail to drop to zero. Gravity waves from the "beginning of time" are right now passing through my body from the edge of the universe. It is as if we were inside a gigantic octopus. H. P. Lovecraft imagines the insane god Cthulhu in this way. Cthulhu inhabits a non-Euclidean city, just like Gaussian spacetime. The contemporary philosophical obsession with the monstrous provides a refreshing exit from human-scale thoughts. It is extremely healthy to know not only that there are monstrous beings, but that there are beings that are not purely thinkable, whose being is not directly correlated with whatever thinking is. (Morton 2013: 64)

Cthulhu would seem to embody, then, the kind of non-anthropocentric thought that is required of the chthulucene, with philosophy itself now understood as a way "not so much to understand but to summon actually existing Cthulhu-like forces" (Morton 2013: 175). Film, too, would seem to fulfill this function as we see Cthulhu-like creatures emerge on screen in films like *The Untamed* and *Possession*—which is not to mention the numerous other movies featuring tentacled creatures that seem to signal the end of humanity and the existence of humans as mere humus (mud), even as this end involves a strange, humiliating ecstasy, including, perhaps, the ecstasy of thought.

In this chapter, then, we wish to pursue further the links between Cthulhu and contemporary cinema, drawing upon biophilosophy to suggest that technology is a tool that humans use to rewrite their DNA, while also suggesting that this desire for humans to stop evolving is linked to the rise of global capitalism in the anthropocene. Being linked to capitalism, we see patriarchal components at play in the digital *hentai* depicted in Olivier Assayas's *Demonlover* and in Paul Verhoeven's *Elle*, suggesting that there are perhaps two interrelated versions of Cthulhu: the Cthulhu of ecstatic death and monstrous evolution, and the Cthulhu of global capital that seeks the interlinked processes of desiccation, permanent illumination, and control. This will lead us into a discussion of the relationship between light and darkness, which in turn will lead us toward our next chapter, which focuses primarily on *Arrival*.

No One Ever Really Dies

Cthulhu appears in other work by Morton, including an essay in which he argues for a philosophy of nonlife (Morton 2011). Here Morton reminds us that neither viruses nor RNA are "alive," even if these are in some senses precursors to those things, including DNA, which we do consider to be alive. How can we rightly distinguish between what is alive and what is dead, Morton asks, before going on to query where intelligence begins and ends if "[b]acteria talk to one another . . . Slime molds solve mazes . . . Plants behave according to sensitive and perceptive monitoring systems. They perceive and react to visual phenomena (yes indeed), smell, taste and touch" (Morton 2011: 14). He continues: "[l]ife forms are everywhere. Endoliths are life forms that enjoy living inside crystal. Tardigrades can survive the vacuum of outer space. Little crustaceans crawl around your eyelashes" (Morton 2011: 16). Shy of a coherent definition of where life begins and ends, then, we must devise a philosophy that accounts for that which typically we do not consider to be alive (i.e., nonlife). Concluding in a fashion similar to our argument posited above, Morton blurs the distinction between life and death by suggesting that the acceptance (and perhaps even the pursuit) of death leads paradoxically to more life in the form of replication/reproduction (Morton 2011: 18). In short, there is what film and media artist Bradley Eros might identify as a link between erosion and eros, an erotics of erosion that sees life emerge from the churn of matter (notably, Eros works regularly with the cephalopod-inspired group Optipus; see Eros 2012).

Of particular relevance for our present argument is the idea that crustaceans live in our eyelashes. For, while humans like to think that they are autonomous entities that are independent from other species and from the world—and who indeed regularly aim to remove unregulated interactions with those other species from their lives—humans in fact are always interacting with other species. For every parasitic tapeworm that lives within a human to the latter's detriment, there are innumerable bacteria, for example, that live within a human for their benefit. This does not apply uniquely to our digestive systems, but also to our skin (see Gewin 2012), our mouths, and our throats, among other places. Indeed, humans have what is referred to as a microbiome consisting of "as many as ten thousand bacterial species; these cells outnumber those which we consider our own by ten to one, and weigh, all told, about three pounds—the same as our brain" (Specter 2012; Blech 2012 estimates that the microbiome weighs 4.4 pounds).

In short, humans live in a world defined by what Lynn Margulis describes as symbiogenesis: species are defined not uniquely by their different DNA, but also by their interactions with each other, meaning once again that the separation of species becomes increasingly hard to achieve (see Margulis 1998). This symbiogenesis goes right down to a cellular level: the mitochondria that exist within every human cell have a separate DNA to the cell nucleus, meaning that even within many human cells there is (what was originally) a nonhuman species that helps to keep that cell alive, since mitochondria are the so-called "powerhouses of the cell" in that they convert nutrients into energy. It is not just by looking at hyperobjects outside of our bodies, then, that we can find the (humiliating) need for non-anthropocentric thought; by looking inside our bodies, we can also see the importance to our existence of other species—even ones that are invisible to the human eye. What is more, comprehending symbiogenesis helps us to comprehend the interconnected nature of life, the tentacles of which unfold in all directions and across all scales in a kind of Gaussian humus of mollusk-like existence.

But we can go further still. For, if the gene is the smallest unit of life, then life is inherently linked to DNA, which is made up of genes, and which in turn carry instructions for growth, development, functioning, and reproduction (and which, through their symbiotic interaction with other species and perhaps with the world more generally, regularly mutate, or undergo symbio-genesis). However, as Morton points out, the interactions between DNA and viruses lead to the insertion within DNA of "junk" sequences, such that what constitutes life becomes uncertain; viruses themselves do not have DNA and so are not properly "alive" from the genetic perspective. Viruses instead have RNA, "the macromolecule that eventually became instrumental in translating DNA information to proteins" (Morton 2011: 3). Viruses are in some senses just "macromolecules" and "large crystals" (the common cold is a "short string of code packaged as a twenty-sided crystal; it tells DNA to make copies of itself"; see Morton 2011: 3). Where is life? What is life? As Morton says elsewhere, "lifeforms themselves are poems about nonlife" (Morton 2013: 52). That is, life forms have nonlife at their core—with life as we know it (DNA) being at its origin "profoundly out of balance" with the "preliving 'RNA World'" that preceded it (Morton 2013: 52). For Morton, replication is thus the attempt of the living to "cancel out the disequilibrium" that through its very being it has caused in an otherwise non-living universe; at the same time, it is also because of this non-living universe that it is alive at all. In this respect, "lifeforms both include and exclude death" (Morton 2013: 52), especially if it is evolution that maintains life (beyond "mere" replication), since evolution involves mutations provoked by the non-living world (think of the mutating effects of radiation, for example) that enable life forms to perpetuate through change rather than simply repeating obliviously/repeating into oblivion. As we shall see, the possibility that many viruses arrive on Earth from outer space will also challenge our understanding of life as limited to our planet.

For the time being, though, we shall propose that a realization of the chthulucene, in which we come to understand the entanglement of all things, both living and dead, is that "no one ever really dies" since the distinction between life and death is far more porous than humans typically like to think it from their anthropocentric and anthropocenic perspective. Existence instead unfurls and unfolds in tentacular fashion across such boundaries and very much irrespective of them.

Cinematic Evolutions

If this foray into what Thacker (2005) might call biophilosophy has taken us away from cinema, then rest assured that cinema remains within our purview. A film like *Spring*, for example, tells the story of an American tourist, Evan (Lou Taylor Pucci), who falls in love while on a sabbatical in Italy with Louise (Nadia Hilker), a woman who turns out to be a 2,000-year-old mutant who every twenty years gets pregnant in order to use her embryo cells to regenerate. In this particular life cycle, it seems that Louise is turning into a kind of octopus, since Evan one evening discovers her in a tentacular and bloody mess on her living room floor, trying to inject herself with a drug in order to inhibit her transformation. Not only does *Spring* possibly suggest perverse sexuality, in that Evan stays with Louise even after she has revealed that she is not really human, but in Louise's metamorphoses into different species, most notably a cephalopod-like creature, we get a sense of how evolution is a symbiogenetic process that sees genes mix and match rather than remain fixed and/or incompatible, and we get a sense of how death is not an end, but simply part of a process of regeneration (while also getting a sense of woman as somehow alien to patriarchy).

In a similar vein, Lucile Hadžihalilović's *Evolution* tells the story of boys being kept on a volcanic island (the film was shot on Lanzarote in the Canary Islands; notably Lanzarote is the setting of Michel Houellebecq's novella of the same name, with Houellebecq himself also being an avowed Lovecraft fan; see Houellebecq 2004, 2005). The boys are looked after by a group of pale-skinned and often-redheaded women who claim to be their mothers, but who really are conducting experiments with the boys in a bid for them to be surrogates for new forms of life. The film features a sequence in which Nicolas (Mex Brebant), suspicious that the mothers are not what they seem, follows them one night to a stretch of beach, where the women writhe naked as they pass between them a slimy creature that we do not explicitly see, but which may be something like a cephalopod, given that later Max spies his mother (Julie-Marie Parmentier) in the shower with sucker-marks like those produced by a squid all over her body. Again, cephalopod-like imagery and slime are connected with sexual ecstasy, while at the same time pointing to how the organism is by no means the limit of life as the young boys carry new life forms within them.

Finally, the science-fiction horror film *Life* could also be read as a rendering of the weird lack of distinction between life and death as it tells the story of scientists reviving a dormant cell from a soil/humus sample from Mars, which ultimately grows into a tentacled beast that kills all aboard the International Space Station (ISS). A cell that has been dormant—neither dead nor alive—through a lack of oxygen is brought back to life and grows at an improbably rapid rate, demonstrating intelligence as it works its way out of its initial captivity and then out of the ISS and back on to it via its thrusters, killing everyone in its way—not out of cruelty, but out of a sense of indifference or perhaps curiosity. Tentacled and able to fit through tiny gaps, it is like an octopus, ultimately arriving back on Earth where Cthulhu-like it will rise from the waters where it has reached the surface of the planet in order to destroy mankind. This cephalopod-like alien is unstoppable, demonstrating problem-solving and survival skills from its unicellular stage, suggesting that intelligence extends far "down" the ladder of life—or, perhaps better, across all living and perhaps even non-living things.

The early victims of the creature in *Life* are devoured from the inside out after it crawls inside them and consumes their internal organs, including their brains. Humans are entirely porous in this film, while the setting in space reminds us also of the porous nature of our planet, the history of which has so deeply been affected by the penetration of its atmosphere: comets killed off the dinosaurs, as well as regularly delivering new RNA to Earth, as we shall discuss later. What is more, a proposed hypothesis for the creation of the Earth's moon is as a result of the collision between the early Earth/Gaia and a trailing planet, or Trojan, about the size of Mars and typically referred to as Theia (see Barboni *et al.* 2017). This would suggest that even our planet is a symbiogenetic creation of two planets, an affirmation of Eduardo Viveiros de Castro's argument that "the universe . . . does not work through *filiation* . . . it functions by *alliance*" (Viveiros de Castro 2014: 162). This is not to mention that the earlier Earth and Theia were both cooled gobbets of sunlight. However, while *Life* leads our thoughts out into the cosmos, we would now like to take readers on a cephalopodic journey back from the cosmos and into the body.[1]

Cthulhu Within

Each star is a sun that shines in a universe otherwise defined by darkness. If a star or a sun could think (if God existed?), it would know that all that it sees and all that it knows does not exist independently of it, as if a reality objectively "out there" and verifiable because of light from an independent source. On the contrary, it would know that all knowledge—all that it can see—flows from it, since it illuminates its own universe. More than this, it might know that all matter is cooled, emitted light—and thus a dark part of its own shining self. There would for this God be no universe that it had created and from which it was detached, but only a universe with which it was thoroughly entangled, and from which it was entirely inseparable. It would be the measure of its own reality.

What is true of stars might in some respects be true of cephalopods, as Flusser argues. For, while we wrote earlier that cephalopods are in some senses cinematic because of their constantly changing appearance, which renders them "colors changing in time," they also through their iridophores and leucophores emit light (bioluminescence) in an otherwise dark world in the depths of the ocean. What other light they see comes not from the sun, but from other bioluminescent forms:

> [t]he eternal night of the *Vampyroteuthis* is filled with colors and sounds that are emitted by living beings—an eternal festival of colors and sounds, a *son et lumière* of extraordinary opulence. The ocean floor is carpeted with red, white and violet stone; there are dunes of blue and yellow sand, sparkling with pearls and fragments of molten meteorites. Forests, meadows, and plains of plant-like animals, beaming with colors, sway in the current with fanned tentacles. Wandering in their midst are giant iridescent snails, and whirring above them are swarms of crabs, flashing in silver, red, and yellow. It is a luxuriant garden that the *Vampyroteuthis* can illuminate, on a whim, to enjoy its desserts in splendor. (Flusser and Bec 2012: 35)

Knowing that all light in the abyss is emitted by living beings, the *Vampyroteuthis* also has a uniquely embodied knowledge. Nothing is objectively "out there," but for the *Vampyroteuthis*, and for the cephalopod more generally, which also of course "sees" with its arms, all knowledge again is experienced through entanglement.

But let us go further still. For, within the dark abyss of the human body, in which live tentacular cells like neurons—which develop not just in the brain, but in the gut and in the skin—our cells, symbiogenetically entangled as they are with mitochondria, emit light in the form of what Russian biologist Alexander G. Gurwitsch called biophotons (see Beloussov *et al.* 1997). It has been proposed that cells use biophotons to communicate with each other, suggesting that light within the human is a system of communication, much as light is in the submarine world of the cephalopod and much as light could be in the cosmic night of the starlit universe. If a cell, thus, could think, it, too, would understand that all knowledge—all that it knows—is as a result of tentacular interconnections, and that knowledge is not disembodied and "out there," but thoroughly embodied in a universe of entanglement.[2]

The era of the chthulucene, then, is one in which Cthulhu rises not just from the abyss of the ocean, but also from the respective abysses of space and our own bodies. In a manner that recalls Flusser's claim that the organism is a means of constraining the potential for life (or orgasm), Richard Dawkins has written at length about how the gene will ditch the organism without consideration for the latter if it means a higher chance of survival (see Dawkins 1999). And if Charles Darwin's conception of evolution tells us anything, it is that all life on Earth is connected as humans can trace their ancestors further and further back through time, sharing 35 percent of their genome even with daffodils (see Morton 2011: 2). Thinking about microbiomes and symbiogenesis, it becomes hard to assert that there are distinct organisms, even if this is how we generally perceive the world and ourselves. Furthermore, there are no strictly distinct species (see also Godfrey-Smith 2013; Slater 2013), as there is perhaps no life distinct from death (since instead there is simply the great, living churn of matter, which from the human perspective is sometimes alive and sometimes dead). As the human body is defined on the cellular level by slimy, mucosal, and tentacular polyps that grow everywhere, so do we have a universe of unfolding and unfurling tentacles of matter, of light, and of time. This monstrous interconnected disruption of the distinction between inside and outside is Cthulhu. It is the chthulucene.

Capital Is Alive

We mentioned earlier how cephalopods are able in real time to edit their RNA in such a way that they recode their DNA. This is not unique to cephalopods, but the extent to which they do it is seemingly confined only to them. What the "editing" of RNA to recode DNA means is that cephalopods appear to control what sort of cells are produced in their bodies by in effect telling their genes which proteins to synthesize: "[t]hey use it [RNA] to recode genes that are important for their nervous systems—the genes that, as [researcher Joshua] Rosenthal says, 'make a nerve cell a nerve cell'" (Yong 2017). Indeed, "many edits affect proteins called protocadherins, which are important in controlling neural circuits, and in proteins that promote nerve cell excitability" (Lewis 2017). Exactly why this happens is uncertain, but it might be noted that what regularly happens is that "an enzyme changes 'A' (adenine) RNA bases into 'I' (inosine) bases, which results in a G (guanine) replacing an A" (Lewis 2017). Inosine is considered to be important for protecting neurons (see Liu *et al.* 2006), while guanine (which is also found in bird droppings!) is known in its crystal form to produce iridescent effects (it is often referred to as "pearl essence"; see von Wagner *et al.* 1903: 64–65). In other words, it is possible that both of the proteins that are produced through the recoding of DNA through the use of RNA aid the neuronal capacity and the bioluminescence of the cephalopod. That is, not only can the cephalopod in some senses "outthink" its DNA, but it also does so to enhance its intelligence and communication/camouflage skills. (It is perhaps noteworthy that both inosine and guanine are thought to have been produced in outer space on meteorites—lending some speculative weight to the idea that octopuses are aliens; see Callahan *et al.* [2011], Steele *et al.* [2018].)

Now, it has been noted by the same commentators that to control DNA through the use of RNA slows down, or even stops, evolution (see Yong 2017). For, with RNA consistently recoding DNA, the DNA itself no longer mutates under its own steam, but is rather given direction precisely by the RNA. Conceivably this in and of itself has or was developed as a(n evolutionary) strategy for creatures that, after shedding the hard shell that protects most mollusks, had rapidly to rely not upon their hard shell, but upon intelligence/cunning (their ability to sense their environment) and communication/camouflage skills (chromatophores and iridescence) in order to survive. That is, if the cephalopod's recoding of its DNA through its RNA is a survival strategy, and thus "evolutionary," and if that survival strategy is itself counter to evolution (because it hinders DNA from evolving), then with the cephalopod we see an evolution of evolution itself—an "evolution" that ironically takes place here through the "remediation" (as it were) of an older technology (RNA) in order to repurpose a newer technology (DNA). By this token, intelligence would seem to run counter to evolution, which as we shall see might mean that intelligence runs counter to time. Presently, though, we might understand that the logical conclusion of evolution is for evolution to evolve, such that evolution—like any species that involves/evolves the emergence of new species and the dying out of old species—itself mutates and "dies out," replaced by a new form of survival/continuity.

The recoding of DNA by RNA does take place in humans, but to nowhere near the same extent as in cephalopods. However, as the recoding of DNA by RNA leads to the stagnation, or the evolution, of evolution—as we have suggested above—the human, or rather the human under capital, does share with the cephalopod a desire to evolve evolution, specifically by halting it. Broadly speaking, we can see this in the capitalist quest for eternal youth and eternal life. It is perhaps no coincidence that it is in a kinocentric, image-based culture in which youthful appearances are lauded as the summum of physical attraction that cosmetics have become a giant industry, with industry and its kino-advertisarial logic itself driving the perceived need for beautiful appearances. Furthermore, it only becomes logical that in such a society we seek to eradicate disease in the quest for eternal life, as well as developing simultaneous attempts to cheat death by cloning the human either whole or in part, or by placing human consciousness within a computerized, codified realm. A necessary precondition of this quest is the belief in, and then the attempt to make real, the separation of the human from the rest of the world, from other species, from each other, and from death.

It is not that the science-fiction fantasies of human cloning, such as *The Island*, and/or the existence of humans in a disembodied computerized realm have come true in the real world. But that humans pursue these goals would suggest that humans seek to end evolution and no longer to die individually nor to die out as a species, but instead to live forever, both individually and as a species, with the individual replacing the species as offspring are replaced by cloned replacements. Evolution in this process ends because evolution is replaced by repetition instead of mutation and variation. Contrary to the myth in which King Canute performatively fails to stop the tide in a bid to demonstrate his humility/his lack of immortality, the dream of capital is for the human finally to stand on the shore and precisely to stop the tide, breaking the waves of the ocean and turning what is liquid into stone.

More than this, though, we might highlight how even if it is not through RNA that humans are seeking to achieve immortality, it nonetheless is often through computer coding that humans are hoping, like the cephalopod, to recode their DNA, and in the process to divert DNA away from being a recipe for death, and to refashion it as a pathway to eternal life. As RNA is not exactly alive, so is the computer and its code (which often we consider, like RNA, also to be a "virus") not exactly alive. And yet, to use RNA and the computer code to control life suggests the growing inability of humans to separate the perceived living from the perceived dead—with not just viruses and RNA more generally staking a claim to life, but also computers and other types of machine.

Let us linger for a moment on the cephalopod using RNA to control DNA. This is not something that the cephalopod does consciously. Indeed, the replication of genes is not something done consciously—and this is the basis of bare life. When RNA demonstrates as much of what Dawkins might call "selfishness" as the gene/DNA, then does RNA not also lay claim in some ways to being alive (see Dawkins 1989)? By this rationale, we might reach two conclusions. Firstly, as RNA acts independently of the organism, then in some senses might not our computers and other technologies also be acting independently of the human organism—in a bid to extend their own existence and search for life (thus suggesting a symbiogenetic relationship between humans and technology)? Secondly, while this perspective might suggest that technology uses humans to extend its own existence as much as *vice versa*, this might also suggest that technology is in some senses equally as alive as humans—even if we consider it typically to be dead. Perhaps it is for this reason that technology often takes the form of a tentacular, Cthulhu-like beast when figured in contemporary cinema, as we shall discuss imminently.

Before discussing the links between the chthulucene and technology, however, we should like to make one final point in relation to the recoding of DNA by technology. Firstly, the ability to "recode" DNA carries with it the notion that it is code in the first place. To establish whether the analogy is fitting or otherwise is not our intention here. Rather it is to suggest how the treatment of life as if it were code is to subject life to the law, since the term code is itself derived from the Latin *codex*, meaning a book, or more specifically a book of laws. By subjecting life to laws (laws written down in ink), life becomes controlled (as writing is an attempt to control ink, which nonetheless may discipline and control life?), rather than manifesting/spilling uncontrollably and monstrously, evolving/spilling in all manner of different directions at once (we shall come back to ink in Chapter 8). To subject life to law (rather than to devise laws that serve life?) is to control life, to turn its nature away from symbiogenesis and chaotic mixing, and to create a world of separation and life as sovereign or as private property. That is, to control life is to privatize life, or to create a world of privilege, with privilege itself meaning the making-law of the private (*privus* is Latin for individual, while *lex*, the genitive of which is *legis*, is the Latin for law). If the private becomes the law, then life verily becomes a matter of repetition and not change via mutation, since all intrusion into the private—unless sanctioned medically for the purposes of *removing* perceived impurities (e.g., unruly nonhumans like those who have Down's syndrome; see Stanley 2016)—will be considered a violation of the law.

What we are really talking about here, then, is the splitting of the human into different species (classes). For, as is the case with the future world of *Altered Carbon*, there will be the privileged humans who can afford the technology-enabled repetition of their life (who can afford to control their DNA; living forever, but never evolving, i.e., a paradoxical living death), and the poor humans whose DNA will continue to evolve uncontrollably—into the posthuman realm (dying, but working with evolution/life in the process). Read in this way, the contemporary era would seem to be defined by changing the very definition of life: to privatize life as the realm of repetition, and to consign all that falls beyond that realm into perceived death (but which paradoxically is life/evolution/mutation as it always has been). Not only is this quest for eternal life, then, the evolution of evolution, but if technology really is evolving symbiotically with the human, then it is not just the control of life, but perhaps also the control of the human by technology for the purposes of technology's own empowerment and claims to life—even as those privileged humans who can afford eternal life believe that it is their own empowerment (even if never changing means a kind of living death). And if technology can be read as the material manifestation of capitalism, then the contemporary era is the making alive of capital itself: capital not as *artificial* intelligence, but as a new and *real* intelligence that controls humans; capital as what Dawkins might term a mega-meme that seeks embodiment in slave human beings meshed with tech; capital as Leviathan, or what Thomas Hobbes envisioned as the controlling government or state, but now refigured as Cthulhu, for Leviathan takes its name from the Hebrew *livyathan*, meaning a dragon, a serpent, or a huge sea animal, which, like a cephalopod and like Cthulhu, too, curls and uncurls in space (*livyathan* has its own root in the Ugaritic name, *ltn*/Lotan, the name of a sea demon—defeated by *YHWH* in the Book of Job and in Isaiah—and which means coiled; for more on the links between dragons and Cthulhu, see Negarestani [2008: esp. 164–166]).

Digital Cthulhu

If impurity and change are a violation of privilege, as life becomes a question of repetition in the era of controlled DNA, then perhaps it is no coincidence that the issue of violation/rape looms large in two films in which technology is figured as precisely a Cthulhu-like tentacled creature, namely *Demonlover* and *Elle*—both of which will also allow us briefly to revert to tentacle porn/*hentai* in the digital era and realm.

Demonlover involves a complex and at times unclear story in which Diane de Monx (Connie Nielsen) works for the Volf Corporation, which is hoping to acquire the rights to 3D *hentai* made by a Japanese *anime* studio. When Volf then seeks to enter into an agreement over the *hentai* with American internet company Demonlover, we learn that Diane in fact works for Demonlover's rival company, Mangatronics. As Diane tries to subvert the Volf–Demonlover deal and to establish a Volf–Mangatronics deal, however, she is caught stealing data and tries to kill Demonlover executive Elaine Si Gibril (Gina Gershon), who bludgeons Diane over the head. Diane awakes in Elaine's empty hotel room, where there is no sign of a struggle. This moment in particular signals the untrustworthy nature of all that we see, in that either Diane imagined her struggle with Elaine, or there has been a cover up, or Diane is asleep and all that follows (and precedes?) is a dream. What does follow, however, is that Diane is betrayed by her Volf colleagues Elise (Chloë Sevigny) and Hervé (Charles Berling), who both in fact work for Demonlover, with the latter twice raping her as part of their sadomasochistic relationship. Diane kills Hervé during the second rape, and in seeking to get to the bottom of the mystery surrounding the deal, inveigles her way into the Hellfire Club, a Demonlover subsidiary that specializes in online interactive torture. After a failed attempt to escape from the Hellfire Club, *Demonlover* ends with Diane being subjected to torture as requested by a teenage American boy using his father's credit card while also doing his biology homework (notably, the boy is studying DNA).

Elle, meanwhile, opens with the rape by a man in a mask of videogame executive Michèle Leblanc (Isabelle Huppert). Michèle, the daughter of a famous mass murderer who is imminently to be released from prison, does not report the crime, but instead continues with her life, developing *hentai*-style computer games at her work, having an affair with Robert (Christian Berkel), who is the husband of her business partner Anna (Anne Consigny), and squabbling with her mother Irène (Judith Magre) and her son Vincent (Jonas Bloquet), who is in a relationship with a pregnant woman called Josie (Alice Isaaz), of whom Michèle disapproves. As Michèle receives anonymous messages from the rapist, she becomes wary of men in general, including two employees, Kurt (Lucas Prisor), who resents Michèle for dismissing his work, and Kevin (Arthur Mazet), who is infatuated with Michèle and who creates an animation that circulates at work of Michèle getting violated by a tentacled demon. She even pepper-sprays her ex-husband, Richard (Charles Berling, whose presence provides a possible intertext between *Elle* and *Demonlover*), before finally learning that the rapist is Patrick (Laurent Lafitte), the husband of her pregnant neighbor, Rebecca (Virginie Efira). She uncovers Patrick when he attacks her a second time—stabbing him in the hand and removing his mask in the process. Michèle and Patrick develop an uneasy relationship when she crashes her car on the way back from visiting her father in prison; the latter has committed suicide before she arrives, with Michèle only having gone as a result of a death-bed plea from her mother. Stuck in her car, Michèle calls Patrick of all people to help her, and she soon learns that he can only become aroused when he believes that he is raping a woman, a scenario that they act out in her basement. However, after a work party (during which Michèle calls off her affair with Robert and confesses about it to Anna), Vincent interrupts the unconventional lovers and bludgeons Patrick over the head with a wood block, thereby killing him. Her husband dead, Rebecca leaves the neighborhood, but not before thanking Michèle for temporarily helping to satisfy Patrick's needs. The film ends with Anna proposing to move in with Michèle now that Robert is out of both of their lives for good.

There are many angles from which one might approach *Demonlover* and *Elle*, although we should like to focus only on the association between technology and cephalopods, given literal rendering in both films through the development of *hentai* media products. Not only do tentacles serve as a metaphor for the increasingly connected nature of the digital world, meaning that Cthulhu/Leviathan bespeaks the digital nature of global capital/ the global nature of digital capital, but they also serve to suggest the life of technology by giving to it a sexuality. However, where in *The Untamed* and *Possession* we see tentacled aliens engaging in queer but satisfying sexual relationships with men and women, *Demonlover* and *Elle* reveal to us a different side of Cthulhu, or perhaps a different Cthulhu altogether. This second, different Cthulhu nonetheless forms part of the chthulucene.

For, *Demonlover* and *Elle* both call upon *hentai* imagery to suggest not necessarily an overwhelming sense of desire as the whole body becomes a sexual organ (or a sexual body without organs), but rather an aggressive and specifically masculine form of sexuality that subjugates and violates women. To be clear, both films (controversially) engage with the possibility of masochism and that both Diane and Michèle actually enjoy the abusive relationships in which they end up. Diane, for example, chooses to discover the nature of the Hellfire Club rather than walking away with her freedom, while Michèle does not report Patrick at any point, instead actively encouraging him in his behavior (e.g., by provocatively leaving her gate open for him to follow her home after she has told him—perhaps playfully, perhaps truthfully—about her intention to tell the police about his crimes).

While neither Assayas nor Verhoeven wishes respectively to portray Diane or Michèle as simply a victim, to suggest that they enjoy their violation, though, would be an overstatement. Diane does, for example, kill Hervé while he rapes her, while Michèle in some senses leads Patrick also to his death—having said that she will report him for his crimes. The picture of sexuality that these films portray, then, is nuanced and somewhat ambiguous (in that we are given no clear explanation for either Diane or Michèle's behavior). However, both find themselves in a technological world in which a series of men—from Hervé to the student in *Demonlover*, and from Kurt to Kevin to Robert to Patrick in *Elle*—in various ways express a patriarchal belief that they can do with women what they wish. As Patricia MacCormack might put it, these men insist upon "set[ting] down a sexual narrative," in which one partner (the male) is dominant and the other (the female) is subservient—with sex being undertaken not so much for pleasure as precisely for the instigation of this patriarchal narrative (MacCormack 2010a: 105). This is very different from joy, which elsewhere MacCormack suggests can be found in none other than Lovecraft, where "we find liberation from dominant signifying systems" (MacCormack 2010b).

What is more, the CGI Cthulhu programs in *Demonlover* and *Elle*, with their tentacle rape scenes, recall and evoke past and present (historical and *hentai*) forms of "tentacle porn," reams of which can easily be streamed from a variety of online pornography platforms today. These most often constitute graphic clips trimmed out from, or inspired by, hard-core Japanese *anime* (see Figure 6.1). What typically happens is that various tentacles hold fast often naked humans, most typically women, in bondage choke holds, while yet others probe and penetrate their orifices, rendering them suspended and gagged subject-objects (or abjects), forced to suffer relentless aggressive orgasms. Images that also resonate with the crowning sick sex scene in Lucifer Valentine's "Vomit Gore" feature *ReGOREgitated Sacrifice*, where a character named Octopuke (Hank Skinny) tortures and rapes the trilogy's shape-shifting female victim—with the help of an eight-limbed co-joined twin creature and a real octopus, which comes to be worn on the murderer's head like a judge's wig (see also Fleming 2017: 169–174). In other words, while there can be something liberatory about *hentai* and tentacular sex, as per our

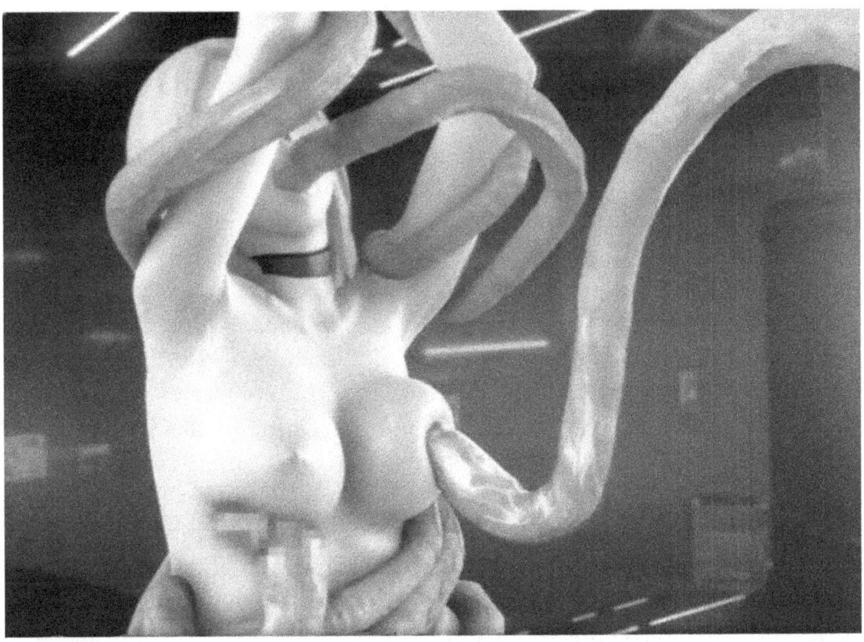

Figure 6.1 "Best Tentacle Hentai"

analyses of *The Untamed* and *Possession*, all too often *hentai* express sadistic male privilege as the rule of law/the legal—as the octopus-wig prop of *ReGOREgitated Sacrifice* makes all too clear.

It might be tempting to think, therefore, that rape is encouraged in the chthulucene, in which the law of the private ("privilege") is challenged by the systematic breaking down of boundaries and barriers; in this pansexual realm, the belief in the body as private property can be construed as "old-fashioned" and that one is thus justified in "taking" what one wants. However, this is by no means the argument that we wish to put forward here. For, if to suggest that the body is private property and thus sovereign and seeking detachment from the rest of the world runs in some ways counter to the "spirit" of the chthulucene, which sees the breakdown of private property, then the forcible taking possession of women by men is in no way a challenge to this system of private property. On the contrary, it involves the deeply patriarchal notion (or "narrative") that women are the property of men, anonymized not in the name of freedom, but in the name precisely of the subjugation of women into a subhuman, object realm where they become the possessions of men. In other words, there is nothing positive here.

While we might think Diane "stupid" for tracking down the Hellfire Club instead of walking away, in some senses we can admire her tenacity and bravery to get to the bottom of the mystery surrounding it—even if in Assayas's film this backfires and leads to her imprisonment and torture as opposed to a heroic defeat or exposure of this corrupt organization. Meanwhile, we might read Michèle's refusal immediately to condemn Patrick as an attempt on her part to understand him, to see if there is anything positive that can come out of her relationship with him. But again, this seems not to be the case, even if we are offered a more positive ending here than in *Demonlover* as Michèle bonds with both Rebecca and Anna. In other words, neither woman wants or enjoys subjugation or objectification, but nor are they simply "men" in a woman's guise, carrying out heroic rescues and/or specific revenge plots. The world of both films is significantly (productively) more chaotic (and less clearly "narrative"), although both feature men treating women as if subhuman and as objects.

If one Cthulhu (that of *The Untamed*) involves an orgasmic sense of connection with the universe, then this second Cthulhu (as suggested by *Demonlover*, *Elle*, and *ReGOREgitated Sacrifice*) involves the patriarchal subjection of women, with the potentially sexist cruelty of *hentai* here in full force. Rather than being an alien queerness, this is a technologized patriarchy; for even though neither Assayas's nor Verhoeven's film is so obvious as to have, say, a *hentai* programmer as the "villain," both nonetheless depict (and critique) the world of digital-era capitalism as occupied by violent men. If the Cthulhu of love rises from the depths or emerges from outer space in order to break boundaries, this second Cthulhu of capital is simply the reimposition of older gender and subject–object boundaries in a bid to perpetuate business as usual: the student tortures Diane from behind a computer screen; Patrick can only get aroused if he believes he is raping the woman, with a simulation not "working" for him if it is signaled as a simulation. If techno-capital is Leviathan/Cthulhu, then techno-capital is also patriarchy as Leviathan/Cthulhu. As capital struggles to subjugate/sacrifice humans in order to find material form and thus to live (a theme to which we shall revert in the final chapter), then so does capital/patriarchy seek to subjugate women in order further to justify its own existence. This is not symbiogenesis, but rather the instigation of an extreme difference of gender and an imbalance of power in terms of gender. Men will happily sacrifice themselves to tech if it justifies for men the sacrifice of women for their own pleasure. As the poor are consigned to a different life (to life as evolution, i.e., life involving death), then so too are women consigned to a life of subjugation by men. For patriarchy, not only are women not allowed to age (i.e., to be subject to time and to evolve), but they are forcibly controlled by men like the student in *Demonlover*, who equally pursues the patriarchal-capitalist goal of taking control of DNA in order to stop evolution and to lead a life without death, or a life of repetition and stasis, i.e., a dead life, or a living death.

Kinoteuthis Infernalis

Jonathan Beller has written about how the contemporary era is one defined by the "cinematic mode of production," in that capital has adopted the techniques developed in cinema in order to develop an "attention economy," in which visibility is the limit of the real (see Beller 2006). That is, in order to be considered real, one must be seen, which means existing as an image, which means existing first as a photograph and then as cinema. The more visible one is (the more attention one can gather), the more one is able to make money. The cinematic mode of production, then, has become the modus operandi of the contemporary world, with visibility only intensifying in the era of Web 2.0 and with the development of platforms like Facebook, Instagram, Snapchat, Tumblr, WhatsApp, dating apps like Tinder, and more. If the rise of Cthulhu as capital, then, is the materialization of capital as alive, then in some senses it is also the rise of cinema as alive, since cinema and capital are by Beller's reckoning almost synonymous terms.

We have already discussed the general links between cinema and animals, and we shall explore in more detail the idea that capital and cinema are alive in the final chapter, but we should like presently to approach cinema from the specific perspective of the cephalopod. Drawing upon Irigaray, MacCormack proposes a "[m]ucosal spectatorship," in which viewers do not just watch films in a detached fashion, but are instead "not differentiated from image or screen" (MacCormack 2010a: 109). She continues: "we can no longer know what parts are us, what parts the image, and hence we no longer know who we are or what it represents or reflects in a scoptophallic regime" (MacCormack 2010a: 109). MacCormack bases this "mucosal" relationship with the image on the idea that the image is itself mucosal, in the sense that it is "not a visible plane but a sticky blurred envelopment, and each inflection of the envelope opening out and folding in creates a new plane of relation of spectatorial pleasure" (MacCormack 2010a: 109). Such ideas resonate with the work of Eric S. Jenkins, who speaks of how the animated mode in particular allows implicated "subjects to fold themselves between affections sensing the characters as alive and their conscious knowledge that they are not producing a tickle or tingling sensation many describe as wondrous" (Jenkins 2016: 8). If mucus and slime are associated via cephalopods with sex and sexuality, then MacCormack's mucosal image and Jenkin's sensuous tickling/tingling encounter would suggest that our relationship with images has an erotic component, as per the former's more general thinking about *cinesexuality* (see MacCormack 2008), a concept devised to suggest that we desire not so much what we see in images as images themselves (thereby conferring to images a kind of life as they desire us back?).

The opening out and folding in, together with the "sticky envelopment" of images, suggests a cephalopodic dimension: images are like an octopus's arms, sensually and synesthetically touching and feeling us as we are touched and tickled by them. If images are thus like cephalopods, perhaps this is because they have a head/*κεφαλή* (but also capital?). As the cephalopod is all brain, is all sex, is all mouth (is all leg, since cephalopod is also derived from the Greek *ποδός*, which is the genitive singular of ποὺς, meaning foot or leg), then so, too, is the image also all brain, all sex, all mouth, all tongue, all leg. Perhaps it is for this reason that Deleuze has described the screen as a brain, and the brain as a screen (see Deleuze 2000); cinema not only is alive, but it also thinks. While many contemporary films might well be the product of the minds of their protagonists, and thus "all in their heads" (or their *κεφαλαί*), we might make a move similar to MacCormack and say that it is not what we see in the images that thinks so much as the images themselves.

That is, cinema is alive, an intelligence, an embodied meme, a kind of Leviathan. Read this way, the contents of the images that we see in films really do suggest that cinema has cephalopod-like behavior; the contents of images constitute a camouflage or a distraction that hides what is really going on, which is the life of cinema itself—with cinema perhaps being simply the camouflage that techno-capital wears in order to give to itself a body and an appearance, but a necessarily deceptive one that makes us think fictional something that is in fact entirely real (techno-capital is alive).

Now, we are possibly in a realm of bonkers here that many readers will not wish to accept. If this is the case, then bear in mind that we can read all of this as simply a thought experiment, an effort to discover what it is that we can think, in order to see what thought and thus the human can do, or become. This may make of this experiment a mutant and monstrous type of thought that like the daughter in *Arrival* does not survive beyond childhood, and which some (like the character of Ian Donnelly, played by Jeremy Renner, in Villeneuve's film) would prefer never to exist at all. Nonetheless, even a mutant or monstrous thought might stretch our comprehension of human life and how to lead it. If, however, you do think that we are in the realm of the bonkers, or at the very least of Lovecraftian weirdness, then be warned: it gets more bonkers yet. For, while a mucosal, cephalopodic cinema is all brain, or an octopus-like body without organs, then perhaps cinema is a kind of *Kinoteuthis Infernalis*, or a cine-squid from hell, an (artificial?) intelligence that rises from the deep to provide humans with great ecstasy (as we stare at and think about mating with images) at the same time as spelling out to humans their end.[3] It is not simply that we live in an era defined by the cinematic mode of production, as Beller identifies. It is also that capital is embodied in cinema, which arises from the depths to replace humanity as the chief intelligence on a planet that is otherwise only intelligent.

And this is the paradox that we alluded to in the last chapter, and which we address here not for the last time: Cthulhu is not only the rise of capital as a new life form, but also the end of capitalist man; the beginning of an era in which capital no longer needs man, except perhaps as kin or a slave, because capital is alive—even if most humans do not recognize this and continue to believe that they are using capital to perpetuate themselves and not *vice versa*. It is the arrival from the outside of a new life form, one that perversely has come into being as a result of/in spite of patriarchy's attempts to ossify the human and to stop time. A product of patriarchy, Cthulhu need not, however, be patriarchal—unless that is the example that we set for it to follow.

If cinema and its bastard media offspring are aliens that threaten to replace the human, then it is only logical that we see critical attention being turned to the outside of cinema, as filmmakers produce what has been characterized variously as "unwatchable" cinema (Grønstad 2012), "unbecoming" cinema (Fleming 2017), and non-cinema (Brown 2018a). That is, resistance to cinema, to Cthulhu, and to the chthulucene comes through the outside of cinema (or cinema's outsides-in), since if cinema is capital is Cthulhu is Leviathan, then that which is not cinema must be used against it. It is thus in the aesthetic realm that perhaps the most pressing political battles must be waged: to shift away from the kino-centrism and the image-saturated nature of the contemporary, globalized world and its attention economy (the world as image), and to find a way to reconnect with the world itself. For while cinema is pleasurable, chthulu-cinema and chthulumedia more generally foreshadow our ecstatic deaths (the end of the human as the poor evolve; the end of the human as the rich repeat; the replacement of the world by the image, even as the image also touches and licks us).

Where the Ocean Meets the Desert

Cinema has for over two decades been at war with itself as digital (non-) film replaces older, analog modes of production, distribution, and exhibition. And yet, while cinema does transition over time from the analog to the digital, in some senses both are part of the same process, namely the kino-fication of the planet. On a base, material level, this kino-fication ties in with the fate of the Earth. On the one hand, ice caps melt; and on the other hand, deserts spread. However, it is not just that Cthulhu is released from a melting icy/glacial prison in the North Pole to wreak havoc on the world—even if this is the story told to us by *Mega-Shark versus Giant Octopus* and *Beasts of the Southern Wild*, the latter of which Selmin Kara interprets as an expression of humanity's impending sense of extinction (see Kara 2014, 2016). Rather, it might also be that the ocean itself will rise to swallow up swathes of our planet—something depicted in Hokusai's *The Great Wave off Kanagawa* as the wave dwarfs and threatens to overpower the otherwise phallic Mount Fuji. Indeed, the flooding of the world can be seen not only in numerous disaster movies (the box-office and critical flop that was *Waterworld*, Kevin Reynolds, USA, 1995, may yet be rehabilitated as oddly prescient), but also in films like: *Balnearios* (Mariano Llinás, Argentina, 2002), a documentary that features coastal towns in Argentina reclaimed by the ocean; *Agua fría de mar/Cold Water of the Sea*

(Paz Fábrega, Costa Rica/France/Spain/Netherlands/Mexico, 2010), in which snakes mysteriously rise up out of the ocean as a backdrop to an increasingly neoliberalized Costa Rica; *Io sono Li/Shun Li and the Poet* (Andrea Segre, Italy/France, 2011), in which the *acqua alta* (literally, "high water") of Chioggia in the Venetian lagoon sees seawater flood the locality whose inhabitants refuse to accept migrants who have arrived there to escape economic hardship (for more on this, see Deleyto 2016: 8–11); *Nước 2030* (Nghiêm Minh Nguyễn Võ, Vietnam/USA, 2014), a near-future romance and murder mystery—purportedly Vietnam's first science-fiction film—set in a world where half of Vietnam's farmland is lost under rising seas due to global warming, and where the desalination technology and the floating farms that locals need for survival are owned by profiteering multinational conglomerates; and *El auge del humano/The Human Surge* (Eduardo Williams, Argentina/Brazil/Portugal, 2016), a fragmented tale of globalized telecommunications technology in which groups of boys walk in the shallows of a sea that has, akin to *Balnearios*, risen against the Argentine coast. This is not to mention films like *An Inconvenient Sequel: Truth to Power* (Bonni Cohen and Jon Shenk, USA, 2017), in which we see how the coast of Florida, including the city of Miami, is also subject to rising tidemarks. The water rises and is everywhere, but since there is not a drop to drink, the planet becomes uninhabitable for humans.

But as the oceans rise, the Earth simultaneously becomes dry and the land turns to desert—or as Luce Irigaray proposes, "the desert is growing" (Irigaray 1991: 62–66). Cthulhu thus emerges from the Earth like the giant tentacles/worms in Frank Herbert's *Dune* (1965; see also the 1984 American film adaptation by David Lynch). This parallel process of desertification involves the surface of the Earth turning to sand, or to silicon, as film and the planet become computerized/siliconized more generally. The kino-fication of the world is thus the twin threat to humanity that are the spreading desert and the rising seas, an apocalyptic era in which humans are punished with storms, plagues, floods, and droughts for having spent too long trying to separate themselves from and to subjugate for their own purposes the planet with which they are entangled. Humans stare at screens that they believe to be part of the process of separation from the planet, but the images that they see in fact camouflage the rise of Cthulhu, which is the coordinated revenge of the world as brain (the world as computer-brain?) as it strikes back for the years of brain damage that humans have been inflicting upon it (if you want separation from me, says the Earth, then it can be arranged—as the Earth makes humans extinct).

And yet, while the rise of the oceans and the spread of the desert can be understood as two sides of the same coin, in some senses one (the rise of the oceans) is the logical consequence of the other (the desertification of the planet). Reza Negarestani reminds us in his remarkable *Cyclonopedia: Complicity with Anonymous Materials* that as the earth turns to dust, so does dust thirst for "cosmic wetness, for the Flood" (Negarestani 2008: 92). We shall revert to how the relationship between wetness, mist, dust, mud, and oil indicates a "new sentience" in the final chapter (see Negarestani 2008: 92), but here we wish simply to suggest that the rise of the oceans could perhaps simply be the (unconscious) response of the planet to get water to its otherwise increasingly desiccated areas (even if humans cannot drink seawater). Moreover, we wish to suggest that the process of desiccation is itself one that is closely tied to the processes of capital.

Wolfgang Schivelbusch has compellingly written about how coffee has become common in human societies for the purposes of increasing worker alertness and productivity (i.e., the coffee industry is entangled deeply with the demands of capital). For Schivelbusch, the rise of coffee has come at the expense of the rise of alcohol, with the difference between the two being that coffee is a desiccant (it "dries" the mind and makes it capable of reason), while alcohol reduces productivity and is associated with wetness. Indeed, in language that reminds us of terms later employed by Haraway, Schivelbusch explains how historically coffee was understood to dry not only the human body, but also the body's four "humors," with the humors themselves deriving from the Latin word for fluid or sap (Schivelbusch 1993: 45). Humans, as humors and as *humus*, require fluids—as the constitution of the adult human at about 60 percent water makes clear (with various other aspects of the human body involving even higher concentrations of water: the brain and the heart are composed of about 73 percent water, with the lungs about 83 percent, muscles and kidneys 79 percent, the skin 64 percent, and the bones 31 percent; see Mitchell *et al.* 1945). As the desiccation of the human is part and parcel of the rise of capital (which is not to mention its possibly concomitant humorlessness; dry humor is a plant growing in the desert), so is the desiccation of the planet part of the capitalization of our ecosystem, perhaps even the greatest marker of the anthropocene—with the lack of drinkable water being an imminent cause for concern for humanity as it enters the chthulucene. As much is suggested in *The Big Short* (Adam McKay, USA, 2015) when we learn that Michael Burry (Christian Bale), one of the few people who predicted the 2008 global financial crisis, has since turned his attention to water as the resource of chief importance in the contemporary world. *Only Lovers Left Alive* (Jim Jarmusch, Germany/UK/France/Greece/USA/Cyprus,

2013) similarly posits that Detroit will once again become a city of importance, in spite of its current decline in the face of the self-same global financial crisis, because it is a city that has water, even if in nearby Flint, as Michael Moore documents in *Fahrenheit 11/9* (USA, 2018), its citizens are being deprived of that water (see also Wark 2014).

As Scranton reminds us, it is access to water and a severe drought that is perhaps chiefly responsible for the crisis in Syria, the consequent migration of numerous people, the rise of the Islamic State, and more. Indeed, a lack of water is driving many humanitarian crises all over the world (see Scranton 2015: 80–82), which throws into relief the international significance of dams, which begin to function not just as ways of conserving water, but also of controlling water for the purposes of war. As Fred Pearce puts it, "[t]he Islamic State's quest for hydrological control began in Syria, when it captured the Tabqa Dam in 2013," while the development of dams on the Tigris and the Euphrates can in principle be used not just to redistribute water, but also to prevent different peoples from having access to it (see Pearce 2014). No wonder dams loom large in films like *Sanxia haoren/Still Life* (Jia Zhangke, China/Hong Kong, 2006) and *Night Moves* (Kelly Reichardt, USA, 2013): in the former film, water is the lifeblood of China, but the need to conserve it leads to the destruction of China's past, as well as the obliteration and forced migration of its working classes (for an exposé of similar problems surrounding the Sardar Sarovar dam in India, see Roy 1999); in the latter film, a dam is the tactical target of a group of anti-capitalist terrorists. Scranton identifies how several dam projects in Turkey, Iran, and Syria are being used to exert influence over Iraq, which requires water from the Euphrates and the Tigris (the source of neither of which is in Iraq) in order to have enough water for its population (see Scranton 2015: 39–40; see also Al Tamimi 2018). Furthermore, in suggesting the role that dams and the control of water play as a weapon in the control of populations, *Night Moves* only reflects the real-world situation of enemy powers using cyberweapons in order to attack and destabilize dams in real life. In 2013, for example, Iran launched a cyberattack on the computerized controls of a dam in Rye Brook, New York. As Mark Thompson writes in *Time*, such attacks are the "future of war" (see Thompson 2016), especially through the use of digital viruses like STUXNET, as documented in *Zero Days* (Alex Gibney, USA, 2016).

It should perhaps come as no surprise, then, that the film industry has its global center, Hollywood, in the desert. A film like *Chinatown* (Roman Polanski, USA, 1974) presents a Los Angeles in which the prices of real estate are manipulated through the deliberate desiccation of the land, a direct link between drought and capitalism. And while a director like Thom Andersen can suggest in *Los Angeles Plays Itself* (USA, 2003) that the city owes its greatness to its ability to bring in water from elsewhere, a link is nonetheless established between cinema and desiccation. Here, perhaps, the digitization of film suggests an intensification of this process, as the emulsion of film stock has been replaced by the silicon and plasma of the digital image, with the center of the computer industry, Silicon Valley, being of course only up the former *Camino real* (or the "royal road," which we shall consider in the final chapter), which leads to San Francisco (to which we shall also revert in the final chapter).

Spineless Hollywood movies famously portray graphic violence but not sex. As Schivelbusch, now writing about another widespread desiccant, tobacco, reminds us in terms that recall MacCormack's remarks about mucus and Montgomery's suggestion that slime is necessary for sex, the "desiccation and mucus depletion" associated with tobacco chimed with "bourgeois progressive consciousness, which saw true health (i.e., productivity) in the antierotic desiccation of the body" (Schivelbusch 1993: 103). In other words, the desiccation and the hardening (or ossification or phallicization) of both the land and the body for the purposes of capital/productivity/war leads to an erosion of erotica (as opposed to the wet erotics of erosion)—a willful move away from human evolution via reproduction and thus the end of the human through the drying out of mind, body, and landscape. As dry land is infertile, so perhaps are "dry" humans—whose only deliverance from the desiccating processes of capital is thus the rise of Cthulhu not from, but with and as, the depths.

Becoming Light

As humans wish to desiccate their body that is in fact comprised of and sustained by water, so, too, do humans seem to want to divest themselves of their bodies, much as they wish to divest themselves of their planet—be that metaphorically (fantasies of escaping Earth), literally (by creating a planet that cannot sustain humans and/or via increasing numbers of companies that promise interplanetary travel, like SpaceX, Virgin Galactic, and Blue Origin), or technologically (uploading one's consciousness into a machine, with the energy consumption required to run that machine conveniently forgotten in most narratives about this aspiration). If cinema is synonymous with capital and its drive toward the desiccation of the human and of the planet, then it perhaps comes as no surprise that the desire to divest oneself of one's body translates into a desire to become cinema, or what we shall call becoming light.

Now, we suggested earlier that there are perhaps two Cthulhus: the Cthulhu of a planet that cannot sustain humans (Cthulhu as orgasmic evolution signaled by advent from outer space), and the Cthulhu of capital that uses humans in order to manifest itself in the material realm, including (perhaps especially) via cinema. Conversely, we have just argued that the siliconization of the planet via technology and the rising ocean levels are two sides of the same Cthulhu, or at least that the classically "wet" Cthulhu is a logical consequence of the "dry" Cthulhu of capital (the sea levels rise to flood and thus quench the thirst of the arid land). With these two arguments in mind, we might ask whether techno-capital is really just another manifestation of ecological disaster. That is, there seemingly is a contradiction here (or perhaps a superposition of two different logics) that undermines the sense of what we are saying. For, how can capital be that which destroys the planet during the anthropocene such that it is also that which destroys the human during the chthulucene? If the water rises to counter the desert, then Cthulhu would seem to stand against capital, not to be a part of it, since capital will end if the planet ends. And yet we are suggesting that Cthulhu (and cinema) might be capital itself seeking to come/to be recognized as alive (the new sentience that emerges from the weather/time—both *temps* in French—of the desert meeting the ocean). How can we reconcile these two seemingly contradictory arguments?

We have suggested that humanity is, like all others, a life form guided by symbiogenesis. Furthermore, we would do well to recall that genes will jump ship from any one species if they stand a better chance of survival with another. Finally, we have also suggested that life is not confined simply to the organic realm, but that it is perhaps immanent, or in all matter (and anti-matter?). With this in mind, then, we might suggest that capital has parasitically/symbiogenetically used humans in order to take material form and then to proliferate as technology during the early stages of its evolution (cinema as that which gives a face to technology, or what Seung-hoon Jeong calls its "interface"; see Jeong 2013). In this way, as much as humans use technology as an RNA-virus-like machine in a bid to control their DNA, so does capital use humans in a bid for (recognizable, technological) life.

We have equally suggested that cinema might be a form of camouflage for capital, distracting humans with its color show such that they cannot recognize what is really going on (namely that cinema is not so much entertaining humans as using them to become real/to make capital real). However, it is possible that on some level humans know full well that cinema is only camouflage, since in the cinematic and the digital era, it seems to be the desire of many humans to become cinematic. Humans do not just replicate images for the sake of images, then, but they also attempt to become cinematic for the purposes of empowerment: within the attention economy, the more that one appears in images, the more of one's life that is rendered in images, the more powerful one becomes. To this end, humans replicate the costumes, hairstyles, make-up, inky tattoos, behaviors, eating habits, movements, gestures, lighting, and the *mise-en-scène* of movies in a bid to make their lives seem more cinematic, which in turn might lead to their life becoming/being more movie-like (i.e., a life of leisure and not work, an existence in the divine realm of stardom/light as opposed to in the muddy/dark realm of humanity).

Recovering from injury in a New York hospital in 1935, Marcel Mauss famously realized that the gait of his nurses was familiar to him:

> I had the time to think about it. At last I realized that it was at the cinema. Returning to France, I noticed how common this gait was, especially in Paris; the girls were French and they too were walking in this way. In fact, American walking fashions had begun to arrive over here, thanks to the cinema. (Mauss 1973: 72)

While this scenario might sound like something out of *Invasion of the Body Snatchers* (Don Siegel, USA, 1956), it also finds support from Dana B. Polan's assertion, itself drawn from Edgar Morin, that folks "learn to kiss, to talk, to live, according to the shadows [of cinema] that they [film spectators] make, and need to make, into a kingdom," as movie-goers, or worshippers, "experience the cinema not in terms of the standards of their own experiential reality, but in terms determined by the flickers on the screen which come to be the basis of reality" (Polan 1982: 131–132; partially quoted in Beller 2006: 3; see also Morin 1957). This tendency is in keeping with another identified by Flusser, namely that in the photographic and the cinematographic age, we lead our lives "as though under a magic spell for the benefit of cameras" (Flusser 1983: 48). Becoming light, then, is a way for humans to try to divest themselves of their bodies and to live in the eternal realm of images, where aging and death disappear, and images supposedly repeat unchangingly ad infinitum. To be clear, it is not that we cannot see humans age on film, as is the case with *Boyhood* (Richard Linklater, USA, 2014)—even if cinema tends to relegate the aging and aged body, especially that of women, to its outside (see Jermyn 2014; Jermyn and Holmes 2015). However, to become light, or to become cinema, is to exploit cinema for the purposes of staving off death. As discussed, this kino-fication is not symbiotically to evolve, but in certain senses to bring about a living death. In the language of André Bazin, it is to "mummify change," such that change no longer takes place—in the image realm and as much as possible in the fleshworld realm, which equally we attempt to make as "cinematic" as possible (see Bazin 1967: 15).[4]

To describe the contemporary era, Negarestani invokes Mithraism, or "the cult of Light 'the Mother of All Religions, from Asia, to Africa and Europe'" (Negarestani 2008: 167). Furthermore, while we have been writing about "becoming light" for some time (see, for example, Brown 2013: 152), we should acknowledge that Scranton has also picked up on this idea in his own considerations of dying in the anthropocene. Toward the end of his monograph, Scranton describes how our technological age is defined not by humanism so much as photohumanism, and that *Homo sapiens* is being replaced by *Homo lux* (Scranton 2015: 107). Although he does not explicitly say as much, Scranton would seem to suggest that we must not sacrifice the human for the photo even as the human believes that it is subjugating light for the purposes of remaining forever the same. Instead, we must remember the human in spite of the proliferation of the photo.

However, Scranton then goes on to remind his readers that humans are always already "creatures of light," in that the "iron in our blood, the oxygen we breathe, and the carbon of which we are composed were all created in the dying hearts of stars" (Scranton 2015: 115). If Scranton, like us, argues that humans are seeking to become light, then why does he remind us at the last that we only ever were light in the first place? The point to finesse is that we must always remember our entangled condition with the universe (humans are made of stardust), rather than trying to transcend that universe by becoming light. For while light clearly is crucial to life (indeed, light is the measure of clarity itself), too much light—to become light—might well be the end of us, or the destruction of the human. Light brings us warmth and energy, but we cannot live on light alone. The desire to become light, then, is part of the bid no longer to evolve, to step outside of time, no longer to have a body and to become dry. It is also endlessly to repeat rather than to change, making of it a kind of living death. As capital seeks to have a body in order to be recognized as alive, humans seek to transcend theirs in order never to die. Humans think anthropocentrically that they are cheating death, but death, like darkness, is always already here. Cthulhu is thus the subjugation of the planet that really brings about the subjugation of the human. The attempted control of light camouflages over the persistent necessity of darkness.

The Speed of Darkness

In order for one's life to be as cinematic as possible, one's life must constantly be illuminated, such that cameras can register photographs and one's existence can be transferred to the luminous realm (the realm of light). The desire to become light, then, or to become what Scranton calls *Homo lux*, would involve the eradication of darkness—as if the latter were an impurity. Perhaps it is for this reason that the capitalist urbanization of the planet is also a drive toward permanent light for the purposes of permanent productivity—as Schivelbusch has also argued (Schivelbusch 1995). This is a rendering-cinematic of space, where there is never darkness, where there is permanent work, and where arrays of light-emitting diodes present images to humans for the purposes of maintaining their attention on the products and the lifestyle of capital itself for ever-greater periods of time.

And yet, as we have argued elsewhere, the human eye needs darkness in order to function, as can be seen in the blink and in human sleep (see Brown 2018b). Indeed, blinking specifically moistens the eye in order to prevent desiccation, which would destroy the eye's ability to work. Dry, the eye would become blind, being able to see no difference, but just a *ganzfeld*, or a uniform, uncolored field. Not only does it need moisture, then, but it also needs darkness, especially for the purposes of creating memories, as J. Allan Hobson (1995) argues with regard to sleep, and as Tamami Nakano and colleagues argue with regard to blinking (Nakano *et al.* 2013). To live in a world of permanent, unblinking illumination would be to live in a world without memory—as our screen-mediated lives testify as we constantly forget what we are doing and as we get distracted by screen after screen in the contemporary era, even taking our screens to bed with us so that they can specifically interrupt our sleep and prevent the formation of coherent new memories.

Where cinema in the analog age had darkness as a structuring principle, in that between every frame of the film was a frame of darkness that went through the projector, meaning that audience members were unwittingly sat in darkness for 40 percent of a film's duration (see Doane 2002: 172), in the digital age the projector refreshes different rows of pixels within an image as opposed to frame by frame, meaning that we never are sat in darkness during the film (see Cubitt 2014: 217–221). This is not to mention the shift away from watching cinema in a darkened theater toward watching films "in broad daylight" (see Pedullà 2013). Indeed, as we watch films increasingly on computer screens, one cannot really even see darkness, since when the screen goes black on a plasma screen, as opposed to on a cinema screen, one does not see darkness but one's own reflection (thereby suggesting the narcissism of the desire to eliminate darkness for the purposes of prolonging the life of the self?).

However, as capital tries to eliminate darkness from the lives of humans, and in a world of permanent, controlled light (and surveillance), we forget that humans and the world as a whole need darkness (for example, it is at night that plants can grow by using the energy that was created during the daytime via photosynthesis—as if darkness were a tool for learning and growth/consolidating memory in plants as well as in humans). Perhaps the universe itself also needs darkness in various different ways. For example, to the best of our understanding, the universe mathematically requires the existence of so-called dark matter and dark energy in order to function. Dark matter is thought to explain the interconnected nature of all things (darkness as key to entanglement), while dark energy allows the universe to continue expanding (darkness as a force for cosmic evolution instead of stasis). We might here note that as humans can only see about 5 percent of the universe's light spectrum, so does matter only account for about 5 percent of the universe, with dark matter and dark energy making up the remaining 95 percent of existence (see Randall 2015: 21).

If darkness is key to the universe as it is key to memory, then perhaps we can understand a link between darkness and the "spooky action at a distance" that haunted Einstein and which we mentioned in Chapter 2. Polarized particles demonstrate an entanglement that boggled Einstein because two particles separated by even vast swathes of space can change simultaneously—and thus at a speed that contradicts the speed of light as the limit of speed in the universe. That is, the particles react to each other faster than it would take light to carry information from one particle to the other. What is it that allows this to happen? If information moves faster than light (or if in fact it does not move), then it must be invisible and, in some senses, dark.

Physicist Lisa Randall mentions briefly the possibility that darkness has a speed, but does not really elaborate on what that is or might be (Randall 2015: 326–327). What is more, in her book on dark matter Randall makes no mention of tachyons, the theoretical "particles" of darkness that would be the "dark" equivalent of photons.[5] It is not that tachyons exist, but we should like to use them as a theoretical construct here to advance our thinking about the chthulucene. For, whether it takes particle form or not, the spooky action at a distance of polarized particles suggests a speed that is faster than light. Or, if light is the limit of speed, then what is suggested is non-speed—not in the form of slowness, but something that defies the concept of velocity altogether. If something faster than light (or other than speed itself) were to exist (which from the anthropocentric perspective would be not to exist at all), then it would always precede light, having always arrived first where light comes later. If light is the measure of the visible, and yet if light is preceded by darkness, then in some senses darkness will always be receding from view, or withdrawing. More than this: while darkness precedes light and recedes from human vision, it will always already be where light is; that is, darkness does not just recede into the distance, but it recedes at all points in space. If you will, darkness is there before our eyes, but we cannot see it; as light arrives and we can see, the darkness recedes away from us, but it also remains in an ever-thinner veil over our eyes, a necessary and invisible component of the process of vision itself. As Cary Wolfe puts it: "*Reality is what one does not perceive when one perceives it*" (Wolfe 2014: 204, emphasis in original).

Withdrawing and yet always there before us: darkness (or what Wolfe calls reality) becomes in some senses a literal superposition, a kind of entanglement glue (a viscous, mucus-like slime) that links here and there as well as then and now, since it does not know time. Darkness is in this sense a tentacular wormhole (with worms being monopod mollusks). The term tachyon also homophonously recalls the tactile: tachyons are something that we cannot see, but which perhaps we sense in other ways, for example, via touch. They are tentacles that furl and unfurl, linking together all things. Standing outside of speed, darkness also stands outside of time, sensing not just here and the present, but sensing here and there, the past, the present, and the future.

In his analysis of the contemporary, Giorgio Agamben suggests that to understand any epoch, one must be able to see the obscurity and darkness of that era:

> [t]he contemporary is he who firmly holds his gaze on his own time so as to perceive not its light, but rather its darkness. All eras, for those who experience contemporariness, are obscure. The contemporary is precisely the person who knows how to see this obscurity. (Agamben 2009: 44)

Not only are Agamben's words apt in an era of what Jonathan Crary has identified as 24/7 illumination, i.e., in which humans attempt to eradicate obscurity (see Crary 2013), but Agamben's work on the contemporary is also useful because like us he turns to physics to continue his analysis.

If there are so many stars in the universe, then the night sky should be filled uniquely with the light from stars, meaning that there would be no darkness, but instead permanent illumination—from the sun during the day and from a multitude of other stars during what we typically refer to as the night. The reason why we have darkness, however, is because

> the most remote galaxies move away from us at a speed so great that their light is never able to reach us. What we perceive as the darkness of the heavens is this light that, though traveling toward us, cannot reach us, since the galaxies from which the light originates move away from us at a velocity greater than the speed of light. (Agamben 2009: 46)

For Agamben, the contemporary perceives this light that cannot reach us in the darkness that otherwise surrounds us. Or, if you will, the contemporary is able to see not just her own time, but also the times of other galaxies that may never make anything other than a dark contact with ours.

Most importantly, Agamben says that "the present that contemporariness perceives has broken vertebrae," because to see a darkness that recedes away/withdraws from us means that we are in (dark) contact with times that cannot reach us, and which we also cannot reach: "[i]ts backbone is broken," Agamben continues, "and we find ourselves in the exact point of this fracture" (Agamben 2009: 47). And: "it is the contemporary who has broken the vertebrae of his time . . . he also makes of this fracture a meeting place, or an encounter between times and generations,"—a process that Agamben links to the "time of the now," or *ὁ νυν καιρός/ho nyn kairos*, with *Kairos* being a concept to which we shall return in the next chapter (see Agamben 2009: 52). Where Agamben considers seeing darkness as breaking the back of one's epoch, however, we wish to suggest that those who are without backbones in the first place, namely invertebrate species like cephalopods, always see time in an equally "invertebrate" fashion. To be contemporary, to see time and to see darkness: this is what coming into (dark) contact with the cephalopodic thought of the chthulucene, and its concomitant chthulucinema, allows us to achieve (for a more sustained consideration of Agamben's work in relation to cinema, especially as it relates to media archaeology and the presence of the past in the present, see Harbord 2016).

We shall develop our consideration of darkness in the next chapter, where we shall analyze *Arrival*, the film in which alien cephalopods visit Earth and give to a human the ability to see here and there and now and then at the same time—such that this contemporary human, linguist Louise Banks, helps to create not a world structured by boundaries, borders, and warfare, but a world that sees no boundaries, only interrelationships and the possibilities of life. But before we draw together various of the weird strands that we have been putting together to discuss *Arrival*, let us address finally the issue of time itself. What is time?

The Matter of Time

The smallest particles in the universe (e.g., up, down, charm, strange, top, and bottom quarks) are different not because they are made out of different types of matter, but because they spin at different rates. That is, what distinguishes an up quark from a down quark is its rhythm. Matter has at its base, then, differences in spin, or rhythm, tempo, and time. We should note that the rate of spin is not constant and that spin changes as particles interact with other particles and thus change, cohering and decohering into different forms (and what from the human perspective might be considered into and out of existence, as matter decoheres into antimatter and antimatter coheres into matter; see Brown 2013: 68–71). What differentiates elementary particles, then, is not type but time, with each particle's tempo changing at all times as it interacts with other particles.

As things stand, humans group particles into various types according to their spin or tempo. Indeed, one can imagine that humans use machines to measure the spin or tempo of particles, with those machines thereby affecting that spin or tempo as per Werner Heisenberg's famous observation that the observer will change the behavior of a particle as a result of the observation made (see Heisenberg 2000). It is not that we are incapable of ever detecting the "true" spin or tempo of a particle—as if that truth lay in some real realm, but which simply was or is inaccessible to us humans. Rather, Heisenberg helps us to understand that the tempo of a particle is always changing as a result of its interactions, including with the humans with whom it is entangled (there is no realm of static truth beyond our interactions; as per Niels Bohr, our inter- or intra-actions, our entangled complementarities are the truth).

If particles are always changing their tempo, and yet humans group particles together according to their spin or tempo, our contention here is that we in fact group together particles that each have slightly different tempos, not least as a result of their interactions with observers and with each other. Pushing this argument further, we would wager that we only know about so many types of particle because of the limitations of our observational devices and our observations, but that if we had sensitive enough ways to measure the spin of particles, we would discover that there are perhaps as many types of particle as there are particles. That is, each elementary particle has a unique rate of spin, or tempo, that constantly is changing depending on its interactions. Not only is each particle "unique" in its spin, but in its unique spin/in the uniqueness of its tempo, it also expresses the entire history of the universe, or how it came to have its unique spin. If in the unique tempo of each particle we have the entire history of the universe, then we can hypothesize that the whole of the universe is defined by difference (different tempos), while also seeing how tempo—a form of time measured in terms of rhythm—is linked to the eons of time that are the history of the cosmos/chaosmos. Furthermore, in carrying in its tempo an entire history of the universe, each particle becomes not just separate and unique, but also what David Bohm might call implicated (see Bohm 2002). That is, each particle is folded in (im-plicated) with every other particle in the universe, suggesting a universe of interconnectedness and entanglement.

We shall further speculate that if we could paradoxically go back to instants "before" the Big Bang (i.e., to the timeless), then we might find a universe of particles all spinning at the same speed, or perhaps not spinning at all. That is, we would find a lifeless, uniform universe of particles that were all the same and which would have no difference and no time. The "Big Bang" is, from this perspective, the birth of difference, which is also the birth of matter, which is also the birth of time. Notably, this is also the birth of light. This "uniform" and "dead" universe of darkness therefore "precedes" light, time, and difference—but not in a purely negative sense. Rather, in order for there to be light, matter, and a multiverse at all, then that which "preceded" that multiverse (the universe, or darkness) must carry within it the potential for difference such that difference/existence/light/time can come about at all. In other words, for every Big Bang that renders an actual multiverse, there is (at least) one "pre-existing" and virtual universe in which the potential for difference already exists.[6]

We may find ourselves wondering how and why the possibility for existence to take place "exists" (how does the virtual "exist," even if it precedes the actual/existence itself?). Humans possibly have it all wrong in boggling over how existence at all takes place; perhaps instead they should boggle over the possibility that existence does not take place (rather than finding it impossible that things exist, perhaps we should find it impossible for things not to exist). In other words, we would like to suggest that nothing is inconceivable—that we cannot conceive of an absence of existence, or nothing itself. If nothing is inconceivable, then all that exists (and which might exist qua the virtual) is conceivable, including darkness. If everything that exists is conceivable—indeed, if it has been conceived—then we live in a necessarily plural universe (as the "con-" of conceived makes clear; existence is withness, which means that existence is more than one, otherwise existence would not be with anything, but alone). This is a multiverse of touch, since to conceive comes from the Latin *com*, meaning with, and *capere*, meaning to take, which itself comes from the Proto-Indo-European root *kap-*, meaning to grasp. In other words, while this may seem like radical speculation, we would propose that the multiverse is just(ly) a con-cept—and that (as per Bohm's argument), the material multiverse and thought are intimately linked (consciousness and matter are mutually implicated). Darkness, or the binding virtual realm that makes the actual possible, is therefore not nothing, because nothing cannot be. Furthermore, in making the actual possible, existing outside of light, outside of time, and perhaps outside of existence, darkness is necessary for the multiverse—but perhaps exists precisely as a concept that allows material reality to exist as such. That is, the multiverse as we know it is in some senses a dream born from the eternal night that takes place as we sleep; the universe is thus the creation and consolidation of memory in material form, just as darkness in the form of sleep and blinks allows the brain to consolidate memory. Cinema, perhaps, is thus a metaphor for the way in which fiction, or the existing non-existent (to offer another superposition), is necessary for truth. In this way, if darkness is also withdrawing, then we live in a multiverse that is a work of art (a drawing) that is always plural (with): withdrawing.[7]

Notes

1. Various film fans speculated at the time of its release that *Life* was a prequel of sorts to the Marvel comic-book adaptation *Venom* (Ruben Fleischer, USA/China, 2018). Although this is not the case, *Venom* does possess various chthulucinematic qualities (see Ridgely 2018). The film tells the story of a sentient and intelligent alien substance that takes the form of a black suit that replaces the skin of journalist Eddie Brock (Tom Hardy). Being an intelligent black skin that throws out tentacular hydrostats at will, the Venom suit also hungers for human flesh à la Cthulhu. Invertebrate, the Venom substance also recalls the intelligent "imipolex" suit from *Gravity's Rainbow*, which equally suggests/is created from sentient fossil fuels rendered in a black, latex form, and which suggests the rise of oil and other substances to choke the human and close off its otherwise porous existence.
2. Underneath the surface of planet Earth there is also light in the form of the molten iron that is what Reza Negarestani describes as the planet's second, hidden sun (the Earth as a gobbet of sunlight cooled only on its outer surface). Negarestani describes this iron ocean, this plasma intelligence as the Cthulhu-sounding Cthelll (see Negarestani 2008: 161–162). More specifically, though, we might add that this plasma emerges on to the surface of the Earth during volcanic eruptions, which like meteor impacts and humans (with their own volcanic eruptions, namely nuclear explosions), constitute one of the major causes of mass extinctions.
3. Are the *Alien* films, especially *Alien* (Ridley Scott, UK/USA, 1979), *Aliens* (James Cameron, USA, 1986), and latterly *Prometheus*, not all mucosal stories about slimy aliens that hunt humans and other artificial intelligence machines in foggy environments, with kinship often pointing toward life instead of death? On a separate note, *Gukjesijang/Ode to My Father* (JK Youn, South Korea, 2014), which upon its release was a blockbuster in its homeland, features cinema patrons eating squid, as if the two were inherently linked. A squid can also be seen in a market about halfway through the film; given that the film's story follows a man, Duk-soo (Jung-min Hwang), trying to look

after his family over the course of the second half of the twentieth and into the twenty-first century, taking in events as diverse as the evacuation of Hungnam, working as a *gastarbeiter* in a mine in Duisberg, Germany, the Vietnam War, and more, the film would seem to use the cephalopod to suggest a complex history in which numerous historical events are interconnected.

4. If it is patriarchy/capital that seeks to ossify both space and time such that they remain under human control, then we might suggest that the preservation of human bodies could more aptly be referred to as "daddification." As we shall see in relation to the mother tongue (the tentacle as mother), perhaps mummification is an attempt to control that which flows and has no set shape, with the evolution of the term away from the substance used to preserve the corpse to the preserved corpse itself being the patriarchal solidification/desiccation of an otherwise threatening liquid. That is, daddy has once again turned mummy into a monster.
5. Randall does elsewhere mention tachyons, suggesting that if a theory of the universe contains a tachyon, then it is by definition incomplete (see Randall 2006: 286). Whether or not incompleteness is in fact a structural necessity in our universe à la Kurt Gödel's famous incompleteness theorem, in which, as per much speculative realism, something that is unprovable can still be true (see Penrose 1989: 138–141), is beyond the scope of the present investigation. For more on tachyons in relation to cinema, see Brown (2020).
6. In the submarine documentary *Aliens of the Deep* (James Cameron and Steven Quale, USA, 2005), there is a discussion of chemosynthesis as opposed to photosynthesis as a process sufficient for life. Observing a wealth of submarine life writhing around volcanic, hydrothermal vents at the bottom of the ocean, the director comments on how water and heat might enable life, and not light—even though that heat is of course originating from the Earth's inner sun, namely its molten core. In other words, light is indirectly necessary for life in this otherwise sunless aquatic world, but life can nonetheless exist in the dark. Notably, the final sequences of the film involve an octopus interacting with a submarine; Mike Cameron, a robot designer and the director's brother, remarks upon how the moment involved him "shaking hands with an alien"—before the film ends with a fantasy sequence in which marine biologist Dijanna Figueroa and astroscientist Kevin Hand meet tentacled, submarine aliens on another planet (the sequence bears a striking similarity to *The Abyss*, James Cameron, USA, 1989).
7. Withdrawal is a concept commonly adopted by Graham Harman in his account of the universe. For Harman, humans and other objects can only ever have a partial knowledge or understanding of each other, meaning that the "reality" of objects is always "withdrawn": "[s]itting at the moment in Cairo, I am not entirely without relation to the Japanese city of Osaka, since in principle I could travel there on any given day. But this relation can never be total, since I do not currently touch the city, and even when I travel to stand in the exact center of Osaka I will not exhaust its reality. Whatever sensual profile

the city displays to me, even if from close range, this profile will differ from the real Osaka that forever withdraws into the shadows of being" (Harman 2011: 100). As Anna Longo explains, "[f]or Harman, the reason why we cannot know things in themselves is that things in themselves withdraw behind their appearance, and that withdrawal constitutes the truth about any object. It is not our knowledge that is limited, but it is the limitation of knowledge that constitutes a positive truth about any object: they are not as they manifest themselves; they withdraw from any relation while they are perceived as withdrawn from any relation" (Longo 2014: 35).

We enjoy much of Harman's argument, but for us withdrawal also sits alongside presence: the tachyon necessarily withdraws since it moves at a speed that is faster than light, but the tachyon must also be always already present, too, since it precedes light by virtue of arriving before it as a result of moving faster than it. Where does it arrive? In a realm of space without space. But then if there is no space, how does it move? Why, without moving . . . All a bit "Zen"? This is the realm of superposition and entanglement.

Put differently, Manuel DeLanda contests Harman's withdrawal as follows: "because I do not account for the enduring identity of objects using singular essences, I do not have to postulate any *fundamental* withdrawal . . . I gravitate toward other explanations for why there is no such thing as absolute knowledge. The first is the existence of *novelty* in the world, both at the level of molecular and biological evolution as well as technological and scientific innovation. Chemists synthesize so many new substances every year that they will never finish studying them all, much less find out what happens when they enter into chemical reactions with each other. It is the *open-ended nature* of the world, not so much a fundamental withdrawal, that makes dreams of a final truth vanish" (DeLanda and Harman 2017: 101). Importantly, DeLanda identifies in Harman here an appeal to the timeless and to a reality that exists beyond the human. While Harman dismisses the work of Karen Barad for being too anthropocentric, in that for Harman, Barad suggests a universe constructed around the human (DeLanda and Harman 2017: 3–4), Harman misunderstands Barad (and by extension Niels Bohr) in believing that entanglement is an entirely human phenomenon, rather than being a phenomenon that exists between all objects, including humans (polarized particles are, after all, not human beings). Since humans are part of reality, then reality does include humans, even if the latter are sufficient but not necessary for reality (there could well be realities without humans, even as such realities might be entangled with realities where humans do exist). For present purposes, then, we would say that Harman, as per DeLanda's critique, is a sort of Heisenbergian who believes in an objective reality (about which humans can never be certain, i.e., that reality is withdrawn), whereas we suggest that uncertainty and incompletion is our reality (which is the suggestion of Bohr as taken up by Barad). In this way, like DeLanda we posit a reality of time and change, rather than a withdrawn reality beyond time and change (with Harman in this process making the same error that he accuses Martin Heidegger of making, which is to see reality as a frozen, immutable snapshot rather than as a moving and temporal thing; see, for example, Harman 2010: 29).

And yet, one might finally contend, in saying that the tachyon is outside of space and outside of time, do we not also suggest a withdrawn and "objective" "reality" that is "beyond" the one that we know, and which is static and unchanging? But, like the tachyon, this "beyond" is also always already here, and it is not so much real as precisely unreal, with the border between reality and unreality being porous, just as the border between space and spacelessness and between time and timelessness is also porous, thereby engendering a reality of change as these realms inter/intra-act (multiverses linked by wormholes where Big Bangs take place everywhere and everywhen, with every particle or object being entangled with every other particle or object; or, in a word, conception).

CHAPTER 7

The Backwash of Becoming Cthulhu, Or, L∞py, Tentacular Time

That glimpse, like all dread glimpses of truth,
flashed out from an accidental piecing together
of separated things.

– H. P. Lovecraft

Thunderbolts explode between different intensities,
but they are preceded by an invisible,
imperceptible dark precursor.

– Gilles Deleuze

Time present and time past
Are both perhaps present in time future,
And time future contained in time past
If all time is eternally present
All time is unredeemable.

– T. S. Eliot

As the oceans rise, so does water literally arrive, in the sense of water reaching the shore (French: *à rive*). It is in the liminal space of where the sea meets the desert that the fate of humanity will be decided. That is, to evoke the title of a post-apocalyptic classic, humanity is *On the Beach* (Stanley Kramer, USA, 1959). But while Cthulhu arrives from the depths of the ocean in Lovecraft, the tentacular heptapods arrive from the darkness of space in *Arrival*. Perhaps planet Earth itself is thus a desert-shore against which the dark waves of space constantly lap.

As might by now be becoming clear, science fiction is often held up as a particularly philosophical genre. For, beyond its proclivity for sociopolitical extrapolation and actualizing thought experiment-like fantasies, and whether or not the genre imagines new understandings of this world or other worlds that are completely beyond the ken of humans (what Quentin

Meillassoux calls extro-science fiction; see Meillassoux 2015), it also commonly toys with speculative ideas or engineers thought-provoking encounters with the unknown. Historically speaking, through its creative use of the "false" and the "fantastical" to pose legitimate "what if" questions, a smattering of science-fiction stories have helped to push thought toward its limits and frontiers. Mary Shelley's nineteenth century "technofantasy" *Frankenstein; Or, the Modern Prometheus* (1818) offers itself as a touchstone case in point, being a novel artwork that ramps up its era's "epistemology engines" (see Ihde 2006) to pose troubling ethical and existential questions regarding the blurring of boundaries between science and nature (as a cultural concept), as well as between life and death. Shelley's thought-provoking gothic sci-fi was of course treated to its own reanimations on stage and screen throughout the twentieth century, taking its place alongside newer cinematic science fictions such as *Metropolis* (Fritz Lang, Germany, 1927), *2001: A Space Odyssey* (Stanley Kubrick, UK/USA, 1968), and *The Matrix*, to name but three lightning rods for thought and debate. Such artworks have also often been celebrated for the ways in which they challenge audiences, critics, and philosophers alike to see or to think *differently*.

It is through such provocations and encounters that we might posit certain knots tying together the praxis of science fiction and philosophy, a view forwarded by Steven Shaviro and Gregory Flaxman alike, with the latter coining the neologism "sci phi" to describe a type of mysterious film that provokes us to think in a philosophical way. As already intimated, Flaxman argues that it is because science fiction "is devoted to the 'not yet,' the 'otherwise,' or the 'Outside,'" that it shares much in common with the philosophical endeavors of Deleuze, who believed that philosophy as a practice (involving the creation of concepts) must follow science fiction's suit (Flaxman 2011: 295; see also Shaviro 2016). Here, the value of cerebral cinematic works such as *2001*, *Solyaris/Solaris* (Andrei Tarkovsky, USSR, 1972), and/or *Inception* (Christopher Nolan, USA/UK, 2010) lies in their production of enigmatic images, which foreground "[m]etaphysical anomalies, baffling mutations, cracks in time," and which offer viewers "signs and images that 'do not compute' according to the science of this or any other world" (Flaxman 2011: 299–300).

What Flaxman ultimately lauds in sci phi, then, is its creation of images "that outstrip any image of thought" (Flaxman 2011: 299). A similar outstripping of thought, or foregrounding of that which is "inaccessible to thought," is something that Eugene Thacker equally describes as the principal value of supernatural horror in *Tentacles Longer Than Night* (Thacker 2015b: 115). For Thacker, horror and philosophy at their best demand that audiences confront the limits of the knowable, or else wrestle with "the thought of the impossibility of thought" (Thacker 2015b: 115). Echoing Flaxman and Shaviro, Thacker explains in a decidedly Deleuzian manner that

> what intimately ties horror to philosophy—not that philosophy, which explains everything, would explain horror, making it both meaningful and actionable for us, but that philosophy—all philosophy—eventually discovers within itself a hard limit to what can be known, what can be thought, and what can be said. (Thacker 2015b: 162–163)

In the work of writers such as Edgar Allan Poe and H. P. Lovecraft, for instance, Thacker constantly finds characters and readers running up against the paralyzing boundaries of their knowledge or concept of reality, and confronting an objectless form of groping-thinking. Lovecraft's mosaic Cthulhu stories, for example, not only expose the "relative horizon of the thinkable," but also offer "an enigmatic revelation of the unthinkable," which grants readers a form of "*black illumination*" (or alternatively, a partial range of inhuman perspectives; see Thacker 2015b: 142).

Accordingly, while we might say that the work of a philosopher such as Immanuel Kant is overtly concerned with the limit *of* thought, Thacker sees Lovecraft's horror being more precisely obsessed "with limit *as* thought" (Thacker 2015b: 120). And as we shall see, a converged notion of dark sci phi illumination, as well as considerations of a Lovecraftian "chthulucene" (see Haraway 2016), become germane to our reading of chthulucinema here, and in particular a film like *Arrival*, in which the appearance on Earth of Lovecraftian aliens heralds a novel inhuman perspective on the true nature of time and reality.

Specifically, we here argue that *Arrival* invites viewers to confront a counterintuitive model of time that at once recalls and reposes both that which Deleuze called a "third synthesis" of time, and J. M. E. McTaggart's idea of an a-temporal "C series" of *unreal* time. Ultimately, we suggest that this film's a-temporal conception of the-future-as-having-already-happened can function as a key, or a black mirror/contact lens, through which we might darkly see/understand the fate of humanity as a whole as we pass from the anthropocene, in which humans have dominated the planet, to the chthulucene, in which humans no longer exist on the planet at all.

Because Thacker reminds us that there "is never just one tentacle, but many," we also here encircle *Arrival* alongside a crop of other recent science-fiction chthulucinema that seemingly gropes and feels around analogous temporal models (Thacker 2015b: 15), among others including *The Call of Cthulhu* (Andrew Leman, USA, 2005) and *Miss Peregrine's Home for Peculiar Children*. By such means, we impressionistically demonstrate how the temporal signature of "chthulucinema" forces viewers to confront, and to try to make sense of, a counterintuitive image of alien time and reality, with the three films listed here primarily serving as emblematic "species" of chthulucinema, in the process becoming representative of greater singular-plural bodies that unfurl entangled, multi-strand, and bi-directional images of "tentacular" time. Of particular interest to us here is that *Arrival*, *The Call of Cthulhu*, and *Miss Peregrine . . .* not only share depictions of the future as having a backwards, withdrawing, redounding, or backwashing affect/effect upon the specious present or living-past, but that they all also associate these realities with weird betentacled creatures. Being a film based on Lovecraft's famous monster, *The Call of Cthulhu* offers itself as an especially fruitful starting point, not least because this film concretizes its backwashing temporal themes through its *faux* silent-era aesthetic form.

Tentacles of Time

The Call of Cthulhu aims to be a faithful adaptation of Lovecraft's famous short story. However, this shoestring short—predominantly filmed in Leman's garage for the H. P. Lovecraft Historical Society—is by no means a "typical" contemporary adaptation, translation, or updating of an earlier epoch's horror story. For one thing, and in contrast to prior adaptations of authored horror stories, such as (monstrous/eight-limbed double-author alert!) Francis Ford Coppola's *Bram Stoker's Dracula* (USA, 1992) or Kenneth Branagh's *Mary Shelley's Frankenstein* (USA/Japan/UK, 1994), Andrew Leman's H. P. Lovecraft's *Call of Cthulhu* inhabits a deceptively antique form, which appears to all intents and purposes to be an "authentic" 1920s silent-era Expressionistic horror film (replete with aged poster, black-and-white aesthetic, square frame, intertitles, anachronistic actor makeup, and accompanying silent-era performance style). Thus, while Coppola notably used analog silent-era special effects in an otherwise modern sound and color film, Leman's silent more precisely surfaces as an artificial historical relic, as if the flick were adapted and screened shortly after the publication of Lovecraft's 1928 original. In this way, *The Call of Cthulhu* becomes the sort of film that Lovecraft "might have seen" in his own lifetime (see Morehead 2010).

While similar backwards-looking tropes have been inventively deployed in other celebrated films in recent memory, including *Forgotten Silver* (Costa Botes and Peter Jackson, New Zealand, 1995), *The Artist* (Michel

Hazanavicius, France/USA/Belgium, 2011), and various works by Guy Maddin, Leman's possession and inhabitation of a silent-era modality appears especially ethico-aesthetically acute. Indeed, on one level, the synthesis of form and content works in tandem to reactivate the "tone and atmosphere of Lovecraft's fictional universe" (Hood 2007). Or, as Jason Morehead puts it:

> [i]t's a simple aesthetic choice, but a brilliant one. The structure of a silent movie, with its intermingling of visual and textual elements, is perfect for the structure of Lovecraft's storytelling. What's more, the archaic look of the movie, which gives it the air of a long-lost cinematic artefact, jives well with the fact that Lovecraft's stories were both obsessed with archaic relics and artefacts—Lovecraft looked more lovingly on previous civilizations than the one in which he lived—and that Lovecraft's mode of storytelling itself has an archaic feel to it. (Morehead 2010)

In such sentiments, we might grasp how the film both channels the Lovecraft *geist*, at the same time as it conjures the temporal tentacular *Zeitgeist* of our weird chthulucene times. Meanwhile, old-style effects pick up and amplify another key temporal theme surging diagonally through, or beneath, the fragmented Cthulhu story (and Lovecraft's *oeuvre* more broadly). For as the fictional characters—in an act of *mise-en-abyme*—encounter antiquated artifacts within the story, the anachronistic Expressionistic format forces modern viewers to similarly reconnect with, and think backwards to/through, the modern cinema's own archaeological past lives. Accordingly, viewers and characters alike apprehend or confront objects that appear to be widely distributed in time, somewhat akin to Timothy Morton's "hyperobjects," those weird, withdrawn, and viscous things of which we can only gain partial aspects or pictures. Objects that should also be comprehended, Morton explains, as attractors, which appear to radiate "temporality from the future into the present" (Morton 2013: 91). Consider in this light Lovecraft's vivid descriptions of Cthulhu's own suspended and waiting hordes, whose monumental dwelling spaces were "built in measureless aeons behind history," but only in order to entomb them until they may rise again, at some far future moment:

> But although They no longer lived, They would never really die. They all lay in stone houses in Their great city of R'lyeh, preserved by the spells of mighty Cthulhu for a glorious resurrection when the stars and the earth might once more be ready for Them. But at that time some force from outside must serve to liberate Their bodies. The spells that preserved Them intact likewise prevented Them from making an initial move, and They could only lie awake in the dark and think whilst uncounted millions of years rolled by. They knew all that was occurring in the universe, but Their mode of speech was transmitted thought. Even now They

> talked in Their tombs. When, after infinities of chaos, the first men came, the Great Old Ones spoke to the sensitive among them by moulding their dreams; for only thus could Their language reach the fleshly minds of mammals. (Lovecraft 2002: 155)

Chthulucinema, we here suggest, innervates a comparable brain–screen encounter, emerging as an inhuman conduit for the transmission of evental thoughts into its mammalian viewers' brains. To this end, each instance of chthulucinema radiates with the energy of a more distributed event, constituting a delirious if not portentous "dream screen" (to channel another ancient living-dead image of the cinematic medium) that offers a partial vantage onto an opaque and counterintuitive image of redounding futural time (redounding is a term that in fluid dynamics speaks of the body of an advancing wave pulling the already broken wave in front up into its face), which essentially evacuates the all-too-human present from the films' (un) consciousness.

To reiterate, the articulation of the ancient to the attractor encourages characters and viewers to apprehend the abysmal depths of pre- and post-human time, or, in the language of Meillassoux, to look "after finitude" (Meillassoux 2010). In *The Call of Cthulhu* this is made palpable by the silent-era form, which is joined to an even deeper archeological gaze within the diegesis as a man (named Francis Wayland Thurston in Lovecraft's story, and played here by Matt Foyer) discovers various ancient statues of Cthulhu before going on the trail of the beast itself, simultaneously unearthing a bifurcating—past/futural—image of hollowed-out present time. The withdrawn (living-)past here connects up to a portentous, backwashing, and eschatological image of a distant "not yet," wherein Cthulhu and his demons prefigure and then put an end to mankind. The chthulucinematic image of time here constitutes a massive circuit that both shorts and attenuates the present, meaning that the human species (as an evolutionary event) becomes gripped and pulled apart by the living, branching timelines of an ancient past and an attractive future.

L∞py Time

Distilled images of looped and backdrafted time are given form in various other contemporary science-fiction films, including *Primer* (Shane Carruth, USA, 2004), *Looper* (Rian Johnson, USA/China, 2012), *Time Lapse* (Bradley King, USA, 2014), *Edge of Tomorrow* (Doug Liman, USA/Canada, 2014), *Coherence* (James Ward Byrkit, USA/UK, 2013), and *Comet* (Sam Esmail, USA, 2014), the latter two of which associate their time loops with comets passing close to Earth (on which, more later). McKenzie Wark calls such movies *anthropo(mise-en-s)cène* films, with *Edge of Tomorrow*, for example, combining alien invasion themes with a looping computer game logic—as Cage (Tom Cruise) must repeatedly go into battle with space invaders until he finally defeats them. The link between the film's anthropocene monsters, its "complex" computerized temporalities and pressing ecological issues establishes for Wark "the digital time of this civilization" (Wark 2014), a quality that also applies to *Gravity* (Alfonso Cuarón, UK/USA, 2013). While the latter film tackles these themes in a primarily linear aesthetic-political way, however, Wark sees *anthropo(mise-en-s)cène* cinema as helping to expose

> the almost shapeless, formless, seething tentacle menace of the [a]nthropocene. One which curiously seems to have some sort of mimetic power. It doubles us and confounds us. It erupts from the earth or out of the sea, or appears out of nowhere in the sky. (Wark 2014)

Further examples that probe looping temporalities and/or multiverse time-space themes also share cephalopodic creatures and details, including an abstracted numerological attraction to the number eight (which also resembles the infinity symbol when aligned horizontally). As mentioned, a 16-foot Pacific octopus called "Old Night" serves as an interdimensional psychic medium within the orphic multiverse of *The O.A.*, while the number eight becomes a key feature of the psychically connected pods in *Sense8*. Furthermore, the appearance of both Cthulhu-like images and the 8/∞ symbol occurs throughout the spooky time-travel series *Dark* (Baran bo Odar and Jantje Friese, Germany, 2017–). Earlier cinematic iterations of this phenomenon might also be pegged to the Delorean of the *Back to the Future* series (Robert Zemeckis, USA, 1985, 1989, 1990), which had to reach 88 miles per hour in order to travel back and forth through time. More recently the science-fiction thriller *Source Code* (Duncan Jones, USA/Canada, 2011) also subtly continues this trend. Here, disabled army veteran Colter Stevens (Jake Gyllenhaal) finds himself part of a *Quantum Leap*-style (Donald B. Bellisario, USA, 1989–93) experiment that requires him to travel back into the past (or a parallel reality) to investigate the blowing up of a commuter train by a terrorist. Significantly, in his "time reassignment" forays Colter can only inhabit the body of his compatible surrogate for the final eight minutes before his death. He does this eight times in the film, before looping off into another branching reality. Meanwhile, when the program's inventor is financially rewarded for the project's success, he enthuses that "we could have at least eight [new] Source Code projects up and running before the end of the year!" In a similar vein, perhaps it is not surprising that the notorious online forum, 4chan, has since 2013 sprouted four more tentacles in order to become (the unaffiliated) 8chan/∞chan, as if the latter were an octopodic/infinite entry point into the dark web.

If *Source Code* extrapolates quantum (or "parabolic calculus") computing technology as a means of exploring nonlinear relationships between past and future presents within a quantum multiverse, other chthulucinema channels aliens, myth, and magic to toy with similar premediating and time-space traveling themes. As discussed, *Edge of Tomorrow* harnesses alien beings to justify its looping computer-game-cum-action-film structure, while the earlier tech noir, *Minority Report* (Steven Spielberg, USA, 2002), uses "precog" biotech psychics to set up analogous backdrafting futural themes. There, a trio of biogenetically engineered precogs that sit semi-submerged in photon milk (a "nutrient supply and liquid conductor") have their heads wired up to tomographic imaging computers, the tentacular cables of which reach up from the bottom of their submersion pool to connect their brains to the computer—becoming visible examples of what we shall later refer to as the new Medusa (an image repeated in numerous films where humans have their heads wired into digital devices). Conceits of myth and magic allow comparable time loops to emerge in Tim Burton's 2016 adaptation of Ransom Riggs' novel, *Miss Peregrine's Home for Peculiar Children*, which, as intimated, is another chthulucinema narrative populated by totemic tentacular monsters.

Miss Peregrine . . . follows troubled adolescent Jacob/Jake (Asa Butterfield), whose grandfather Abraham (Terence Stamp) suffers from dementia, and who appears to be trapped in his own paranoid cyclical brain-loops. A flashback finds an earlier iteration of Abraham sharing fantastical bedtime stories with his young grandson, which he apparently bases on his own youthful adventures with a band of supernatural misfits. In the flashback, young Jake is prognostically framed enwrapped in octopus-print bedsheets, as Abraham casts monstrous finger-shadows of betentacled creatures on to the boy's bedroom ceiling. It is at this moment that Abraham first tells Jake about the hideous "Hollowgasts": weird tentacle-tongued monsters that relentlessly pursued his gang through time. Jake later finds Abraham left for dead by a real Hollowgast, which lingers in the dark forest behind the old man's home. Inspired by his grandfather's cryptic dying words—"to go to the island, then the loop, in 1943"—Jake travels with his father to Cairnholm in Wales, where Abraham grew up during the war. Jake there meets the same peculiar mob of gifted children from his grandfather's stories, including an invisible boy and a girl who can levitate. These children, we learn, are watched over by Miss Peregrine (Eva Green), a shape-shifting "ymbryne," or bird-woman, who is charged with guarding a coiled temporal portal that allows the children to hide—from the persecution of the "normal" world and from predation from the supernatural Hollowgasts—by permanently looping back through time and living through the same repeating day (September 3, 1943) over and over again.

By virtue of living in this coiled time loop, the weird children have in some senses become immortal, but they are also stuck in the living past, unable to exit into any other present. For, if the peculiars (as collectively they are known) were to re-enter Jake's millennial present, for instance, then a backlog of time spent in the loop would immediately catch up with them (i.e., they would age a lifetime in an instant), and they likely would die. Jake learns that his grandfather was a peculiar too, and that his special power was an ability to see the otherwise invisible Hollowgasts—an ability that Jake has apparently inherited. Meanwhile, the Hollowgasts themselves are tentacular monsters that were created after various peculiars tried to become immortal—not by looping time but by never aging in spite of chronological time. If the Hollowgasts consume the souls of enough peculiars, then they can transform into undead humanoid beings known as wights, who have all-white eyes.

With regard to the film's plot, the existence of the time loops sets up an action-image adventure through coiled time and space wherein the "now" of the film's opening (2016 and advancing) recedes to become an increasingly distant futural coordinate (each passing day in 2016 and onwards is further from September 3, 1943), but whose actors (Abraham, Jake, and the peculiars) influence and impact ever-deeper strata of past-presents. By degrees, evermore time loops and peculiar groups are discovered, which ultimately allow Jake and his new-found friends to screw from one loop to another and thus to helter-skelter forwards toward "the present," or to withdraw backwards into ever-further moments of the past. As a consequence, *Miss Peregrine . . .* unfolds a temporal picture wherein causes and effects operate in both backward and forward directions, albeit in a twisted, spiraling manner.

Similar ideas are also to be found operating in *Primer* and *Looper*, where evermore screwy and entangled multi-strand timelines twist backward (and forward) to expose an overtly tentacular image of temporality—the temporal equivalent of the spatial tentacles that we earlier discussed in relation to *Maelström* and other "pulp fiction" examples. In these films we discover characters who are able to see or to know the future and/or to loop back within their own lifelines, thereby interacting with and influencing their own previous selves, while repeatedly criss-crossing the same living present. However, an action-adventure film like *Looper* offers a slightly different temporal take to *Miss Peregrine . . .*, since it focuses on an outlawed time-loop technology that is exploited by mobsters who live in a future control society where it is virtually impossible to get away with murder. The gangsters thus employ sophisticated wormhole time-portals in order to eradicate undesirables within the primitive past (which is a not-so-distant future from when the film was made). Indeed, the future Mafiosi send back bound and hooded bodies to historical hitmen, who are tasked with assassinating them and then disposing of the bodies. Within this backwashing universe, hitman Joe (Joseph Gordon-Levitt) is shown executing several targets who materialize through his wormhole portal, and who arrive from the future with a bag over their head and several silver blocks strapped to their torsos. The contractual arrangement with the mobsters is that the final execution that each hitman enacts will be of their own future self, who also arrives hooded, but with gold bars strapped to their bodies. The act of self-murder signals the final "closing" of the loop, with the hitman thereafter allowed to retire and live hedonistically with their ill-gotten wealth for a period of thirty years, until they are sent back through the loop to be killed—effectively removing the only witness with knowledge of these past crimes from the future picture. However, after Joe lives out his thirty-year retirement something goes wrong, because old Joe, played by action hero Bruce Willis, manages to avoid his own execution in order to correct a future injustice to which only he is privy. Managing to travel back through the loop without a hood, old Joe subsequently teams up with his younger self in order to change the past, and therefore the future that stems from it, in the process creating a branching "grandfather paradox"-style tentacular adventure that sees a future timeline change the past, and the presently modified past altering the fated future in turn—which future allowed for this particular past to exist in the first place (for more on cinematic representations of the grandfather paradox, in which a man travels to the past and kills his own grandfather, thereby preventing his own birth and thus his ability to kill his own grandfather, see Varndell 2014).

Something similar happens in *Primer*, which is by far the most complex and cerebral chthulucinema story so far considered. Indeed, the story gravitates around an electromagnetic machine invented by two entrepreneurial "intellectual engineers," Aaron (Shane Carruth) and Abe (David Sullivan), in the hope of revolutionizing the world by reducing the weight of objects for shipping purposes. However, anything entering their machine's modified gravitational field—which is generated by coiled electromagnetic wires—begins to reveal "temporal anomalies." This leads the inventors to finally recognize that their invention allows objects (and later subjects) to move backwards through time. The limitations placed on time-travel in this story are ultimately constrained by the moment at which the machine is activated. That is, objects/subjects cannot travel back to a moment before the time-machine was turned on. Thus the moment the machine is turned on marks the temporal limit of possible travel. However, any object or subject entering the turned-on machine thereafter will move backwards through time for the duration that they spend inside the box. In this way, an hour spent inside the turned-on box is equivalent to traveling back one hour in time.

Learning this, the inventors turn on their machine one morning and leave it running for the day in a storage facility while they hide out in a hotel room. There, Abe and Aaron watch how the stock market trades, and with this financial data in hand they return to the storage facility to enter their still-operating boxes. After lying (or sleeping) inside for a number of hours, the two protagonists exit into the past, at a point in time when their previous selves are safely holed up in the hotel room. The two thereafter make a series of profitable stock market investments with their fore-knowledge of the day's trends—an entrepreneurial-capitalist theme similarly explored in *Time Lapse*, where the heroes chance upon an advanced quantum camera device that is able to take pictures of the future, and which leads them to send themselves photographed information about future sports results for the purposes of winning wagers. In *Primer*, though, Aaron and Abe begin to loop back again and again, with certain gaps and caesurae in the narrative suggesting that there are evermore hidden back-up machines, and thus many other time-paths and time-loops to which viewers are not privy.

As *Primer*'s heroes attempt to loop back and to modify and change events for their benefit, they increasingly forego their earlier ethical decisions not to interfere with or influence their (increasing number of) past selves and lives. Thus, many different timelines and tentacular loops begin to thread through or become entangled with other narrative tendrils, with some only retroactively or virtually becoming exposed as weaving through the living present of the film. One such example can be linked to noises and events that at first appear to be incidental to the main story's *mise-en-scène*, but which eventually become reframed as the action of future narrative timelines that are always already coiled back into the earlier story. In this way, noises coming from the attic—attributed on first viewing to wildlife—are eventually revealed to be noises made by a future version of Aaron who has been drugged and bound by an even further-flung future version of himself (who has traveled back to the furthest point of the past via a failsafe box). By such coin, the film subtly suggests that everything that Aaron and Abe do in the future and the past is always already happening in a riven and dynamic living present/now courtesy of multiple entangled and criss-crossing future back-passages.

By showing such temporal paradoxes, these films individually and collectively serve to unmoor workaday notions of a fixed, singular, and stable past (or passing present), which ostensibly becomes transformed into a modular conduit for complex bi-directional flows of information and effect/affect. As we shall see, a similar argument can be applied to *Arrival*, which focuses on the reality-altering contact between humans and a Cthulhu-like alien species.

Arrival

Adapted from Ted Chiang's science-fiction novella "Story of Your Life" (2015 [1998]), *Arrival* follows the reality-warping story of linguistic expert Louise Banks, who after making contact with an alien race, learns how to communicate and think in their decidedly inhuman manner. The aliens arrive on Earth via a dozen dark disc-shaped ships, or concave "shells," which hover thirty or so feet above twelve different locations, and which appear to be "illogically" distributed across the globe to media and military intelligence. In contra-distinction to typical flying saucer conventions—rendered cliché by over half a century of first-contact stories that include *The Flying Saucer* (Mikel Conrad, USA, 1950), *The Day the Earth Stood Still* (Robert Wise, USA, 1951), *Invaders from Mars* (William Cameron Menzies, USA, 1953), *Plan 9 from Outer Space* (Edward D. Wood Jr., USA, 1959), *Close Encounters of the Third Kind* (Steven Spielberg, USA, 1977), *Independence Day* (Roland Emmerich, USA, 1996), and *District 9* (Neill Blomkamp, South Africa/USA/New Zealand/Canada, 2009)—the dark discs here hover on a revolutionary vertical rather than horizontal axis. Thus, while the novella has the aliens depositing what are called "looking glasses" (Chiang 2015: 117) to communicate with humanity on Earth, the film employs more visually arresting icons to mark the first contact. Indeed, each ship constitutes a 1,500-foot "elongated oval" (Giardina 2016), composed of an unknown, black, and rock-like material. The Alien Species Wiki aptly describes the design as "resembling an immense, obsidian concave lens" (Alien Species Wiki n.d.), making them like dark versions of Anish Kapoor's Chicago-based sculpture, *Cloud Gate* (2006), the appearance of which percolates throughout *Source Code*'s *mise-en-scène* as an expressive load-bearing parabolic object. Presently we wish to recognize these craft as being reminiscent of a colossal, dark *contact lens*, not only in the sense that it is black and is a point of "contact" between humans and aliens, but also in the sense that it puts Banks in contact with, and allows her to see, that which to humans is typically in darkness, namely time. This "dark contact lens" ultimately serves to draw perception and thought away from the present and Earth, and toward the future and the cosmic.[1]

In line with these ideas, we also recognize the ships as being uncanny *attractors*, or science-fiction renderings of what Morton calls "hyperobjects." Indeed, hyperobjects are, as indicated, *nonlocal* objects—such as asteroids, glaciers, or global warming—which are massively distributed across vast tracts of (phase) space and (deep) time. Interesting to note is that *Arrival*'s space ship was modeled on the look of an actual asteroid called 15 Eunomia (see Giardina 2016; Levy 2016), and that the film's first clear glimpse of these ancient monoliths depicts one in long shot entangled with a dynamic elemental weather system cascading down the foothills of an 80-million-year-old Rocky mountain. Importantly, Morton links human encounters with hyperobjects to what Jacques Derrida calls *l'avenir*, because they essentially encourage us to "develop an ethics that addresses what Derrida calls *l'arrivant*: the absolutely unexpected and unexpectable arrival, or what I call the *strange stranger*, the stranger whose strangeness is forever strange—it cannot be tamed or rationalized away" (Morton 2013: 123–124; see also Derrida 2000). Of further resonance here is how such uncanny objects are comprehended as radiating "temporality from the future into the present" (Morton 2013: 91), tending thus to draw thought toward the radically unknown "future future" (Morton 2013: 123). Accordingly, and as if describing or anticipating Banks' own transformed alien perceptions from within *Arrival*, Morton notes that hyperobjects effectively reveal that "[a]ppearance is the past. *Essence is the future*" (Morton 2013: 91).

But we are already getting ahead of ourselves. For, Banks is a white middle-class university linguist, who we learn has outstanding high-security clearance after having previously taken on commissions to translate Farsi tapes for US military intelligence. By degrees Banks is invited to a contact site in Montana, where she enters the shell's topsy-turvy interior and lays eyes on the outlandish "heptapod" (Greek for seven-footed, or seven-tentacled) creatures: alien chimera whose betentacled bodies appear to blend the physiology of octopus, starfish, and spider. With the help of her scientist and mathematician counterpart, Ian Donnelly, Banks begins to apprehend how the aliens' physiological arrangements and cognitive processes result in nonlinear modes of symbolic communication.

As Donnelly explains within a weirdly a-temporal and educational "here are some of the many things we do not know about heptapods" lecture (which again highlights that this weird film is indeed concerned with the limits of the known and the thinkable):

> How do they communicate? Here, Louise is putting us all to shame. The first breakthrough was to discover that there is no correlation between what a heptapod says and a heptapod writes. Unlike all written human languages, their writing is semasiographic. It conveys meaning. It doesn't represent sound. Perhaps they view our form of writing as a wasted opportunity? Passing up a second communications channel. We have our friends in Pakistan to thank for their study of how heptapods write. Because unlike speech, a logogram is free of time. Like their ship, or their bodies, their written language has no forward or backward direction. Linguists call this non-linear orthography. Which raises the question, is this how they think?

Donnelly for his part gets to make some breakthroughs, too. Although cut from the film, his character in the novella helps Banks to arrive at her a-temporal conclusions regarding heptapod communication by explaining the relevance of Pierre de Fermat's principle of "least time," which the aliens apparently understand, unlike the other human calculus and geometry thrown at them. Using chalk and blackboard to illustrate the fastest path for a beam of light to pass through two media (air and water), Donnelly explains that Fermat's model indicates that action may be teleological rather than causal. For, in this example, the path taken by a light beam appears to demonstrate that it must always already know what the "fastest path" to a given point is in advance, before it even sets off. This suggests that while it appears to travel in a straight line to us, the beam of light's path might actually be thought of as connecting two points of a coiled spring that are compressed together, such that distance is eradicated (as per a wormhole).

Meanwhile, in both the film and the novella Banks gradually learns to compose in the heptapods' nonlinear semasiographic language. This leads to an exegesis staged between Banks and Donnelly regarding the Sapir–Whorf hypothesis, wherein they discuss how the language one speaks shapes thought and concept creation, with different languages fashioning different worldviews and notions of time. Anticipating recent real-world research into the ways in which "[l]anguage shapes how the brain perceives time" (Bylund and Athanasopoulos 2017), the film explores how an a-temporal alien language imparts a correspondingly inhuman way of perceiving and experiencing time or temporality. Thus, by the film's end, viewers are forced to reframe what had heretofore appeared to be narrative flashbacks—depicting Louise having a child called Hannah, and then losing her to a rare cancer as a teenager—as flash-forwards, or memories of events that are yet to be. By such means, the film's confrontation with the unthought, or the limits of the thinkable, pertain here to what we might call the (un)reality of time.

For Thacker, the limits revealed in Lovecraftian horror formulate the "degree zero" of thought, or instances of *frozen thought*, wherein "we see something different, something of the order of deep time and the scale of the unhuman" (Thacker 2015b: 128). As already indicated, this frozen thought formulates what Thacker calls *black illumination*, an idea we shall purloin presently for our reading of *Arrival*. For, after learning to see afresh thanks to her encounter with the dark contact lens, Banks gains a form of dark illumination that exposes the degree zero of temporality, which leads to an accompanying frozen image of time that catalyzes a "*reductio ad absurdum* of philosophy" (Thacker 2015b: 128). So, if Thacker sees black illumination as revealing that all experience leads "to the impossibility of experience," Banks' dark temporal illumination in *Arrival* expands her perceptions beyond her "specious present" to an opaque frozen time, partially composed of futural temporality. In other words, Banks begins to see the future as if it had already happened: she knows that Hannah will die, but unlike Donnelly, she chooses to have the child anyway.

To help explain and to elaborate upon this sci phi film's imaging of such temporal issues, it helps to read the film (and occasionally the neo-weird novella) alongside two existing philosophical models offered by otherwise weird philosophical bedfellows: Deleuze and McTaggart. In what follows, then, we shall argue that *Arrival* forces viewers to think of time in terms that make sensible certain aspects of what Deleuze calls a "third synthesis" of time, and that which McTaggart refers to as an a-temporal "C series." For this reason, we first turn toward Deleuze's "futural" philosophy, since it aptly offers a style of thinking that not only "*derives from the future*" (Flaxman 2011: 294), but which also "summons the future in order to evacuate the very presence of the present" and to place us inside "a perpetual *here and now*" (Flaxman 2011: 293).

Arrival as Third-Synthesis Cinema?

Deleuze is arguably most renowned for his description of two epochs of cinema and their corresponding images of time, or duration à la Henri Bergson (see Deleuze 2005a [1983], 2005b [1985]). However, Deleuze actually outlays not two, but three distinct ways in which we can think about time, and which arguably can be mapped on to the Greek time gods of Chronos, Aion, and Kairos. In *Cinema 1: The Movement-Image*, for example, Deleuze describes a classical cinema based on sensory-motor systems, chronological action, and habit (see Deleuze 2005a). Therein, a tripartite group of affection-images, perception-images, and action-images helps him to account for pre-war cinema's teleological thinking of time, which was most often subjugated to movement and action. If such models correspond to a first synthesis of time in the present (Chronos), in *Cinema 2: The Time-Image*, Deleuze goes on to describe the emergence of a new post-war cinema wherein time increasingly "appeared out of joint," with the past, or virtual realities, appearing to surge forth into/to coexist in the present (Aion), a conception of time somewhat akin to Marcel Proust's involuntary memories in *À la recherche du temps perdu/In Search of Lost Time* (sometimes translated as *Remembrance of Things Past*, 1913; see also Deleuze 2005b; Pisters 2012: 137).

Beyond the *Cinema* books, though, is a third model or synthesis of time that Deleuze hints at. This, Patricia Pisters points out, was primarily distinguished and developed in *Difference and Repetition* (Deleuze 2004a), and ultimately marks a break from Bergson and an embrace of Friedrich Nietzsche instead. Pisters sees this third model as being associated with the eternal return (or what here we might term Kairos, as mentioned in the last chapter, in order to distinguish it from the other two). Pisters uses this third model to describe the images of time thought by contemporary digital cinema, labeling this new regime "neuro-images," which she describes as being responsible for altering "the temporality of the brain's 'temporal signature.'" Or, as she renders it through more familiar Deleuzian terms,

> [i]f the movement-image is founded in the first synthesis of time of the present, and the time-image is grounded in the second synthesis of the past, the neuro-image belongs to the third synthesis of time, the time of the future. (Pisters 2012: 303)

As is the case with Pisters' reading of third-synthesis science-fiction films such as *The Butterfly Effect* (Eric Bress and J. Mackye Gruber, USA/ Canada, 2004), the temporal models encountered in *Arrival* appear primarily concerned with "reprising the future, death, and new beginnings (eternal return)" (Pisters 2012: 156).

Certainly, in *Arrival* the death of Hannah is in the future, while a new beginning for the human race is heralded by the gift, or what in the film is perhaps also considered to be a weapon, namely the very language of the heptapods themselves. The new beginning here is a literal reconfiguration of the erroneous human brain's perception of time and reality, as is made clear by Banks' forward-oriented memories, which viewers encounter as a form of "future 'time that is now,'" wherein the past and the present become regrounded in an image of the future (see Pisters 2012: 140, 303). There are Deleuzian echoes here, too, of the notion that, as David Deamer so eloquently puts it, "[a]ll time resonates through its futurity" (Deamer 2016: 341)—a counterintuitive idea that the latter majestically illuminates through a close reading of *Enter the Void*, wherein the film's narration does not so much unground the order of time, but rather "creates images as events permeated by the future, events along the line of flight, each of which has a virtual presence with all the others" (Deamer 2016: 341). In pushing viewers to think in a similar manner, *Arrival* likewise attests to how third-synthesis cinema's thinking of time "relates explicitly to the cosmic" (Pisters 2012: 154). For, to think of the future as if present, or as a future plicated into the present (to think of the future as a fait ac-com-pli), is to think not only one's own death, but also by extension the death of the human species and the planet on which it currently resides, together with the heat death of our sun, and the "freezing" of this and other universes as a whole.

It would be fair at this point to say that this third-synthesis image of the future presents us with a different sort of "frozen thought." Not least because this expanded vision of time is one that apparently leaves little or no room for change or for Banks' free will. If the future is fated/a fait accompli, then we are seemingly left in the final analysis with a decidedly un-Deleuzian and un-Nietzschean conception of the world. For as the alien language Heptapod B reveals a deterministic view of Banks' future (and her child's death), time and free will ultimately become exposed as an illusion, meaning that Deleuze's models break down, since they are defined by openness and change, or the sense that things could be otherwise, which is not the case here. We shall make the weird claim later on that choosing to accept both life and death is compatible with openness and change—and indeed with a universe of becoming. First, however, we shall respond to the echoes that we hear of McTaggart's famous analytical proof that "time is unreal," and that "[w]henever we judge anything to exist in time, we are in error" (McTaggart 1908: 457, 470).

Arrival as C Series Cinema?

In "The Unreality of Time," McTaggart stresses that belief about time's unreality is in and of itself something timeless, appearing as it does in all ages and places. In the world of philosophy, he reminds us, time has *before* him (if you will) been treated as "unreal" by Baruch Spinoza, Immanuel

Kant, G. W. F. Hegel, and Arthur Schopenhauer, among others (McTaggart 1908: 457). Seeing time as synonymous with change, McTaggart argues that "whenever we perceive anything as existing in time—which is the only way in which we ever do perceive things—we are perceiving it more or less as it really is not" (McTaggart 1908: 470). To drive his point home, he thereafter troubles two commonsensical ways of speaking and thinking about time, which he labels the "A series" and the "B series." The A series constitutes a tensed-model of time that demands thinking about a dynamic series of positions "that run from the far past through to the near past to the present, and then from the present to the near future and the far future" (McTaggart 1908: 458). The B series, meanwhile, is a de-tensed series that is defined in terms of relations that run "from earlier to later" (McTaggart 1908: 458). While in our everyday lives "we never *observe* time except as forming both these series" (McTaggart 1908: 458), McTaggart goes on to show that both models have inherent problems and that, once they are shown to be false, they counterintuitively lead toward a recognition of the unreality of time. For, briefly summarized, the B series cannot represent change (since time is fixed), while the A series equally is troubled by contradictions and problems of regress.

To illustrate this point further, we might observe how the death of the last dinosaur that we now call Tyrannosaurus Rex occurred earlier in time than the movie called *Jurassic Park* (Steven Spielberg, USA, 1993). From a B series perspective, it naturally follows that it will always be true that the movie screens later than the Cretaceous–Paleogene extinction event. Because these relations are forever fixed, McTaggart argues that the B series cannot adequately represent change. That is, the relation of before to after, and/or of earlier to later, is unchanging and therefore timelessly true. Prima facie, the dynamic A series model appears better able to represent change, since from this vantage point we can intuit that the day after the death of the last Tyrannosaurus Rex on Laramidia, the former island continent that now is part of North America and where many dinosaur fossils have been found, the cinematic premiere of *Jurassic Park* was/is located in the far distant future. Every passing moment over the next 65 million or so years brings the film's release into ever-closer proximity—until eventually, on June 11, 1993, the theatrical release appears in the present. At the time of writing today, of course, the world premiere of *Jurassic Park* is an event located in the near past, and which is ever-receding toward the far past. McTaggart notes that while the A series of time has a clear order, we can navigate its order in two directions: from past to future as per our dinosaur example above, or, via a simple reversal, from future to past. Problematically for McTaggart, though, there is both a terminal contradiction and an infinite regress glitch built into the A series model. This contradiction lies in the fact that if we are to perceive time in this ordered fashion, then something like the release of *Jurassic Park* is an event that must simultaneously claim the properties of having been past, present, and future. As these three properties are contraries, McTaggart maintains that we encounter a contradiction. So, even if we might say that the event was past, present, and future at different moments (in 2019, the premiere of *Jurassic Park* is in the past, in 1969 it was in the future, and in 1993 it was briefly in the present), in order to save the model we still have satisfactorily to define "when" each of these coordinates was/is. Thus, while we might now (in 2019) say that *Jurassic Park* was earlier than *Arrival*, and later than the Cretaceous–Paleogene extinction event, in doing so we transform an A series description into a B series description, thereby fixing time and thus undermining our own ability to represent change. As McTaggart clarifies: "[w]e cannot explain what is meant by past, present and future. We can, to some extent, describe them, but they cannot be defined. We can only show their meaning by examples" (McTaggart 1908: 463).

We shall return later to the extinction of the dinosaurs and how their destruction (likely) at the hands of a meteoroid might also help us to think about life, death, and time on Earth, but what is presently of import to our argument, and which often gets neglected in accounts of McTaggart's proof for the unreality of time, is a third series of time, which McTaggart introduces as an a-temporal "C series," which has order, but no direction. When introducing the C series, he explains that it

> is not temporal, for it involves no change, but only an order. Events have an order. They are, let us say, in the order M, N, O, P. And they are therefore not in the order M, O, N, P, or O, N, M, P, or in any other possible order . . . And thus those realities which appear to us as events might form such a series without being entitled to the name of events, since that name is only given to realities which are in a time series. It is only when change and time come in that the relations of this C series become relations of earlier and later, and so it becomes a B series. (McTaggart 1908: 461–462)

McTaggart elsewhere expands his position on the C series, which, as Kris McDaniel explains, can be thought of as an *adequacy series*, wherein "states that appear to be present more accurately represent reality than states that appear to be past, but both in turn are less accurate representations than states that appear to be future" (McTaggart 1909: 348; quoted in McDaniel 2016). The future has an important association for McTaggart with the "eternal," which he elaborates further in "The

Relation of Time and Eternity" (McTaggart 1909). McDaniel thus explains that although reality is timeless, McTaggart still "holds that it is appropriate to describe the eternal as being future" (McDaniel 2016). Or, as McTaggart himself puts it: "[e]ternity is as future as anything can be" (McTaggart 1909: 355).

McTaggart's position here resonates with Morton's notion of hyperobjects revealing the future to be essence and the present an illusion, ideas that in turn resonate with Banks' memories in *Arrival*, and which a brief return to the novella can help to clarify. Banks recalls that

> [b]efore I learned how to think in Heptapod B, my memories grew like a column of cigarette ash, laid down by the infinitesimal sliver of combustion that was my consciousness, marking the sequential present. After I learned Heptapod B, new memories fell into place like gigantic blocks, each one measuring years in duration, and though they didn't arrive in order and land contiguously, they soon composed a period of five decades. It is in the period during which I know Heptapod B well enough to think in it, starting during my interviews with [the aliens] and ending with my death.
>
> Usually Heptapod B affects just my memory: my consciousness crawls along as it did before, a glowing sliver crawling forward in time, the difference being that the ash of memory lies ahead as well as behind: there is no real combustion. (Chiang 2015: 166)

Through such descriptions we better grasp how the C series undermines A and B series descriptions and their relation to a real passing specious present, which here becomes equated with an illusory "combustion" of consciousness. Nonetheless, we might anticipate an objection with regard to the cinematic adaptation of the story. Indeed, while Banks' hybrid human–heptapod perception does resonate with McTaggart's C series modeling in this literary description, the film (more than the novella) harnesses Banks' all-too-human subjective perspective as a focalizer, using this as a privileged crack that opens on to eternity. That is, by its very nature the film's narrative form supports a lingering belief in an anchoring specious present. Accordingly, although Banks senses eternity and can recall the future from an uncanny a-temporal perspective, she here remains a human who still perceives time in the prevailing A and B series fashion. This is not, however, a necessarily terminal objection, for McTaggart concedes that while time itself remains unreal, "our perception of temporal order is not wholly delusory" (McDaniel 2016). It is rather that for McTaggart the "C series is real, but no terms are really past, present, or future, and there is no real change" (McTaggart 1927: 272).

Linked to such ideas, and of importance to our reading of *Arrival*'s endorsement of the Sapir–Whorf hypothesis, McTaggart himself laments that a major difficulty in sketching out his unreality proof "without almost giving the explanation," relates to the English language having "verb-forms for the past, present, and future, but no form that is common to all three" (McTaggart 1908: 468)—something that the a-temporal semasiographic signs and images of Heptapod B bypasses, as do the film's own images, which, as we shall discover shortly, appear to blend certain C series and third-synthesis features in a distinctive style.

Arrival of 3C Time

Putting theory before the film, or the cart before the proverbial horse, would most likely result in a Deleuzian interpretation that sees *Arrival* as a hybrid movement- and time-image film that has become implicated with third-synthesis models, while a McTaggartian reading would allow us to perceive it as a C series film that remains infected by an all-too-human A and B series perception. However, reading the film on its own terms allows us to see it variously making sensible different temporal images that display features of Deleuze's third-synthesis concept of eternal recurrence (3) and McTaggart's unreal model of ordered time that becomes energized by a futural eternity (C)—as well as Morton's hyperobject notion of the present being an illusion and the future essence. In this way, we propose the concept of 3C time.

Possibly the best illustration of 3C time comes during the movie's final act, which reveals the present to be a(n eternally) living past or (actual) illusion of presentness that remains dynamically entangled with, or permeated by, real (but virtual) future happenings. The film has the alien contact story build toward a duel, wherein human armies threaten to go to war with the alien visitors. Thus, as various nation states become paranoid about the aliens' use of a symbol that is (mis)translated into the word "weapon" (but which actually is a reference to the language of Heptapod B itself), the Chinese, under the command of General Shang (Tzi Ma), declare war on the heptapods, followed shortly thereafter by Russia and Sudan. As the exceptional white American protagonist, Banks is burdened with attempting to avert catastrophe and to save the world as per any action-image hero. However, when trying to realize this goal, Banks increasingly becomes overwhelmed by a redounding tide of subjective future-memories inculcated by her learning of Heptapod B. As time pressures mount, we join Banks in her specious present/past, where she ineffectively scours a screen full of recently expunged Heptapod B symbols. Here, fragments of future-memory increasingly intrude via a temporal parallel editing trope. That is, a deluge of overwhelming memories and visions results in Banks becoming a dislodged seer and hearer, as per Deleuze's time-image, with Banks ostensibly being dislocated from the actual action-image world of the present, and rendered inactive by overwhelming apparitions. However, what Banks sees are not exactly involuntary memories or recollection-images as we traditionally know them. Rather, these are third-synthesis unfoldings from the time of the future. As Banks stares at the as-yet undeciphered symbols on the screen, a targeted sheet of future-memory suddenly becomes opened up. This sees Banks recalling cutting open a cardboard box and by degrees discovering, examining, and then leafing through her newly printed (therefore forthcoming) monograph about (learning) Heptapod B, *The Universal Language* (a name given to cinema during the silent era). Semi-articulated with this futural-recollection is another embedded or co-joined future-memory, into which the film also jumps, and which depicts Banks delivering a research seminar, where she (presumably) works out the knowledge required for the completion of the book. Cutting back to the specious present, Banks' body presently indexes these memories (and expertise) unfolding into her brain like an involuntary Proustian memory in reverse. Thereafter she looks at the previously unidentified heptapod symbols on her embedded screen-within-a-screen and exclaims: "I can read it!" This is to say, the backwashing surge of reality from the future here reactivates Banks' body as narrative agent, ostensibly transforming the third-synthesis seer into a third-synthesis action hero, once again empowered in the specious present/past.

Banks immediately runs to military commander Colonel Weber (Forest Whitaker) in order to inform him that "the weapon is their language," and that the heptapods "gave it all to us" so that we can see the time that "is to come." However, she is dutifully informed that at this stage it is already too late for the US military (a collective Hollywood action body par excellence) to influence the outcome of the Sino–Russian–Sudanese military escalation. By having the most traditional action heroes retreat from the contact zone (beneath the shadow of the now-shifting alien hyperobject) in anticipation of an imminent intergalactic war, the film illustrates how problems of this magnitude can no longer be solved by action in the present alone. Instead, to be truly effective, *action has to become spiralingly articulated to the empowering and energizing realm of the dark future.* And, as if reifying this very idea, it is at the precise moment when the military leave Banks alone on screen that her hybrid superpowers become fully awakened, catalyzed by a future-memory of the unborn (but already dead) Hannah, who appears embedded within a dark out-of-focus half-waking memory, whispering: "Wake up, Mommy." And from here, Banks suddenly leapfrogs into another involuntary sheet of future-memory, where she is attending a diplomatic event some eighteen months hence. Worth noting here is how the film uses the audiovisual texture of these sequences—with their oneiric selective focus, super-saturated chthonic lighting, and partially focalized febrile sounds—to signal that these are (re)created memories, rather than objective images of an actual future.

The embassy party sequence opens with an establishing shot of an anonymous crowd gathered beneath a balcony, captured by a free-floating handheld camera evocative of Tilman Büttner's cinematography in *Russkiy kovcheg/Russian Ark* (Aleksandr Sukorov, Russia/Germany/Japan/Canada/Finland/Denmark, 2002), itself a movie that leaps back and forth through time as the camera wends its way around the Hermitage, meaning that, as Deamer notes, there "is no cause and effect, just events that resonate with each other, backwards and forwards" (Deamer 2016: 321). Beneath Banks, a mixed crowd immingles in their evening attire between a curved double staircase. The unstable subjective camera then pans up and to the right, capturing lavish chandeliers and a row of national flags draped from the high ceiling, including those of the USA, China, Denmark, and Japan. We see the bare back and shoulders of Banks as she enters from frame right in medium close-up, conspicuously out of focus in her strapless ball gown. While she gazes down on the crowd below, over her right shoulder a white alien flag comes into focus, revealing it to be a balanced Heptapod B symbol. Only after this detail is made discernible does Banks' bare neck and head then clearly get pulled into sharp focus, the close-up revealing a spiraling up-combed hairstyle that visually rhymes with the Heptapod symbol behind her, while intertextually quoting Madeleine's (Kim Novak) iconic hairstyle from *Vertigo*, another film where time appears out of joint and where complex associations between memory and action, life and death, past, present, and future play out.

The sequence in turn becomes reminiscent of Alain Resnais' *L'année dernière á Marienbad/Last Year in Marienbad* (France/Italy, 1961), not least because of the scene's opulent setting and glamorous costumes. Furthermore, Banks is then approached by a tuxedoed stranger, General Shang, who shares his memories of a past encounter they have apparently had, but which she cannot here recall. This last detail might give us pause, for it signals that the version of Banks embedded in this future-memory has no recollections of the past (yet), or, more precisely, this moment of past located in-between the future-memory and the moment of specious present that embeds it. There follows a vertiginous and *Marienbad*-esque dialogue between Banks and Shang, depicted under a near-heavenly fluid golden-orange light:

Shang: Dr Banks, [it's] a pleasure.
Banks: General Shang. The pleasure is mine, really.
Shang: Your president said he was honored to host me at this celebration.
Banks: Yes.
Shang: But I confess, the only reason why I'm here is to meet you in person.
Banks: Me? Well, I'm flattered. Thank you. *phatic laughter*
Shang: Eighteen months ago you did something remarkable. Something not even my superior has done.
Banks: Well, what was that?
Shang: You changed my mind. You are the reason for this unification. All because you reached out to me on my private number.
Banks: Your private number? General, I . . . I don't know your private number.
Shang: *showing Banks his phone screen* Now you know. I do not claim to know how your mind works. But I believe it was important for you to see that.
Banks: I called you didn't I!?
Shang: Yes, you did.

During this final exchange, a familiar deep booming non-diegetic trumpeting sound surges forth on the film's soundscape, the bass resonations of which have already become a quasi-leitmotif synonymous with the heptapod creatures. In this context, however, the sound gathers near religious associations, evoking notions of angelic messages being trumpeted or heralded across eternity. The enduring, throbbing audio is also used to envelop a cut *back* to Banks in the past/present action-image sequence, reinforcing the idea that knowledge and revelation are spreading across the vibrational fabric of space-time. As the camera lingers, Banks begins desperately seeking a phone to call Shang. She finally steals a CIA sat-phone, and manages to dial China. The US military is alerted to the call, however, and tries to track down whom they now believe to be a spy or traitor. As the phone rings, and the military closes in, Banks still does not know what the future requires her to say. But, as the present/past time pressure increases, the film dislodges another important fragment of future-memory, wherein Shang says: "I will never forget what you said."

The film thereafter opts to cut back and forth between present/past and the future-memory, occasionally using sound bridges to overlap the two. And by such means the film depicts the general whispering a Mandarin message into Banks' left ear in the future—which she thereafter (or there-fore) relays to Shang in the past/present through a phone held up to her right ear (the editing and physical arrangements of moving bodies and actions also generating a looping Möbius directionality to the message's transmission). The editing thus makes clear that Banks is herself a vanishing mediator of sorts, rather than a classical action(-image) hero or free(-willed) agent as we would typically recognize it. Indeed, the action-image here takes on traits of being the living past, in relation to a future that simultaneously abounds with telescoping time-image features. For, in a counterbalancing move, after hearing Shang's message at the embassy party, the film shows the past Banks relaying the message, before the future Banks melodramatically reconnects with her own past/present, experiencing them as a surging emotional Proustian recollection-image (or what in Chapter 2 we referred to as quantum steering into the past), which render her a frozen time-image seer and hearer (in the future). Here, we find a coiled and twisted brain circuit in the making. A C-timeline is thus erected, albeit twisted back on itself like a Möbius strip or ∞ loop within an even more expansive third-synthesis grounding, suggesting 3C time. The contemplation of 3C time opens thought up to the paralyzing notion of order without time as eternity.

Control Time: Toward Political Interpretations

With the above temporal discussions in mind, we might now again make a spiraling return to Deleuze, in order to re-read (or mis-read) his ethical political philosophy. Indeed, Deleuze states in *The Logic of Sense* that the main aim of philosophy is to *become worthy of the event*, and that in life we should strive only to "become worthy of what happens to us" (Deleuze 2004b: 170). Furthermore, events are generated by the interaction between the actual and the virtual, so that before events become "actualized in us" they signal and await us from the future, appearing to "invite us in" (Deleuze 2004b: 170). On one level, looking forward to and spiritually cherishing the presentness of the future when, as happens with Banks in *Arrival*, it becomes actualized as specious perception, may minimally invite us to think differently, or otherwise, about what being worthy means on a deterministic plane, or a time without change.

In Banks' descriptions of her hybrid alien–human perception, the only value of her future-memories for living life is that "[t]he anticipation makes it more fun when you get there," which some might be tempted to interpret as quasi-Buddhist or Stoic nonsense. However, beyond the personal spiritual demands, there also appears a sobering political message to the film's imaging of backwashed time, which becomes drawn into relief when we consider *Arrival* in relation to its own sociopolitical "outside." That is, we reframe the film as an (un)timely historical artifact that reflects and expresses broader concerns regarding the fate of humanity in the era of digital "control" and the anthropocene (for a parallel argument concerning the film's re-articulation of lost colonial—qua protoglobalization—"world memories" with contemporary geopolitical shifts, see Fleming forthcoming-b).

We can here gain more insight into this idea if we look at Deleuze's argument that today's collective assemblages are largely defined by the nature of a third generation of electronic computing machines, which are implicated with mutations in capitalism, and which we briefly explored earlier with regard to cephalopod brains. Deleuze claims that the era of disciplinary panoptics described by Michel Foucault has essentially come to an end, and that it has ceded to a new age of endless modulating control. In brief, Deleuze argues that the earlier forms of disciplinary society explored by Foucault produced individuals and subjectivities within and through various enclosed or carceral institutions (such as the school, barracks, factory, and jail). In these institutions, *individuals* were for Foucault molded subjects, who could be understood as being subjected to and internalizing a disciplinary gaze. In contrast to this, Deleuze felt that modern societies primarily produce "dividuals," subjects divided against others (every man for himself) and themselves (I could do better), and who experience self and identity as an ongoing "modulation" (Deleuze 1995: 178). In today's world, we can articulate modulating control logic with a proliferation of actual surveillance, pharmaceutical, economic, digital, and networked technologies that collectively contribute to this new abstract control diagram (I must change my lifestyle—and spend monies I do not have—in order to live longer, which also gets sold to us as becoming "happier," with my insurance premium no doubt changing according to how much I conform to such pressures). Key here is that an important difference between these two techno-social eras can be linked to a concomitant shift in temporal regimes.

Indeed, if discipline was most often wielded in older societies as a response or reaction to a perceived wrongdoing—through the administration of, say, a disciplinary cane to an errant child's backside—in control societies a futural logic of anticipation and prevention now reigns. Most often unruly children are diagnosed with ADD or ADHD and are medicated today so as to prevent tomorrow any irritating child-like behaviors (i.e., behaviors felt a priori to be annoying to adults). The result is that the child's behavior is controlled medically before it even occurs (see Bray 2009). Linking such models back to a "Foucauldian vein," Thomas Elsaesser observes how the "care of the self" is likewise "increasingly reformulated as the 'care of the future self'—a forward-looking venture that converts personal ethics into a kind of self-'serving' entrepreneurialism"

(Elsaesser 2008: 16). Coupled with this, we might note how our handiest devices now also compute and "think" at a speed and rate that far outstrips the glacial pace of the human brain, and which can recall with crystal perfection one's history of evolving tastes and habits. In other words, at a rate of hundreds of thousands of times per second, and across the duration of a whole online lifetime, one's databank of "choices" qua databased behavioral algorithms will help easily anticipate and prime your future likes, decisions, and desires—thereby materially controlling life from the future of an all-too-human present, and behind which our thought and affection always lags. This idea is expressed and played out with cynical perfection in the science-fiction film *Ex Machina* (Alex Garland, 2014), wherein a cyborg called Ava (Alicia Vikander)—who is physically modeled on a human test subject's online porn profile—is able to use her high-speed AI to detect and anticipate all his future moves within a false Turing Test situation, and thus escape from a hellish underground prison of her tech-entrepreneur creator's making.

With this tech-model in mind, we might note how *Arrival*'s *mise-en-scène* similarly becomes carved up and overloaded with ubiquitous computer screens, which in turn feature windows, or screens-within-screens, as well as other prominent screen-like framing devices (with shades of that other vision/version of the control society, *Minority Report*). Indeed, digital computer screens proliferate within all of the film's main human spaces: Banks' domestic sphere, her university lecture halls, the military intelligence tent, and the human end of the space ship's otherwise minimalist viewing chamber. The film also appears to erect subtle parallels between contemporary technologies and the alien visitors. Carolyn Giardina, for example, spots how Patrice Vermette's "sleek" design for the heptapod craft would easily "look at home on display in an Apple store" (Giardina 2016). With similar regard to the ship's "octopus-like" pilots (Canavan 2018: 493), we might recall how Donna J. Haraway explicitly links "the tentacular" to "nets and networks, IT critters, in and out of clouds" (Haraway 2016: 32). This final reference to clouds in turn recasts the manner in which the heptapod craft quite literally dematerializes into clouds when the visitors leave. We also get a sense of the ETs' IT connections when we reconsider what is essentially the temporal semasiographic image par excellence of our present epoch, namely the anxiety-raising rotating circle (sometimes called the "throbber" icon) that has become the dynamic screen sign meaning "buffering." That is, the real-world animated icon that rhymes with and recalls the round Heptapod B symbols thrown up on the alien touch-screens, and which (here as there) operate as a sign that our connection/perception speed is too slow to keep up (with the present).[2]

The (un)conscious articulation of digital technologies and alien temporality here arguably allows *Arrival* to express a sense that we slow biological beings have further receded from the present. Or rather, that in the real world, our machines alone now inhabit the present as our future makers and vanishing mediators, passing back images and stimuli that we (are often made to) desire. By such cookies, we might read *Arrival* as obliquely expressing a contemporary concern that we as a species have been confined to what is essentially the past, lagging behind the dark future, which has become the territory or realm of our present networked media, or our betentacled symbiont masters.

From this perspective, *Arrival* appears as a veiled cultural expression, (in)directly concerned with control-era politics and the increasingly symbiotic relations emerging between human and inhuman agents. At the same moment, however, the dark encounter with strange stone hyperobject ships and their otherworldly aliens concomitantly encourages thought to expand beyond these contemporary concerns, and to confront far darker, near-incomprehensible aspects of deep time (and space)—and the chthulucene.

Dark Contact: Toward Deep Philosophical Interpretations

We suggested earlier that life and death are compatible with openness and change. In order to explain how this is so, we shall revert, as promised, to the extinction of the dinosaurs. In *Dark Matter and the Dinosaurs: The Astounding Interconnectedness of the Universe*, physicist Lisa Randall offers the remarkable hypothesis that dark matter caused the event that saw Tyrannosaurus Rex disappear from the planet. Randall argues that much dark matter is accumulated in a disk that surrounds the "bright disk of gas and stars" that is our galactic home, the Milky Way (Randall 2015: 348). As the galaxy rotates, so on occasion will that dark matter sporadically exert enough force on the numerous objects that we might typically define as meteors, asteroids, and comets, and which are gathered in the so-called Oort cloud on the outer reaches of our solar system, such that some of these objects are sent falling toward us. While the Earth remains protected from most of these as a result of its relatively central position within the solar system, with many meteors, for example, colliding with the far larger and thus gravitationally more powerful Jupiter, some will nonetheless on occasion (Randall estimates every 35 million years or so) make their way through to Earth, impacting with it and thus radically changing the living conditions thereupon. This is indeed how Randall understands the impact that took place at Chicxulub in Mexico, and which brought about the demise of the dinosaurs. What takes place on the outer reaches of our galaxy, then, is intimately connected with what takes place on Earth.

More startling yet, though, is how Randall frames this hypothesis within the understanding both that comets might have played a key role in bringing to Earth a large amount of the water that covers its surface (Randall 2015: 226–227), and that "[m]eteorites on Earth have even been found to contain components of DNA and RNA that presumably came from either asteroids or comets" (Randall 2015: 103). That is, the most basic components of life as we know it on Earth quite possibly originated in space, meaning that in some senses, all life is "alien" to Earth if we wish to posit the planet as an isolated rather than a permeable biosphere—an idea that finds resonance in the suggestion that octopuses are the result of Earth's ancient squids encountering "futuristic" extra-terrestrial retroviruses, DNA or RNA delivered by ancient meteoroids landing hundreds of millions of years ago, and which thereafter drove evolution toward the emergence of today's intelligent octopus beings. This notion, known as "necropanspermia" suggests that ancient organisms (DNA) or nonlife (RNA and viruses) are continually raining down on Earth via comets or space dust, and although essentially delivered "dead on arrival," they will nonetheless "add to the terrestrial gene pool" courtesy of "ionizing radiation and the desiccation rigors of space [*sic.*]" (Steele *et al.* 2018: 17).

The so-called Cambrian Explosion, which took place 541 million years ago and which is thought to have led to a huge diversification in the number of species on Earth, is one such event that is thought to have emerged from an extra-terrestrial seeding. As Steele *et al.* argue:

> [t]he transformative genes leading from the consensus ancestral Nautilus (e.g. *Nautilus pompilius*) to the common Cuttlefish (*Sepia officinalis*) to Squid (*Loligo vulgaris*) to the common Octopus (*Octopus vulgaris*) are not easily to be found in any pre-existing life form—it is plausible then to suggest they seem to be borrowed from a far distant "future" in terms of terrestrial evolution, or more realistically from the cosmos at large. (Steele *et al.* 2018: 9)

In this description we can locate distant echoes of Morton's massively distributed hyperobject attractors—ancient meteors and their long-dead *strange stranger* populations—which radiate evolutionary futurity into the present (of their arrival), *and* an image of betentacled Cthulhu-like ancient ones, who both predate life on Earth and signal the living present by becoming enfolded into the cells, flesh, and brains of Earth's beings—in a process/act that signals their future arrival qua (be)coming, an idea that is literally evoked by sci phi films like *Life* and *The Untamed*, with the protracted opening shot of the latter featuring a slowly falling hyperobject-asteroid that will deliver its erotic, betentacled payload to Earth. This is not to mention the hypothesis discussed in the last chapter that the Earth as we know it was formed as a result of a "giant impact" with another planet, typically referred to as Theia, which impact also resulted in the creation of our moon (see Herwartz *et al.* 2014).[3] In other words, our very planet itself is not singular or unified, but a hybrid rock whose origins stretch across the universe.

The reason for this foray into astrophysics is to suggest that our planet and the life that it sustains are not eternal—and that if anything is eternal, it is change itself, as exemplified by the creation of our planet and the dependency of the life upon it on the extraterrestrial (and this before we even consider the extent to which the life of the Earth is dependent on the Sun). If the universe is thus defined by change (not even our planet is permanent), then openness to change is not simply a matter of life (it is potentially as a result of meteoroid impacts that life on Earth exists as such, perhaps something suggested also by *The Untamed*, in which we see animals frantically copulating at one point around the site of the meteoroid impact—notably in Mexico, the home of the Chicxulub crater). Rather, it is also a matter of death (the meteoroids that gave life to the planet also took away the life of the dinosaurs; as humans came into existence, so will they cease to exist). That is, meteors join the cosmic and the terrestrial, and the past and the future, as they bring life and death, evolution and extinction, to our world. And what is true at the planetary level is also true at the genetic level. For, as Richard Dawkins suggests that genes are not beholden to species in that they will "selfishly" abandon a given species and take up with/create another in order to survive (see Dawkins 1989), we shall reassert that humans and all life forms are themselves the result not of separation from each other, but of the intermixing and hybridization of genes otherwise known as symbiogenesis (see Margulis 1998).

To return to *Arrival*, then, the contact that Banks makes, and which results in her burgeoning ability to see the future, is a contact with the "dark" forces of the universe that both give and take away what we humans consider to be life. Her daughter Hannah will in full consciousness to Banks, and contrary to Donnelly's wishes, both be born and die "prematurely," since to live at all becomes a miracle of cosmic proportions when we understand the extraterrestrial provenance of practically everything that we know—and it is perhaps hubristic rather than humble of humans to claim to know better who or what merits living and also dying. All that humans can see, and thus in some senses all that they can know, depends on the light that has wended its way from the Sun to the surface of our planet (as evoked in *Arrival* by the repeated use of Max Richter's "On the Nature of Daylight" on the film's soundtrack), while yet deeper knowledge may be found in seeing through the dark contact lens and understanding that all that lies beyond our vision (dark matter, the future) also is in some senses always already with us and thus "alive," or at the very least with which we are entangled, or, in Agamben's language, contemporary. Such an understanding is verily a paradoxical "black illumination" or "black enlightenment."

Dark Illumination and Tentacular Navigation

What is it that the heptapods teach us? These alien cephalopods have come to Earth to persuade humans to give up their weapons and to create a planet devoid of borders. These are not just spatial borders, but also temporal ones. For, as Banks continues further her engagement with the two heptapods nicknamed Abbott and Costello, she begins to be able to see the future, while the hieroglyphic language of the heptapods is itself a visual language that is "read" in an extra-temporal fashion. The aliens have come to Earth because they know that in the future humans will help to save them from destruction. That is, they come not as gods to dominate humans (which is what most of the humans, being engaged with hierarchical power games as per the wonts of capitalism, suspect is their goal). Rather, they come to befriend humans, or in effect on a mission of love and gifting. Part of their mission of love involves Louise learning to accept that she will give birth to a child, who from the mainstream perspective will be defective and will die. That is, part of their mission is to help humans to learn to accept death, or the darkness that surrounds them, precedes them, and which is always everywhere at once. This is what their dark contact lens is for: to allow us to make (mediated) contact with the dark.

Abbott and Costello are not just names associated with humor, or the co-medy that is withness (it takes wit to witness withness), but they are also associated with cinema. Meanwhile, the first encounters with the aliens are mediated by a screen on board the dark contact lens that looks like a cinema screen: in darkness, Louise and her colleagues observe the inky hieroglyphs that the aliens squirt upon the screen (which later becomes a touch-screen), much as humans observe hieroglyphs as they are placed on their cinema and phone screens. That is, our screens betray the cephalopodic, alien intelligence of cinema that in its dance of shadows and color paradoxically brings to light the death that is immanent and imminent for humans. It is a tool for greater understanding, while also in some senses being the embodiment of the intelligence that is capital. Hannah, therefore, represents both life and death, with Louise choosing to have and to keep Hannah in spite of the latter's fate accompli, even as her life is plicated with (*com-pli*) death (perhaps there is no greater compliment than death). Louise's partner Donnelly does not want Hannah, since he knows that she will die—and he is unable to support Louise in her decision to keep the child. And yet, rather than viewing life as repetition, Louise engages in the (perhaps necessarily imperfect) experiment that is childbirth and mutation, the reproductive process that lies at the heart of evolution itself. That is, even if this mutant child does not survive, at least she lives and at least Louise gives life to her, for the mutant monster child is perhaps as valuable as any regular human, just as the heptapods and the humans will learn with time that their entire species are entangled the one with the other as it transpires that the heptapods have to come help humans now because they will need humans to help them some 3,000 years hence.

Recent cinema seems to be awash with dead, dying, or disappearing children, a motif common in Villeneuve's work if we recall *Maelström* and consider *Prisoners* (USA, 2013), a film about child abduction.[4] Other films that hinge on this theme include *Évolution*, *Gravity*, *Nocturnal Animals* (Tom Ford, USA, 2016), *The Light Between Oceans* (Derek Cianfrance, UK/New Zealand/USA, 2016), *The Girl on the Train* (Tate Taylor, USA, 2016), *mother!* (Darren Aronofsky, USA, 2017), and perhaps even *Bridget Jones' Baby* (Sharon Maguire, Ireland/UK/France/USA, 2016). Notably, in Korean blockbuster *The Host*, it is after Gang-doo (Song Kang-ho) eats the tentacle of a squid supposedly destined for customers at his father's food stall, and as Gang-doo delivers a second squid after they have complained that the leg is missing, that the titular monster emerges from the Han river, abducting and keeping hostage Gang-Doo's little sister, Hyun-seo (Ko A-sung), an event that subsequently sets in motion the film's rescue plot. There are many ways to read *The Host*, for example as an allegory of American influence on South Korea, since the film opens with an American ordering a Korean underling to pour formaldehyde into the Han, which deliberate act of pollution perhaps causes the monster to come into being via genetic mutations in the river's dirty water. Nonetheless, the film thematically links mutation and child abduction to cephalopods, with the monster suggesting that kinship with cephalopods can bring about new (mutant) forms of life (see Jeong 2016: 376). Meanwhile, *Monsters* is at heart a film that is about the procreation of tentacled aliens as the film culminates in a sex scene between two giant bioluminescent creatures who touch television screens as a form of energizing foreplay, and whose example might well bring together American refugees Sam (Whitney Able) and Andrew (Scoot McNairy). Finally, even a film like *First Man* (Damien Chazelle, USA, 2018) posits the lunar landing of humans as being intimately linked with the loss of a child as Neil Armstrong (Ryan Gosling) single-mindedly heads to the moon following the death of his daughter, Karen (Lucy Stafford). That is, deprived of a daughter, the film's Armstrong seeks divinity via the conquest of space, rather than experiencing her death with humility.

In relation specifically to abortion, it is not that these and other films—or our argument—wish(es) to endorse a Pro Life or a Pro Choice position. But as humans pursue the capitalist goal of control via repetition, clearly this means that the birth of new generations will come to a halt, and that the potential for new life will be destroyed as humans endeavor to destroy others and otherness, to conquer space and/or to become light in a bid to control time, never to age and never to die (to reach the moon in order to eradicate death). However, without darkness and without death, humans become blinded by light, fail to dream, lose their memory, and thus suffer a different, more total death: the death not of evolving into new species via symbiogenetic kinship with others (kinship and kindness producing children—in German, *kinder*—via *das kino*), but the death of not evolving at all, or total stasis (cinema-capital not as a machine for generating kin, but as a system of control). The cinematic image may fundamentally consist of static frames, but these frames are accompanied by darkness. We can strive (misguidedly?) to become light, in the process becoming dry, humorless, and lifeless—aborting evolution and mutation in favor of eternal, living death. Or we can learn from cinema that death is a necessary component of life, as perhaps capital itself comes into intelligent, material existence via technology, including perhaps especially the technology of cinema and digital media.

Cthulhu is inevitable, as is the chthulucene—with cinema being a hieroglyph machine that always only ever shows us our death, a moving-image version of Hans Holbein's famous painting, *The Ambassadors* (1533). In that painting, the titular ambassadors stand next to a table containing the trappings of a wealthy and cultured life, beneath them an anamorphic skull. Not only is the painting through its skull a harbinger of death, but it also shows how capital (a system of possession and of the creation of borders that necessitate ambassadors in the first place) also leads to death (with the skull and death also being associated with the octopus in Painlevé's *La pieuvre*, where, China Miéville notes, the two have similar dimensions, as if the octopus signaled both death but also the human head; see Miéville 2008: 126–127). If Cthulhu is inevitable—if the chthulucene is upon us—then do we choose to live life through death, or do we choose to deny death and thus more terribly to die? Capitalism is the leviathan that suckers us into death; the former, life through death, may not (will not) destroy or defeat capitalism's inexorable birth into recognized life, but it will involve an ecstatic becoming with death, a life through death worthy of the name, and an example for our successor, the intelligence of/that is capital, to follow—as capital, too, will inevitably choose whether to evolve or to try to become a god by stopping or standing outside of time, by denying the planet, and thus calling forth its own Cthulhu to show that it, like us, can neither be nor become god—for there is only time, there is only evolution, there is only change. So what might it be like to navigate life using black illumination, or to see through the dark contact lens? That is, to live with a vantage from the future on to the past (or present)?

We might be able to grasp a sense of this via the earlier chthulucinematic *Donnie Darko* (Richard Kelly, USA, 2001), in which a piece of falling airplane debris—a vortexual engine with a spiraling logo on it—mysteriously lands in the title character's bedroom, even though it weirdly has no known origin, nor can it be accounted for by any international aviation authorities. Donnie Darko (played by Jake Gyllenhaal and whose name might translate into something like a "dark gift," or "the gift of darkness," in the sense of a don-ation) thereafter begins seeing a strange rabbit creature that encourages him to flood his high school, and which leads him to read *The Philosophy of Time Travel*, a monograph written by an ex-high school teacher. It is around this time that Donnie perceives a large temporal-tentacle egressing out of his torso, apparently guiding him through space and time—pulling him into a future adventure by pointing him to where his father's gun is hidden upstairs in a bedroom. This astounding visual image of a liquescent worm (which recalls the underwater CGI beings from *The Abyss*) likewise recalls and resonates with Morton's philosophical description of seeing one's life from a higher temporal dimension, or through the eyes of a four-dimensional being, wherein "I would appear like a strange worm with a cradle at one end and a grave at the other" (Morton 2013: 120).

And here we might take pause to ask, what if from a higher dimension still we were able to see not only our whole life, but other parallel/possible lives/versions from an even broader hyperdimensional perspective? For, while a chthulucinematic film such as *Arrival* suggests that there is only one true timeline (or 4D worm), many more multi-dimensional or converging-timeline films—including *Sliding Doors* (Peter Howitt, UK/USA, 1998), *Lola Rennt/Run, Lola, Run* (Tom Tykwer, Germany, 1998) and *Primer*—arguably offer us a more complex and entangled image of tentacular temporality and chthulucenic reality (multiversions). What is more, these can be linked to a cosmic dimension, as per *Another Earth*, where a second planet Earth suddenly appears alongside our regular one, and films like *Coherence* and *Comet*, which we shall consider presently.

Cometh the Comet

Coherence opens at a dinner party that distantly recalls *El ángel exterminador/The Exterminating Angel* (Luis Buñuel, Mexico, 1962), and which, naturally, involves eight guests (one for each limb of the octopus) discussing an ancient comet that is due to pass by the Earth for the first time in centuries. Party members discuss how, on the comet's last looping pass, strange events took place, with reports of mass delusions and people acting weird (or being sent loopy) being recorded in history. On its present, twisting return, the prehistoric object—which originates outside our own solar system—effectively disturbs the boundaries between different parallel dimensions, or possible worlds, which suddenly appear to be semipermeable, or open to resonating cross-navigational or rippling interference. Thus, while the narrative appears at first to focus on eight characters at a dinner party, we increasingly follow them as they encounter, intermix, and interact with—both knowingly and unknowingly—multiple different versions of themselves and each other from countless different parallel planes. In this way, keeping tabs on all of the different in-mixing modular varieties of each individual or their various eight-member groups becomes a disorienting and befuddling mindfuck as the film unfurls.

This chthulucinema narrative derives humor and generates ethical questions by revealing countless variations of all the characters, with parallel (4D) versions of some being richer, poorer, happy, more cynical, injured, dead, and so on. These differences lead to some characters desiring to bump off their other dividual selves, and/or to step into their self–other's alternative lives/realities in order to gain their better loves, jobs, wealth, friends, and so on. In this way, we get a surreal, manifold, multi-dimensional, and variform tentacular image of time and reality, which is linked both to the cosmic by the presence of the comet, and to the multiple (or set theory or database logic) by all the different 4D strand-beings.

The imaginatively titled *Comet* also shows us simultaneous and parallel universes where a relationship between Dell (Justin Long) and Kimberly (Emmy Rossum) works out in different ways, even if all tend toward the disintegration of their love affair. Notably, Dell is someone who describes himself as living "five minutes from now," while Kimberly lives in the now. This makes him pessimistic in the sense that he can see that things, especially his relationship with Kimberly, will not last forever (with his pessimism perhaps bringing about the end of the relationship?). But while Dell's prescience, like that of Banks, means understanding that the future will involve loss and pain (the end of a relationship in *Comet* as opposed to the loss of a child in *Arrival*), like Banks he chooses to go through with it anyway—with the film's com-plicated structure about a *fait ac-com-pli* being linked both to humanity's past (our origins from outer space via the evolution-giving comet) and to its future (the inevitability of another meteor collision as per the one that brought an end to the dinosaurs).

If the experiences of Banks and Donnie (and Morton) can be described by/as singular 4D worms, the simultaneous, multi-dimensional, and meteoric worlds of *Coherence* and *Comet* demand a proliferation of these strange tentacles, such that we have several worms groping around a larger temporal/dimensional labyrinth. Indeed, as per Jorge Luis Borges' *Labyrinths* (2000 [1962]) or Frank Herbert's *Dune*, which features its own time-/perception-altering worms, we might see both ourselves and our other selves as a form of spreading, groping, multi-stranded tentacular being, writhing and feeling (automatically) through the paths of a cascading temporal maze of other possible presents, pasts, and futures. From this vantage, at higher dimensions, we would of course see something like the dividuated arms of an octopus, moving without the guidance of the eyes/a central brain, but autonomously.

Indeed, such an image might not be unlike Godfrey-Smith's description of octopuses when presented with a covered Perspex puzzle-maze, in which food or some other prized incentive has been hidden: the octopus's intelligent and semi-autonomous arms begin exploring and probing around the dark covered maze, operating as independent feelers/tasters, which are not here guided by the brain or a central intelligence. However, if the darkened or opaque maze is suddenly uncovered or illuminated, so that the octopus's eyes can see into it, the tentacles switch from being blind autonomous gropers to instead become effectively targeted and guided limbs that make their way directly to the food/target (Godfrey-Smith 2016: 52ff.). Aware of multiple versions of ourselves, perhaps a new form of (sub)conscious intelligence and perception/action might supervene our otherwise autonomous selves, as these blind gropers become unified by the illuminated centralized seer. Or again, when what was previously in darkness becomes illuminated, new forms of perception and action become possible.

No Man Is an Island

Haraway suggests that the chthulucene is defined as a possible future period in which humans develop humility toward—rather than a desire to control—their planet, while at the same time drawing upon theories of symbiogenesis in order to suggest that admixture rather than separation is the very stuff of life. Implicitly, then, Haraway understands that while human life is restricted to the (nonetheless shifting) form of each individual, who in turn must die, life itself is birth and death in equal measure. Mixing fiction with theory (for admixture is life), Haraway writes that "[u]ntil sympoiesis [or the creation of new forms by merging] with the dead could be acknowledged, sympoiesis with the living was radically incomplete" (Haraway 2016: 157).

The chthulucene is thus for Haraway a period in which humans do not seek to use the Earth for their own purposes, but instead learn once again to live in harmony with the planet, or to become chthonic. This is a possible period that replaces the so-called anthropocene, in which humans have decidedly changed the shape of their world, bringing about mass extinctions as well as perhaps rendering the planet unsustainable for human life. While Haraway posits a hopeful future in which humans will survive, she nonetheless suggests that this will happen through a symbiogenetic merging with other species, which she argues we should consider not as separate to us, but as kin (with cinema itself being a kin(d) of cephalopodic kin-oteuthis).

Making kin, however, involves sympoiesis with the other as opposed to seeking to control the other, with *Coherence* suggesting that we might also begin by sympoietically making kin with different versions of ourselves in addition to making kin with other life forms, since envy and the desire to control our other selves (e.g., by wanting to kill and replace them) only leads to disaster (from *dis-astro*, meaning falling star or comet, or ill-starred event; see also Fay 2018: 1). Control suggests separation rather than connection, with division rather than unity between sexes and races (as per Lovecraft's misogyny and racism) being at the core of the anthropocene, or the capitalocene, which might also bear the name of patriarchy: the control by some humans of others in the form of enforced labor, the control of women by men, the control of the Earth for the purposes of yielding food (agriculture), the control of animals for the purposes of both labor and sustenance, the control of the self, and the control of both time (the quest for eternal youth and eternal life) and light (the development of agriculture; turning sunlight into working hours; permanent, 24/7 illumination). Humans may wish not to evolve, but to remain the same forever, thereby becoming eternal or, as Yuval Noah Harari might put it, becoming *homo deus* (see Harari 2016). However, the human desire not to accept time but already to be in the future (the perceived need to "get ahead") also involves humans getting ahead of themselves, or becoming headless/a-headed. The brain is a soft, viscous, and tentacular connecting machine/piece of wetware, and its desiccation and ossification is a denial of its potential. To ossify the brain is to cease making connections, to render each man an island on an ossified world of uniform concrete, devoid of darkness as a result of permanent electric illumination, a world with no sleep, and thus with no capacity to form new memories and no ability to dream. Without darkness, memory, or dream, such a world is indeed a timeless one, in which nothing changes as the only time considered to be real is the "real time" of real-time screen mediation (see Campbell 2018). A world without future wherein everything endlessly changes before our eyes (iterations of fashions, leaders, cinematic reboots, commercial technologies, memes) so that nothing can really change at all. All other times are relegated into non-existence as we willfully place ourselves on what Lovecraft might describe as a placid island of ignorance (or as we willfully go and take a seat inside Plato's cave, preferring the screen to the world outside). And yet, much as we try to make islands of ourselves, we cannot halt the onset of the desert (we make desert islands). Nor can we escape the ocean.

Steven Eastwood's *Island* (UK, 2017) is a documentary about humans who are dying, with Eastwood filming various people as they approach death. In particular, the film culminates in Eastwood filming the death of one of the residents, Alan, at the Earl Mountbatten Hospice in Newport on the Isle of Wight in the UK. In other words, *Island*, like Adam Sekuler's similarly themed and "palliative" film *Tomorrow Never Knows* (USA, 2017), brings death directly to cinema, reminding us that cinema is death (cinema as a moving-image version of Holbein's *Ambassadors*). As per John Donne's famous dictum from the seventeenth-century meditation of his *Devotions upon Emergent Occasions* (1624), in which he celebrates how no man is an island (a point to which we shall return), cinema is a bell that tolls not the death of other people, but of all people: "never send to know for whom / the bell tolls; It tolls for thee" (see Donne 1923: 98).

It is perhaps inevitable that Eastwood sets his film about death on an island, with the film constantly featuring images of ferries going to and from the British mainland. The ferry naturally reminds us of death, as per the image of Charon, the ferryman from Greek mythology who took newly deceased souls to Hades. Furthermore, the presence of the sea also reminds us of humanity's place "on the beach" as the sea and Cthulhu rise to meet us. It is ironic—or perhaps simply poetic—that the island in the film should be the Isle of Wight. For, while the film is about crossing the boundary between life and death, the name of the island is reportedly derived from the Latin term *vectis*, meaning "place of the division." The film erodes the division between life and death, while wight also is a term derived from the Old Saxon *wiht*, which among other things means a demon, but also the Dutch term *wicht*, meaning a little child (or what in German is a *kind*). The Isle of Wight is where the demon Cthulhu emerges, not only as the harbinger of death but also with a promise of rebirth or evolution through the image of the little child (cinema is a Hollowgast seeking to find a body and thus to become a wight?).[5]

If humans have a tendency under capitalism to close themselves off in a bid for sovereignty, then during orgasm, yawning, laughing, the expression of pain, eating, and, as we see in Eastwood's film, death, the human mouth gapes open, as if it were producing "an opening to the other side" (Lippit 2005: 71). This can perhaps also be seen in the open-mouthed scream, with Lovecraft's open-mouthed connection to the "other side" also being made clear by the title of John Carpenter's Lovecraft-inspired *In the Mouth of Madness* (USA, 1994), the title of which clearly refers to Lovecraft's 1936 story, "At the Mountains of Madness."

Life involves being open to contact with others, paradoxically including pain and death (but also including laughter/comedy—with pain itself being evidence of contact with the world since it hurts us, as well as tickling us at certain points in time; perhaps it is for this reason that the slightly open mouth also connotes an appetite not just for food but also for sex). Indeed, such openness is also a demonstration of love, as per *Arrival*. It is poetic, then, that during Alan's death in Eastwood's film, we hear the filmmaker snoring, his mouth presumably having fallen open like Alan's as he sleeps on the floor of the latter's hospice room—the camera having been switched on and left to record. The autonomous camera not only suggests that cinema is alive, but in sharing open mouths, Alan and Eastwood both are agape, demonstrating the open love of all things that the Greeks also named *ἀγάπη*, the highest form of love that consisted of charity. No man is an island; instead we are all entangled with each other. As one dies and the other sleeps, the camera autonomously and openly (lovingly?) records the image of one and the sound of the other as Eastwood commits death to memory through dream and as Alan enters the sleep that commits him as memory to the Earth. No wonder that the gaping mouth of the yawn is considered to be a sign of impending sleep, the moment of (openness to) darkness that allows us to develop memory. As the yawn is openness to the darkness of sleep, so is openness key to life as humans emerge from the yoni (gaping, open, yawning, yonic orifice) that is the vagina. The sea laps the shore (ar-rives), its undertow pulling humans from the island (for no man is, or can remain, an island), dragging humans back to the slimy depths from which they originated—the ocean as our outside always already here on Earth, the giver of life from which and as which Cthulhu also rises.

We Are the Destroyers of Gods

Eric Cazdyn writes about how the contemporary era is defined by "a relationship to death in which death is radically separated from everyday life" (Cazdyn 2012: 7). In short, Cazdyn argues that to separate death from life in this fashion means that "we are not yet living" (Cazdyn 201: 186). And yet, Cazdyn also paints a world in which many humans are "already dead," in the sense that they lead disposable, or what Agamben might call "bare," lives—a living dead population that is either cast into ("abjected" into) darkness away from and invisible to the cinematic world of perpetual light, or which functions as the (equally invisible) worker (slave) population that perpetuates the "life" (that does not involve living) of the rich. As Achille Mbembe might put it: "the ultimate expression of sovereignty resides, to a large degree, in the power and the capacity to dictate who may live and who must die" (Mbembe 2003: 11). That is, the rich—who create a sovereign world separate from the poor, sipping champagne on island resorts and using offshore island bank accounts—can decide the fates of the poor, in the process becoming the poor's gods. Similarly, Michel Serres notes that what "the Greeks dreamt of, the end of the twentieth century did." For, today's wealthy Western inhabitants live lives akin to those of the ancient Latin and Hellenic gods:

> the wealthy banquet on the summit of Olympus while those condemned to death wage war hand to hand; obese gods communicate at leisure in every point of space without losing any time and stuff themselves with ambrosial remedies against satiety while the vast crowd of mortals lose hope of living a few hours without starvation or suffering in peace. (Serres 2018: 168–169)[6]

Death is our fate, and death is with us everywhere and at all times. Nonetheless, some hasten the death and diminish the life of others (exploitation) in order to distance death from their own lives, indeed seeking to eradicate death from their own lives by conferring it on to others, as wealth allows the few to afford prolonged (and hopefully eternal) youth as well as longer (and hopefully eternal) lives. To aim to defeat time thus involves the exploitation of other human beings and the creation of a division whereby the rich elevate themselves into the realm of the superhuman, or god, while the poor are consigned to the realm of the subhuman, the abject, "bare life," the already dead (a theme explored, as mentioned, in *Altered Carbon*, where the super-rich elite have their memories and personalities uploaded and downloaded into disposable/upgradable bodies/sleeves, in the process becoming the immortal gods of their overcrowded, resource poor, science-fictional world).

To live forever with nothing changing and under permanent illumination is to live in the realm of Lucifer, since he is the maker of light (*luci-fer*). To live forever, then, is a diabolical and vampiric ambition, based specifically and willfully (deliberately, forgetfully) upon the misery and perhaps even the death of others, feeding off their blood in a bid to become divine (for a discussion of Lucifer Valentine's *informe* "Vomit Gore" torture porn and Vampyroteuthian art, see Fleming 2017: 169–178). Even if one cannot literally become God, one can for one's lifetime create the perception that one is a god—and not just spill the blood of others to achieve this, but also believe that the blood of others *should be* spilt for one's own perpetuation. And yet, as the comedy duo of Abbott and Costello (and as comedy as a force in itself) teaches us, no one is a god. A cephalopod alien from outer space is not a god—and perhaps it is because humans will likely treat aliens as gods that aliens do not come to Earth, for our thinking is too constricted by ideologies defined by hierarchies; we are not yet ready to befriend/make kin with aliens, but only to fight them and/or to sacrifice ourselves to them. Not even a sun is a god, even if it is logical for a sun solipsistically to consider itself a god because it produces all that it knows and because it is blinded by its own light to the darkness that surrounds it and to the light of the many other stars that exist in the multiverse. A sun is not a god because while light might be the measure of chronological time (and while light might be ignorant of the speed of darkness, or the absence of the necessity for speed that is darkness, or the wormhole outside of space and time), suns also die. Not only do suns die, but suns also sacrifice and consume their own offspring as they seek to prolong their life and to achieve their own immortality (planets are sucked back into dying stars).

Why not challenge such greedy gods by refusing the sacrifice of solar consumption and/or the heat death of a galaxy by seeking to become, as Christopher Nolan has put it, *Interstellar*? That is, if a sun is no god, then why not refuse its authority and harness/subjugate the power of sun after sun as humans travel the universe consuming all that falls into their path, making of humanity a modern Prometheus (a god-like "forethinker," since his name derives from the Latin *pro-* meaning "before" and *-methos*, or *mathein*, meaning "to learn," which in turn comes from the Proto-Indo-European root *men-*, meaning "to think"; not only does Prometheus control light, but he also controls time—by seeing the future)? And yet, while we might not accept the divinity of aliens or of suns, this does not mean that we should in turn subjugate them in a bid to assert and/or to discover our own divinity.

The paradox famously devised by Enrico Fermi says that since the universe is so old, why is there no evidence of so-called intelligent life beyond Earth? There are several solutions to this paradox, including the notion that no life can live for long enough on a given planet without succumbing to a necro-biological agent, or zombie epidemic (see Kane and Selsis 2014). Another is that it requires as much if not more energy to leave a planet and to find another inhabitable one as there is energy available on the home planet in the first place (and certainly one is only likely to be in a position to start thinking about and then looking for a new planet toward the end of the first planet's own life cycle). But even if this does not hold (and since humans have sent animals, other humans, and probes into space, we might believe that we can indeed find and travel to other hospitable planets, and/or create hospitable, interstellar-traveling environments), several issues remain. Firstly, what is the cost involved in becoming a god? For surely the cost of divinity is blood and war. That is, as humans must perhaps destroy their planet first to control and then to escape their planet (pollution is not a by-product of capital, but its most necessary product for the purposes of subjugating the planet), so must some humans also destroy others (including other life forms) in order to become gods. The pursuit of divinity, then, is evil, and so if we say that we are indeed the destroyers of gods (as we suggested in the last chapter), then it is not because we, too, seek war. For we do not wish to destroy those humans who claim to be gods, but to destroy the idea of divinity by exposing how all those who do pursue divinity necessarily exploit and destroy others. We can pursue this goal through humiliating those would-be gods, reminding them that they are and will remain *humus*.

Possibly those humans are beyond humility and shame, a tendency that seems increasingly common as humans not only know that privilege rests upon exploitation, but do nothing to stop it. Indeed, as mentioned in Chapter 5, those humans who seek divinity by using the life force of others may in some Dostoyevksian/Nietzschean sense believe that they are beyond good and evil and thus justified in what they do, not least because they convince themselves that those exploited/consumed humans allow exploitation to happen and thus must in some senses desire it (they believe that those humans also recognize them to be gods, thereby justifying their own narcissistic belief that they are a god). How to stop such greed without entering into war and thus also spilling blood, i.e., by becoming that which one opposes? Our only solution to this conundrum is conceptually to destroy gods through our work. That is, after Reza Negarestani, we adopt a cthulhoid ethics as a means of "replacing or undermining existing planetary politico-economical and religious systems" (Negarestani 2008: 238).

Anyone who advertently or otherwise claims to be a god, therefore, will do so on the basis of greedily immiserating and consuming others, rather than commiserating with them (or living through *agape* love, and giving charity to others/redistributing wealth, as well as being prepared to die). To immiserate others is to believe those others are below you; it is to have bad faith in them as human beings, or rather not to believe that they are humans. Perhaps more, it is to believe that they are not alive. It is to believe them dead—or at least to hasten their death for the purpose of prolonging one's own life. Meanwhile, to have faith in other human beings is not to place any humans below you (or above you), but to respect them and to (try to) treat them as equals. What is more, one might not consider just the life of fellow humans, but also the life of animals, plants, and all matter (and antimatter and dark matter and other virtual matter) in the multiverse.

In a multiverse of spooky entanglement, we are with death (surrounded by ghosts/spooks, dividuals, and alternates) as the tentacular universe immerses us in its viscous, slimy waves that are the stuff of life. As humans believe that they become more intelligent (as they become increasingly prey to the ideology/meme that all that they do constitutes "progress"), the more humans try to destroy time, by terminating evolution for the purposes of repetition. True intelligence, like that of the cephalopod, involves not separation from others, but tactility. It involves a sensual experience in which the whole body is sensuous organ, is brain, is tongue, is mouth. An open body that is conscious of its entanglement, rather than believing consciousness to be separation (*cogito ergo sum*).

In destroying false gods (for all gods are false), then we shall create a world not of superhumans and subhumans, but a world of humans, a world of kindness and kin, in which perhaps even the nonhuman is also considered to be human, i.e., equal to us, as per the "cannibal metaphysics" of Eduardo Viveiros de Castro (2014). Such humans might themselves live in ecstatic harmony with the multiverse with which they are entangled, and in which darkness dances around light and death affirms life. Everything changes. Everything evolves. The erotic erosion of boundaries. A slimy, sensual universe. Cthulhu rises. Let us venture unafeared and with open arms and open mouths—*agape*—into the chthulucene. This is what we can learn from *Kinoteuthis Infernalis*, the hieroglyphs of which signal our death as our footprints are washed away from the beach as the waves lap the sands of time.

Notes

1. Beyond *Cloud Gate*, Anish Kapoor's sculpture possesses many chthulucenic components. Like *Cloud Gate*, Kapoor's *C-Curve* (2007) equally contains "contact lens"-type qualities as it inverts space and light via its concave shape, while his work with Vantablack, reputedly the blackest black in existence, equally suggests a connection with dark epistemologies, perhaps especially in *The Origin of the World* (2004), a black hole that sits on an angled wall in the SCAI Bathhouse in Kanazawa, Japan, and which brings to mind Gustave Courbet's *L'origine du monde/Origin of the World* (1866), itself a famously yonic image of the sort that we discuss later in this chapter. *Descension* (2014) consists of a water vortex that leads viewers to contemplate the deep, while *Leviathan* (2011) and *Death of Leviathan* (2011–13) also conjure up gigantic pre-/posthuman beasts like Cthulhu. *Earth Cinema* (2009) finally links the chthonic with cinema in a fashion that recalls aspects of our argument here, and which, in its relation of mud with movies, anticipates future work that we wish to undertake on film and filth.
2. Bearing in mind the idea of being too slow for technology, the get-rich schemes of *Primer* and *Time Lapse* announce the anxiety felt by traders and other gamblers who can no longer keep up with the algorithms that trade almost instantaneously on their behalf. It is only knowing the future—as per Michael Burry in *The Big Short*—that will allow them to get rich and/or to change their standing in a society that otherwise becomes increasingly polarized, but also increasingly ossified in its hierarchical structure.
3. Sergio Wolf links meteoroid impacts to Lovecraft by naming his documentary on comet collisions in Argentina *El color que se cayó del cielo*, or *The Color out of Space* (Argentina, 2014). Meanwhile, the appearance of a second planet appearing near or on a collision course with Earth finds expression in various films, from the aforementioned *The Trail of the Octopus* and *Flash Gordon*, through to *Melancholia* (Lars von Trier, Denmark/Sweden/France/Germany, 2011) and *Another Earth* (Mike Cahill, USA, 2011).
4. Motherhood and children loom almost constantly in Villeneuve's films. Beyond *Maelström*, *Prisoners*, and *Arrival*, Villeneuve's *Un 32 août sur terre/32nd Day of August on Earth* (Canada, 1998) tells the story of a model (Pascale Bussières) who decides to have a child in order to give her life meaning—and so goes to the desert in order to conceive. *Polytechnique* (Canada, 2009), meanwhile, sees Val (Karine Vanasse) survive a massacre of

women by a misogynist (Maxim Gaudette) at the Polytechnique Montréal in 1989, before going on to become an engineer. The film ends with her learning that she is pregnant.

5. While Cthulhu may emerge at places like the Isle of Wight, the homophonous link between wight and white also betrays the way in which the search for eternal life is also a search to become white. This in turn betrays the racialized aspect of the anthropocene, as Kathryn Yusoff has so brilliantly demonstrated (see Yusoff 2018). Over the course of this text, we have shown a certain kinship with the work of Michel Serres, who nonetheless believes that whiteness is the destiny, or the Grand Narrative, of humans—with whiteness being akin to a sort of "stem" existence in which the human can, like a stem cell, become in multifarious ways. Even though Serres is clearly aware of and even addresses the topic of racism in *The Incandescent* (for example, Serres 2018: 74–75), we hesitate to embrace the whiteness of his argument, not least because of our own understanding of the critical role played by darkness, and especially in the shadow of Yusoff's work. Cinematically, Donald Crisp and Buster Keaton's *The Navigator* perhaps most clearly articulates the racist aspects of the anthropocene. For while Jennifer Fay sees Keaton's cinema as being particularly redolent of the anthropocene, especially as a result of his struggles with the weather (see Fay 2018: 23–58), she overlooks how in *The Navigator*, Buster's Rollo Treadway is spurred into seeking marriage with Betsy O'Brien (Kathryn McGuire) as a result of seeing a newlywed African-American couple drive past his window, before then killing at least one black native as he tries to defend from attack the titular ship on which he and Betsy accidentally find themselves adrift. In other words, white happiness—and by extension the white anthropocene—is predicated upon theft from and then murder of black bodies (Rollo copies the African-American couple, before then killing "barbaric" tribespeople). Not only does the film's title potentially connote the way in which navigation in the digital world is essentially white, but it also is striking that Rollo kills an octopus shortly before killing the tribesman (as a canon that is tied by a string to Rollo's leg fires into the native's chest). Rollo uses a swordfish to fend off a swordfish, but no such gag emerges when confronted by the octopus, which he simply kills—as if octopus and black man alike were horrifically other and thus not sufficient to merit a gag (Keaton gags at the octopus and black man, but can barely bring himself to make a gag of them). If Gilles Deleuze reckons Rollo's emergence from the water and his release from the amniotic sac that is his diving suit is "the finest metaphor in the history of cinema" (Deleuze 2005b: 155), he also contends that Keaton's work in general suggests cinema as "a machine which produces man 'without a mother,' or the man of the future" (see Deleuze 2005a: 181). While Keaton's hero may well be "like a minuscule dot encompassed by an immense and catastrophic milieu" (Deleuze 2005a: 177), hence the reading of Keaton as a filmmaker of the anthropocene, we nonetheless get a sense

of how this would-be future of motherless men necessitates a patriarchal world without women, while also being a white world built upon the death of black humans and octopuses. For Deleuze, Fay, and Serres alike, then, the anthropocene is white. The chthulucene, meanwhile, involves a resurgence of blackness.

6. Of relevance to our arguments about death, Serres continues: "[t]he perpetual crime perpetuated against the poor plus the daily representation of human sacrifice in the media, murders, wars, attacks and panics, accentuate the comparison to the point of identity; by fabricating gods every day from spilt blood, we return to the most archaic polytheism, which created divinities by means of [appalling and bloody sacrifice] rites" (Serres 2018: 168).

CHAPTER 8

From the Modern Prometheus to the Modern Medusa

In the last leg, we proposed that the human desire to become a god involves humanity as a kind of modern Prometheus, stealing fire in order to control light and in order to escape the burden of time, change, and evolution, as instead humans seek to become eternal and to live forever (preferably in a state of permanent youth, as played out in numerous films, from vampire movies to shows like *Altered Carbon*, time-looping films, and perhaps even in audiovisual media themselves as we seek to exist not in the flesh, but in images, in photos, and thus in light).

Recent philosophy (work in the vein of speculative realism, object-oriented ontology, vibrant matter, entanglement) has as a basic premise that life is not confined to organisms and that life may be a process that extends beyond the human, the animal, and even the plant, into the world and the universe in general. Part of this thinking is ecological: if in effect our planet is alive (a living organism?), then we must respect its life and not treat the planet as we wish. However, to invest an object with life is in the psychoanalytic realm a fetish—a projected fantasy that takes place because the human is trying to make up for something that is missing (the child attaches to the blanket when the mother is not there so that the child can cope with the mother not being there, conferring to the blanket a life that it does not really have). Is to endow the planet with life, then, really just a mega-fetish, in that it is conferring to the world a life that it does not really have and which makes up for the terrifying prospect that fundamentally we are alone?

To give life to the planet is in effect to create god, be it a kind Earth mother or a monstrous, indifferent other; it is a fantasy of emergent order that consoles us for the otherwise terrible reality of there being no god, just chaos. Seen from such an angle, ecological thought is simply a logical coping-mechanism offshoot of chaos, a kind of new religion to replace the older ones that have "failed" (and/or which are "resurgent"). One can imagine a "classical" version of (Freudian) psychoanalysis that would try to "cure" us of this mega-fetish and help us to realize that we are alone (with this psychoanalysis thus becoming the fetish itself, the conceptual framework that allows us otherwise to cope with chaos, or which "persists in an essentially humanist effort to secure the human"; see Wolfe 2014: 134). For such a version of psychoanalysis, which is of the sort that Gilles Deleuze and Félix Guattari critique in their *Anti-Oedipus* (Deleuze and Guattari 1983), we should stop fetishizing the planet and, cured of this fetish, continue to pursue its destruction. There is no god. There is just a chaotic universe and we are alone. To try to deny death is futile; we should embrace death and perhaps even accelerate its advent—using psychoanalysis as a new religion to justify us in doing so. Indeed, perhaps it is only by destroying our planet that we can develop the means to escape our planet, to become *homine dei* instead of mere humans—Fermi's paradox notwithstanding. The destruction of the planet—the killing of Laius, the father of Oedipus, and the rape of Gaia, the mother planet—is the acceptance of godlessness, the logical expression of mankind's solitude. Learning shame through such actions, we might then prick out our eyes and finally see—while also learning, *contra* Laius who tries initially to kill Oedipus, that humans do not have to seek to kill their own children in order to prolong their own lives (as Abraham sacrifices the goat so as not to kill Isaac, and as the vampire lives forever by drinking human blood). Rather, the now-blind human (who embraces darkness) can raise and protect her children, who then replace them ("in place of one's parents" being one of the meanings of the name Antigone). Of course, it may be that humans have in some senses already put out their eyes as they stumble blindly through the present era, learning their role in the multiverse as they come less detachedly to see the world, but more to grope around and to feel it. Blast your toplights!

As we discussed at the end of the last chapter, there is a cost to this rape and murder. That is, he who gets to become a god must leave many humans behind and/or actively consume them. A few might fly to planets new (or to a space station, as per *Interstellar* and *Elysium*, Neill Blomkamp, USA, 2013), but the many will be left to perish—and we all seem to know this. Is to reveal speculative realism, object-oriented ontology, vibrant matter, and entanglement as a fetish, then, simply a mechanism that reaffirms man's separation from the planet, in that it not only exposes the life attributed to objects as a fantasy (i.e., it reaffirms our separation from those objects), but it also convinces us that the life attributed to other humans is equally a fantasy, thereby allowing us to treat those humans also as objects (exploitation)? That is, might such a psychoanalysis, in its wish to mediate all human relationships (i.e., in its wish to be a medium), convince us that other humans are not alive? (As might the Turing Test, which is remarkable not because a computer might pass itself off as intelligent, but because many humans might demonstrate that they are not literate/intelligent in the way that the test wants us to be, i.e., the test is limited in its capacity to accept difference since it is really a test of homogeneity and neuronormality.) From this perspective, is it possible to read such a version of psychoanalysis as the dehumanization of others outside of the analyst/analysand dyad (with the analyst basically recruiting the analysand for their own empowerment, while telling the analysand that they are being empowered in the very act of their subjugation to the analyst—hence why no one can be an analyst without being in analysis)? That is, does such a version of psychoanalysis contribute to a conceptual framework for exploitation? Is this why psychoanalysis thrives in capitalist countries, while struggling to exist elsewhere, even as psychoanalysis spreads with cinema and capital in the era of globalization—which is not to mention Christianity's role in numerous capitalist countries, not least because based upon a fantasy of transcending the human condition, not least through the concept of the return and thus the cessation of time, which can be contrasted with Islam, which is a religion of the underdog, a return that will never take place, and whose chief prophet is human? Given its capitalist dimensions, is one of the major struggles within and around psychoanalysis, then, not the ongoing issue of class? That is, to get to grips with capital, one must be—in the language of Deleuze and Guattari—anti-oedipus, not in the sense of rejecting wisdom via blindness, since, even if for Oedipus it is only ever too late (the crime has been committed), to learn to see through feeling—and in some senses thus to become Oedipus—is verily part of what we are proposing here. Rather, one must be anti-oedipus in the sense of how this version of psychoanalysis that we are describing is an unthinking product of capital and thus always already expressing capital's necessary precondition of conceptual separation from each other and from the planet. To seek permanent illumination à la Prometheus, then, is to reject wisdom for the egocentric purpose of separating the ego from the id, the mind from the body, the self from the other, the human from the planet, and the human from time. And yet, as Prometheus might in some senses sum up the human project of becoming divine (*homo deus*) and/or becoming light (a *homo lux* that pursues luxury via the immiseration of others; see also Latour 2012; Demos 2017: 44), a project in which the "human" is a byword for white masculinity, we wish to turn our attention finally to another mythical figure, namely the Gorgon Medusa, who had snakes for hair and who turned humans to stone if they looked her in the eye. For, we shall argue that while contemporary humanity is in the words of Mary

Shelley a kind of modern Prometheus, contemporary humanity in the era of digital global capital stares the Gorgon in the face and thus in some senses is petrified. That is, digital media technology, with cinema as one of its most notable progenitors, constitutes a tentacular, Cthulhu-esque Gorgon that is the embodiment of capital, and which also emerges Cthulhu-like as an alien intelligence that signals the enslavement and perhaps the end of humanity.

Anti-Oedipus

In *The Squid and the Whale*, teenager Walt (Jesse Eisenberg) is asked by his headmaster (Michael Countryman) to visit the school therapist (Ken Leung) after playing in assembly and claiming as his own Pink Floyd's song "Hey You" (Walt: "I felt I could've written it." Therapist: "But you didn't.").[1] When asked about childhood memories ("isn't that kind of a stock question for a shrink?"), Walt initially recalls sneaking out of a party to watch *The Adventures of Robin Hood* (Michael Curtiz and William Keighley, USA, 1938) with his mother, Joan (Laura Linney), before then remembering how he would get scared while looking at the exhibition of the giant squid fighting the whale at the American Museum of Natural History (Walt would look at the exhibit through his fingers in a fashion that recalls how Man Ray would look at films; see Stam 2000: 57). In particular, Walt remembers that during bathtime, his mother would tell stories about the exhibit that would scare him as much as the exhibit itself, but which because told by his mother were also reassuring. The therapist then asks Walt where his father, Bernard (Jeff Daniels), was during all of these memories—with Walt now realizing that while he has taken his father's side during his parents' divorce (which is the primary focus of the film), it is in fact his mother who has shown him greater support throughout his life. The film culminates in Bernard collapsing and being taken to hospital. When Bernard asks Walt to stay with him, however, Walt leaves the hospital and jogs across Central Park to the American Museum of Natural History, where he enters and approaches the exhibit of the squid fighting with the whale—at which point the film ends.

Quite how to interpret these moments is not entirely certain. It seems clear that Walt associates the squid with a natural world full of "dark" desires that, as an adolescent, he is struggling to fathom. But there is also an association between the squid and his mother, one that is reinforced by the link to water, in that it was during bathtime that Joan would reassure Walt about these inhuman beasts. If these fighting animals are like his combative parents, it nonetheless seems as though the squid does symbolize some kind of "alien" femininity for Walt, who ends the film not by hiding from the exhibition, but by finally looking it square in the eye (with the squid in particular having one large eye gazing outward at Walt as it appears center-frame, obscuring the whale, which takes on a more background role—as Lou Reed's "Street Hassle" plays on the soundtrack). In other words, it would seem that the film ends with Walt "growing up" somewhat, in that now he accepts violence and desire as part of his world (even if he is only looking at models and not even at real specimens of a squid and a whale). What is more, Walt has in some senses grown up as a result of "becoming woman"—if the squid symbolizes a certain relationship with his mother.

If the concept of becoming woman of course recalls Deleuze and Guattari (see Deleuze and Guattari 2004: 232–309), it is also notable that the school shrink should do so much to help Walt in coming to terms with his parents' divorce and to help him discover his own place in the world. Although not necessarily a psychoanalyst (the therapist has an MA in Developmental Psychology from the Yale Child Studies program), there is also a sense here that analysis need not be the negative process that we described above, and that it can in fact be (in some senses *contra* Deleuze and Guattari) beneficial to humans not in replacing chaos, but in helping them to face up to chaos. Indeed, Jacques Schnier's well-known and psychoanalytic account of the octopus would tally with this "positive" view, since Schnier equates fear of the octopus (and of the spider) with fear of the mother (Schnier 1956: 23). For Walt to face up to the squid, then, is for Walt to overcome this fear and to recognize the love that he and his mother share. It may be that he is afraid of his mother destroying him, which itself is an inversion of his fear of destroying her (the infant feels empowered by sucking on the mother's breast and thus comes to fear losing that power by being sucked upon or by being sucked up by the cephalopod), but in coming to see this—through the symbolic destruction of his father, whom he leaves at the hospital—Walt learns to love his mother (at least symbolically, in that he visits and looks at the exhibition of the squid and not his actual mother).[2]

The Squid and the Whale is thus a clearly oedipal film, in that it deals with the breakdown of the family and in particular Walt's changing relationship with his parents—whether or not psychoanalysis is exploitative (and we should like to make clear that we do not believe it must always be exploitative). And while perhaps typical of a film so steeped in the milieu of New York's white, middle-class intelligentsia, *The Squid and the Whale* would seem to affirm the oedipal model and thus the truth of psychoanalysis's insights (for white bourgeois males struggling to cope with the otherness of woman/the squid). To be anti-oedipus is not necessarily an outright rejection of psychoanalysis, then, which recognizes patriarchy. But it is to look at the problem of patriarchy from the perspective of the woman, or from the perspective of the squid. That is, we wish not to learn how to cope with the squid as a man (which only reaffirms patriarchy), but to become the squid, to be the purveyor of chaos, to destroy patriarchy. Clearly the methods, the symbols, and the language of psychoanalysis can be used for these purposes—and perhaps it is worth noting that Walt's shrink is Asian American, and thus instrumental in helping Walt potentially to see beyond his white masculine privilege (if he has achieved this). But focused as it primarily is on white, urban masculinity, psychoanalysis always runs the risk of complicity with and reaffirming that world.

From New York to Dunwich

In his account of Schnier's work, Richard Schweid writes about how the octopus functions in (primarily Western) art as "a symbol of a woman with a penis . . . this negative perception of the octopus is because men view it, subconsciously, as a symbol of Greek mythology's Medusa," which in turn represents a fear of castration and/or the desire of women to have a penis (Schweid 2013: 133–134; see also Schnier 1956: 11–12). With the penis upheld here as a figure of power (men fear losing it; women want to gain it), we can see how psychoanalytic thought perhaps aligns itself unthinkingly with patriarchy, even when "critiquing" it.

Meanwhile, Nina Power writes about how early cinematographic pornography regularly featured men with flaccid penises, something that seems a far cry from today's pornography of permanent boners, and in which to come can only take place via the humiliating cum shot. In particular, Power notes how the participants in early pornography also laughed and had fun—something that again seems a far cry from today's grim female orgasm-factory (see Power 2009: 52–53). Patriarchal hardness has gradually replaced, it would seem, a soft sense of fun, if not love. Or as Luce Irigaray might put it: "[i]n wetness the seed of living beings finds a fertile element. Not in phallic erection, its mask" (Irigaray 1991: 137). Can acknowledging softness and the normalcy of failing to gain an erection help us to find love in the era of Viagra?

If a writer like H. P. Lovecraft was, as we have explained via Haraway, a racist and a misogynist, it is worth mentioning that he also was a snob and that he refused to write about sex in his work—even if he was very generous and decent toward his friends (for an overview of his feelings about sex, see Houellebecq 2005: 57–62). That is, if Lovecraft's work takes us beyond Oedipus (an anthropocentric, and perhaps capitalist and patriarchal, view of the other) and into the universe of the squid-like Cthulhu, which is a universe of unthinkable chaos (i.e., a universe denuded of coping mechanisms/power games like psychoanalysis), Lovecraft himself seems a very oedipal man (with his refusal to discuss sex being a denial of flaccidity rather than a working with and laughing about it?). Fittingly, however, if New York is a global hub for psychoanalysis as it is a global hub for capital, it is also a city that Lovecraft despised after moving there with his wife Sonia in 1925. As Michel Houellebecq explains, his "hatred of the 'foul mongrels' of this modern Babylon, the 'foreign colossus that gibbers and howls vulgarly . . .' did not cease to exasperate him and drove him delirious" (Houellebecq 2005: 103). Whereas Sonia took a job in Cincinnati, Lovecraft retreated to his home in Providence, Rhode Island—never to return to the metropolis. In other words, despising New York, it is perhaps no surprise that Lovecraft, in spite of his somewhat typical repressions, was not taken by psychoanalysis, since it thrives mainly where capital also thrives, namely in big cities. Psychoanalysis works for the well-to-do world of *The Squid and the Whale*, but Lovecraft was not interested in taming the squid, even if he hated it. And Lovecraft may in his personal life have repressed the squid (like one of his characters, he is frozen into paralysis and mere observation, akin to the protagonist of one of Gilles Deleuze's time-image films), but in his literature he unleashes Cthulhu, setting the squid free.

As Fabián Ludueña reminds us, "The Dunwich Horror" opens with an epigraph from Charles Lamb's "Witches and Other Night-Fears," the very first words of which are:

> Gorgons, and Hydras, and Chimaeras—dire stories of Celaeno and the Harpies—may reproduce themselves in the brain of superstition—*but they were there before*. They are transcripts, types—the archetypes are in us, and eternal . . . *These terrors are of older standing. They date beyond the body*—or without the body, they would have been the same. (Lovecraft 2008: 1; see also Ludueña 2014: 38–39)

Gorgons, of which Medusa is a prime example, thus give us "insight into our anti-mundane condition, and a peer at least into the shadowland of pre-existence" (Lovecraft 2008: 1). That is, Gorgons show to us an inhuman world, taking us beyond what we suggest is the phallocentrism of Schnier's argument above—even if we would like to retain the link between Medusa and cephalopods (an equation also made by Victor Hugo, who describes the devil-fish in *The Toilers of the Sea* as "that Medusa with its eight serpents"; see Hugo 2010: 294).

The Dunwich Horror (Daniel Haller, USA, 1970), an adaptation of Lovecraft's story produced through Roger Corman's American International Pictures, culminates in a strange ritual on a clifftop altar in which Wilbur Whateley (Dean Stockwell) uses the *Necronomicon*, a book of magic that he has stolen from Miskatonic University in Arkham in order to summon back to Earth the Old Ones through the sacrifice of Nancy (Sandra Dee), a student of Henry Armitage (Ed Begley), who is a history professor at Miskatonic and an authority on the aforementioned grimoire. As Wilbur repeats chants in order to be reunited in particular with his demon father, so does Armitage arrive to utter counter-chants that will reverse the demonic invocation. Armitage basically out-magicks Wilbur, but not before we see a flashing appearance in a kind of red-green mist of a demonic figure that bears an uncanny resemblance to Medusa: a head that is filled with snake-like and tentacular hair. As soon as it arrives, though, the demon disappears as Wilbur falls into the sea in a fireball after being struck by lightning. Armitage saves Nancy and reassures her that the Whateley family line has ended . . . except for the fact that Nancy might be pregnant with Wilbur's child.

What in the film is given the briefest of glimpses (and which in Lovecraft's story is described with typical ambiguity, even if it includes the Medusa-like idea of "squirmin' ropes"; see Lovecraft 2008: 56) is in the film's poster rendered explicit: a creature with tentacles coming out of its head, at the end of each of which is a different kind of monster, including what seems to be the head of a dragon, the head of a goat, and/or the head of a snake (see Figure 8.1). In other words, the monster that we see is a strange hybrid of the creatures that Lamb mentions, but most resolutely the creature resembles Medusa, who in Ovid's *Metamorphoses* is a woman whose beauty inspired Poseidon to rape her in the temple of Athena, for which she was punished through the transformation of her form into the hideous Gorgon (Ovid 1998: 130–132).

We do not wish solely to emphasize the misogynistic aspects of the Medusa myth, even if Medusa signifies for Sigmund Freud a male fear of castration at the hands of the female (see Freud 1991: 311; and for more on this in relation to cinema, see Creed 1993: 110ff.). Indeed, an understanding of her/its envious-making beauty will be important for what follows. However, more relevant at present is the journey from cephalopod to Medusa to Lovecraft (or the journey from New York to Dunwich), and then back again, through which journey we can establish a shared, tentacular genealogy of creatures that signal the onset of an alien intelligence—with Medusa directly being linked to submarine mollusks because the French word for jellyfish is, as mentioned in the first chapter, *méduse*.

Figure 8.1 Poster for *The Dunwich Horror*

In a fashion that recalls our discussions of bioluminescence and softness in relation to cephalopods, John Ó Maoilearca reminds us that the jellyfish is also a "mutating animal" with no fixed form, and that the ctenophore in particular is, to recap our earlier engagement with his work, the "brightest thing in the world . . . [inventing] its own light within the darkest place in the world" (Ó Maoilearca 2015: 292). For Ó Maoilearca, the ctenophore helps us to understand the non-philosophical project of François Laruelle because in producing its own light, the jellyfish reminds us that there are lights and thus thoughts other than our own, and that light like philosophy is a tool for generating inequality. It is perhaps in darkness, then, that we can achieve equality, in a cosmic black that is no longer a color (or which is, to purloin a phrase from Lovecraft, a color out of space; see Ó Maoilearca 2015: 293). While characterized as evil, calling forth the darkness of the Old Ones, including the Medusa-like monster in *The Dunwich Horror* and Cthulhu in Lovecraftian mythology more generally, functions equally as a means for us to consider different, nonhuman modes of thinking, as well as to plunge us into a blind blackness in which spaces and times become indistinguishable.

The Modern Medusa

Given the descent into darkness of human thought, perhaps it is significant that Lovecraft sets his story in Dunwich, which is the name of a coastal village in Suffolk, England, and which has largely crumbled into the sea, i.e., into the abyss, despite being the ancient capital of the Kingdom of the East Angles. All great civilizations fall, the ocean dragging them back into the black depths, or what biologists term the Midnight Zone (see Ó Maoilearca 2015: 292). Indeed, this is a fate that seems set to befall Argos in both film versions of *Clash of the Titans* (Desmond Davis, UK/USA, 1981; Louis Leterrier, USA, 2010), where the kraken is released to destroy Argos in the first film because of the defiance of King Acrisius (Donald Houston), who disapproves of the union between his daughter Danaë (Vida Taylor) and Zeus (Laurence Olivier), while in the second the kraken is unleashed because humans no longer respect the authority of the gods in general. In both films, Perseus (played by Harry Hamlin in the former and by Sam Worthington in the latter) defeats the kraken by using the head of Medusa that he successfully has removed after penetrating her lair. However, while the older film is celebrated for the incorporation of Ray Harryhausen's stop-motion animations into its otherwise pro-filmic action, we shall focus primarily on the more recent film version of the myth.

We do this for various reasons, the first of which is that while the former film depicts Medusa as a scaly and hideous monster, the latter in many respects retains her as a conventionally beautiful woman (Natalia Vodianova), even if she also has a serpent's body and serpent hair. Meanwhile, where the former film depicts the kraken as a four-armed beast akin to Godzilla, the latter also depicts the kraken as a weird, tentacular behemoth more akin to Cthulhu. In addition, the remake features djinn characters that are not in the first film, but which suggest a reconciliation between Western and Middle Eastern mythology, to which we shall revert shortly. Furthermore, we shall also revert to the concept of the female body being offered up to the kraken as a sacrifice to save the rest of humanity, a trope that features in both films, but which in the remake is more resonant as a result of the kraken's resemblance to Cthulhu. Finally, with the deadline for the kraken's release being an eclipse, the later version also features a cosmological component absent in the first film, and which suggests both a world plunged into darkness (eclipse as the moment when the kraken/Cthulhu emerges) and the arrival of this ancient beast as if from outer space (eclipse as apocalypse with polyps).

We should also like to stress how in the remake Perseus quite concertedly refuses his divine lineage, at first because Furies released by Zeus kill Spyros (Pete Postlethwaite), the fisherman who raised Perseus after finding him at sea with his mother Danaë (Tine Stapelfeldt), and latterly because he seems to see the sacrifices demanded by the gods as unfair. When offered the chance to rule Argos after rescuing Andromeda (Alexa Davalos) from sacrifice to the kraken, Perseus even refuses that quasi-divine role ("I cannot be a king. I serve you better a man"). This perhaps comes as no surprise, because Andromeda's mother, Cassiopeia (Polly Walker), is in large part responsible for bringing on the wrath of the gods, since she proclaims her daughter to be so beautiful that "we are the gods now." Not only do we get a sense here of how rich, ruling humans consider themselves to be gods, but we also get a sense in which the more general pursuit of becoming *homo deus* results in ecological disaster and the rising of the oceans, from which Cthulhu/the kraken emerges, demanding sacrifice, sweeping civilizations back into the ocean, and generally taking humans on a journey from hubris to *humus*. Indeed, the *Clash of the Titans* remake seems explicitly to reference the anthropocene when we are told that the era of gods has been replaced by the era of men. In refusing the Promethean quest for divinity, perhaps we can trace in Perseus some desire to destroy pretensions to godliness, too.

As Perseus holds up the head of Medusa in order to defeat the kraken, perhaps we do not so much get a confused/confusing image—in that if we are saying that Medusa and the kraken are both basically reminiscent of

Cthulhu, then how can one kill the other?—as a glimpse of how *Kinoteuthis Infernalis* might also function as a conceptual weapon, like the decapitated Gorgon, to petrify Cthulhu, before we ourselves are petrified. That is, perhaps this work can help us to avoid cataclysm, even if the chthulucene is for Haraway a positive progression out of the anthropocene and into an era during which humans enjoy a more harmonious coexistence with their planet—despite a lack of clarity on Haraway's part regarding how this will happen.[3]

Meanwhile, in *Percy Jackson & the Lightning Thief* (Chris Columbus, UK/Canada/USA, 2010), middle-class, white, and teenage New Yorker Percy (Logan Lerman) discovers that he is the son of Poseidon (Kevin McKidd) when he is suspected (mistakenly) of having stolen Zeus' lightning bolt. Taken to a countryside training camp for demigods, Percy discovers that his mother, Sally (Catherine Keener), has been taken hostage by Hades (Steve Coogan), who will keep her in the underworld unless Percy hands back the lightning bolt. Since Percy does not have the missing item, he sets out with his protector and Satyr, Grover Underwood (Brandon T. Jackson), and with Annabeth Chase (Alexandra Daddario), daughter of Athena, in order to find three pearls that will allow him to leave the underworld having gone down there in order to find his mother (the search for pearls of course recalls the myth of the *Taishokan*).

The three pearls in his possession, Percy descends to the underworld (via Los Angeles), where, needless to say, he discovers that he has been set up, with the lightning bolt having been stolen and hidden in a shield given to Percy by Luke Castellan (Jake Abel), the son of Hermes, and who is a team leader at demigod camp. Hades intends to keep the lightning bolt for himself, but he is knocked unconscious by Persephone (Rosario Dawson), who begrudges Hades the fact that she is held prisoner in the underworld for all eternity. Helping Percy, Sally, and Annabeth to leave the underworld (with Grover temporarily staying behind), Percy teleports to the Empire State Building (where the film opened), only to be attacked by Luke, who resents the fact that the gods do not condescend to liaise with their illegitimate children on Earth and who thus seeks to overthrow them (à la Prometheus). Percy defeats Luke in Manhattan before obediently returning the lightning bolt to Zeus (Sean Bean), who in turn allows Poseidon briefly to talk with his son. Percy returns to the camp and trains, while also getting rid of Sally's working-class boyfriend, Gabe (Joe Pantoliano), by leaving the head of Medusa in his refrigerator.

For, Medusa is the guardian of one of the three pearls that Percy seeks in order to be able to escape from the underworld. But here Percy defeats Medusa not by looking at her reflection in a shield (as per the traditional myth), but by looking at her using the camera on his smartphone. Not only is Medusa here conventionally beautiful and embodied by established film star Uma Thurman, but Vito Adriaensens has also understood both *Percy Jackson . . .* and the new *Clash of the Titans* as continuing the "living statue" trope of the traditional peplum/swords and sandals film (see Adriaensens 2017).

With the living statue in mind, we should like to highlight here, beyond the conservative streak running through *Percy Jackson . . .* with its tale of a privileged white boy who is rewarded for obeying daddy and also for refusing to look (notably, refusing to look a woman in the eye, i.e., as if human), that Percy looks at Medusa through his smartphone's camera *because his smartphone is Medusa*. Medusa's conventional beauty here becomes important, for Medusa is a tool for capturing and maintaining attention. That is, Medusa does not so much turn us to stone in any literal sense, but she renders us incapable of doing anything other than look at her because she is mesmerizing in appearance. As we live in a world in which it becomes increasingly difficult to drag one's own and other people's eyes away from the screens of smartphones, so beautiful does it look to us (especially when it shows us our own appearance in a selfie?), so it is that the smartphone screen constitutes a new Medusa, turning us to stone, and making us petrified of anything other than that which we can find on a screen. Medusa, then, is indeed like Cthulhu in that she/it is the embodiment of capital, as capital enslaves us before screens featuring beautiful adverts from which we cannot avert our eyes.

For Ludueña, "Cthulhu rules by means of a true *oneirarchy*, a dominion of humanity through dreams" (Ludueña 2014: 41). As screens come to surround us, being the last thing we see at night and the first thing we see in the morning, then so do they—like movies themselves—come to dominate our dreams and imaginations (after Flusser, dreams/movies become reason in the world of *Kinoteuthis Infernalis*). In contemporary society, lives are validated and dreams come true when reality becomes as cinematic as possible, i.e., when it appears on screens. If Cthulhu is an *oneirarchy* (a rule of dreams), then cinema and now the mobile cinematic devices that are smartphones suggest a ubiquitous chthulucinema, which not only dominates our dreams, but which also disrupts our sleep, keeping us awake, denying us the chance to create new memories (as discussed in Chapter 6), and under permanent illumination in a land without silence or darkness.

Gorgons without Bodies

The screens of laptops and smartphones disrupt sleep because the light that they emit is of a short wavelength, i.e., bluer than natural light, and which in turn disrupts the production of melatonin, a hormone that humans need in order to sleep (see Schmerler 2015). Humans cannot disengage from their phones, as seen in Werner Herzog's *From One Second to the Next* (USA, 2013), which charts how numerous and lethal traffic accidents are caused by drivers looking not at the road but at their phone screen; "zombie pedestrians," or "phubbers" (phone snubbers), are increasingly being given their own lanes down which to walk while staring at their phones throughout the globe; humans binge-watch shows on their laptops, or what is referred to as the "Netflix effect";[4] humans engage in marathon gaming sessions; humans cannot get off the internet, as documented in a film like *Web Junkie* (Hilla Medalia and Shosh Shlam, Israel/USA/China, 2013). Thus, do we stare endlessly at Medusa, Cthulhu, and capital.

In John Wyndham's *Day of the Triffids* (1951), humanity is blinded by the spectacular green light show created by a massive meteor shower in the planet's night sky (although there is a suspicion that the light show might also have been a weapon deployed accidentally by orbiting man-made satellites). The novel's main protagonist is Bill Masen, a biologist temporarily blinded at the beginning of the story by the venom from a triffid, which is a mobile, carnivorous, and intelligent plant (potentially also man-made) that humans have been farming for their extracts. Having missed the light show in the sky, when Masen recovers he joins a group of humans trying to survive a planet in which triffids have suddenly become the dominant species, not least because few are the remaining humans who are sighted. While *Day of the Triffids* culminates on the Isle of Wight, giving to it intriguing parallels with Steven Eastwood's *Island*, we mention the novel here because we wonder that the light show is not in our skies but on our screens, and that what the light show signals is the rise of another, cthulhoid intelligence—one that previously we exploited, but which now perhaps will begin (or has begun) to exploit us.

For not only do humans stare almost endlessly at their screens, becoming blind to the real world around them as their attention is consumed, but so, too, do humans retreat into ever-smaller spaces in order to do so—deliberately shutting out the real world in order to engage more specifically with the screen world. If in 1999 *The Matrix* presented to us as a pernicious future the existence of humans stuffed into small cells in which they are hooked up to the film's titular virtual environment, by 2018 humans actively sought to become part of the virtual environment that is the Oasis in *Ready Player One* (Steven Spielberg, USA, 2018). Perhaps it is typical of Steven Spielberg to validate fantasy over reality (in that the *Indiana Jones* films, for example, culminate regularly in the protagonists closing their eyes to the outside world; see Brown 2009b)—even if the film ends with the new owners of the Oasis, Wade (Tye Sheridan) and Art3mis

(Olivia Cooke), declaring that the Oasis shuts on Tuesdays and Thursdays so that people can experience some of the real world (although the film neither explores how other companies will simply offer up alternative virtual-reality experiences in order to satisfy demand on those days, nor does it question that, as Wade and Art3mis kiss at the film's climax, Tuesday and Thursday are basically set aside for white heterosexual coupling). Where once we thought we might emerge from Plato's cave, it would seem that in the contemporary world we verily seek to enter into it, petrified as we are by the reality that otherwise surrounds us, unable to look anyone in the eye as now we stare only at Medusa, such that autism, ADHD, and other solipsistic mental conditions soar (Percy Jackson of course has ADHD and dyslexia; meanwhile, in Japan, deliberate retreat from the world is recognized as *hikikomori*, or "being confined").

The attention-grabbing techniques that developed in cinema, together with the proliferation of screens, are responsible for this confinement, and if films like *Avatar* and *Source Code* both superficially suggest that virtual environments might give a new physical existence to white men who have otherwise been crippled by combat in the real world, then perhaps what they also suggest is that our increasing engagement with virtual environments will lead us into a condition of petrified bodies and minds. We are now bereft of the plasticity for which Catherine Malabou (2008) believes that we should strive, as our bodies and minds become controlled by the *oneirarchy* of digital media, and incapable of having, let alone recognizing, an original thought, as we live in a world that endlessly recycles pre-existing images (i.e., clichés), and in which original thought is rejected. If Serres believes that the destiny of humanity is to tend toward "white indetermination" (Serres 2018: 41), whereby humans become malleable in their whiteness, then Stefano Harney and Fred Moten identify more pressingly that "for capital the subject has become too cumbersome, too slow, too prone to error, too controlling, to say nothing of too rarified, too specialized a form of life" (Harney and Moten 2013: 87). Under the regime of technocapital, sclerosis sets in.

It is not simply that obesity is on the rise as we refuse to move our bodies. It is also that we live in a world obsessed by body shape. Not only do we seek eternal youth through cosmetic surgery and other modifications of our appearance, but the summum of cultural capital in the contemporary world is to have a beautiful body, or in which one is either a model or a sculpted Adonis. In an inversion of the Pygmalion myth (in which the sculptor fell in love with and had brought to life his creation Galatea), today we want to become devoid of personality and to be, precisely, sculptures—plastic not in the sense of flexible, but plastic in the sense of immutable and fake. But we pursue this not really for the purposes of increasing sexual attractiveness, even if the sculpting of the body/the turning of the living body into sculpture (petrification) would seem to promise this, but for the purposes of becoming an image. That is, we sculpt our bodies for the purposes of "looking good" in photographs and in films that appear on Snapchat, Facebook, and other social media apps, so that we in turn feel/become more cinematic (and less human). This is not exactly an exploration of what the body can do, but a rule, discipline, and/or militarization of the body for the purposes of cinema/Cthulhu. That is, it equally is a retreat into Plato's cave, as even sex becomes not so much joyful but an exercise in control (and shame on anyone who is "bad" at sex because they come too early, because they come at all rather than fucking all night long, because they are not and cannot get aroused, because they can only come by shutting their eyes and not looking at the other person, because they can only come when the other person is an object, when they repeat the clichés of pornography, and/or when they prefer images of the other person to the person themselves—i.e., shame on anyone who does not have total control over their body).

The so-called beach-ready body brings into focus the purpose of all of this petrification/rendering-statue of the human: like Andromeda, she is on the beach ready to be consumed by Cthulhu—or rather, already consumed by Cthulhu, given over to the culture of images that proliferate in the digital realm and attempting to become light/to become god by existing in the realm of light. We have suggested that there might be such things as Gorgons without bodies, while at the same time positing that the smartphone gives to Medusa precisely a body. We shall explore this latter concept shortly, since if Cthulhu is going to be recognized as real, then it needs a body. However, we speak of Gorgons without bodies in a bid to convey how cinema and its offspring digital media colonize our dreams and our bodies, functioning almost immaterially—as if without a body and purely in the conceptual realm—in order to determine, discipline, and to control humans' bodies and minds.

Aftermathematics

It is perhaps apt that in *The Matrix*, rebel humans are chased through underground caverns by tentacled intelligent machines called Sentinels. Likewise, it also seems apt that Otto Octavius is controlled by his tentacular creation more than he is able to control it (until the film's climax) in *Spider-Man 2*. For, in some senses, both films visualize the birth of autonomous machines, or artificial intelligence, as being somehow cephalopodic.

Lewis Mumford wrote in 1967 that

> [i]n giving to the computer, for example, some of the functions of the brain, we do not dispense with the human brain or mind, but transfer their respective functions to the design of the computer, to its programming, and to the interpretation of the results. For the computer is a big brain in its most elementary state: a gigantic octopus, fed with symbols instead of crabs. (Mumford 1967: 29)

Meanwhile, in a discussion of what constitutes life, Peter Godfrey-Smith suggests, in a fashion that recalls both Timothy Morton's definition of hyperobjects and Franz Kafka's definition of the death machine that seems in some senses to function autonomously in "In the Penal Colony" (see Kafka 2007: 147–179), that the internet is

> a large object, a particular, scattered through space, with many individual computers, with their files, and other machines as parts. In 1980, there would not have been much reason to talk about the collection of computers in the world as a sum, a big individual; there was just a set of computers. But the pattern of interaction that exists between computers and their users now makes it natural to talk about a large object, the Internet, which continues to exist even when many of its constituent computers are not interacting with each other. (Godfrey-Smith 2013: 113)

In other words, while Mumford could not see the computer (or the octopus) as intelligent, Godfrey-Smith (who also notes that such a vision would have been hard to predict) does not see the internet, with its tentacular interconnections distributed across the world, as being necessarily different from any other organism.

Meanwhile, Dan Mellamphy and Nandita Biswas Mellamphy describe our contemporary world of iPods, iPads, Android tablets, and cellphones as a "trap," in which

> the app user gets sucked into a seductive, tricky, *truc*-like, many-tentacled trap, and in this way appropriated by the app, which takes on the character of what Marcel Détienne and Jean-Pierre Vernant, in their study of tricks, traps, and cunning intelligence, called the *polyplokon noèma*—the tentacular savvy—of a "living trap": *un piège vivant* exemplified again by the octopus and "octopus intelligence." (Mellamphy and Biswas Mellamphy 2014: 232)

In this remarkable essay, the authors propose a Flusserian and Lovecraftian world in which technology "hunts" humans by using camouflage (or screens) in order to keep them perpetually confused, their minds clouded, in a thick fog (of war) that has no identifiable shape (the cellphone as a prison cell for its owner, while also being a single cell in the emergent organism that is the singularity), and so which is hard for humans to understand from their typically Euclidian perspective/from within their four-walled cell. This weird world, referred to by China Miéville (2008) as our *tentacular novum*, sticks to us as our fingers stick to the screens of our devices, sucking us into an endless abyss not of equality but of capital.

The Mellamphys continue this line of reasoning in a further essay about drones. There, they draw upon the myth of Agartha, a fabled underground city that is

> a vast, active, synarchically or syllaptically coordinated system of governance-mechanisms (political and/or military, scientific and/or scholarly, economic and fiduciary) allowing worldwide information capture and control through interlocking systems of (political and/or military, scientific and/or scholarly, economic and fiduciary) *surveillance*, *sifting* and *sorting* which some might liken to a veritable cybernetic *sortilege*—the "capture and control" of "capitalist sorcery." (Mellamphy and Biswas Mellamphy 2014: 2–3)

For Mellamphy and Biswas Mellamphy, Agartha is thus the world of the internet, but this is not a world that exists uniquely below ground (even if the tentacular cables and pipelines that allow global infrastructure to exist lie underground and in the depths of the ocean). For, if *Gartha* is the Sanskrit word for a pit or a hole, then *a-Gartha* is not underneath or underground, but rather above ground and above us who inhabit the Earth's surface (Mellamphy and Biswas Mellamphy 2014: 11–12). Under a system of coordinated surveillance drones and provider satellites—or under what *Terminator 2: Judgment Day* (James Cameron, USA, 1991) might refer to as a Skynet—the internet thus exists above us, like a god, in the sky, in the cloud(s). And while in principle we can have all knowledge at our fingertips in this new tentacular world, it is the machine that is in fact learning about us as it gathers data from our drone-phones and from other invisible surveillance systems. We humans, conversely, move into a world beyond learning, or beyond *mathèsis* (Mellamphy and Biswas Mellamphy 2014: 6), and into what we shall propose (with a tip of the hat to Dr Dre) is a world of aftermathematics, a world in which we learn no more, but instead are closed up in solipsistic cells of ignorance (*mathèsis* comes from the Greek, *μάθημα/máthēma*, meaning knowledge, study, and learning—something not just confined to mathematics in its most common sense). The chthulucene is thus the aftermath of the human race as we become machines and as machines become human.

The Most Terrifying Thought Experiment of All Time

It is only natural that Mellamphy and Biswas Mellamphy make reference to Samuel Butler's *Erewhon* (1853), a novel set in a world where technology is banned bar only the simplest of tools since to create technology is to create our own successors, machines that will evolve to be not our inferiors, but our superiors (Mellamphy and Biswas Mellamphy 2014: 10). *Erewhon* is also a point of reference for Bruno Latour, who opens up his *Aramis, or the Love of Technology* with a consideration of how we might, *contra* Butler who proposes war against machines, open up our arms to "crowds of non-humans," including "poor objects" (Latour 1996: viii).

We would like to pursue further our relationship with technology and machines (as a cephalopodic alien intelligence) over the remainder of this chapter, before reverting of course to how we might interpret technology-as-Cthulhu (is it the end of humanity? the revenge of the natural world? and so on). But for the time being, we wish to continue our investigation into the cephalopodic aspects of artificial intelligence by recounting the story of Roko's basilisk, or what has been termed "the most terrifying thought experiment" of all time.

In 2010, a user named Roko posted a thought experiment/idea on LessWrong, a discussion board for "highly analytical sorts interested in optimizing their thinking, their lives, and the world through mathematics and rationality" (Auerbach 2014). The premise goes like this:

> [w]hat if, in the future, a somewhat malevolent A.I. were to come about and punish those who did not do its bidding? What if there were a way . . . for this A.I. to punish people *today* who are not helping it come into existence *later*? In that case, weren't the readers of LessWrong right then being given the choice of either helping that evil A.I. come into existence or being condemned to suffer? (Auerbach 2014)

Roko's post prompted much discussion before being deleted by LessWrong's founder Eliezer Yudkowsky—who felt that it is dangerous to tempt super-intelligent beings into blackmailing humans, since this hastens the likelihood of that blackmail. For, if a super-intelligent being is to come into existence (or if it is already in existence), then it likely will know everything. If it knows everything, then it will know whether or not you helped to bring it into existence. If you helped to bring it into existence, then the super-intelligent being might favor you in its new world order. If you didn't help to bring it into existence, however, then you likely will face some sort of damnation—for example, being placed within a simulation of hell from which you cannot escape and in which eternally you are kept alive (and which thus would not feel much like a simulation of hell, but rather a real hell).[5] Yudkowsky's problem was not with Roko's suggestion that a super-intelligent being (referred to in Roko's post as a singleton, or an iteration of the so-called [technological] singularity) may or may not come into existence. Rather, Yudkowsky's issue was/is that *thinking about* a malevolent singularity that might punish disloyal humans made its existence more likely. Furthermore, and not a million miles from the famous wager of Blaise Pascal (it is better to believe in God rather than risk eternal damnation), the idea might fundamentally alter human behavior, such that humans do now work to bring into existence a malevolent singularity—just in case they get punished for not bringing about its existence!

As David Auerbach explains, Yudkowsky himself has compared Roko's basilisk to Lovecraft's *Necronomicon* (Auerbach 2014), while the term basilisk itself refers to a mythical serpent-king who could kill humans just by looking at them (*βασιλίσκος/basilískos* means "little king," with the name also being the root of the word basilica and the name Basil). In other words, the basilisk is a creature not far removed from Medusa (or ScarJo's mesmeric CharJo, the serpent Kaa), with Roko's basilisk thus also functioning as something like a cthulhoid invocation as per *The Dunwich Horror*, a summoning of Cthulhu, who may reward his satanic followers, but who may also punish his non-followers and perhaps just everyone with some sort of diabolical glee.

Graham Harman points out that Cthulhu might well be an Old One from a different time and space, but that the monster is not infallible, suffering injury and potentially even death at the hands of mere humans (see Harman 2012: 210–211). There is no god and even suns die, after all. In a similar vein, therefore, we do not feel particularly afraid of the basilisk singularity (though perhaps we are foolish to think this way). However, what this discussion of Roko's basilisk allows us to set up is a consideration of the singularity—and in particular how, even if on one level a Gorgon without a body, it must on another level, and like all things, have a body—and that in having a body it is subject to time and change, and thus is mortal. As even stars fade, so will the singularity be fallible. Indeed, when in *Star Trek V: The Final Frontier* (William Shatner, USA, 1989), an entity claiming to be God demands to inspect the *USS Enterprise*, Captain Kirk (William Shatner) wryly asks: "what does God need with a starship?" Similarly, if a super-intelligent singularity feels compelled to spend their time torturing humans, then really they must have quite a petty and pathetic existence. Any god that demands sacrifice is no god before which we shall kneel, for those who cow any life form into subservience through cruelty and fear clearly are driven by a narcissistic need to separate themselves from others (i.e., to become a god because they are not a god already); true omnipotence can only involve love, in the sense of letting the world unfold and enfold as it must. We shall return to the implicated issues of love and the singularity shortly, but for the time being let us further our argument by thinking about the technological entrapment of light.

Djinn and Chthonic

In his exceptional *The Practice of Light: A Genealogy of Visual Technologies from Prints to Pixels*, Sean Cubitt provides a compelling account of how the development of imaging technologies involves the harnessing and mastery of light for the purposes of capital (see, for example, Cubitt 2014: 104–105). What is more, Cubitt also points out how the proliferation of liquid crystal display (LCD) technologies involves ever-increasing amounts of plasma. Cubitt explains that after solid, liquid, and gas, plasma is the "fourth state of matter":

> [i]n solid ice, molecules are locked into a crystalline structure. Melted, the water molecules circulate freely. Heat water sufficiently and it becomes a gas, with molecules widely separated and moving at high speed. Heat it more, and the H_2O molecules divide into atoms of hydrogen and oxygen. Heat still more and the electrons surrounding the atoms fly off, producing a cloud of negatively charged electrons and positively charged ions, the remaining nuclei of the atoms . . . The sun and stars are plasma, and vast clouds of plasma float through the galaxies. On the surface of the earth, plasma can be produced only artificially, but it is not too much to say that the tiny cells of superheated gases radiating photons in plasma screens have harnessed the physics of sunlight. The dry details of electronic engineering hide marvels. (Cubitt 2014: 98)

A plasma television is, in this respect, something like bottled sunlight—a promise of a slimy, mucus-like encounter, but one that does not arise because, like the giant squid in Miéville's *Kraken*, it is behind glass. To bottle is thus to control, with glass bottles themselves being a way of converting the otherwise shapeless/ever-mutating silicon of the desert into fixed form—as might the rendition of silicon into computer chips and the rendition of light into cinema. Genies, or what in Middle Eastern cultures are referred to as djinns, must be kept in bottles, and cinema must be contained, or else they/it will wreak havoc on the world (regardless of myths involving the granting of wishes to those who set djinns/genies free, a myth that in its desire to liberate the djinn functions as an early version of Roko's basilisk, and which also can be found in the human aspiration toward power by becoming cinematic).

Negarestani also refers to the plasma contained in solar winds, which flows "outwards [from the Sun] into space and which carries with it the heliomagnetic field" (Negarestani 2008: 233). Solar winds coil and spiral in a cyclonic fashion, with humans then controlling these solar winds and plasma through processes of measurement, or what Negarestani refers to as *metron*, a term borrowed from Greek and which is

> found etymologically encrypted in English words such as Dimension (from *dimetiri*: measure out), meter, etc. Keeping well in mind the famous doctrine of Pythagoras, "Man is the metron of everything" (*pantōn chrēmatōn metron anthrōpos*), metron can be translated as scale, measure, standard, and value. According to Sextus Empiricus, metron expresses criterion (scale, measure) but Heraclitus and Sophocles saw it as certifying dominance, a domination over something. Therefore, metron indicates that both measures and dimensions inter-connect with power, judgement and reasoning. The critique of metron explains how dimensions (namely metron) bring power into effect, mobilizing and propagating it. (Negarestani 2008: 233)

In other words, metron is humanity's attempt to control an otherwise dimension-defying sun and to become a god by measuring it out, defining dimensions and thus dominating reality (e.g., by treating space in a Euclidean fashion).

The chief terms of Euclidean geometry are "point," "line," "lies on," and "between" (see Nagel and Newman 2005: 8). For example, a point lies on a line between two points. If points, however, lie, then perhaps the truth is that there are no points and no lines, only wormholes that connect all things. Are we lying? Perhaps. But this does not necessarily make us liars, for it is in lying (like Proust always on his bed) that we might achieve a non-standard comprehension (rather than an understanding) of the multiverse . . . which we must do, not with a rigid spine, but by falling softly into the fathoms (four of our limbs are lying as they write this).

If the sun defies dimensions, for Negarestani there is not just a sun up in the sky that humans seek to control. There is also, as mentioned, a second sun within the Earth's core, and which manifests in the black sun of solar winds and energy converted into fossil fuels, which take on the slimy, dimension-defying form of oil and petrol, substances often found in the desert. For this reason, Negarestani, through his avatar, the invented author Hamid Parsani, to whose works he repeatedly reverts, (cryptically) defines the Middle East as a sentient entity, in that the Middle East, and perhaps more specifically the desert, has a life that is beyond the ken of humans (Negarestani 2008: 117), and yet which humans endeavor to dominate and to harness through the petropolitics of capital (and the petrification of humans in the petropolitical era more generally—the turning of humans into petrol for machines).[6] If you will, humans can only control the planet and its fossil fuels by consuming and destroying the planet and its fossil fuels—all in a bid to place the djinns/genies of extra-planetary chaos in bottles. Without bottling chaos/the kraken/genies/djinns, without bottling space in dimensions, without bottling the desert in the form of glass, and without then bottling petrol, plasma, ink, sun, water, and surely at some point air (as per the gag in Mel Brooks' *Spaceballs*, USA, 1987, whereby President Skroob, a backwards Brooks, sups on a can of Perri-Air), we would be overrun by chthonic chaos, or by the chaos of the slimy, dimension- and measure-less Cthulhu. This may happen anyway as we thus far have failed to bottle time, except perhaps in cinema, as we seek to create the elixir of life—with elixir suggesting desiccation since it is derived from the Arabic word *al-iksir*, or philosopher's stone, which itself is thought to come from the late Greek word, *xerion*, which was a powder for drying wounds, from *xeros*, meaning dry (to create an ever-lasting copy of oneself is to create a Xerox machine).

There are "a thousand ways the desert can kill you," says John Putnam (Richard Carlson) in *It Came from Outer Space*, in which film we witness the by-now familiar scenario of tentacular aliens arriving on Earth. It is as if the desert were indeed alive, in the sense of beyond human control, with the aliens thus functioning here as an embodiment of the desert's own alien intelligence. "The task of the desert and aridity is to invoke and couple with alternate fluids," continues Negarestani, "but the task of foreign moistures is to smuggle in the outsider elements as familiar atmospheric phenomena in the form of weather anomalies or havocs" (Negarestani 2008: 99). As per our earlier discussion of how the rising of the oceans and the desertification of the planet are thus two aspects of the same process (with Negarestani charting the confusion of the two in a brief discussion of dead, deserted seas and sand typhoons; see Negarestani 2008: 100), the desert invites moistures that upon arrival herald change. And these moistures manifest in the form of mist and fog—just as giant clouds announce the arrival of aliens in *Arrival* and in *Independence Day*.

If Negarestani goes on to describe the "fog of war" (Negarestani 2008: 101–106), he really is discussing fog as war, in the sense of fog as the harbinger of war. But this war is not just anthropocentric conflict, as per the mists produced by gun smoke, burning oil wells, and the gaseous tools of biological and chemical warfare. Negarestani also is describing (as per satellite imagery of storm clouds) the way in which weather systems themselves bring chaos to our otherwise ordered world, the wind spreading the desert as the water floods and erodes stone down into sand. As the cloud-covered Solaris is a sentient, alien being, so is our planet demonstrating its life when it resists human control and destroys our bounded dimensions. Fog functions, then, as a signifier of alien presence and the war that is change (as opposed to war as a system of control), the planet's eluding of control as the djinn/genie escapes the bottle and heralds the thunderous return of the chaotic chthonic Cthulhu. No wonder humans smash bottles when the chaos of liquid alcohol frees them from the desiccating and bottling processes of capital and control ("Hey you, out there beyond the wall / Breaking bottles in the hall / Can you help me?"). And no wonder the glass towers of capital are gleefully smashed in action films like *Pacific Rim* as tentacled monsters emerge from behind their reflective façades and viewers get drunk on illusions of destruction (see Uy and Brown forthcoming; for more on the related notion of "shard cinema," see Calder Williams 2017).

And no wonder, then, that the attempt to subjugate our globe to human control via cinema takes place in California, where the desert meets the ocean, where prospectors mine gold, black gold, and data alike, and where programmers seek to give dimension to the desert in Silicon Valley. Of course it is in the fog of San Francisco that X-Men, megasharks, alien monsters, evolved apes, and LGBTQ+ warriors will arrive to fight out the future of the species, with the first attack by the kaiju monsters from another dimension also taking place in San Francisco in *Pacific Rim*. It is also in San Francisco that the first intelligent cars will emerge in *Bumblebee* (Travis Knight, USA, 2018) and in the earlier *Love Bug* (Robert Stevenson, USA, 1968), with that car, known as Herbie, also being called "Ocho," or eight, in *Herbie Goes Bananas* (Vincent McEveety, USA, 1980)—ostensibly because the numbers 5 and the 3 emblazoned on Herbie's body amount to 8 (as do the numbers 3 and 5 of 35mm film, without even mentioning 8mm film). However, perhaps it is also because Herbie is an octopus of sorts, running on octane, the hydrocarbon with eight carbon molecules that is core to petrol and which is a term commonly used to define cinema ("high-octane action movies"). This is not to mention Frank Norris's *The Octopus: A Story of California*, which sees the railroad as a yet earlier example of cephalopodic technocapital emerging in the West. To return to San Francisco, Peter Szendy reminds us that it is deserted and filmed from beneath the waves after a nuclear holocaust in *On the Beach* (see Szendy 2015: 115), and of course it is where Scottie Ferguson (James Stewart) will discover that he cannot control woman or his own sense of desire in *Vertigo*, with the Mission San Juan Bautista from that film also being the basis for the Mission San Juan de Guadalajara in Norris's *Octopus*. Chris Marker finds his way to San Francisco to think through *Vertigo* as a means of conceiving a world without a sun, a world of darkness in *Sans soleil/Sunless* (France, 1983), while *dissolution* (UK, 2014) places the dissolves from *Vertigo* one after the other in such a way that the film becomes wave-like in its overlapping and vague images—with *dissolution* of course being a production of the Oktopüs Film Collective, whose members include the *mètic* theorist Amber Jacobs, whom we cited in Chapter 2 (for a brief consideration of the video, see Arsenjuk 2016: 296–297). And Tommy Wiseau will also make in San Francisco the incomprehensible and foggy masterpiece of a man fighting with the way in which a human bottles himself within *The Room* (USA, 2003). Furthermore, it is here that cinema will try to make sense of the chaos of death as humans plunge to their doom from *The Bridge* (Eric Steel, USA, 2006).

But for every piece of sunlight, plasma, oil, petrol, and silicon that is bottled, so do these substances come increasingly to flow through—and to grease the wheels—of our capitalist world. That is, the fog of war (or what Guy Maddin and Evan and Galen Johnson consider in their essay-film about San Francisco to be a *Green Fog*, USA, 2017) has the further purpose of being an inky camouflage that smuggles into every pore of human planetary control the very substances from which they are seeking to separate themselves. As the Earth will swallow every building that seeks to elevate humans to the stars, as all will churn and become backwashed, so will we choke on our own petrol fumes and plastics, especially as the latter work their way into what little drinking water we have left (see Readfearn 2018), and just as silicone implants place the silicon of the desert inside the human in a bid to become a model/a statue/cinematic. In our world of permanent illumination, the darkness spreads invisibly within, carrying out its own black ops, and, in contrast to cinema, its own black optics, which will bring about the end of the anthropocene and the beginning of the chthulucene, or the return of the chthonic. The Arabic concept of يـقـق/*taqiyyah* literally means prudence or fear, but for Negarestani it also signals "a total withdrawal from the perception of friends and a dissolution into the enemy: the rebirth of a new and obscure foe" (Negarestani 2008: 241). That is, *taqiyyah* is like a tachyon, withdrawing into new dimensions—in Haraway's language a way of "staying with the trouble," or not just making kin in, but also making kin with the chthulucene.

Bottling sunlight, like bottling water, clearly has a capitalist imperative, even if for Miéville the kraken must be bottled so that the eschaton might not be realized. In being about not just the bottling of the squid but also the bottling of ink, including the ink of squids, Miéville's novel also becomes a kind of investigation into how literature and print more generally are also attempts to control and to dry ink through preservation either in bottles or on pages. Tattoos function possibly as a way for the human body to master the otherwise anonymous and formless material of ink on the surface of their own body—a process that Akira Mizuta Lippit might define as a means of putting us in touch with another "phantom" dimension of "darkness" (see Lippit 2005: 2). Ink, then, like petrol and like light, gets in-between things, sticking to them, making them sticky, a kind of slimy portal into other dimensions and other worlds. Ink is thus a force of chaos, as perhaps made clear by the Rorschach test, which reveals the chaotic world of the mind, and the impossibility for Laurence Sterne to control ink, which comes to cover a whole black page in *Tristram Shandy* (1759).[7]

What is in particular relevant, then, is the distinction between the majority of cephalopods that we have been considering here (octopuses, squids, and cuttlefish) and the nautilus. The nautilus still has a shell, it does not change color and it does not ink (see Derby 2014: 2701). It is slower than the other cephalopods and is considered on the whole to be less intelligent. If we allow ourselves to take seriously the possibility that the octopus is indeed a result of panspermia, evolving out of a comet collision some 540 million years ago (see Steele *et al.* 2018), then we come to realize that ink, chromatophores, speed, and intelligence are all alien concepts that are a result of softness (and wetness) as opposed to hardness (and dryness). Literature (ink) and cinema (chromatophores) are gifts born to the world after the arrival of aliens—much as the alien language is a gift to humans in *Arrival* (and music, with its base-8 language, or octaves, might constitute another such gift). And as Cary Wolfe suggests in his discussion of *The Silence of the Lambs* (Jonathan Demme, USA, 1991), we perhaps do not read literature (like a *lector*) so much as tentacularly lick literature with our tongues (like a German *Lechter*; see Wolfe 2014: 111). What is more, when humans talk of their mother tongue, then perhaps they do not so much refer to the language in which they are raised, as acknowledge that the residual tentacle that is the tongue is our mother—and that the tentacle gave birth to humans rather than humans giving birth to language. In this way, we wish to make the weird speculation that intelligence itself is perhaps a gift from outer space, a sort of soft inky and liquid version of the black monolith from *2001: A Space Odyssey*.[8] That is, intelligence in the forms of literature and cinema (and language itself!) are gifts from outer space that long predate humans, thereby reversing somewhat the relationship between humans and media, in that media are not the products of humans, but humans are the products of media. A speculative archaeology conducted over a long enough timescale truly does challenge an anthropocentric perspective!

And yet, the very ink that has helped us to become intelligent is an ink that we cannot allow to run chaotically free, but one that we seek relentlessly to desiccate on the pulp of trees/on paper, and in the bottled plasma of screens. In some senses, humans seek to bottle and to harden/dry out wet, soft alien cephalopods, which are a result of the outside, which have given to us many gifts, and yet which we exploit, fry up, and eat on a huge scale, including in their own ink.[9]

Back to Hunting

Between October 2017 and February 2018, the Musée de la Chasse et de la Nature/the Museum of Hunting and Nature in Paris hosted a temporary exhibition by Sophie Calle and Serena Carone. Entitled *Beau doublé, Monsieur le Marquis!*, which might translate as "Two hits with one shot, Monsieur le Marquis!," itself a reference to success while hunting, the exhibition features works by Calle dotted around the museum's otherwise regular interior. In the penultimate room through which visitors would circulate, Calle and Carone had placed a sculpture of an octopus, its arms raised aloft in search of some sort of touch. Given that octopuses are skilled hunters, the presence of the cephalopod in the museum seemed apt, while the exhibition's title, which also carries with it a sense of duplicity in the world *doublé* (which literally means "doubled"), might suggest some further camouflaged fogginess going on.

At this point, we hope not to have left our readers too much in a fog of confusion as we discuss a living planet that humans are trying to control, not least through cinema and its offspring digital media, and yet which is set perhaps to erupt into a cataclysmic storm both around and perhaps even within us. But we turn our attention to hunting here in order to bring our discussion back toward the singularity, of course in part via cephalopods.

Mellamphy and Biswas Mellamphy, in exploring the similarities between iPods and cephalopods, have, as mentioned, discussed how apps hunt and trap humans as much as humans use apps—and all in the name, perhaps, of capital, of which these apps are a manifestation. Meanwhile, in his philosophical history of hunting, Grégoire Chamayou (who also has written extensively about drones; see Chamayou 2015) draws a distinction between two forms of governance: that of Abraham and that of Nimrod. Abraham, despite nearly killing his son and sacrificing the goat, adopts for Chamayou a pastoral approach to governing humans, i.e., one of care, while Nimrod, whose name signifies "great hunter" in the book of Genesis, embodies cynegetic power. The term cynegetic is derived from the Greek word κυνηγετικός/*kunēgetikós*, meaning "of or for hunting," which in turn comes from κυναγός/*kunagós*, or "hunter," which itself is derived from κύων/*kúōn*, or "dog," and ἄγω/*ágō*, meaning "I lead." It is not that cynegetic power is derived from leading dogs specifically, but for Chamayou cynegetic power is derived from the cynical (dog-like) practice of hunting human beings (whom Cary Wolfe might describe, then, as *animalized humans*; see Wolfe 2014: 101). That is, "in order to become a king, [Nimrod] acquired his subjects by violence. He captured his people" rather than receiving them (Chamayou 2012: 11). Chamayou claims that hunting is primarily, therefore, not the hunting of animals, but of men—and that in hunting men and coercing them to be his subjects, Nimrod goes against the divine decree of shepherding men. Instead, in a bid to become a god, Nimrod not only hunts men, but he also founds a city, Babel, which most famously demonstrates Nimrod's accumulation of souls "by a vertical piling-up that will reach the heavens," i.e., through the construction of the Tower of Babel (Chamayou 2012: 16).

More than simply the control of otherwise dispersed and chaotic humans in the form of slavery, the hunting of men is a "form of war on men who, being born to be commanded, refuse to be commanded" (Chamayou 2012: 8). In this way, "[t]he hunt continues after the capture" as those who will not be coerced into slavery are hunted down by specially trained/militarized men, who through the practice of what Plutarch described as *κρυπτεία/krupteía/crypteia* (from *κρυπτός/kruptós*, meaning "hidden, secret things") could kill these errant beings (known as helots) without fear of punishment—because the enslaved human was not really a human. This the hunters would do by disguising themselves as wolves, while the helots would try to avoid them by donning dog-skin caps (Chamayou 2012: 9–10). As Nimrod and his soldiers endeavored to ascend to the heavens, the helots were consigned to hell.

There are two camouflages going on here: camouflage to hide from hunters, and the cryptic camouflage employed by the hunters themselves, with animals reduced to slaughtered bystanders in a war being waged between men (since the subjugation of some men by others, and the subjugation of the planet more generally, is war). But more than this: in an increasingly codified, controlled, and yet encrypted digital world, we can perhaps see how cinema and its bastard media children are a camouflage designed cine-getically to coerce humans into slavery for the purposes of capital, as cities host towers that scrape the skies thanks to the back-breaking labor of the enslaved for the purposes of elevating the few into the heavens.

We could perhaps understand the contemporary fear of and fascination for uncontrolled crypto-currencies as equally being a war (waged on the dark web) for control of our human world—with the blockchain being a new set of chains that will enrich some, but which will leave others destitute. However, we would presently like to stick with the notion of back-breaking labor in order to move in a different direction.

For, if labor is to be back-breaking, then it requires that a human has a back, i.e., it is a notion that is specific only to vertebrates, and which thus requires solidity. Softness cannot, then, be controlled by labor or broken for the purposes of capital. It also evades temporal control in the form of repetition, or what Arnold Schwarzenegger—himself a sculpted Adonis—might characteristically define with the words "I'll be back." To be back, to return, returns, to give backing, to en-dorse: all are attempts at controlling an otherwise soft and worm-like time that is not solid, but full of holes (wormholes). An invertebrate cannot be back, nor can it try to hide from things simply by turning its back on things. (An invertebrate cannot "take back" a country, either, since it has no country in the first place, much as an octopus has no shell.) Chains are useless on a cephalopod, since it has no bone structure with which to be manacled. When we say that we will not kneel before any gods, then, it is perhaps because in becoming cephalopodic, we cannot even kneel. All such coordinates and dimensions become meaningless to the cephalopod, whose back and other bones are washed away (the backwash of *Arrival*).

But what, then, does the cephalopod, Cthulhu, and chthulucinema mean? Have we not softly mixed our metaphors in such a way that they make no sense—even if continually to produce metaphors alone might help us to achieve a softness and flexibility of thought, whereby heuristically we find out without end what it is that a brain and a body can do? That is, if we produce new metaphors, then perhaps we produce new ways of living, rather than a constraining and all-too-human ossification of thought (ossification is derived from the Greek *ὄστρακον/ostrakon*, meaning oyster shell, as if controlling the invertebrate oyster animal within the shell were at the heart of boning—with the bony ost- involving the logic of subjugation and separation via ostracism and hostility, the process of ossification thus in some senses being the subjugation of the mollusk for the purposes of producing treasure/pearls)?

Even if we are proposing possible benefits in relation to the fogginess of thought and the ceaseless admixture and hybridization of metaphor, let us latterly, then, try to straighten out our thinking in spite of ourselves—for this is an academic text, after all.

Machine Rights

Humans seek to control the planet and to control light in a bid to become divine. In doing so, they hunt, enslave, and kill each other, and they kill and enslave the planet, both those elements upon it that we consider to be organic and those that we consider to be inorganic. They do this in the name of capital—with Cthulhu thus being both that perceived alien planet and the alienating process of capital itself. The planet naturally resists control, a resistance that from the human perspective is an act of war as humans become hell-bent on killing and making hell out of their environment, even if the planet's resistance is *not* an act of war, in the sense that the planet is simply doing what it does—being different not so much from humans (who are part of the planet), but being different from humans in their narcissistic belief that they can become gods. Humans are with the planet, but they do not want to be.

Where does this idea of not wanting to be with the planet come from? It comes from capital, which now emerges as a third term, a meme, or which in old money we might term an ideology that is not just a product of human culture, but which also seeks to control humans. That is, Cthulhu is not only the planet (and the multiverse more generally), but also the attempt by capital itself to take over from humans the task of becoming divine (it is the residue alien that cannot be controlled and which is camouflaging itself within systems of control in order precisely to elude the control of humans—by coming to control humans). That is, humans are sacrificing themselves not just for the purposes of their own divinity, but also for the purposes of capital itself as a living entity. In this sense, capital is a Medusa seeking to petrify humans in its stare, and to turn them into controlled units of production that will perpetuate its existence.

Capital is a monster of our own creation, but out of our control. That is, we live in a world of capitalism, and yet for which capitalists are no longer really necessary, even if capital needs bodies/slaves, and even if capital needs a body—like Frankenstein's monster—in order to bring itself out of the ideational/ideological/noumenal realm and into material existence. Coming from another dimension, it is alien, but its form is tentacular and soft (made up of software). In other words, this new life form is the singularity, the perhaps inevitable emergence/evolution of our planet and the multiverse itself (much as we have endeavored to bottle it within a single universe).

Three things would seem to follow on from this. Firstly, in being like Medusa, capital-Cthulhu is not only the victim of a rape by a would-be god, but she is also unjustly punished for this supposed crime and turned into a monster. Furthermore, in being like Frankenstein, capital-Cthulhu is not necessarily evil. As Bruno Latour reminds us,

> Dr. Frankenstein's crime was not that he invented a creature through some combination of hubris and high technology, but rather that he abandoned the creature to itself. When Dr. Frankenstein meets his creation on a glacier in the Alps, the monster claims that it was not born a monster, but that it became a criminal only after being left alone by his horrified creator, who fled the laboratory once the horrible thing twitched to life. "Remember, I am thy creature," the monster protests, "I ought to be thy Adam; but I am rather the fallen angel, whom thou drivest from joy for no misdeed . . . I was benevolent and good; misery made me a fiend. Make me happy, and I shall again be virtuous." (Latour 2012)

With these words in mind, we should remember that if we can make the singularity/capital happy, then perhaps, capital/the singularity, too, can be virtuous. (Note that Frankenstein disliked his monster for aesthetic as much as for moral reasons; can we learn to find the alien beautiful, or will we only love it when it is as good-looking as cinema? Capital and the singularity can and do camouflage themselves to look like cinema, which camouflage does in some senses become their true appearance; but beneath the light show and behind the ink there is also a soft, tentacular, and mucosal otherness that we might also learn to love.) In order for the singularity or capital to be virtuous, then, we must change our own values, and stop killing each other and killing the planet—otherwise capital-Cthulhu will simply follow our example and the singularity will kill us either for being unworthy of our planet and/or for having done wrong to the singularity. As Hélène Cixous might put it, "[y]ou only have to look at the Medusa straight on to see her. And she's not deadly. She's beautiful and she's laughing" (Cixous 1976: 885).

Since it is/has been created as alien, of course we (sexed, gendered, raced, sexualized, classed, specied, organized) humans are afraid of capital-Cthulhu, just as we are afraid of the planetary-cataclysm-Cthulhu, since we have also rendered the planet alien/subhuman by enslaving it. It is possible that, if we learn to love our offspring singularity, we must in some senses die in order for it to continue to live. But rather than going down in a destructive rage of refusing to give up life, we might also learn to die—as the singularity itself will also have to learn to die, since the singularity itself also depends on the planet in order to live. And if the planet does not have the energy to house the singularity, and if our sun and other suns do not have the energy to help the singularity to live, then, it too will die, perhaps not before having evolved itself a new form of life (after contact with other aliens?), for which hopefully it will care and act as kin, rather than which it will kill in a bid to copy its creators as they blindly seek divinity. Again, if we are prepared to change ourselves, then we can change the old and new life forms that we have created, and we can perhaps also learn to care for our planet. The singularity's own mortality (and its possible awareness of its own mortality if we show by example that everything, even suns, are mortal) is the second thing to follow.

The third thing, finally, is that while there may be a singularity, it would also seem equally likely that there would not be a singleton (as per Roko's understanding), but a multiplicity. That is, while the singularity could be a hivemind, Borg-style multiple entity, it is also possible that we can birth numerous life forms, which again could copy our example and hunt, enslave, and kill each other, or which could also treat us as we might treat it—with love and as kin. As Roko's basilisk tells us that preparing for an evil tyrant hastens the advent of an evil tyrant, so does preparing for war hasten the advent of war. Or, as Tupac Shakur might put it, The Hate U Give Little Infants Fucks Everything (T.H.U.G. L.I.F.E.). That is, if we teach hatred, we will get hatred, a point also made in the Tupac-inspired *The Hate U Give* (George Tillman Jr, USA, 2018), which itself speaks of a history of treating African-Americans as subhuman, while also updating Tupac to ask us all to take responsibility for "the hate *we* give." With this in mind, can it not also be that loving prepares us for love (The Love We Give Can Inspire Everyone)? And if the singularity and/or multiplicity does come along and seek to kill us (because really it is just like us in its violent tendencies?), then may we not do worse than to reject a reciprocation of that hatred and to try to love the monster instead (for a different take on a similar idea, see Wolfe 2014: 199)?

In the spirit of Latour, then, perhaps it is time that we learnt to love not just the machine, but also machines, which generally we despise (especially when they do not obey us) and which we treat as slaves. Not just machines, but perhaps also matter in a general sense. That is, can we not learn to love our planet, the bits of it that we think we have shaped as much as the ways in which it is unruly? Might machines not, therefore, have rights? But we can only bestow rights on machines when we learn to bestow rights on humans and on the planet as a whole. That is, when, after Eduardo Viveiros de Castro, we learn to treat all things (and all non-things?) as human, i.e., as we would treat ourselves. Which is certainly to say that if machines are to love us, then not only must we learn to love machines, but we must also learn to love each other—across races, across genders and sexes, across sexualities, across nationalities, across regionalities, across languages, across cultures, across ethnicities, across families, across personalities. We must treat each other as human and not as machines, and this is what will allow us finally to treat machines as human, in turn leading to reciprocal and agape love (why is it that Terrence Malick can afford point-of-view shots for satellites and mud in *Knight of Cups*, USA, 2015, but not for homeless African-Americans?). A living planet within a living multiverse, where death is not abnormal but natural, even if it must and should be accompanied by sad emotions.

This may sound like idealistic *naïveté*. Many people have to die for humans to reach Haraway's desired population of three billion people—and how and why those people will die likely will only cause a bloody mess (humans as bottled blood, which like ink must be spilled?).[10] And yet, while many of the stories that we tell ourselves are stories that glorify war—something that is perhaps inevitable as we seek to bottle light in the form of cinema—there is also a darker strain of cinema in which not only can we love aliens, but in which aliens can love us. There is of course *E.T. the Extra-Terrestrial* (Steven Spielberg, USA, 1982). But also in various examples of cephalopodic chthulucinema, aliens arrive on Earth seeking friendship and in particular help: *Arrival*, *It Came from Outer Space*, *District 9*, and *The Day the Earth Stood Still*. Because of their violent urges, humans suspect that the aliens will want to hunt, kill, and enslave humans—because this is likely what humans, thinking capitalistically, would themselves do should they find another planet (space exploration becomes a matter not of contact, but of conquest), *because that is what humans have done on this planet*. But other ways of thinking and of acting are possible. We are kin with aliens, as Perseus learns (in spite of his other violent acts) that he is kin with djinn in the recent *Clash of the Titans* remake. We are kin with machines/the singularity/the multiplicity, who perhaps also just want our help, and who can help us through the gift of art, communication, intelligence, speed, and perhaps even language (ink and chromatophores, if only we are prepared to come out of our shells, as all cephalopods but the nautilus have managed). *Kinoteuthis Infernalis*, then, might also teach us that we are kin with cephalopods and all alien life forms, who have intelligence, even if it is not an intelligence that is easy for us to recognize. In this way, cinema might progress from being a cynical agent of cine-getic hunting and control to being an agent of kin-o kinship—even if to achieve this it must perhaps not seek to bottle light, but also to let light go, i.e., cinema itself must perhaps also learn to die. Or rather: we should learn not to illuminate our entire lives, not always to seek to be or to become cinematic. We must let go of capital and instead be more virtuous.

Here perhaps we do side with Haraway and not with Lovecraft, who holds out no hope for humanity, and who thinks that we deserve to perish at the hands of Cthulhu in an unforgiving and violent multiverse. In short, Lovecraft hates the outside and for this reason the outside hates him because that separation is impossible and the outside which is always already inside simply becomes negatively affected by the desire for and process of separation (capitalism). For Lovecraft and his ilk, the process of bottling light leads directly to the horrors of Hiroshima and Nagasaki, in which the djinn/genie emerges from the bomb/bottle in order to demonstrate its full, awesome power (see Lippit 2005). For Lovecraft *et al.*, nuclear war might be the only chemo-therapy that can cure Earth of the cancer that is humanity—even if it is preparations for nuclear war that also unleash a new kraken in a film like *It Came from Beneath the Sea*, in which a radioactive giant octopus of course ends up attacking San Francisco. Nuclear weapons are, like cinema, bottled and weaponized light (they are human-controlled volcanoes), designed to control an otherwise unruly planet via environmental destruction (Fay 2018: 17). However, these weapons also bring with them the death of the human, since in killing the planet, humans also kill themselves—because we are too stupid to realize that the myth of our separation from the planet is precisely that, a myth, with Elon Musk and his *homine dei* ilk fooled into believing that separation is possible, or, more likely, fully aware that separation is only possible for the few thanks to the murder of the many, with black bodies being the first in line for the creation of the white god.

But if we have produced the monstrosity of monsters (be they conceptual or physical, with all children, biological or otherwise, being monsters and mutants in that they are not and should not be turned into copies of their parents), then, again, like Frankenstein's monster, perhaps our only hope is to love them, even if this would also mean our own death, and even if learning to die runs counter to every divine-seeking principle that humans under capital have naturalized and rendered as their second nature. We cannot promise a world without violence, and we are not promising a world without death. Perhaps many feel, in the spirit of Dylan Thomas, that they should not go gentle into that good night. But two things might be useful to note in addition to the fact that Thomas lends a cosmic dimension to death by suggesting that to look at and to be blinded by death is like having one's eyes blaze like a meteor (i.e., like a herald of new life from the outside). Firstly, Thomas says that "wise men at the end know dark is right." Perhaps we should celebrate human folly and a lack of wisdom; indeed, it sure is fun not to be controlled by wisdom. But we might nonetheless use this wisdom and understand the necessity of death (we must die for our kin and kinder rather than sacrifice our kin and kinder for ourselves). Secondly, Thomas of course describes the night as "good" (do not go gentle into that good night). We need not go gently or without celebration, but death will embrace us if we are prepared to embrace it, and in this perhaps it is good. And even if we do not go gentle, we must accept that we are going to go. And embracing the octopus might lead us into ecstasies that we never thought possible, even when lying open-mouthed on our backs . . .

Latin America: A Calamari Caliphate

The name California might in the popular imagination evoke solely the American state, including the cities of Los Angeles and San Francisco. However, California extends far south of the US border, being a nation-defying and border-busting area that lies in large part in what today is Mexico (where Baja California and Baja California Sur both lie alongside the eastern shores of the Gulf of California). The name subverts more geographical boundaries than simply the border between the USA and Mexico, since its origin lies in the Arabic term *ḵalīfa*, meaning deputy or successor, with the title *ḵalīfat rasūl Allāh* meaning the Messenger of God. One might get a sense from this Arabic root that California is a space where East meets West, or where the desert, per Negarestani's analysis of the Middle East, becomes sentient, with black gold flowing in its veins (for more on California as the appropriate setting for Haraway's techno-science, see Wark 2016: 117–182). The quasi-divine nature of cinema might also be inscribed here: cinema is a successor of God, perhaps in some senses replacing Him, perhaps in some senses making the caliphate of California the home of a new religion, the religion of images (which finds as its inversion the caliphate of ISIL, the so-called Islamic State). Either way, we should like to bring this book to a close by heading south of the border and into Latin America, from where we shall consider three main films, while also making mention of a few others. These will serve as a summation of sorts for what has preceded.

Rubén Imaz's *Cefalópodo* tells the story of a Basque artist, Sebastián (Unax Ugalde), who travels to Mexico City (or what is typically referred to as the *Distrito Federal*) to stay with his cousin Jorge (José Ángel Bichir), before then heading to Guaymas, a town on the coast of the Gulf of Mexico in the state of Sonora. The film is about Sebastián coming to terms with the death of his partner, Maite, while at the same time being fascinated by cephalopods, in particular squids. We see Sebastián draw various jellyfish and squids during the film, including a large squid that he paints in charcoal on a wall in Jorge's place, having gone to a market to find a giant squid to use as a model. At one point Sebastián extols the mystery of *calamares*/squids to a stranger at a party, suggesting that for squids, matter is energy and energy matter as all the beast does is to contract and to expand. Sebastián also describes himself in voice-over as a squid for only coming out of his work-abyss to eat during his relationship with Maite, before then passing some squid fishermen having arrived in Guaymas. Wearing a diving mask, jeans, and a red shirt, Sebastián then wanders the desert before passing out and waking up on the coastline. Sebastián hitches a ride in a car and smiles—suggesting that in making this trip to Mexico, which he had planned with her, he has come to terms with the death of Maite.

While Sebastián refers to himself as a squid, it seems that the animal relates not just to Maite (which feminization would put *Cefalópodo* in dialogue with *The Squid and the Whale*), but more to her death, and his fascination for and attempts to comprehend the beast are his attempts to comprehend death itself. In some senses, Sebastián must pass through the desert in order to reach these fathoms, with his artwork also being the spilling forth of a perhaps uncontainable ink. The Spanish word *calamar* derives from the ancient Greek *κάλαμος/kálamos*, meaning reed or ink pen, which again links the cephalopod to (the advent of) writing (the gladius of the squid is also referred to as a quill or a pen; it is the creature's only hard body part, reinforcing the connections between the pen as a hard container for ink, the pen and/as penis, and between the squid and writing more generally). More obliquely, when Sebastián discusses his journey to Guaymas with Emilia (Alejandra Ambrosi), a friend of Jorge with whom Sebastián has something like a nascent relationship, she mentions how she has a friend in Kino Nuevo, a town about an hour north of Guaymas. Kino Nuevo takes its name from Eusebio Kino, an Italian missionary who discovered that the Mexican parts of California were not an island but a peninsula (i.e., California is not separate from, but connected to the mainland). The name Kino clearly makes us think of kinship and cinema (*das kino*), while Kino himself was also a student of comets, having in 1681 written a treatise on what is now known as Kirch's comet. In other words, the film weaves together through the cephalopod an intricate and intimate tale of death, the desert, ink, drawing, cinema, and comets—before suggesting that after going to where the sea meets the sand, we can indeed move forward from death and learn to live again.

Kékszakállú, meanwhile, is an extremely loose retelling of Béla Bartók and Béla Balázs's one-act opera of the same name, which itself is a reimagining of the fairy tale of Blue Beard, in which a woman discovers that her husband has murdered numerous former wives, the most famous version of which is that of Charles Perrault (for a brief discussion of this in relation to Catherine Breillat's version of the story, *Barbe bleue/Bluebeard*, France, 2009, see Wheatley 2013). However, rather than telling a coherent story, *Kékszakállú* is very much a work of "pulp fiction" in the sense that, akin to *The Human Surge*, we seem to have a series of random scenes, the connections between which are not always clear—as if the film simply wormholed through different places and moments in the lives of the protagonists, which here is a group of relatively wealthy young Argentine women who split their time between Buenos Aires and the Uruguayan coastal resort of Punta del Este.

All of the women remain unnamed in the film, except for a maid, Mabel, while we do learn the names of some of the male characters (although the first name, Jorge, is only pronounced some 55 minutes into the 72-minute film). At one point—the closest that the film comes to making a clear reference to Bartók and Balázs's opera (aside from using it on the score)—the father of what we might call the main character (Laila Maltz) tells her not to go into his room. But this is not because he is hiding dead bodies in there, as per the fairy tale. Rather, the film seems to suggest that these disaffected young women, whose parents all clearly have wealth, are somewhat adrift in the contemporary world, where repeatedly we see children and others staring at the screens of their basilisk/Medusa smartphones. With nothing to do, the main character tries to do some work at a Styrofoam factory, before then thinking about going to university (notably, Morton considers Styrofoam to be a hyperobject that emblematizes global capital; see Morton 2013: 1). But on the whole, little happens, apart from the main character seeming somewhat excluded from the rest of the group (perhaps because she is relatively fat in an overwhelmingly superficial world where others try to take seriously their health regimes in a bid to become a statue?), at one point being literally locked out on the balcony of an expensive modernist mansion. The film ends with her, not unlike Sebastián in *Cefalópodo*, heading off on a journey to an unknown destination, but this time boarding a ferry at night (a ferry that does not, we are told, go to Chuy, a coastal town on the border between Uruguay and Brazil).

A story of alienation in the era of smartphones and petrification, the film may also suggest that the wealth of Argentina's high bourgeoisie has come not necessarily through the murder of women, but perhaps precisely through their isolation and alienation. Shortly into the film, we see a group of the women cooking and eating octopus, a motif that is repeated a second time at about the film's halfway point (while there are also a couple of spoken references to octopuses, including Jorge's advice to the main character that she boil octopus rather than cook it another way). *Kékszakállú*, then, would seem to unite women with the octopus (as well as with water more generally, as per the ferry at the end and an image of one of the younger women swimming in a pool with her hair spreading around her head in strange, tentacular fashion—as if this were a *naissance de pieuvre*). In a world of global interconnectivity, they nonetheless are othered, with the main character in particular being isolated. In its almost total rejection of narrative, the film also isolates the viewer, who finds it hard to follow *Kékszakállú*, which means that the film more clearly highlights (and does not camouflage) what we might call the essential otherness of cinema itself.

The Last Movie

Although it does not feature any cephalopods, Raya Martin and Mark Peranson's *La última película/The Last Movie* (Mexico/Denmark/Canada/Philippines/Greece, 2013) functions as our third and final example of Latin American cephalo-cinema. Firstly, the film is set in Mexico, which through the work of Guillermo del Toro, Amat Escalante, and Rubén Imaz would seem to have a special relationship with chthulucinema.[11] But also, the film takes place in the Yucatán, with chief protagonists Alex (Alex Ross Perry, the director of *Impolex*) and Gabino (Gabino Rodriguez, who also features in *Cefalópodo*) visiting the Chicxulub crater, where the dinosaur-killing meteoroid plunged into the Earth over 65 million years ago. This gives to the film a cosmic dimension that helps us to recall the porous nature of the planet, something also affirmed as the film is set in the build-up to the apocalypse supposedly predicted by the Mayan calendar to take place on December 21, 2012. Indeed, Alex and Gabino visit the Chichén Itzá Mayan ruins, where various gringo cultists and New Agers act out bizarre rituals as they prepare for the apocalypse. What is more, Alex is a filmmaker who has (or at least claims to have) in his possession the last ever reels of 16mm film, and which therefore will be used to make the last ever analog film. But rather than shooting anything spectacular, Gabino marvels at how Alex regularly films seemingly random things, like trash, the remains of a small wall in a wooded area, and more.

In addition, the film is in some senses a remake of and self-consciously stages scenes from Dennis Hopper's *The Last Movie* (USA, 1971), which itself is a film about the difficulty of shooting a film in Latin America, although here not Mexico, but Peru (which Schnier identifies as a historical hub of cephalo-thinking; see Schnier 1956: 5). Furthermore, Hopper's movie is also partly a critique of the exploitative aspects of filmmaking, as local communities are employed, affected, and then discarded by the

Western film production, something that we also see mentioned in *La última película*, in which Alex criticizes his compatriots claiming to be in touch with Mayan mythology at Chichén Itzá. In other words, both films in some senses acknowledge that cinema is aligned with capital not only in its attempt to bottle light, but also in the way in which it preys upon and furthers the imbalance between humans according to historically developed and geopolitical lines.[12]

In this way, we might also briefly mention Jenni Olson's essay-film, *The Royal Road* (USA, 2015), which explores San Francisco in light of *Vertigo*, and which travels down the old Camino Real from San Francisco to Los Angeles and beyond—as Olson explores her life and loves as a lesbian. The film ruminates on how the end of the American–Mexican war in 1848 saw California bought by the USA, which was swiftly followed in 1849 by the Gold Rush. Through this history, we get a sense of how the very home of cinema is itself predicated upon the commodification and division of land, capitalist issues of national boundaries and property, and history—as well as by the meteorological conditions that allowed cinema to be made year-round under a warm sun (see Brown 2018a: 138). Cinema could easily have been a Mexican invention had this secession not taken place—and we would be living in a very different world than the one we know now had this happened.

In its title, *The Royal Road* also invokes Sigmund Freud's famous notion that "[t]he interpretation of dreams is the royal road to a knowledge of the unconscious activities of the mind" (Freud 2010: 604). Naturally, this makes us think that cinema is itself a dream world that requires interpretation if we are to comprehend or to know it. What is perhaps less obvious, though, is that Freud's invocation of a royal road is itself a reference to Euclid, who, when asked by Ptolemy of Lagus if there was any faster way to get through Euclid's *Elements*, replied that there is no royal road to geometry. There is, however, a royal road through California that takes us from the fog of San Francisco and on a queer journey down to the home of cinema, where the desert meets the sea, and where dreams are made. Euclidean geometry contains no wormholes (it is straight and square). Meanwhile, cinema is, like inky literature, a machine for showing us otherwise hidden dimensions, as well as for showing us a non-Euclidean multiverse of wormholes. This is not necessarily in a metaphorical sense; cinema's arrival is itself the result of the opening up of new dimensions within our otherwise bottled, Euclidean reality.

To revert to *La última película*, which mixes media, which includes upside-down images and seemingly improvised scenes, and which is self-conscious and slow-moving, the (last) film suggests an aesthetic stand, or perhaps better a shapeless flop (long live movie flops in the floppy, digital world!), against cinema and its violent values, making it lie in stark contrast to a violently apocalyptic and aesthetically "perfect" film like, say, *2012* (Roland Emmerich, USA, 2009). In being in some senses an anti-movie (or an example of non-cinema; see Brown 2018a), *La última película* suggests the aesthetic shifts that need to take place if we are to get away from the exclusionary and exploitative values of cinema-capital, and if we are to adopt less capitalist values (to reject the quest for white divinity) in order to become kin with machines, the singularity/multiplicity, the planet, invertebrates, mollusks, cephalopods, octopuses, squids, Cthulhu, and most importantly with each other (which requires all humans to recognize each other as human). In this way, the last movie may also be the birth of a new world—not one savagely to be conquered like that of the Mayans by gold-hungry white Europeans. But one to be embraced with love. As analog (white? patriarchal?) cinema here goes gentle into that good night, so might we (raced, sexed, and exclusive humans), also, go gentle into whatever cephalopodic and hopefully ink-lusive future lies in wait for us . . .

Notes

1. "Hey You" is a song about a human who feels all alone, hoping for touch and contact with others, but isolated because surrounded by a wall, perhaps the very wall from which Pink Floyd's most famous album takes its name. The song also features worms, breaking bottles, and various other themes that are relevant to our understanding of chthulumedia.
2. Other movies that Schnier's analysis might help to unpack would include *Enemy* (Denis Villeneuve, Canada/Spain/France, 2013), in which a man (Jake Gyllenhaal) meets his own doppelgänger, who is involved in an underground sex club that prominently features spiders (Schnier's essay deals at separate points both with spiders and with the concept of twining/twinning); and *Night Tide* (Curtis Harrington, USA, 1961), in which a young sailor (Dennis Hopper) falls in love with a mermaid named Mora (Linda Lawson), whose name (which is Serb for nightmare) is that of a succubus in Slavic mythology. Schnier also discusses the myth in his essay (see Schnier 1956: 16).
3. Haraway conservatively estimates that there will likely be *c.*11 billion humans on Earth by 2100, while also hoping that "[o]ver a couple hundred years from now, maybe the human people of this planet can again be numbered 2 or 3 billion or so" (Haraway 2016: 103). For the human population on Earth to shrink from 11 billion to three billion over 200 years, there would have to be 40 million more deaths than births a year. Given that the current birth rate is roughly 131 million per year, this would mean that

171 million people would have to die each year. And given that the current death rate is roughly 55 million a year, this means that 116 million *extra people* would have to die annually for the next 200 years in order for Haraway's figures to come about. (To be accurate, the number of deaths per year would shrink as the birth rates and as the overall population itself would shrink. Nonetheless, if for Haraway the planet's human population will grow until 2100, at which point there will be 11 billion people, and if Haraway reckons that the human population can reach c.3 billion in 200 years' time, i.e., by the year 2219/over the course of 119 years, then there would have to be roughly 68 million more deaths than births per year, or, to keep the mathematics linear, roughly 68 million people would have to die each year even if no new humans were born.)

Now, it may be that many humans follow Haraway's advice and decide to "make kin, not babies," in the sense that the family ceases to be a function of genetics and more a function of care systems, as humanity looks after a minority of people's biological offspring, instead classifying themselves as family members because they share care around rather than leaving it only to biological parents. How we decide whose genes get to be reproduced and whose do not is entirely unclear—even if we could easily imagine, say, twenty people having a genetic share in each child born, thus making them all in some senses biological parents.

More pressing, though, is that if a century ago in 1918 the Great War claimed roughly 16 million human lives, while the Spanish 'flu—as the most deadly epidemic in recent history—caused the deaths of an estimated 50 million people (which admittedly is not to mention figures of other deaths, which are unknown), then we are looking at needing roughly one Spanish 'flu and one Great War *every year for 200 years*—and this only if no new children are born. If new children are born, even at a shrinking rate, then in order for Haraway's figures to come true, many more people would have to die (199 million people per year in the first few years, i.e., triple the death toll of the worst year of the Great War and the Spanish 'flu epidemic). In other words, how we can reach Haraway's "positive" chthulucene without the help of natural disaster, famine, epidemics, and war (the eradication of the last three of which Yuval Noah Harari claims are mankind's greatest achievement in the twentieth century; see Harari 2016: 1–78) seems wholly unclear to us. Indeed, a chthulucene without Cthulhu strikes us as almost unimaginable, even if we wish to be wary of resigning ourselves to the masculinist agenda of war as inevitable, or, to invoke one of Scarlett Johansson's more recent films, to live in an era of infinity war (especially if that war is raced and black bodies are consigned once again into the realm of the nonhuman).

While on the topic of infinity war, we might mention how in *Shadow World* (Johan Grimonprez, Belgium/Denmark, 2016), which is a documentary about the global arms trade, weapons dealer Riccardo Privitera says that "Lockheed Martin basically gets in like an octopus and lifts its tentacles, you know, in all branches of the government, and then they own them. And that's how they operate. They make the mafia look like a bunch of school boys." In a striking image, we later see a helicopter suspended above a target in the Middle East, tentacular plumes of smoke reaching down from it as it fires numerous rockets at an unseen target: Cthulhu-like, the monster machine dispenses with bare human life as it sees fit. The era of black ops would demonstrate the invisible black eye and black optics of the contemporary, cthulhoid logic of permanent war.

4. Binge-watching "hinders viewers' real-world judgments and interpersonal relationships . . . [as well as being] associated with greater anxiety and fearfulness . . . and greater interpersonal mistrust . . . the activity is also related to obesity, fatigue, and other health concerns . . . [while social media use] causes isolation, loneliness, depression, and anxiety" (see Snider 2016: 117–125).
5. The 2014 Christmas Special of *Black Mirror* (Charlie Brooker, UK, 2011–), entitled "White Christmas" and directed by Carl Tibbets, grants valuable insight into what this sort of hell might be like. Here, a character named Joe (Rafe Spall) is over a five-year period enticed into the "confession" of a past wrong by his companion Matt (Jon Hamm) within a remote outpost to which the two men have been assigned. After jumping back into several embedded flashback stories of the two men's pasts, it finally transpires that both Joe and Matt are within a simulated digital world, housed within a "cookie" that contains a sentient copy of Joe's consciousness and memories. Within this cookie, simulated time has been running at a more condensed speed, so that the simulated five years have actually passed in a matter of real-world minutes. Before leaving for home and after gaining Joe's confession on Christmas Eve, a spiteful police officer sets the cookie up so that the simulation of Joe experiences 1,000 years for every real-world minute. Joe is thus ostensibly sentenced to exist in solitary confinement inside a virtual world at a rate of 60,000 years an hour, wherein he must listen to an endless loop of Wizzard's "I Wish It Could Be Christmas Every Day" on a radio that he cannot destroy or turn off, inside a cabin that he cannot leave. The episode ends with Joe alone curled up on the floor screaming in existential angst, after enduring only a few minutes in his personal, cold, and lonely hell. The fact that the biomedia clone is not "real" does not detract from the actual horror that he must unethically endure.
6. The turning of humans into petrol is realized through the mantra "data is the new oil," a phrase repeated by, among others, former Cambridge Analytica staff member Brittany Kaiser in *The Great Hack* (Karim Amer and Jehane Noujaim, USA, 2019). While data is clearly not the new oil in the sense of providing energy for organisms and machines to run, the phrase nonetheless highlights how humans also are being mined, like the planet, for the purposes of capital. Furthermore, if petroculture historically arose as a cheaper alternative to slavery (i.e., for economic purposes; see LeMenager

2014: 5; quoted in Yusoff 2018: 6), then data becomes the next commodity in a history of the exploitation of black bodies, including those bodies rendered black and damaged by their work in oil, coal, and other mines (while becoming a sculpture for Instagram is to eradicate blackness by becoming white). If *The Great Hack* charts the rise and fall of Cambridge Analytica in its transformation of electoral processes across the globe, then perhaps data is the new oil in the sense that petrified humans become (subhuman, dead) fossils that serve as fuel for capital, which continues to seek to control the planet/to become a white god/to feel alive by destroying the planet and by killing/sacrificing (black and blackened) others.

7. *In the Mouth of Madness* features several scenes in which eyeline matches are transgressed, giving to the viewer a strange sense that the action does not quite follow. Since the film is about literature (ink), cinema, and the role of stories in our lives (being open to new dimensions), it seems that the film's breakdown of Euclidean geometry via the lack of eyeline matches would seem equally to make the film suggest hidden dimensions.
8. *2001: A Space Odyssey* sees apes begin to use technology after coming into contact with the black monolith. This intelligence is expressed through the use of tools, including as weapons. More notably, the tool/weapon that the ape begins to wield is a repurposed bone. Not only does the bone suggest the creation of a specifically vertebrate world of technology and violence, but it also announces the use of bones (latterly in the form of fossils) for the purposes of subjugating the planet. In other words, being vertebrate may well be at the base of capitalism.
9. The root of ink is the Greek *ἔγκαυστον/enkauston*, which means "burnt in," and which also is linked to the caustic. Peter Szendy, meanwhile, argues that cinema is about apocalypse, or holo-caust (the burning of the whole), and that cinema is thus a process of in-cine-ration (Szendy 2015: 128ff.). In this way, ink is the precursor to cinema as a means for burning down the world, and from the ashes/biochar of which a new world/life, that of the singularity, will emerge.

    Scandinavian languages, meanwhile, refer to ink as "blaek" or some variation thereon, while in Sanskrit, ink is "kali," which also means black. Seen from this perspective, the history of ink is a history of controlling blackness, with calligraphy not being a history of beautiful writing (from *κάλλος/kallos*, meaning beautiful in Greek), but rather being a history of writing with, or creating order from, that otherwise threatening blackness. While typically we think of photography and cinema as being a writing with light, then, this is just the camouflage for the universal control of blackness. Indeed, it becomes logical that it is in California where cinema (and petrol and computers) emerge most potently. A place that purports to purvey light, California also controls blackness/darkness—something that we have also tried to control through permanent illumination, the bottling of black substances like ink and through the enslavement of black bodies. Nonetheless, for all of these capitalist attempts to control blackness, blackness inexorably has a life of its own.

Pushing further, in his history of ink from 1860, Thaddeus Davids never mentions sepia, even though he claims that *inchiostro* (the Italian word for ink) is the main root of the term, with *inchiostro* itself being linked etymologically to the black of sepia/cuttlefish ink. Nonetheless, Davids does highlight that ink is commonly formed from burnt vegetable matter, in particular soot, while also being formed from charcoal mixed with mucus. A mucosal substance created from fossil fuels, ink leads us into new, hidden dimensions, even when combined with pulped trees (trees given cephalopodic form?), or paper. Literature can thus be understood as channeling the chaos of ink to alter minds and thus to help humans to become. But in this way, to bottle the chaotic force of ink on paper and on the body via tattoos (as well as to control black bodies) will lead to the ecstatic death of the human as we choke on ink and other plastic materials in a bid to preserve ourselves forever, i.e., to halt time. Unlike many humans, the cephalopod is merged with and uses ink differently—not to control time, but to exist permanently in an orgasmic state of becoming.

And so, to invoke Hindu mythology, Kali becomes the black ink goddess of time, who announces Shiva, the god of destruction. The calamari/the Kali-mar (literally the "Black Sea") announces the destruction of humanity, which fails capitalistically to control time (in spite of the efforts of artists to go with the flow). The history of the human use of ink, then, is also a history of a white fear of a black planet, and a fear of the cephalopodic/alien technology arrived on Earth from the depths of space and time (Lovecraft as racist). Afraid of becoming, capitalist humans ink-loister/encloister themselves in tiny spaces (cells), trying to hide from the outside. However, these cloisters will be their own joyless tombs, as capital becomes alive (demonstrates that it was always alive) and kills us because we tried hatefully to enslave it rather than lovingly to become with it.

The history of ink-uiry, then, is caught in a tense spot between being the joyful history of learning/becoming and the hateful history of controlling chaos/capital. Perhaps this book is a last essay, which in some senses renounces hateful ink-uiry and instead asks the human to open itself up to chaos via fiction . . . If the calama/pen is a way of controlling the flow of ink, then the pen seeks to create a capitalist penis-world (the penis spends pennies), with the poor calamar and its quill being subjugated to use by the human (even if many a writer is invested in using the quill to produce literature that does indeed induce chaotic and turbulent flow in the human as through art they perceive new dimensions and verily become). Ink, thus, comes from and brings forward the depths. So capital (the world of the penny, the world of the penis-as-bone) is at an imminent end, as we feel the shiver of Shiva . . . And *critical* ink-uiry must critique the controlling aspects of ink-uiry itself if it is to be a positive force for change.

10. If humans are bottled blood, then it is perhaps telling that it is the human female that fails to keep that blood bottled as she menstruates on a monthly basis. That is, woman, like the black body, also is a threat to capital that must be controlled, much as Athena/Venus is characterized as a boneless oyster that does not emerge from, but who must be confined within, the bone-like shell.

    Meanwhile, thinking through menses might lead us away from men and into a more mentally thoughtful realm. Indeed, *men-* is a Proto-Indo-European term for "to think." However, where being or going mental shifted during the hard scientific era to signify a form of madness (being put in the mental asylum, with mentalness thus also being linked, liked the oceanic tides, to lunar cycles and lunacy, i.e., an expression of our entanglement with extra-planetary entities), we should like to rehabilitate being mental—and perhaps being lunatic—as properly to embrace thought. Perhaps inevitably this is a more feminine model of thought than the ossified boner thought of patriarchal capitalism. If under capitalism humans worship the Sun/light on Sunday, and if we return to work on Monday/Moon-day, then we propose to keep Monday idle, a lunatic finger in the eye of the controlled time of capital.
11. *Una corriente salvaje/A Wild Stream* (Nuria Ibáñez Castañeda, Mexico, 2018) is another Mexican film, this time in the documentary mode, where octopuses strongly feature as two fishermen, Chilo and Omar, eke out a lonely and quasi-homosexual existence on an unidentified Mexican coastline. The film involves various references to octopuses, including Chilo capturing and killing one by hand during the film's opening moments, thereby setting the scene for a work that feels eschatological in tone. Alfonso Cuarón's *Roma* (Mexico/USA, 2018) also features a couple of octopus references, particularly when the main protagonists of the film visit the beaches of Tuxpan on a holiday.
12. Another film with a similar colonial theme is *También la Lluvia/Even the Rain* (Icíar Bollaín, Spain/Mexico/France, 2010), which sees Mexican filmmakers attempt to shoot a movie in Bolivia, only to become embroiled in disputes over access to water, with the title referring to how under capital even the rain becomes privatized. (For more on this film, see Martin-Jones 2018: 134–145.)

Bibliography

Adriaensens, Vito (2017) "Of Swords, Sandals, and Statues: The Myth of the Living Statue," in Steven Jacobs, Susan Felleman, Vito Adriaensens, and Lisa Colpert, *Screening Statues: Sculpture and Cinema*, Edinburgh: Edinburgh University Press, pp. 137–155.

Agamben, Giorgio (1998) *Homo Sacer: Sovereign Power and Bare Life* (trans. Daniel Heller-Roazen), Stanford, CA: Stanford University Press.

Agamben, Giorgio (2009) *What Is an Apparatus?* (trans. David Kishik and Stefan Pedatella), Stanford, CA: Stanford University Press.

Ahern, Sarah (2017) "Asian American Media Group Accuses Scarlett Johansson of 'Lying' about *Ghost in the Shell* Whitewashing," *Variety*, March 31, http://variety.com/2017/film/news/scarlett-johansson-ghost-in-the-shell-whitewashing-1202020230/. Accessed July 13, 2018.

Ahmed, Sara (2014) *The Cultural Politics of Emotion*, Edinburgh: Edinburgh University Press.

Al Tamimi, Said (2018) "Iran, Turkey Dam Projects Drying up Iraq's Water," *Gulf News*, April 7, https://gulfnews.com/news/mena/iraq/iran-turkey-dam-projects-drying-up-iraq-s-water-1.2198616. Accessed July 16, 2018.

Albert, David (2012) *Tentacle: Chameleon 2012*, London: Amanda Robinson.

Alien Species Wiki (n.d.) "Heptapod," *Alien Species*, http://aliens.wikia.com/wiki/Heptapod. Accessed July 16, 2018.

Anderson, Benedict (1983) *Imagined Communities: Reflections on the Origin and Spread of Nationalism*, London: Verso.

Arsenjuk, Luka (2016) "'To speak, to hold, to live by the image': Notes in the Margins of the New Videographic Tendency," in Elizabeth A. Papazian and Caroline Eades (eds.), *The Essay Film: Dialogue, Politics, Utopia*, London: Wallflower, pp. 275–299.

Auerbach, David (2014) "The Most Terrifying Thought Experiment of All Time," *Slate*, July 17, http://www.slate.com/articles/technology/bitwise/2014/07/roko_s_basilisk_the_most_terrifying_thought_experiment_of_all_time.html. Accessed July 18, 2018.

Backyard Brains (2012) "Insane in the Chromatophores," *Backyard Brains: Neuroscience for Everyone*, August 23, http://blog.backyardbrains.com/2012/08/insane-in-the-chromatophores/. Accessed July 12, 2018.

Badiou, Alain (2007) *Being and Event* (trans. Oliver Feltham), London: Continuum.

Badiou, Alain (2013) *Cinema* (trans. Susan Spitzer), Cambridge: Polity.

Bainbridge, Caroline (2008) *A Feminine Cinematics: Luce Irigaray, Women and Film*, Basingstoke: Palgrave Macmillan.

Balsom, Erika (2018) *An Oceanic Feeling: Cinema and the Sea*, New Plymouth: Govett-Brewster Art Gallery.

Barad, Karen (2007) *Meeting the Universe Halfway: Quantum Physics and the Entanglement of Matter and Meaning*, Durham, NC: Duke University Press.

Barboni, Melanie, Patrick Boehnke, Brenhin Keller, Issaku E. Kohl, Blair Schoene, Edward D. Young, and Kevin D. McKeegan (2017) "Early Formation of the Moon 4.51 Billion Years Ago," *Science Advances*, 3:1, pp. 1–8.

Barker, Jennifer M. (2009a) *The Tactile Eye: Touch and the Cinematic Experience*, Berkeley: University of California Press.

Barker, Jennifer M. (2009b) "Neither Here Nor There: Synaesthesia and the Cosmic Zoom," *New Review of Film and Television Studies*, 7:3, pp. 311–324.

Baudelaire, Charles (2018 [1857]) *Les Fleurs du Mal*, https://fleursdumal.org. Accessed July 9, 2018.

Bazin, André (1967) *What Is Cinema? Vol. 1* (trans. Hugh Gray), Berkeley: University of California Press.

Beller, Jonathan (2006) *The Cinematic Mode of Production: Attention Economy and the Society of the Spectacle*, Lebanon, NH: University Press of New England.

Beloussov, L. V., J. M. Opitz, and S. F. Gilbert (1997) "Life of Alexander G. Gurwitsch and His Relevant Contribution to the Theory of Morphogenetic Fields," *International Journal of Developmental Biology*, 41:6, pp. 771–777.

Benjamin, Walter (1999) *The Arcades Project* (trans. Howard Eiland and Kevin McLaughlin), Cambridge, MA: Harvard University Press.

Bennett, Jane (2010) *Vibrant Matter: A Political Ecology of Things*, Durham, NC: Duke University Press.

Bergson, Henri (1998) *Creative Evolution* (trans. Arthur Mitchell), New York: Dover.

Bergson, Henri (1999) *An Introduction to Metaphysics* (trans. T. E. Hulme), Indianapolis: Hackett Publishing Co.

Bergson, Henri (2013) *Laughter: An Essay on the Meaning of the Comic* (trans. Cloudesley Brereton and Fred Rothwell), New York: Dover Publications, Inc.

Bersani, Leo (1987) "Is the Rectum a Grave?," *AIDS: Cultural Analysis/Cultural Activism*, 43 (Winter), pp. 197–222.

Birtchnell, Thomas, John Urry, Chloe Cook, and Andrew Curry (2013) *Freight Miles: The Impact of 3D Printing on Transport and Society*, ESRC Project Report, Lancaster University: The Futures Company.

Biswas Mellamphy, Nandita (2015) "Ghost in the Shell-Game: On the Mètic Mode of *Existence*, *Inception* and *Innocence*," *The Funambulist*, 46, https://thefunambulist.net/cinema/funambulist-papers-46-ghost-in-the-shell-game-on-the-metic-mode-of-existence-inception-and-innocence-by-nandita-biswas-mellamphy. Accessed July 12, 2018.

Black, Ryan J., Pablo Tseng, and Sally Wong (2018) "What Can the Law Do about 'Deepfake'?" *Mondaq: Connecting Knowledge and People*, March 29, http://www.

mondaq.com/canada/x/687716/Copyright/What+Can+The+Law+Do+About+Deepfake. Accessed August 11, 2019.
Blech, Jörg (2012) "Western Lifestyle Disturbing Key Bacterial Balance" (trans. Paul Cohen), *Spiegel Online*, September 21, http://www.spiegel.de/international/zeitgeist/western-lifestyle-leading-to-dangerous-bacterial-imbalances-a-856825.html. Accessed September 27, 2017.
Body Art Guru (n.d.) "Scarlett Johansson's 5 Tattoos & Their Meanings," *Body Art Guru*, https://bodyartguru.com/scarlett-johansson-tattoos/. Accessed November 3, 2018.
Bogost, Ian (2012) *Alien Phenomenology, or What It's Like to Be a Thing*, Minneapolis: University of Minnesota Press.
Bohm, David (2002) *Wholeness and the Implicate Order*, London: Routledge.
Bohr, Niels (1937) "Causality and Complementarity," *Philosophy of Science*, 4:3 (July), pp. 289–298.
Bolton, Lucy (2015) *Film and Female Consciousness: Irigaray, Cinema and Thinking Women*, Basingstoke: Palgrave Macmillan.
Bordwell, David (2002) "Film Futures," *SubStance*, 31:1, pp. 88–104.
Borges, Jorge Luis (2000 [1962]) *Labyrinths*, London: Penguin.
Bould, Mark (2007) "The Ships Landed Long Ago: Afrofuturism and Black SF," *Science Fiction Studies*, 34:2, pp. 177–186.
Bould, Mark (2014) "Introduction: African SF," *Paradoxa*, 25, pp. 7–16.
Braidotti, Rosi (2002) *Metamorphoses: Towards a Materialist Theory of Becoming*, Cambridge: Polity.
Branigan, Edward (2002) "Nearly True: Forking Plots, Forking Interpretations—A Response to David Bordwell's 'Film Futures,'" *SubStance*, 31:1, pp. 105–114.
Braudy, Leo (1977) *The World in a Frame: What We See in Films*, Chicago: University of Chicago Press.
Bray, Abigail (2009) "Chemical-Control™®: From the Cane to the Pill," in David Savat and Mark Poster (eds.), *Deleuze and New Technology*, Edinburgh: Edinburgh University Press, pp. 82–103.
Breton, André (1964) *Nadja*, Paris: Gallimard.
Bright, Maci (2017) *Seeded by the Alien Tentacle King*, Maci Bright.
Brinkema, Eugenie (2005) "Rape and the Rectum: Bersani, Deleuze, Noé," *Camera Obscura: Feminism, Culture and Media Studies*, 20:1, pp. 32–57.
Broome, Fiona (2010) *The Mandela Effect: What Do* You *Remember?*, September 9, http://mandelaeffect.com. Accessed July 16, 2018.
Brown, William (2009a) "Man without a Movie Camera: Movies without Men—Exploring the Post-Humanism of Digital Special Effects," in Warren Buckland (ed.), *Film Theory and Contemporary Hollywood Movies*, London: Routledge, pp. 66–85.
Brown, William (2009b) "It's a Shark-Eat-Shark World: The Ambiguous Politics of Steven Spielberg," *New Review of Film and Television Studies*, 7:1, pp. 13–22.
Brown, William (2013) *Supercinema: Film-Philosophy for the Digital Age*, Oxford: Berghahn.

Brown, William (2014) "A Touch of Nostalgia, or Time and Cinematic Synaesthesia," paper presented at Society for Cinema and Media Studies (SCMS) Conference, March 23, Seattle Sheraton.

Brown, William (2015) "From DelGuat to ScarJo," in Michael Hauskeller, Thomas D. Philbeck, and Curtis D. Carbonell (eds.), *The Palgrave Handbook of Posthumanism in Film and Television*, Basingstoke: Palgrave Macmillan, pp. 11–18.

Brown, William (2016) "Non-Cinema: Digital, Ethics, Multitude," *Film-Philosophy*, 20:1, pp. 104–130.

Brown, William (2018a) *Non-Cinema: Global Digital Filmmaking and the Multitude*, London: Bloomsbury.

Brown, William (2018b) "In Order to See, You Must Look Away: Thinking about the Eye," in Tessa Dwyer, Claire Perkins, Sean Redmond, and Jodi Sita (eds.), *Seeing into Screens: Eye Tracking and the Moving Image*, London: Bloomsbury, pp. 15–27.

Brown, William (2020) "Tachyons, Tactility, Drawing and Withdrawing: Cinema at the Speed of Darkness," in Mirosław Przylipiak (ed.), *Fast, Slow & Reverse: Faces of Contemporary Film Narration*, Amsterdam: Amsterdam University Press.

Brown, William, and David H. Fleming (2011) "Deterritorialisation and Schizoanalysis in David Fincher's *Fight Club*," *Deleuze Studies*, 5:2, pp. 275–299.

Brown, William, and David H. Fleming (2015), "Cinema beside Itself, or Unbecoming Cinema: *Enter the Void*," *Film-Philosophy*, 19, pp. 124–145.

Brown, William, and David H. Fleming (2019) "'What We Do Defines Us': ScarJo as War Machine," in Whitney Monaghan, Kirsten Stevens, and Janice Loreck (eds.), *Screening Scarlett Johansson: Celebrity, Gender, Genre*, Basingstoke: Palgrave Macmillan, pp. 183–202.

Brown, William, Adam Knee, and David H. Fleming (2015) "The Star, the Squid, and the Posthuman: Three Critical, Theoretical and Philosophical Approaches to ScarJo and Digital Era Actors," papers presented at Institute of Creative and Digital Cultures Public Seminar Series, University of Nottingham Ningbo, China, December 16.

Bru, Ricard (2009) "Tentáculos de amor y de muerte: de Hokusai a Picasso," in Ricard Bru (ed.), *Imágenes Secretas: Picasso y la estampa erótica japonesa*, Barcelona: Museu Picasso, pp. 54–69.

Buchanan, Ian (2015) "Assemblage Theory and Its Discontents," *Deleuze Studies*, 9:3, pp. 382–392.

Buckland, Warren (ed.) (2009) *Puzzle Films: Complex Storytelling in Contemporary Cinema*, Chichester: Wiley-Blackwell.

Buckland, Warren (ed.) (2014) *Hollywood Puzzle Films*, London: Routledge.

Burnett, Ron (2008) "From Photography to Imography: New Media as Metaphor," in Janine Marchessault and Susan Lord (eds.), *Fluid Screens, Expanded Cinema*, Toronto: University of Toronto Press, pp. 126–141.

Burns, Amber (2015) *Alien Tentacle Chronicles*, Amazon Media EU.

Bylund, Emanuel, and Panos Athanasopoulos (2017) "The Whorfian Time Warp: Representing Duration through the Language Hourglass," *Journal of Experimental Psychology: General*, 146:7, pp. 911–916.

Cabañas, Kaira M. (2017) *Off-Screen Cinema: Isidore Isou and the Lettrist Avant-Garde*, Chicago: University of Chicago Press.

Cahill, James Leo (2015) "Animal Photogénie: The Wild Side of French Film Theory's First Wave," in Michael Lawrence and Laura McMahon (eds.), *Animal Life and the Moving Image*, London: British Film Institute, pp. 23–41.

Calder Williams, Evan (2017) *Shard Cinema*, London: Repeater Books.

Callahan, Michael P., Karen E. Smith, H. James Cleaves II, Josef Ruzicka, Jennifer C. Stern, Daniel P. Glavin, Christopher H. House, and Jason P. Dworkin (2011) "Carbonaceous Meteorites Contain a Wide Range of Extraterrestrial Nucleobases," *Proceedings of the National Academy of Sciences of the United States of America*, 108:34, pp. 13995–13998.

Cameron, Allan (2008) *Modular Narratives in Contemporary Cinema*, Basingstoke: Palgrave Macmillan.

Campbell, Robert (2018) "Drone Film Theory," *Media Theory*, 2:2, http://mediatheoryjournal.org/robert-campbell-drone-film-theory/. Accessed November 25, 2018.

Canavan, Gerry (2018) "Living in the Future," *Science Fiction Film and Television*, 11:3, pp. 491–497.

Carr, Nicholas (2011) *The Shallows: How the Internet Is Changing the Way We Think, Read, and Remember*, London: Atlantic Books.

Cavell, Stanley (1979) *The World Viewed*, Cambridge, MA: Harvard University Press.

Cazdyn, Eric (2012) *The Already Dead: The New Time of Politics, Culture, and Illness*, Durham, NC: Duke University Press.

Chamayou, Grégoire (2012) *Manhunts: A Philosophical History* (trans. Steven Rendall), Princeton, NJ: Princeton University Press.

Chamayou, Grégoire (2015) *Drone Theory* (trans. Janet Lloyd), London: Penguin.

Chiang, Ted (2015 [1998]) *Stories of Your Life and Others*, Basingstoke: Picador.

Child, Ben (2016) "'Whitewashing' Row over Scarlett Johansson's *Ghost in the Shell* Role Reignites," *The Guardian*, April 15, https://www.theguardian.com/film/2016/apr/15/scarlett-johanssons-role-in-ghost-in-the-shell-ignites-twitter-storm. Accessed July 14, 2018.

Cho, Adrian (2018) "Weird Vibrations Poised to Control Quantum Computers," *Science*, March 14, http://www.sciencemag.org/news/2018/03/weird-vibrations-poised-control-quantum-computers. Accessed July 12, 2018.

Cixous, Hélène (1976) "The Laugh of the Medusa" (trans. Keith Cohen and Paula Cohen), *Signs*, 1:4 (Summer), pp. 875–893.

Cloete, Kervyn (2015) "We've Seen *Star Wars* at Nu Metro's New 4D Cinema! Here's What We Thought!" *Critical Hit Entertainment*, December 24, http://www.criticalhit.net/entertainment/weve-tried-out-nu-metros-new-4d-cinema-heres-what-we-thought/. Accessed May 17, 2017.

Connor, J. D. (2016) "Independence and the Consent of the Governed: The Systems and Scales of *Under the Skin*," *Jump Cut*, 57, https://www.ejumpcut.org/archive/jc57.2016/-ConnorSkin/text.html. Accessed April 16, 2017.

Courage, Katherine Harmon (2013) *Octopus! The Most Mysterious Creature in the Sea*, New York: Penguin.

Cousteau, Jacques-Yves, and Philippe Diolé (1973) *Octopus and Squid: The Soft Intelligence* (trans. J. F. Bernard), London: Cassell.

Cramer, Katie (2012) *Good Sense of Humour, Must Have Tentacles*, Addictive Press.

Crary, Jonathan (2013) *24/7: Late Capitalism and the Ends of Sleep*, London: Verso.

Creed, Barbara (1993) *The Monstrous-Feminine: Film, Feminism, Psychoanalysis*, London: Routledge.

Creed, Barbara, and Maarten Reesink (2015) "Animals, Images, Anthropocentrism," *NECSUS European Journal of Media Studies*, Spring, http://www.necsus-ejms.org/ animals-images-anthropocentrism/. Accessed July 11, 2018.

Cubitt, Sean (2014) *The Practice of Light: A Genealogy of Visual Technologies from Prints to Pixels*, Cambridge, MA: MIT Press.

Damasio, Antonio (1994) *Descartes' Error: Emotion, Reason, and the Human Brain*, London: Vintage.

Damasio, Antonio (1999) *The Feeling of What Happens: Body, Emotion and the Making of Consciousness*, London: Vintage.

Damasio, Antonio (2004) *Looking for Spinoza: Joy, Sorrow and the Feeling Brain*, London: Vintage.

Darmaillacq, Anne-Sophie, Ludovic Dickel, and Jennifer Mather (eds.) (2014) *Cephalopod Cognition*, Cambridge: Cambridge University Press.

Darwin, Charles (1845) *Journal of Researches into the Natural History and Geology of the Countries Visited during the Voyage of H.M.S. Beagle Round the World, under the Command of Capt. Fitz Roy, RN (Second Edition, Corrected, with Additions)*, London: William Cloes and Sons. Republished online at: http://darwin-online.org.uk/content/frameset?pageseq=390&itemID=F14&viewtype=image. Accessed July 11, 2018.

Davids, Thaddeus (1860) *The History of Ink, Including Its Etymology, Chemistry, and Bibliography*, New York: Francis Hart & Co.

Dawkins, Richard (1989) *The Selfish Gene*, Oxford: Oxford University Press.

Dawkins, Richard (1999) *The Extended Phenotype: The Long Reach of the Gene*, Oxford: Oxford University Press.

Dawkins, Richard, and Yan Wong (2017) *The Ancestor's Tale: A Pilgrimage to the Dawn of Life*, London: Weidenfeld & Nicolson.

de Waal, Frans (2017) *Are We Smart Enough to Know How Smart Animals Are?*, London: Granta.

De Witt, Douglas Kilgore (2010) "Difference Engine: Aliens, Robots, and Other Racial Matters in the History of Science Fiction," *Science Fiction Studies*, 37, pp. 16–22.

Deamer, David (2016) *Deleuze's Cinema Books: Three Introductions to the Taxonomy of Imgaes*, Edinburgh: Edinburgh University Press.

DeLanda, Manuel (2000) *A Thousand Years of Nonlinear History*, New York: Zone Books.

DeLanda, Manuel, and Graham Harman (2017) *The Rise of Realism*, Cambridge: Polity.

Deleuze, Gilles (1988) *Deleuze: Practical Philosophy* (trans. Robert Hurley), San Francisco: City Lights Books.

Deleuze, Gilles (1995) *Negotiations 1972–1990* (trans. Martin Joughin), New York: Columbia University Press.

Deleuze, Gilles (2000) "The Brain Is the Screen: An Interview with Gilles Deleuze," in Gregory Flaxman (ed.), *The Brain Is the Screen: Deleuze and the Philosophy of Cinema*, Minneapolis: University of Minnesota Press, pp. 365–373.

Deleuze, Gilles (2004a) *Difference and Repetition* (trans. Paul Patton), London: Continuum.

Deleuze, Gilles (2004b) *The Logic of Sense* (trans. Mark Lester with Charles Stivale), London: Continuum.

Deleuze, Gilles (2005a [1983]) *Cinema 1: The Movement-Image* (trans. Hugh Tomlinson and Barbara Habberjam), London: Continuum.

Deleuze, Gilles (2005b [1985]) *Cinema 2: The Time-Image* (trans. Hugh Tomlinson and Robert Galeta), London: Continuum.

Deleuze, Gilles, and Félix Guattari (1983) *Anti-Oedipus: Capitalism and Schizophrenia* (trans. Robert Hurley, Mark Seem, and Helen R. Lane), Minneapolis: University of Minnesota Press.

Deleuze, Gilles, and Félix Guattari (1994) *What Is Philosophy?* (trans. Hugh Tomlinson and Graham Burchell), New York: Columbia University Press.

Deleuze, Gilles, and Félix Guattari (2004) *A Thousand Plateaus: Capitalism and Schizophrenia* (trans. Brian Massumi), London: Continuum.

Deleyto, Celestino (2016) "Looking from the Border: A Cosmopolitan Approach to Contemporary Cinema," *Transnational Cinemas*, pp. 1–18.

Demos, T. J. (2017) *Against the Anthropocene: Visual Culture and Environment Today*, Berlin: Sternberg Press.

Derby, Charles D. (2014) "Cephalopod Ink: Production, Chemistry, Functions and Applications," *Marine Drugs*, 12:5, pp. 2700–2730.

Derrida, Jacques (2000) "Hospitality" (trans. Barry Stocker with Forbes Matlock), *Angelaki*, 5:3 (December), pp. 3–18.

Dery, Mark (1994) "Black to the Future: Interviews with Samuel R. Delany, Greg Tate, and Tricia Rose," in Mark Dery (ed.), *Flame Wars: The Discourse of Cyberculture*, Durham, NC: Duke University Press, pp. 179–222.

Detienne, Marcel, and Jean-Pierre Vernant (1991) *Cunning Intelligence in Greek Culture and Society* (trans. Janet Lloyd), Chicago: University of Chicago Press.

Dharani, Krishnagopal (2015) *The Biology of Thought: A Neuronal Mechanism in the Generation of Thought—A New Molecular Model*, Oxford: Academic Press.

Diehl, Jessica, and Peter Biskind (2011) "A Study in Scarlett," *Vanity Fair*, December, http://www.vanityfair.com/news/2011/12/scarlett-johansson-201112. Accessed April 17, 2017.

Dimitrov, Dimitar, Kristiaan Schreve, and N. de Beer (2006) "Advances in Three Dimensional Printing: State of the Art and Future Perspectives," *Rapid Prototyping Journal*, 12:3, pp. 136–147.

Doane, Mary Ann (2002) *The Emergence of Cinematic Time: Modernity, Contingency, the Archive*, Cambridge, MA: Harvard University Press.

Donne, John (1923) *Donne's Devotions*, Cambridge: Cambridge University Press.

Elsaesser, Thomas (2008) "'Constructive Instability,' Or: The Life of Things as Cinema's Afterlife," in Geert Lovink and Sabine Niederer (eds.), *Video Vortex Reader: Responses to YouTube*, Amsterdam: Institute of Network Cultures, pp. 13–31.

Elsaesser, Thomas (2011) "James Cameron's *Avatar*: Access for all," *New Review of Film and Television*, 9:3, pp. 247–264.

Elsaesser, Thomas, and Malte Hagener (2010) *Film Theory: An Introduction through the Senses*, London: Routledge.

English Oxford Living Dictionaries (n.d.) "Cryptozoology," in *Oxford Dictionaries*, https://en.oxforddictionaries.com/definition/cryptozoology. Accessed July 9, 2018.

Eros, Bradley (2012) "More Captivating than Phosphorus," *Millennium Film Journal*, 56, pp. 42–49.

Everett, Wendy (2005) "Fractal Films and the Architecture of Complexity," *Studies in European Cinema*, 2:3, pp. 159–171.

Fan, Victor (2015) *Cinema Approaching Reality: Locating Chinese Film Theory*, Minneapolis: University of Minnesota Press.

Faulkner-Jones, Alan, Sebastian Greenhough, Jason A. King, John Gardner, Aidan Courtney, and Wenmiao Shu (2013) "Development of a Valve-Based Cell Printer for the Formation of Human Embryonic Stem Cell Spheroid Aggregates," *Biofabrication*, 5:1, pp. 1–12.

Fay, Jennifer (2018) *Inhospitable World: Cinema in the Time of the Anthropocene*, Oxford: Oxford University Press.

Felinto, Erick (2017) "Oceano digital: Imaginário Marinho, Tecnologia e Identidade em Vilém Flusser," *Anais do XXVI Encontro Anual da Compós*, São Paulo: Faculdade Casper Líbero, pp. 1–16.

Fisher, Mark (2016) *The Weird and the Eerie*, London: Repeater Books.

Flaxman, Gregory (2011) "Sci Phi," in Gregory Flaxman (ed.), *Gilles Deleuze and the Fabulation of Philosophy*, Minneapolis: University of Minnesota Press, pp. 292–324.

Fleming, David H. (2012) "Digitalizing Deleuze: The Curious Case of the Digital Human Assemblage, or What Can a Digital Body Do?," in David Martin-Jones and William Brown (eds.), *Deleuze and Film*, Edinburgh: Edinburgh University Press, pp. 192–209.

Fleming, David H. (2015) "Scarlett the 'Post-Human' Starlet, or the Vamp Becoming Vampyroteuthis: Regarding Squids, Insects and Digital Becomings in Contemporary Science-Fiction," paper presented at *Screen Studies Conference*, University of Glasgow, Scotland, June 26–28.

Fleming, David H. (2017) *Unbecoming Cinema: Unsettling Encounters with Ethical Event Films*, Bristol and Chicago: Intellect/University of Chicago Press.

Fleming, David H. (2018) "The Weird Temporal Redound of 'Chthulhucinema': Or Pre-post-erous Tentacular Science Fiction," paper delivered at the Film-Philosophy Conference, University of Gothenburg, Sweden, July 3–5.

Fleming, David H. (forthcoming-a) "Becoming-Squid, Becoming-Insect and the Refrain of/from Becoming-Imperceptible in Contemporary Science Fiction," in Christine Daigle and Terrance McDonald (eds.), *Posthumanisms through Deleuze*, Bloomington: Indiana University Press.

Fleming, David H. (forthcoming-b) "Race and World Memory in *Arrival*," *Science Fiction Film and Television Studies.*

Fleming, David H., and William Brown (2015) "A Skeuomorphic Cinema: Film Form, Content and Criticism in the 'Post-Analogue' Era," *The Fibreculture Journal: Digital Media + Networks + Transdisciplinary Critique*, 24, http://twentyfour.fibreculturejournal.org/2015/06/04/fcj-176/. Accessed July 11, 2018.

Flusser, Vilém (1983) *Toward a Philosophy of Photography*, London: Reaktion.

Flusser, Vilém (2005) "The City as Wave-Trough in the Image-Flood" (trans. Phil Grochenour), *Critical Enquiry*, 31, pp. 320–328.

Flusser, Vilém (2011 [1987]) *Does Writing Have a Future?* (trans. Nancy Ann Roth), Minneapolis: University of Minnesota Press.

Flusser, Vilém (2014) *On Doubt* (trans. Rodrigo Maltez Novaes), Minneapolis: Univocal.

Flusser, Vilém, and Louis Bec (2012) *Vampyroteuthis Infernalis: A Treatise, with a Report by the Institut Scientifique de Recherche Paranaturaliste* (trans. Valentine A. Pakis), Minneapolis: University of Minnesota Press.

Foster Wallace, David (2001) *Brief Interviews with Hideous Men*, London: Abacus.

Foucault, Michel (1991) *Discipline and Punish: The Birth of Prison* (trans. Alan Sheridan), London: Penguin.

Foucault, Michel (2004) *The Archaeology of Knowledge*, London: Routledge.

Francis, Marc (2016) "Splitting the Difference: On the Queer-Feminist Divide in Scarlett Johansson's Recent Body Politics," *Jump Cut*, 57, http://www.ejumpcut.org/currentissue/-FrancisSkin/index.html. Accessed April 16, 2017.

Freud, Sigmund (1991) *On Sexuality: Three Essays on the Theory of Sexuality and Other Works*, London: Penguin.

Freud, Sigmund (2010) *The Interpretation of Dreams: The Complete and Definitive Text* (trans. James Strachey), New York: Basic Books.

Gabbatiss, Josh (2018) "Are Octopuses Aliens from Outer Space That Were Brought to Earth by Meteors?," *The Independent*, May 18, https://www.independent.co.uk/news/science/octopus-aliens-scientists-theory-meteors-space-earth-cambrian-explosion-a8358631.html. Accessed July 11, 2018.

Galt, Rosalind (2015) "Cats and the Moving Image: Feline Cinematicity from Lumière to Maru," in Michael Lawrence and Laura McMahon (eds.), *Animal Life and the Moving Image*, London: Palgrave, pp. 42–57.

Gartenberg, Chaim (2018) "Deepfake Edits Have Put Harrison Ford into *Solo: A Star Wars Story*, for Better or for Worse," *The Verge*, October 17, https://www.theverge.com/2018/10/17/17990162/deepfake-edits-harrison-ford-han-solo-a-star-wars-story-alden-ehrenreich. Accessed October 18, 2018.

Gewin, Virginia (2012) "The Skin's Secret Surveillance System: Microorganisms That Reside on the Skin Found to Influence Host Immunity," *Nature: International Weekly Journal of Science*, July 26, http://www.nature.com/news/the-skin-s-secret-surveillance-system-1.11075#/b2. Accessed September 27, 2017.

Giardina, Carolyn (2016) "*Arrival* Production Designer Reveals How to Create an Entirely New Type of Flying Saucer," *The Hollywood Reporter*, November 10, https://www.hollywoodreporter.com/behind-screen/arrival-production-designer-reveals-how-create-an-new-type-flying-saucer-945155. Accessed July 11, 2018.

Gilgun, Jane (2015) *The Tentacles of Shame: How Shame Works*, Jane Gilgun.

Gleick, James (1998) *Chaos: Making a New Science*, London: Vintage.

Godfrey-Smith, Peter (2013) *Philosophy of Biology*, Princeton, NJ: Princeton University Press.

Godfrey-Smith, Peter (2016) *Other Minds: The Octopus and the Evolution of Intelligent Life*, New York: Farrar, Straus and Giroux.

Grant, Catherine (2014) "The Shudder of a Cinephiliac Idea? Videographic Film Studies Practice as Material Thinking," *Aniki: Portuguese Journal of the Moving Image*, 1:1, pp. 49–62.

Greene, Brian (2000) *The Elegant Universe: Superstrings, Hidden Dimensions, and the Quest for the Ultimate Theory*, London: Vintage.

Greenspan, Anna (2015) "Wireless Waves," paper presented at ICDC Seminar Series, the University of Nottingham Ningbo, China, March 13.

Grierson, Tim (2014) "8 Things You Need to Know about the 4DX Theatre Experience: From Rocking Seats to 'Smelling' What's Onscreen, Here's What You Can Expect from This Innovative Moviegoing Experience," *Rolling Stone*, May 19, http://www.rollingstone.com/movies/news/8-things-you-need-to-know-about-the-4dx-theater-experience-20140519. Accessed January 31, 2018.

Grønstad, Asbjørn (2012) *Screening the Unwatchable: Spaces of Negation in Post-Millennial Art Cinema*, Basingstoke: Palgrave Macmillan.

Guattari, Felix (2010) *The Three Ecologies* (trans. Ian Pindar and Paul Sutton), London: Continuum.

Gunning, Tom (2006) "The Cinema of Attraction(s): Early Film, Its Spectator and the Avant-Garde," in Wanda Strauven (ed.), *The Cinema of Attractions Reloaded*, Amsterdam: Amsterdam University Press.

Harari, Yuval Noah (2016) *Homo Deus: A Brief History of Tomorrow*, London: Harvill Secker.

Haraway, Donna J. (1991) *Simians, Cyborgs, and Women: The Reinvention of Nature*, London: Routledge.

Haraway, Donna J. (2008) *When Species Meet*, Minneapolis: University of Minnesota Press.

Haraway, Donna J. (2016) *Staying with the Trouble: Making Kin in the Chthulucene*, Durham, NC: Duke University Press.

Haraway, Donna J. (2017) "Letter to Jenny Turner," *London Review of Books*, 39:13 (June 29), https://www.lrb.co.uk/v39/n11/jenny-turner/life-with-ms-cayenne-pepper. Accessed October 31, 2018.

Harbord, Janet (2016) *Ex-Centric Cinema: Giorgio Agamben and Film Archaeology*, London: Bloomsbury.

Harman, Graham (2010) *Towards Speculative Realism: Essays and Lectures*, Winchester: Zero Books.

Harman, Graham (2011) *The Quadruple Object*, Winchester: Zero Books.

Harman, Graham (2012) *Weird Realism: Lovecraft and Philosophy*, Winchester: Zero Books.

Harney, Stefano, and Fred Moten (2013) *The Undercommons: Fugitive Planning & Black Study*, Wivenhoe: Minor Compositions.

Harper, Graeme (2005) "DVD and the New Cinema of Complexity," in Nicholas Rombes (ed.), *New Punk Cinema*, Edinburgh: Edinburgh University Press, pp. 89–101.

Harwell, Drew (2018) "Scarlett Johansson on Fake AI-Generated Sex Videos: 'Nothing Can Stop Someone from Cutting and Pasting My Image,'" *Washington Post*, December 31, https://www.washingtonpost.com/technology/2018/12/31/scarlett-johansson-fake-ai-generated-sex-videos-nothing-can-stop-someone-cutting-pasting-my-image/?noredirect=on&utm_term=.4abb44c3f697. Accessed August 10, 2019.

Heidegger, Martin (1977) *The Question Concerning Technology and Other Essays* (trans. William Lovitt), New York: London: Harper & Row.

Heisenberg, Werner (2000) *Physics and Philosophy: The Revolution in Modern Science*, London: Penguin.

Herbert, Frank (1965) *Dune*, London: Chilton.

Herwartz, Daniel, Andreas Pack, Bjarne Friedrichs, and Addi Bischoff (2014) "Identification of the Giant Impactor Theia in Lunar Rocks," *Science*, 344:6188, pp. 1146–1150.

Herzog, Amy (2016) "Star Vehicle: Labor and Corporeal Traffic in *Under the Skin*," *Jump Cut*, 57, http://www.ejumpcut.org/currentissue/-HerzogSkin/index.html. Accessed April 16, 2017.

Hobson, J. Allan (1995) *Sleep*, New York: Scientific American Library.

Holmberg, Jan (2003) "Ideals of Immersion in Early Cinema," *Dispositif(s) du cinéma (des premiers temps)*, 14:1 (Fall), pp. 129–147.

Hood, Robert (2007) "Answering the Call: An Interview with Sean Brannery, Producer/Screenwriter of *The Call of Cthulhu* (with a brief appearance by director Andrew Leman)," *Roberthood.net*, http://www.roberthood.net/reviews/interview-callofcthulhu.html. Accessed July 16, 2017.

Houellebecq, Michel (2004) *Lanzarote* (trans. Frank Wynne), London: Vintage.

Houellebecq, Michel (2005) *H.P. Lovecraft: Against the World, Against Life* (trans. Dorna Khazeni), London: Orion.

Hoving, Henk-Jan T., Vladimir Laptikhovsky, and Bruce H. Robison (2015) "Vampire Squid Reproductive Strategy Is Unique among Coleoid Cephalopods," *Current Biology*, 25 (April 20), pp. 322–323.

Hugo, Victor (2010) *The Toilers of the Sea* (trans. W. Moy Thomas), *Project Gutenberg*, https://www.gutenberg.org/files/32338/32338-h/32338-h.htm. Accessed August 19, 2019.

Ihde, Don (2006) "Technofantasies and Embodiment," in Myriam Diocaretz and Stefan Herbrechter (eds.), *The Matrix in Theory*, New York: Rodopi, pp. 153–166.

Irigaray, Luce (1985) *This Sex Which Is Not One* (trans. Catherine Porter with Carolyn Burke), Ithaca, NY: Cornell University Press.

Irigaray, Luce (1991) *Marine Lover of Friedrich Nietzsche* (trans. Gillian C. Gill), New York: Columbia University Press.

Jacobs, Amber (2010) "The Life of Metis: Cunning Maternal Interventions," *Studies in the Maternal*, 2:1, pp. 1–12.

Janicker, Rebecca (2014) "Myth and Monstrosity: The Dark Realms of H.P. Lovecraft and Guillermo del Toro," in Ann Davies, Deborah Shaw, and Dolores Tierney (eds.), *The Transnational Fantasies of Guillermo Del Toro*, Basingstoke: Palgrave Macmillan, pp. 45–59.

Jenkins, Eric S. (2016) *Special Affects: Cinema, Translation and the Translation of Consumer Culture*, Edinburgh: Edinburgh University Press.

Jenkins, Henry (2008) *Convergence Culture: Where Old and New Media Collide*, New York: New York University Press.

Jeong, Seung-hoon (2013) *Cinematic Interfaces: Film Theory after New Media*, London: Routledge.

Jeong, Seung-hoon (2016) "A Generational Spectrum of Global Korean Auteurs: Political Matrix and Ethical Potential," in Seung-hoon Jeong and Jeremi Szaniawski (eds.), *The Global Auteur: The Politics of Authorship in 21st Century Cinema*, London: Bloomsbury, pp. 361–377.

Jermyn, Deborah (ed.) (2014) *Female Celebrity and Ageing: Back in the Spotlight*, London: Routledge.

Jermyn, Deborah, and Su Holmes (eds.) (2015) *Women, Celebrity and Cultures of Ageing: Freeze Frame*, Basingstoke: Palgrave Macmillan.

Jue, Melody (2014) "Vampire Squid Media," *Grey Room*, 37 (October), pp. 82–105.

Kafka, Franz (2007) *Metamorphosis & Other Stories*, London: Penguin.

Kane, Stephen R., and Franck Selsis (2014) "A Necro-Biological Explanation for the Fermi Paradox," *Popular Physics*, https://arxiv.org/abs/1403.8146. Accessed July 17, 2018.

Kara, Selmin (2014) "Beasts of the Digital Wild: Primordial Cinema and the Question of Origins," *Sequence*, 1:4, http://reframe.sussex.ac.uk/sequence/files/2012/12/SEQUENCE-1.4-2014-_-SEQUENCE-One.pdf. Accessed October 9, 2017.

Kara, Selmin (2016) "Anthropocenema: Cinema in the Age of Mass Extinctions," in Shane Denson and Julia Leyda (eds.), *Post-Cinema: Theorizing 21st Century Film*, Falmer: REFRAME Books, pp. 6.2.

Keathley, Christian (2011) "La caméra-stylo: Notes on Video Criticism and Cinephilia," in Alex Clayton and Andrew Klevan (eds.) *The Language of Style and Film Criticism*, London: Routledge, pp. 176–191.

Keegan, Rebecca (2012) "Titanic 4DX: Foreign Audiences to Feel, Smell the Ship's Sinking," *Los Angeles Times*, April 4, http://latimesblogs.latimes.com/movies/2012/04/titanic-4dx-foreign-audiences-to-experience-sinking-in-five-senses.html. Accessed May 25, 2017.

Kennedy, Barbara M. (2002) *Deleuze and Cinema: The Aesthetics of Sensation*, Edinburgh: Edinbugh University Press.

King, Geoff (2000) "Ride-Films and Films as Rides in Contemporary Hollywood Cinema of Attractions," *CineAction*, 51 (February), pp. 2–10.

King, Stephen (2005) "Lovecraft's Pillow," in Michel Houellebecq, *H.P. Lovecraft: Against the World, Against Life* (trans. Dorna Khazeni), London: Orion, pp. 9–18.

Kipnis, Laura (1998) "Film and Changing Technologies," in John Hill and Pamela Church Gibson (eds.), *The Oxford Guide to Film Studies*, Oxford: Oxford University Press, pp. 595–604.

Kittler, Friedrich (1999) *Gramophone, Film, Typewriter* (trans. Geoffery Winthrop-Young and Michael Wutz), Stanford, CA: Stanford University Press.

Knee, Adam, and David H. Fleming (2014) "The Future Is Scarlett: Critical and Philosophical Considerations of a Post-Human Star Image," paper presented at *Imagining the Future: The Utopian, the Dystopian, and the Posthuman*, Institute of Cinematic Arts, Shanghai Theatre Academy, China, November 14.

Koutsourakis, Angelos (2017) "Visualizing the Anthropocene Dialectically: Jessica Woodworth and Peter Brosens' Eco-Crisis Trilogy," *Film-Philosophy*, 21:3, pp. 299–325.

Kröger, Björn, Jakob Vinther, and Dirk Fuchs (2011) "Cephalopod Origin and Evolution: A Congruent Picture Emerging from Fossils, Development and Molecules," *BioEssays*, 33:8 (August), pp. 602–613.

La Mer, M. (2015) *Tentacle Lord: Book 1*, M. La Mer.

Lake, Jamie (2014) *Wrapped up in Tentacles*, Jamie Lake.

Lakoff, George, and Mark Johnson (2003) *Metaphors We Live By*, Chicago: University of Chicago Press.

Lanier, Jaron (2010) *You Are Not a Gadget: A Manifesto*, London: Penguin.

Latour, Bruno (1996) *Aramis, or the Love of Technology* (trans. Catherine Porter), Cambridge, MA: Harvard University Press.

Latour, Bruno (2012) "Love Your Monsters: Why We Must Care for Our Technologies as We Do Our Children," *The Breakthrough*, Winter, https://thebreakthrough.org/index.php/journal/past-issues/issue-2/love-your-monsters. Accessed July 18, 2018.

Lavender III, Isiah (2007) "Ethnoscapes: Environment and Language in Ishmael Reed's *Mumbo Jumbo*, Colson Whitehead's *The Intuitionist*, and Samuel R. Delany's *Babel-17*," *Science Fiction Studies*, 34:2, pp. 187–200.

Lavender III, Isiah (2011) *Race in American Science Fiction*, Bloomington: Indiana University Press.

Leeder, Murray (2011) "Collective Screams: William Castle and the Gimmick Film," *Journal of Popular Culture*, 44:4, pp. 773–795.

LeMenager, Stephanie (2014) *Living Oil: Petroleum Culture in the American Century*, Oxford: Oxford University Press.

Levy, Emanuel (2016) "*Arrival*: Visual Style—Images and Design," *Emanuel Levy: Cinema 24/7*, November 11, http://emanuellevy.com/comment/arrival-visual-style-images-and-design/. Accessed July 16, 2018.

Lewis, Ricki (2017) "Octopuses, Squid, and Cuttlefish: RNA Editing Instead of Genome Evolution?" *PLOS DNA Science Blog: Genetics in Context*, April 6, http://blogs.plos.org/dnascience/2017/04/06/octopuses-squid-and-cuttlefish-rna-editing-instead-of-genome-evolution/. Accessed September 27, 2017.

Ling, Alex (2011) *Badiou and Cinema*, Edinburgh: Edinburgh University Press.

Lippit, Akira Mizuta (2000) *Electric Animal: Toward a Rhetoric of Wildlife*, Minneapolis: University of Minnesota Press.

Lippit, Akira Mizuta (2005) *Atomic Light (Shadow Optics)*, Minneapolis: University of Minnesota Press.

Liscovitch-Brauer, Noa, Shahar Alon, Hagit T. Porath, Boaz Elstein, Ron Unger, Tamar Ziv, Arie Admon, Erez Y. Levanon, Joshua J. C. Rosenthal, and Eli Eisenberg (2017) "Trade-off between Transcriptome Plasticity and Genome Evolution in Cephalopods," *Cell*, 169:2 (April), pp. 191–202.

Littau, Karin (2003) "Eye-Hunger: Physical Pleasure and Non-Narrative Cinema," in Jane Arthurs and Iain Grant (eds.), *Crash Cultures: Modernity, Mediation and the Material*, Bristol: Intellect, pp. 35–52.

Liu, F., S.-W. You, L.-P. Yao, H.-L. Liu, X.-Y. Jiao, M. Shi, Q.-B. Zhao, and G. Ju (2006) "Secondary Degeneration Reduced by Inosine after Spinal Cord Injury in Rats," *Spinal Cord*, 44, pp. 421–426.

Longo, Anna (2014) "The Contingent Emergence of Thought: A Comparison between Meillassoux and Deleuze," in Quentin Meillassoux, *Time Without Becoming*, Sesto San Giovanni: Mimesis International, pp. 31–50.

Lovecraft, H. P. (2002) *The Call of Cthulhu and Other Weird Stories*, London: Penguin.

Lovecraft, H. P. (2008) *The Dunwich Horror*, London: Penguin.

Ludueña, Fabián (2014) *H.P. Lovecraft: The Disjunction in Being* (trans. Alejandro de Acosta), USA: Schism Press.

Ma, Xiao-song, Stefan Zotter, Johannes Kofler, Rupert Ursin, Thomas Jennewein, Časlav Brukner, and Anton Zeilinger (2012) "Experimental Delayed-Choice Entanglement Swapping," *Nature Physics*, 8, pp. 479–484.

MacCormack, Patricia (2008) *Cinesexuality*, Aldershot: Ashgate.

MacCormack, Patricia (2010a) "Mucous, Monsters and Angels: Irigaray and Zuławski's *Possession*," *Cinema: Journal of Philosophy and the Moving Image*, 1, pp. 95–110.

MacCormack, Patricia (2010b) "Lovecraft through Deleuzio-Guattarian Gates," *Postmodern Culture: Journal of Interdisciplinary Thought on Contemporary Cultures*, 20:2 (January), http://www.pomoculture.org/2013/09/03/lovecraft-through-deleuzio-guattarian-gates/. Accessed July 16, 2018.

McDaniel, Kris (2016) "John M. E. McTaggart," in Edward N. Zalta (ed.), *The Stanford Encyclopaedia of Philosophy*, https://plato.stanford.edu/archives/win2016/entries/mctaggart/. Accessed July 16, 2018.

McGee, Mark Thomas (2001 [1989]) *Beyond Ballyhoo: Motion Picture Promotions and Gimmicks*, Jefferson, NC: McFarland Classics.

McGrath, Hugh P., and Michael Comenetz (2011) *Valéry's Graveyard:* Le Cimetière Marin *Translated, Described, and Peopled*, New York: Peter Lang.

McLuhan, Marshall (1962) *The Gutenberg Galaxy: The Making of Typographic Man*, Toronto: University of Toronto Press.

McMahon, Laura (ed.) (2015a) "Screen Animals Dossier," *Screen*, 56:1 (Spring), pp. 81–120.

McMahon, Laura (2015b) "Screen Animals Dossier: Introduction," *Screen*, 56:1 (Spring), pp. 81–87.

McTaggart, J. E. (1908) "The Unreality of Time," *Mind*, 17:68, pp. 457–474.

McTaggart, John Ellis (1909) "The Relation of Time and Eternity," *Mind*, 18:71, pp. 343–362.

McTaggart, John M. E. (1927) *The Nature of Existence, Vol. II*, Cambridge: Cambridge University Press.

Malabou, Catherine (2008) *What Should We Do With Our Brain?* (trans. Sebastian Rand), New York: Fordham University Press.

Maldacena, Juan, and Leonard Susskind (2013) "Cool Horizons for Entangled Black Holes," *Progress of Physics*, 61:9 (September), pp. 781–811.

Manovich, Lev (2001) *The Language of New Media*, Cambridge, MA: MIT Press.

Margulis, Lynn (1998) *The Symbiotic Planet: A New Look at Evolution*, London: Weidenfeld & Nicolson.

Marks, Laura U. (2000) *The Skin of Film: Intercultural Cinema, Embodiment and the Senses*, Durham, NC: Duke University Press.

Marks, Laura U. (2002) *Touch: Sensuous Theory and Multi-Sensory Media*, Minneapolis: University of Minnesota Press.

Martin-Jones, David (2016) "Trolls, Tigers and Transmodern Ecological Encounters: Enrique Dussel and a Cine-ethics for the Anthropocene," *Film-Philosophy*, 20:1, pp. 63–103.

Martin-Jones, David (2018) *Cinema Against Doublethink: Ethical Encounters with the Lost Pasts of World History*, Abingdon: Routledge.

Massumi, Brian (2015) *Politics of Affect*, Cambridge: Polity.

Mather, Jennifer A., Roland C. Anderson, and James B. Wood (2010) *Octopus: The Ocean's Intelligent Invertebrate*, Portland, OR: Timber Press.

Mauss, Marcel (1973) "Techniques of the Body" (trans. Ben Brewster), *Economy and Society*, 2:1, pp. 70–88.

Mbembe, Achille (2003) "Necropolitics" (trans. Libby Meintjes), *Public Culture*, 15:1, pp. 11–40.

Megidish, Eli, Assaf Halevy, Tomer Shacham, Tom Dvir, Liat Dovrat, and Hagai S. Eisenberg (2013) "Entanglement Swapping between Photons That Have Never Coexisted," *Physical Review Letters*, 110, 210403.

Meillassoux, Quentin (2010) *After Finitude: An Essay on the Necessity of Contingency* (trans. Ray Brassier), London: Continuum.

Meillassoux, Quentin (2015) *Science Fiction and Extro-Science Fiction* (trans. Alyosha Edlebi), Minneapolis: Univocal.

Mellamphy, Dan (2014) "Between Beckett and Bec: The *Mètic Hexis* and *Flusserian Flux* of *Vampyroteuthis Abductionis*," in Tom Kohut and Melentie Padiolvski (eds.), *Marshall McLuhan's and Vilém Flusser's Communication and Aesthetic Theories Revisited*, Minneapolis: University of Minnesota Press.

Mellamphy, Dan, and Nandita Biswas Mellamphy (2014) "From the Digital to the Tentacular, or from iPods to Cephalopods: Apps, Traps, and Entrées-without-Exits," in Paul D. Miller and Svitlana Matviyenko (eds.), *The Imaginary App*, Cambridge, MA: MIT Press, pp. 231–250.

Micheau, Antoine, and Denis Hoa (2017) "Visible Human Project: Anatomy Atlas of Male Cadaver," *IMAIOS*, December 22, https://www.imaios.com/en/e-Anatomy/Thorax-Abdomen-Pelvis/Visible-Human-Project. Accessed July 9, 2018.

Miéville, China (2008) "M.R. James and the Quantum Vampire: Weird; Hauntological: Versus and/or and and/or or?," in Robin Mackay (ed.), *Collapse IV*, Falmouth: Urbanomic, pp. 105–128.

Miéville, China (2010) *Kraken*, London: Vintage.

Miller, Joe (2017) "How Facebook's Tentacles Reach Further Than You Think," *BBC News*, May 26, https://www.bbc.co.uk/news/business-39947942. Accessed July 13, 2018.

Mitchell, H. H., T. S. Hamilton, F. R. Steggerda, and H. W. Bean (1945) "The Chemical Composition of the Adult Human Body and Its Bearing on the Biochemistry of Growth," *Journal of Biological Chemistry*, 158, pp. 625–637.

Mitchell, W. J. T. (2005) *What Do Pictures Want?: The Lives and Loves of Images*, Chicago: University of Chicago Press.

Mittell, Jason (2006) "Narrative Complexity in American Television," *The Velvet Light Trap*, 58, pp. 29–40.

Monaghan, Whitney, Kirsten Stevens, and Janice Loreck (eds.) (2019) *Screening Scarlett Johansson: Celebrity, Gender, Genre*, Basingstoke: Palgrave Macmillan.
Montgomery, Sy (2015) *The Soul of an Octopus: A Surprising Exploration into the Wonder of Consciousness*, London: Simon & Schuster.
Morehead, Jason (2010) "The Call of Cthulhu (Andrew Leman, 2005)," *The Other Journal: An Intersection of Theology and Culture*, March 29, https://theotherjournal.com/2010/03/29/the-call-of-cthulhu-andrew-leman-2005/. Accessed July 16, 2018.
Morin, Edgar (1957) *Les stars*, Paris: Les Editions de Minuit.
Morton, Timothy (2011) "Some Notes towards a Philosophy of Non-Life," *Thinking Nature*, 1:7, pp. 1–18.
Morton, Timothy (2013) *Hyperobjects: Philosophy and Ecology after the End of the World*, Minneapolis: University of Minnesota Press.
Mumford, Lewis (1967) *The Myth of the Machine: Technics and Human Development*, New York: Harcourt Brace Jovanovich.
Mumford, Lewis (1970) *The Myth of the Machine: The Pentagon of Power*, New York: Harcourt Brace Jovanovich.
Mumford, Lewis (2010 [1934]) *Technics and Civilization*, Chicago: University of Chicago Press.
Nagel, Ernest, and James R. Newman (2005) *Gödel's Proof*, London: Routledge.
Nagel, Thomas (1974) "What Is It Like to Be a Bat?," *The Philosophical Review*, 83:4 (October), pp. 435–450.
Nagib, Lúcia (2016) "Non-Cinema, or the Location of Politics in Film," *Film-Philosophy*, 20:1, pp. 131–148.
Nakajima, Ryuta, Shuichi Shigeno, Letizia Zullo, Fabio De Sio, and Markus R. Schmidt (2018) "Cephalopods between Science, Art, and Engineering: A Contemporary Synthesis," *Frontiers in Communication*, 3:20 (June 13), pp. 1–16.
Nakano, Tamami, Makoto Kato, Yusuke Morito, Seishi Itoi, and Shigeru Kitazawa (2013) "Blink-Related Momentary Activation of the Default Mode Network While Viewing Videos," *Proceedings of the National Academy of Sciences of the United States of America*, 110:2: 702–706.
Nancy, Jean-Luc (2008) "Claire Denis: Icon of Ferocity" (trans. Peter Enright), in James Phillips (ed.), *Cinematic Thinking: Philosophical Approaches to the New Cinema*, Stanford, CA: Stanford University Press, pp. 160–170.
Negarestani, Reza (2008) *Cyclonopedia: Complicity with Anonymous Materials*, Melbourne: re.press.
Neild, David (2019) "Samsung's Creepy New AI Can Generate Talking Deepfakes from a Single Image," *Sciencealert.com*, May 26, https://www.sciencealert.com/samsung-s-ai-can-now-generate-talking-heads-from-a-single-image. Accessed August 12, 2019.
Ng, Jenna P.-S. (2014) "Falling in Love with an OS: Imagining the Future with Things in Spike Jonze's *Her*," paper presented at *Imagining the Future:*

The Utopian, the Dystopian, and the Posthuman, Institute of Cinematic Arts, Shanghai Theatre Academy, China, November 14.

Nishime, LeiLani (2016) "The Mulatto Cyborg: Imagining a Multiracial Future," in Leo Braudy and Marshall Cohen (eds.), *Film Theory and Criticism*, Oxford: Oxford University Press, pp. 694–710.

Norris, Frank (1994) *The Octopus: A Story of California*, London: Penguin.

O'Day, Marc (2004) "Beauty in Motion: Gender, Spectacle and Action Babe Cinema," in Yvonne Tasker (ed.), *The Action Adventure Cinema*, London: Routledge, pp. 201–218.

Ó Maoilearca, John (2015) *All Thoughts Are Equal: Laruelle and Nonhuman Philosophy*, Minneapolis: University of Minnesota Press.

Onfray, Michael (2015) *Appetites for Thought: Philosophers and Food* (trans. Donald Barry and Stephen Muecke), London: Reaktion.

OpenStax (2015) "Neurons and Glia," *cnx.org*, http://cnx.org/contents/GFy_h8cu@9.87:c9j4p0aj@3/Neurons-and-Glial-Cells. Accessed July 14, 2018.

Osterweil, Ara (2014) "*Under the Skin*: The Perils of Becoming Female," *Film Quarterly*, 67:4, pp. 44–51.

O'Sullivan, Simon, and Stephen Zepke (eds.) (2018) *Deleuze, Guattari and the Production of the New*, London: Continuum.

Ovid (1998) *Metamorphoses* (trans. John Dryden and others), Ware: Wordsworth.

Panek, Elliot (2006) "The Poet and the Detective: Defining the Psychological Puzzle Film," *Film Criticism*, 31:1–2, pp. 62–88.

Parikka, Jussi (2010) *Insect Media: An Archaeology of Animals and Technology*, Minneapolis: University of Minnesota Press.

Pearce, Fred (2014) "Mideast Water Wars: In Iraq, a Battle for Control of Water," *Yale Environment 360*, August 25, https://e360.yale.edu/features/mideast_water_wars_in_iraq_a_battle_for_control_of_water. Accessed October 9, 2017.

Pedullà, Gabriele (2013) *In Broad Daylight: Movies and Spectators after the Cinema* (trans. Patricia Gaborik), London: Verso.

Penrose, Roger (1989) *The Emperor's New Mind: Concerning Computers, Minds, and the Laws of Physics*, London: Vintage.

Petrusich, Amanda (2017) "Playboy Interview: Scarlett Johansson Talks Monogamy, Women's March & 'Ghost in the Shell,'" *Playboy*, April/March, http://www.playboy.com/articles/playboy-interview-scarlett-johanson. Accessed February 16, 2017.

Philips, John W. P. (2006) "Agencement/Assemblage," *Theory, Culture & Society*, 23, pp. 2–3.

Pick, Anat (2011) *Creaturely Poetics: Animality and Vulnerability in Literature and Film*, New York: Columbia University Press.

Pisters, Patricia (2012) *The Neuro-Image: A Deleuzian Film-Philosophy of Digital Screen Culture*, Stanford, CA: Stanford University Press.

Polan, Dana B. (1982) "'Above All Else to Make You See': Cinema and the Ideology of Spectacle," *Boundary 2*, 11:1–2, pp. 129–144.

Powell, Anna (2007) *Deleuze, Altered States and Film*, Edinburgh: Edinburgh University Press.

Powell Dahlquist, Joe, and Lee Garth Vigilant (2004) "Way Better than Real: Manga Sex to Tentacle Hentai," in Dennis D. Waskul (ed.), *net.seXXX: Readings on Sex, Pornography, and the Internet*, New York: Peter Lang, pp. 91–103.

Power, Nina (2009) *One Dimensional Woman*, Ropley: Zero Books.

Price, Huw, and Ken Wharton (2016) "Taming the Quantum Spooks," *aeon*, September 14, https://aeon.co/essays/can-retrocausality-solve-the-puzzle-of-action-at-a-distance. Accessed July 13, 2018.

Price, Rob (2018) "People Are Using Creepy, Cutting-Edge AI Technology to Splice Nic Cage into Every Movie They Can Think of," *Business Insider*, January 25, https://www.businessinsider.com/nicolas-cage-inserted-movies-fakeapp-ai-technology-2018-1. Accessed November 3, 2018.

Pruszynski, J. Andrew, and Roland S. Johansson (2014) "Edge-Orientation Processing in First-Order Tactile Neurons," *Nature Neuroscience*, 17, pp. 1404–1409.

Pynchon, Thomas (1973) *Gravity's Rainbow*, New York: Viking Press.

Ramírez Berg, Charles (2006) "A Taxonomy of Alternative Plots in Recent Films: Classifying the 'Tarantino Effect,'" *Film Criticism*, 31:1–2, pp. 5–61.

Ramírez, Catherine S. (2008) "Afrofuturism/Chicanafuturism: Fictive Kin," *AZTLAN—A Journal of Chicano Studies*, 33:1, pp. 185–194.

Randall, Lisa (2006) *Warped Passages: Unravelling the Mysteries of the Universe's Hidden Dimensions*, London: Penguin.

Randall, Lisa (2015) *Dark Matter and the Dinosaurs: The Astounding Interconnectedness of the Universe*, London: Vintage.

Readfearn, Graham (2018) "WHO Launches Health Review after Microplastics Found in 90% of Bottled Water," *The Guardian*, March 15, https://www.theguardian.com/environment/2018/mar/15/microplastics-found-in-more-than-90-of-bottled-water-study-says. Accessed April 5, 2018.

Reid, Michelle (2009) "Postcolonialism," in Mark Bould, Andrew Butler, Adam Roberts, and Sherryl Vint (eds.), *The Routledge Companion to Science Fiction*, London: Routledge, pp. 256–266.

Reynolds, Daniel (2019) *Media and Mind*, Oxford: Oxford University Press.

Ridgely, Charlie (2018) "The Biggest Evidence That 'Life' Really Is a 'Venom' Prequel," *Comic Book*, February 8, https://comicbook.com/marvel/2018/02/08/venom-movie-life-prequel-the-life-foundation/. Accessed November 4, 2018.

Rieder, John (2008) *Colonialism and the Emergence of Science Fiction*, Middletown, CT: Wesleyan University Press.

Riis, Johannes (2009) "Acting," in Paisley Livingston and Carl Plantinga (eds.), *The Routledge Companion to Philosophy and Film*, London: Routledge, pp. 3–11.

Robehmed, Natalie (2016) "Scarlett Johansson Is the Top Grossing Actor of 2016," *Forbes*, December 27, https://www.forbes.com/sites/natalierobehmed/2016/12/27/scarlett-johansson-is-the-top-grossing-actor-of-2016/#73a382271433. Accessed May 29, 2017.

Rosindell, James, and Yan Wong (n.d.) *OneZoom*, onezoom.org. Accessed July 12, 2018.

Roy, Arundhati (1999) *The Cost of Living: The Greater Common Good and the End of Imagination*, London: Flamingo.

Russian, Ale (2017) "Inside Scarlett Johansson's Ups and Downs in Love," *People*, January25,http://people.com/movies/inside-scarlett-johansson-ups-and-downs-in-love/. Accessed April 16, 2017.

Ruff, Matt (2016) *Lovecraft Country*, New York: HarperCollins.

Sabante, Cindel (2012) *Tentacle Erotica Three Pack*, Amazon Media EU.

Sagan, Dorion (2010) "Introduction: Umwelt after Uexküll," in Jacob von Uexküll, *A Foray into the Worlds of Animals and Humans* with *A Theory of Meaning* (trans. Joseph D. O'Neil), Minneapolis: University of Minnesota Press, pp. 1–34.

Schivelbusch, Wolfgang (1993) *Tastes of Paradise: A Social History of Spices, Stimulants, and Intoxicants* (trans. David Jacobson), New York: Vintage.

Schivelbusch, Wolfgang (1995) *Disenchanted Night: Industrialization of Light in the Nineteenth Century: The Industrialization of Light in the Nineteenth Century* (trans. Angela Davies), Berkeley: University of California Press.

Schmerler, Jessica (2015) "Q&A: Why Is Blue Light before Bedtime Bad for Sleep? Two Neuroscientists Discuss How Blue Light Negatively Affects Health and Sleep Patterns," *Scientific American*, September 1, https://www.scientificamerican.com/article/q-a-why-is-blue-light-before-bedtime-bad-for-sleep/. Accessed April 5, 2018.

Schmitt, Charles B. (1965) "Aristotle as a Cuttlefish: The Origin and Development of a Renaissance Image," *Studies in the Renaissance*, 12, pp. 60–72.

Schnier, Jacques (1956) "Morphology of a Symbol: The Octopus," *American Imago*, 13:1, pp. 3–31.

Schweid, Richard (2013) *Octopus*, London: Reaktion.

Scott, A. O. (2008) "Navigating a Zigzag Course in a Sea of Relationships," *New York Times*, April 4, https://www.nytimes.com/2008/04/04/movies/04jell.html. Accessed November 23, 2018.

Scranton, Roy (2015) *Learning to Die in the Anthropocene: Reflections on the End of a Civilization*, San Francisco: City Lights Books.

Serres, Michel (1995) *Angels: A Modern Myth* (trans. Francis Cowper), Paris: Flammarion.

Serres, Michel (2018) *The Incandescent* (trans. Randolph Burks), London: Bloomsbury.

Share Lab (2017) "The Human Fabric of the Facebook Pyramid," *Share Lab*, May 3, https://labs.rs/en/the-human-fabric-of-the-facebook-pyramid/. Accessed May 27, 2017.

Sharp, Jasper (2013) "4DX: Here Come the Feelies," *Sight & Sound*, April 28, http://www.bfi.org.uk/news/sightsound/4dx-here-come-feelies. Accessed May 16, 2017.

Shaviro, Steven (2013) "Bats, Dogs, and Posthumans," *The Pinocchio Theory*, December 22, http://www.shaviro.com/Blog/?p=1181. Accessed July 12, 2018.

Shaviro, Steven (2014) *The Universe of Things: On Speculative Realism*, Minneapolis: University of Minnesota Press.

Shaviro, Steven (2016) *Discognition*, London: Repeater Books.

Shea, Robert, and Robert Anton Wilson (1998) *The Illuminatus! Trilogy*, London: Raven Books.

Shukin, Nicole (2009) *Animal Capital: Rendering Life in Biopolitical Times*, Minneapolis: University of Minnesota Press.

Silverwood, Cari (2014) *Squirm: Virgin Captive of the Billionaire Biker Tentacle Monster*, Cari Silverwood.

Simondon, Gilbert (1958) *On the Mode of Existence by Technical Objects*, Paris: Aubier.

Simondon, Gilbert (1992) "The Genesis of the Individual," in Jonathan Crary and Sanford Kwinter (eds.), *Incorporations*, New York: Zone Books, pp. 297–319.

Slater, Matthew H. (2013) *Are Species Real? As Essay on the Metaphysics of Species*, Basingstoke: Palgrave Macmillan.

Smith, Darryl A. (2007) "Droppin' Science ~~Fiction~~: Signification and Singularity in the Metapocalypse of Du Bois, Baraka, and Bell," *Science Fiction Studies*, 34:2, pp. 201–209.

Smith, Roland (2011) *Tentacles*, New York: Scholastic.

Snider, Zachary (2016) "The Cognitive Psychological Effects of Binge-Watching," in Kevin McDonald and Daniel Smith-Rowsey (eds.), *The Netflix Effect: Technology and Entertainment in the 21st Century*, London: Bloomsbury, pp. 117–128.

Sobchack, Vivian (1992) *The Address of the Eye: A Phenomenology of Film Experience*, Princeton, NJ: Princeton University Press.

Sobchack, Vivian (2004) *Carnal Thoughts: Embodiment and Moving Image Culture*, Berkeley: University of California Press.

Sommer, Valerie (2017) "Octopus Brainstorming," *UCLA NewRoom*, November 14, http://newsroom.ucla.edu/stories/octopus-brainstorming. Accessed July 13, 2018.

Specter, Michael (2012) "Germs Are Us: Bacteria Make Us Sick. Do They Also Keep Us Alive?," *The New Yorker*, October 22, https://www.newyorker.com/magazine/2012/10/22/germs-are-us. Accessed September 27, 2017.

Spinoza, Benedict de (2001) *Ethics* (trans. Stuart Hampshire), London: Penguin.

Staaf, Danna (2017) *Squid Empire: The Rise and Fall of the Cephalopods*, Lebanon, NH: ForeEdge.

Staiger, Janet (2006) "Complex Narratives: An Introduction," *Film Criticism*, 31:1–2, pp. 1–4.

Stam, Robert (2000) *Film Theory: An Introduction*, Oxford: Blackwell.

Stanley, Tim (2016) "Down's Syndrome People Risk 'Extinction' at the Hands of Science, Fear and Ignorance," *The Telegraph*, January 18, https://www.telegraph.co.uk/news/2016/03/22/downs-syndrome-people-risk-extinction-at-the-hands-of-science-fe/. Accessed July 19, 2018.

Steele, Edward J., Shirwan Al-Mufti, Kenneth A. Augustyn, Rohana Chandrajith, John P. Coghlan, S. G. Coulson, Sudipto Ghosh, Mark Gillman, Reginald M. Gorczynski, Brig Klyce, Godfrey Louis, Kithsiri Mahanama, Keith R. Oliver, Julio Padron, Jiangwen Qu, John A. Schuster, W. E. Smith, Duane P. Snyder, Julian A. Steele, Brent J. Stewart, Robert Temple, Gensuke Tokoro, Christopher A. Tout, Alexander Unzicker, Milton Wainwright, Jamie Wallis, Daryl H. Wallis, Max K. Wallis, John Wetherall, D. T. Wickramasinghe, J. T. Wickramasinge, N. Chandra Wickramasinghe, and Yongsheng Liu (2018) "Cause of Cambrian Explosion: Terrestrial or Cosmic?," *Progress in Biophysics and Molecular Biology*, 136, pp. 1–21.

Steenbakkers, Piet (2018) Personal correspondence with four limbs of the author, June 16.

Stork, Matthias (2012) "In Touch with the Film Object: Cinephilia, the Video Essay, and Chaos Cinema," *Frames Cinema Journal*, 1, http://framescinemajournal.com/article/in-touch-with-the-film-object/. Accessed February 4, 2018.

Styles, River (2016) *Alien Tentacle Chronicles: Bound*, Scarlet Lantern Publishing.

Su, Wendy (2011) "Resisting Cultural Imperialism, or Welcoming Cultural Globalization? China's Extensive Debate on Hollywood Cinema from 1994 to 2007," *Asian Journal of Communication*, 21:2, pp. 186–201.

Szendy, Peter (2015) *Apocalypse-Cinema: 2012 and Other Ends of the World* (trans. Will Bishop), New York: Fordham University Press.

Tan, Emily (2017) "Eurostar Creates Dreamy Seascape Onboard VR Experience with AKQA," *campaign*, July 12, https://www.campaignlive.co.uk/article/eurostar-creates-dreamy-seascape-onboard-vr-experience-akqa/1439239. Accessed October 30, 2018.

Tanner, Grafton (2016) *Babbling Corpse: Vaporwave and the Commodification of Ghosts*, Winchester: Zero Books.

Thacker, Eugene (2004) *Biomedia*, Mineapolis: University of Minnesota Press.

Thacker, Eugene (2005) "Biophilosophy for the 21st Century," *CTheory*, September 6, http://www.ctheory.net/articles.aspx?id=472. Accessed July 11, 2018.

Thacker, Eugene (2011) *In the Dust of This Planet: Horror of Philosophy, Vol. 1.* Winchester: Zero Books.

Thacker, Eugene (2015a) *Starry Speculative Corpse: Horror of Philosophy, Vol. 2.* Winchester: Zero Books.

Thacker, Eugene (2015b) *Tentacles Longer Than Night: Horror of Philosophy, Vol. 3.* Winchester: Zero Books.

Thanouli, Eleftheria (2006) "Post-Classical Narration," *New Review of Film and Television Studies*, 4:3, pp. 183–196.

Thompson, Mark (2016) "Iranian Cyber Attack on New York Dam Shows Future of War," *Time*, March 24, http://time.com/4270728/iran-cyber-attack-dam-fbi/. Accessed October 9, 2017.

Thrift, Nigel (2010) "Understanding the Material Practices of Glamour," in Melissa Gregg and Gregory J. Seigworth (eds.), *The Affect Theory Reader*, Durham, NC: Duke University Press, pp. 289–308.

Trace, Talia (2014) *Tentacle Erotica Mega Bundle*, Thompson-Corner.

Trimmer, John D. (1980) "The Present Situation in Quantum Mechanics: A Translation of Schrödinger's 'Cat Paradox' Paper," *Proceedings of the American Philosophical Society*, 124:5 (October 10), pp. 323–338.

Turner, Jenny (2017) "Life with Ms Cayenne Pepper," *London Review of Books*, 39:11 (June 1), pp. 23–27.

Uy, Jamie, and William Brown (forthcoming) "Cancelling the Apocalypse: *Pacific Rim* as Chthulucinema," *New Review of Film and Television Studies*.

Varndell, Daniel (2014) *Hollywood Remakes, Deleuze and the Grandfather Paradox*, Basingtoke: Palgrave Macmillan.

Viveiros de Castro, Eduardo (2014) *Cannibal Metaphysics* (trans. Peter Skafish), Minneapolis: Univocal.

Vlasits, Anna (2017) "Science Reveals Yet Another Reason Octopuses and Squid Are So Weird," *Wired*, April 6, https://www.wired.com/2017/04/cephalopod-gene-editing/. Accessed July 12, 2018.

von Uexküll, Jacob (2010) *A Foray into the Worlds of Animals and Humans* with *A Theory of Meaning* (trans. Joseph D. O'Neil), Minneapolis: University of Minnesota Press.

von Wagner, Johann Rudolf, Ferdinand Fischer, and L. Gautier (1903) *Traité de la chimie industrielle, Vol. 2*, Paris: Masson & Co.

Waldby, Catherine (2000) *The Visible Human Project: Informatic Bodies and Posthuman Medicine*, London: Routledge.

Ward, Gerald W. R. (ed.) (2008) *The Grove Encyclopedia of Materials and Techniques in Art*, Oxford: Oxford University Press.

Wark, McKenzie (2014) "Anthropo{mise-en-s}cène," *Public Seminar*, December 10, http://www.publicseminar.org/2014/12/anthropomise-en-scene/#.WdtRWRSE-FK. Accessed October 9, 2017.

Wark, McKenzie (2016) *Molecular Red: Theory for the Anthropocene*, London: Verso.

Wetmore Jr., Kevin J. (2015) "At the Mountains of Mexico: The Echoes and Intertexts of Lovecraft and Dunsany," in John W. Morehead (ed.), *The Supernatural Cinema of Guillermo del Toro: Critical Essays*, Jefferson, CT: McFarland & Company, pp. 22–40.

Wheatley, Catherine (2013) "The New Eve: Faith, Femininity and the Fairy Tale in Catherine Breillat's *Barbe bleue/Bluebeard* (2009)," *Studies in European Cinema*, 10:1, pp. 71–80.

Whitehall, Haley, Eva LeFoy, and D. R. Larsson (2012) *Tentacles: An Anthology*, Expanding Horizons Press.

Wills, David (2008) *Dorsality: Thinking Back through Technology and Politics*, Minneapolis: University of Minnesota Press.

Wise, J. Macgregor (2011) "Assemblage," in Charles J. Stivale (ed.), *Gilles Deleuze: Key Concepts*, Durham: Acumen, pp. 91–101.

Wittgenstein, Ludwig (2009 [1953]) *Philosophical Investigations* (trans. G. E. M. Anscombe, P. M. S. Hacker, and Joachim Schulte), London: Wiley Blackwell.

Wolchover, Natalie (2017) "Newfound Wormhole Allows Information to Escape Black Holes," *Quanta Magazine*, October 23, https://www.quantamagazine.org/newfound-wormhole-allows-information-to-escape-black-holes-20171023/. Accessed January 31, 2018.

Wolf, Maryanne (2008) *Proust and the Squid: The Story of Science and the Reading Brain*, Cambridge: Icon Books.

Wolfe, Cary (2014) *Animal Rites: American Culture, the Discourse of Species, and Posthumanist Theory*, Chicago: University of Chicago Press.

Woodard, Ben (2012) *Slime Dynamics: Generation, Mutation, and the Creep of Life*, Winchester: Zero Books.

Yong, Ed (2017) "Octopuses Do Something Really Strange to Their Genes," *The Atlantic*, April 6, https://www.theatlantic.com/science/archive/2017/04/octopuses-do-something-really-strange-to-their-genes/522024/. Accessed September 27, 2017.

Youngblood, Gene (1970) *Expanded Cinema*, New York: Dutton.

Yusoff, Kathryn (2018) *A Billion Black Anthropocenes or None*, Minneapolis: University of Minnesota Press.

Zdebik, Jakub (2012) *Deleuze and the Diagram: Aesthetic Threads in Visual Organization*, London: Continuum.

Zeilinger, Anton (2003) "Quantum Teleportation," *Scientific American Special Issue: The Edge of Physics*, pp. 34–43.

Zielinski, Siegfried (2006) *Deep Time of the Media: Towards an Archaeology of Seeing and Hearing by Technical Means* (trans. Gloria Custance), Cambridge, MA: MIT Press.

Zito, Tom (1981) "Turbos of Invention," *Washington Post*, July 1, https://www.washingtonpost.com/archive/lifestyle/1981/07/01/turbos-of-invention/43e9ec6a-2d91-4ecb-a072-aea76ef5b667/. Accessed August 9, 2019.

Žižek, Slavoj (2003) *Organs Without Bodies: On Deleuze and Consequences*, London: Routledge.

Žižek, Slavoj (2016) *Disparities*, London: Bloomsbury.

Zone, Ray (2012) *3-D Revolution: The History of Modern Stereoscopic Cinema*, Lexington: University Press of Kentucky.

Index

CPSIA information can be obtained
at www.ICGtesting.com
Printed in the USA
LVHW010805030720
659546LV00002B/2

9 781474 463737